Oracle Data Integra

Cookbook

Over 60 field-tested recipes for successful data integration projects with Oracle Data Integrator

Christophe Dupupet

Peter C. Boyd-Bowman

Denis Gray

Julien Testut

BIRMINGHAM - MUMBAI

Oracle Data Integrator 11*g* Cookbook

First published: May 2013

Production Reference: 2060613

Published by Packt Publishing Ltd.
Livery Place
35 Livery Street
Birmingham B3 2PB, UK.
ISBN 978-1-84968-174-2

www.packtpub.com

Cover Image by Karl Moore (karl@karlmoore.co.uk)

Credits

Authors

Christophe Dupupet

Peter C. Boyd-Bowman

Denis Gray

Julien Testut

Reviewers

Uli Bethke

Hans Forbrich

Kevin Glenny

Maciej Kocon

Ray McCormack

Acquisition Editors

Edward Gordon

Erol Staveley

Lead Technical Editor

Neeshma Ramakrishnan

Technical Editors

Saijul Shah

Sayali Mirajkar

Hardik B. Soni

Project Coordinator

Arshad Sopariwala

Proofreader

Paul Hindle

Indexer

Monica Ajmera

Production Coordinator

Aparna Bhagat

Cover Work

Aparna Bhagat

Foreword

In 1998, when Sunopsis first opened its door to begin development of the product that would become ODI, the technology landscape was very different from today. There were very few data warehouses over 10 terabytes, and both the underlying hardware and software were struggling to keep up with the load and query demands placed upon them. As a result, the warehouses only included the most critical transactional data from the few key systems. The prevailing ETL approach of the day was to hand-build highly optimized flows, which executed in dedicated hardware, and then spoon-feed the results into the data warehouse. In this context, the founding principles of ODI were extraordinarily bold: leverage the data warehouse itself as the transformation engine and enable developers to work at a much higher level of abstraction, counting on the tool to generate an optimized execution plan.

Viewed with hindsight 15 years later, these principles seem prescient. Data warehouses have grown to be petabytes in size, and the hardware that houses them is often the most powerful in the data center — 100s of processor cores, terabytes of RAM, and 10s of terabytes of Flash. After many years of concerted effort, and with thousands of mappings to show for it, many enterprises have added far more transaction systems into their warehouses, and they are now looking to bring in data sets that have hitherto been dark (for example, server logs, social media feeds), and may be best preprocessed on open source distributed frameworks such as Hadoop. The world has finally caught up to ODI.

Congratulations on your decision to take a different approach to bulk movement and transformation of data within your business. For developers experienced on traditional ETL tools, you will discover yourself doing far less mundane work once you grasp a few of the key ODI concepts such as topologies, knowledge modules, and set-based transformation. This book will be an excellent companion for you on this journey. Written by four experts on the product (with decades of experience among them), including key product managers who are continuing to drive ODI's evolution, this book complements the product documentation with a variety of practical recipes. In addition to all of the common tasks required in populating a data warehouse (for example, change data capture, slowly changing dimensions), readers will also find valuable information on using ODI within a web service environment, and how to use its powerful APIs to programmatically author ODI artifacts.

Since its acquisition, ODI has become the key bulk data technology within Oracle products and within our cloud offerings. I hope you find it as impactful in your business as it has been in ours.

Brad Adelberg

Vice President, Development for Data Integration

Oracle Corp.

About the Authors

Christophe Dupupet is a Director in the Fusion Middleware Architects Team, where he leads the expertise on ODI. The team works closely with strategic customers that implement ODI, and helps define best practices on the product in terms of architecture, implementation, and operations.

Prior to Oracle, Christophe was part of the team that started the operations for Sunopsis in the US, where he lead the technical team (presales, support, and training). Sunopsis was acquired by Oracle in 2006.

Christophe holds an Operations Research degree from EISTI in France, a Masters Degree in Operations Research from Florida Tech, and a certificate in Management from Harvard University.

Christophe is a co-author of the book *Getting Started with Oracle Data Integrator 11g: A Hands-on Tutorial*.

There would be no book if we did not have a fantastic product and customers to trust us with this product. I want to particularly thank all the individuals that have helped this product become what it is today: the architects and software engineers that work and have worked on ODI for their vision and production; our support engineers that help our customers every day and help shape best practices with a forever growing knowledge base (`support.oracle.com` is truly a goldmine if you are looking for information on how to use ODI); our sales engineers and product managers that help customers and partners in their selection of our product.

Peter C. Boyd-Bowman is a Technical Director and Consultant with the Oracle Corporation. He has over 30 years of software engineering and database management experience, including 12 years of focused interest in data warehousing and business intelligence. Capitalizing on his extensive background in Oracle database technologies dating back to 1985, he has spent recent years specializing in data migration. After many successful project implementations using Oracle Warehouse Builder, and shortly after Oracle's acquisition of the Sunopsis Corporation, he switched his area of focus over to Oracle's flagship ETL product: Oracle Data Integrator. Peter holds a BS degree in Industrial Management and Computer Science from Purdue University and currently resides in North Carolina.

Denis Gray is a Director of Product Management for Data Integration at Oracle. Denis has over 15 years of experience in the data-integration field. For the past seven years, Denis has been an integral part of Oracle Development Organization as a Product Manager within Fusion Middleware, delivering data integration solutions. Prior to this, Denis was a data integration consult for Hyperion Solutions (Oracle). Here, Denis worked at many of the largest Fortune 100 companies, building data warehouses and implementing business intelligence solutions. Denis has a Bachelor's Degree in Computer Science from the University of Missouri and currently resides in St. Louis, MO. Denis also co-authored the Packt book *Getting Started with Oracle Data Integrator 11g: A Hands-on Tutorial*.

I would like to thank my beautiful wife Tracy and my sons, Tad and Charlie, for their support, understanding, and above all their love and faith. There were many nights where I was missing in action; however, I never heard a complaint. Also a special thanks to my co-authors for their help and guidance throughout this process.

Julien Testut is a Product Manager in the Oracle Data Integration group focusing on Oracle Data Integrator. Julien has an extensive background in Data Integration and Data Quality solutions and is a co-author of *Getting Started with Oracle Data Integrator 11g: A Hands-on Tutorial*. Prior to joining Oracle, he was an Applications Engineer at Sunopsis, which was then acquired by Oracle. Julien holds a Masters degree in Software Engineering.

To my daughter Olivia, who was born while I was working on this book and who has been filling my life with joy since then. Thanks to my wife Emilie for her help and patience throughout this book's writing process. I couldn't have done it without you. I would also like to take this opportunity to express my gratitude to my co-authors. It's always a pleasure to collaborate with you! Finally, I would like to thank my family and friends for their support as well as my colleagues who help make Oracle Data Integrator a better product with every release. Thank you!

About the Reviewers

Uli Bethke has been working with ODI since 2007. After some initial difficulties familiarizing himself with the tool, he quickly realized the huge potential of ODI. A couple of great innovations went into ODI and it is light years ahead of any of its competitors. It is one of those tools that really make a difference. Uli has been working in data integration and data warehousing for more than 13 years. Verticals include Finance, Retail, Pharma, and Education.

Uli is a managing partner and owner of a small but growing BI consultancy in Dublin, Ireland. He offers expert services on ODI including training. He also consults on data warehousing, data integration, and enterprise architecture. If you want to avail of any of his services, you can contact him through his blog `http://www.bi-q.ie` or directly via e-mail.

Uli has also been a reviewer of the book *Getting Started with Oracle Data Integrator 11g: A Hands-on Tutorial*, published by Packt.

> The last time I reviewed a Packt book, my baby boy Ruairi had just been born. Recently, we have welcomed Una as another member to the family. Una, Ruairi, and Helen, you really make my day.

Hans Forbrich has been working with, consulting on, and teaching Oracle products for 30 years. He is experienced in data integration using Oracle Warehouse Builder and Oracle Data Integrator, as well as with the SOA and OSB technologies. Hans has been enthusiastic about ODI since the Sunopsis acquisition by Oracle, and regularly teaches the Oracle University ODI courses in North America through his partner, ExitCertified Corp.

Hans has been an Oracle ACE since 2005 and an Oracle ACE Director since 2008. For more information about the Oracle ACE program, see `http://www.oracle.com/technetwork/community/oracle-ace/index.html`.

Hans is a frequent reviewer of Packt Publishing's Oracle books, spanning the range of OracleVM and Oracle Scheduler through Oracle SOA Suite.

I'd like to thank my wife Susanne for her patience while I hide behind my computer screen, editing or writing. Also, thanks to my colleagues, especially Dan Morgan and Aman Sharma, for their assistance over the years, and the challenging questions that keep me motivated in our ever expanding field of Information Technology.

Kevin Glenny has international Oracle Technical Architecture experience integrating large scale real-time systems. His most notable projects include the European Grid Infrastructure (EGI) supporting the particle physics large data generated by CERN.

He specializes in the area of scalable OLAP and OLTP systems, building on his Grid computing background. He is also the author of numerous technical articles and his industry insights can be found on his company's blog at `http://oracle.gridwisetech.com/`.

GridwiseTech, Oracle Partner of the Year 2013, is the independent specialist on scalability and large data. The company delivers robust IT architectures for significant data and processing loads. GridwiseTech operates globally and serves clients ranging from Fortune Global 500 companies to government and academia.

Maciej Kocon has been in the IT industry for over 12 years. He began his career as a database application programmer and quickly developed a passion for SQL language, data processing and analysis.

He entered the realm of BI and data warehousing, and has specialized in the design of various data integration frameworks for high data volumes. His experience covers the full data-warehouse lifecycle in various sectors including Financial Services, Retail, Public Sector, Telecommunications, and Life Sciences.

He first came across the tool in 2005 when it was Sunopsis product and has been gradually spending more time on it since. For the last 4 years he has worked full-time on ODI, performing heavy customizations made for enterprise class data warehouse implementations.

He believes the template architecture, which ODI is built upon, is the perfect solution giving the best from both worlds (flexibility and reusability), offering practically limitless possibilities

Maciej is managing partner and owner of a small but growing BI consultancy in Dublin, Ireland. He offers consulting services on data warehousing and data integration architectural solutions tailored for enterprises. He is a contributor to the blog `http://www.bi-q.ie` that focuses on data integration and ODI in particular.

If you want to avail of any of his services you can contact him through that website or via e-mail: `maciej.kocon@gmail.com`

Maciej has also been a reviewer of the book *Getting Started with Oracle Data Integrator 11g*, published by Packt.

I'd like to personally thank Gosia for her patience and encouragement. Reviewing this book is just a little drop in the sea of work I bring home, which would not be possible to accomplish without her huge support.

Ray McCormack was introduced to databases 12 years ago, and since that time he has been synchronizing his on-job and off-job interests with database programming. He has a comprehensive background in database application design, development, business process mapping, systems integration, and leading teams of developers.

Originally from a development background, Ray is very passionate about Business Intelligence and Data Warehousing solutions. He has complete end-to-end expertise in all facets of BI/DW including project management, dimensional modeling, performance tuning, ETL design and development, report and dashboard design and development, as well as installation and administration. He has vast experience in various roles across industry sectors such as pharmaceutical (Icon PLC), education (University of San Diego), scientific (National Instruments), and broadcasting (RTE).

Ray's hobbies include spending time with his family, all sports, and playing with the latest technological gadgets. He loves traveling, having worked in California for 8 years.

Table of Contents

Preface

After our collaboration on the ODI book *Getting Started with Oracle Data Integrator 11g: A Hands-on Tutorial, we thought that there might be a need for a more advanced book on the same subject. So when Packt Publishing approached us to see if it would be possible to write a Cookbook on ODI, we knew that we had the medium for this new adventure. Our objective with this book was to avoid any repetition from the first book and to offer recipes that go beyond what is readily available in the ODI documentation and on the Web. Hopefully, you will agree that we have achieved our goal.*

What this book covers

Chapter 1, Installation, Deployment, and Configuration, answers several deployment questions that we have been asked by ODI users over time. A hands-on approach to these topics allows the reader to learn the answers that we regularly give to our counterparts.

Chapter 2, Defining the Oracle Data Integrator Security, expands the descriptions available in the ODI documentation with "how-to" examples by providing recipes to implement several different aspects of ODI security.

Chapter 3, Advanced Topology, delves into Topology beyond the definition of servers and schemas. These recipes will explore specific elements of Topology that are not typically explored by the average ODI user: definition of new technologies and datatypes, use of actions, and controlling case sensitivity.

Chapter 4, Using Variables, expands the use of variables by implementing them in ways not often documented within the product, such as using variables in resource names and how to best use variables as parameters.

Chapter 5, Knowledge Module Internals, will shed new light on what is possible with KMs, explaining how substitution methods are processed by ODI and even experimenting with Java code inside the KMs.

Chapter 6, Inside Knowledge Modules – SCD and CDC, offers an opportunity to expand on the concepts covered in the previous chapter by focusing on KMs that may not be well known or well understood. We will also experiment with a few alterations of these KMs to provide an even more hands-on experience.

Chapter 7, Advanced Coding Techniques, begins by looking into code generation that can be performed directly from the models using diagrams. This chapter then explores specific advanced topics such as temporary interfaces, embedded SQL queries, pivots, and partition exchange loading.

Chapter 8, Package Loop and File Processing, was written because we noticed that too many users limit their workflows by not knowing how to use them for more mature integration techniques. The recipes in this chapter demonstrate some of the more sophisticated integration techniques, including a focus on flat files processing that will help a developer greater take advantage of ODI orchestration.

Chapter 9, XML and Web Services, discusses two areas of growing importance within ETL processing: using XML files as input and using web services. Recipes will start with the basics of the definition of an XML file and go all the way to invoking web services with callbacks.

Chapter 10, Advanced Coding Techniques Using the SDK, is rich in sample code that automates tasks usually done with the graphical interface, including installation, development, and execution monitoring.

Chapter 11, More with ODI, is a catch-all chapter that addresses questions we've often had to answer, including misconceptions on how the product should be used, and little known secrets that we didn't want to leave aside.

What you need for this book

Since Oracle is one of the leading database platforms, it has been used throughout this book as the primary database technology. By using the DDL installation scripts available through the publisher (see the following section, *Downloading the example code*), all of the required source and target tables can be created and populated in two of the schemas referenced throughout the book. Please note that should you choose to follow along using an alternative technology and/or schema, you will most likely need to adjust the syntax and options accordingly. The following scripts are available:

- `CREATE_USER.sql`: (creates the two cookbook demo user accounts)
- `CREATE_SRC.sql`: (creates the source tables)
- `CREATE_TRG.sql`: (creates the target tables)
- `LOAD_SRC_SCHEMA.sql`: (populates the source tables)
- `LOAD_TRG_SCHEMA.sql`: (populates the target tables)

Some of the recipes within this book will also be referencing flat files, so it will be necessary to establish a folder/directory within the reader's environment and to copy the available (`*.txt`) files into this location. For example, create a directory location called `C:\Temp` and copy the `SRC_AGE_GROUP.txt` and `SRC_SALES_PERSON.txt` files into that folder.

Once all the schemas have been created and the database schemas have been loaded, the reader should start up ODI and perform the following preliminary tasks:

- On the **Topology** tab and within the **File** technology, create a physical data server, physical schema, and logical schema for the `DEMO_FILE` schema. Note that the physical location should be `C:\TEMP`.
- On the **Topology** tab and within the **Oracle** technology, create a physical data server, physical schema, and logical schema for the `DEMO_SRC` schema.
- On the **Topology** tab and within the **Oracle** technology, create a physical data server, physical schema, and logical schema for the `DEMO_TRG` schema.

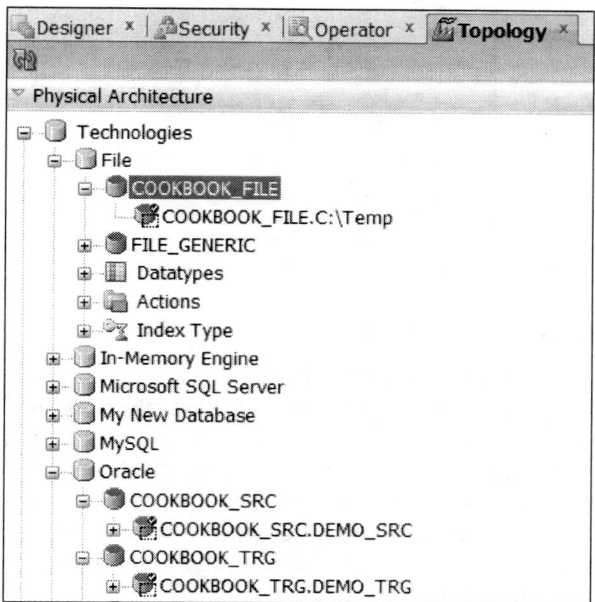

- On the **Designer** tab, create a data model `DEMO_FILE` logical schema.

  Import the `SRC_AGE_GROUP` data store using the available XML file.

  Import the `SRC_SALES_PERSON` data store using the available XML file.
- On the **Designer** tab, create a data model and reverse engineer the `DEMO_SRC` logical schema.

- On the **Designer** tab, create a data model and reverse engineer the `DEMO_TRG` logical schema.

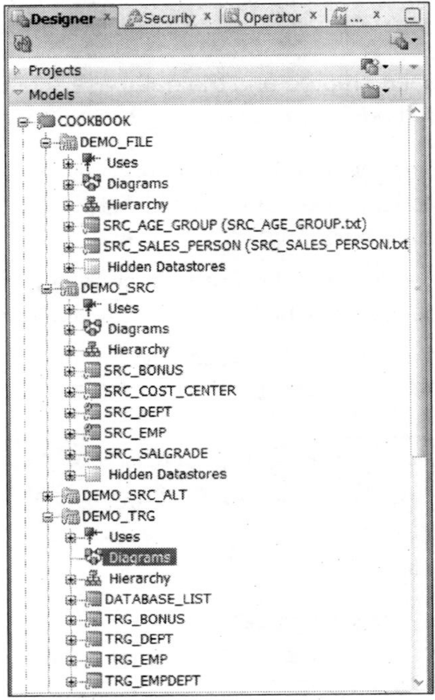

Who this book is for

This book has been designed to present the reader with solutions to specific problems that sometimes challenge even the most accomplished ODI developer. As such, it is not meant to teach the fundamentals of the ODI product, but rather to extend the reader's understanding of Oracle Data Integrator's capabilities. In order to expedite the presentation of the material within this book, there is an assumption that the reader already has a basic understanding of the ODI product and has ready access to a database. For those readers looking for an introduction to ODI, we recommend the book *Getting Started with Oracle Data Integrator 11g: A Hands-on Tutorial* by Packt publishing.

Conventions

In this book, you will find a number of styles of text that distinguish between different kinds of information. Here are some examples of these styles, and an explanation of their meaning.

Code words in text are shown as follows: "A default `jps-config.xml` file named `odi-jps-config-jse.xml` is delivered with the installation of ODI Studio and located within the `ODI_HOME\oracledi\client\odi\bin` directory."

A block of code is set as follows:

```
<serviceProvider type="IDENTITY_STORE" name="idstore.ldap.
provider" class="oracle.security.jps.internal.idstore.ldap.
LdapIdentityStoreProvider">
            <description>LDAP-based IdentityStore Provider</
description>
</serviceProvider>
```

Any command-line input or output is written as follows:

```
Map: oracle.odi.credmap
Key:ODI_AGENT
User_Name:CN=Admin
Password:weblogic1
```

New terms and **important words** are shown in bold. Words that you see on the screen, in menus or dialog boxes for example, appear in the text like this: " Select **File** then **New** from the menu ".

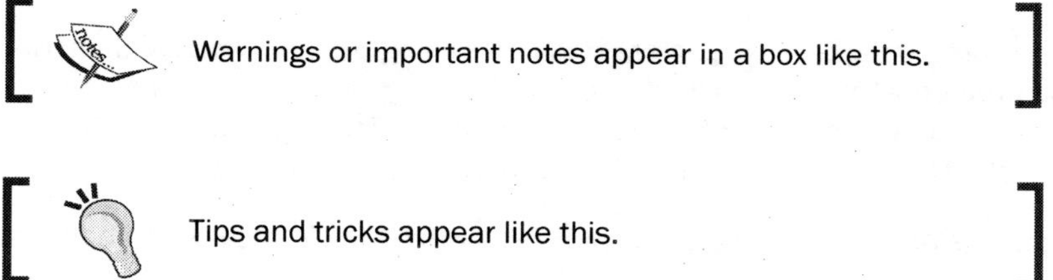

Warnings or important notes appear in a box like this.

Tips and tricks appear like this.

Reader feedback

Feedback from our readers is always welcome. Let us know what you think about this book—what you liked or may have disliked. Reader feedback is important for us to develop titles that you really get the most out of.

To send us general feedback, simply send an e-mail to `feedback@packtpub.com`, and mention the book title via the subject of your message.

If there is a topic that you have expertise in and you are interested in either writing or contributing to a book, see our author guide on `www.packtpub.com/authors`.

Customer support

Now that you are the proud owner of a Packt book, we have a number of things to help you to get the most from your purchase.

Downloading the example code

You can download the example code files for all Packt books you have purchased from your account at `http://www.packtpub.com`. If you purchased this book elsewhere, you can visit `http://www.packtpub.com/support` and register to have the files e-mailed directly to you.

Errata

Although we have taken every care to ensure the accuracy of our content, mistakes do happen. If you find a mistake in one of our books—maybe a mistake in the text or the code—we would be grateful if you would report this to us. By doing so, you can save other readers from frustration and help us improve subsequent versions of this book. If you find any errata, please report them by visiting `http://www.packtpub.com/submit-errata`, selecting your book, clicking on the **errata submission form** link, and entering the details of your errata. Once your errata are verified, your submission will be accepted and the errata will be uploaded on our website, or added to any list of existing errata, under the Errata section of that title. Any existing errata can be viewed by selecting your title from `http://www.packtpub.com/support`.

Piracy

Piracy of copyright material on the Internet is an ongoing problem across all media. At Packt, we take the protection of our copyright and licenses very seriously. If you come across any illegal copies of our works, in any form, on the Internet, please provide us with the location address or website name immediately so that we can pursue a remedy.

Please contact us at `copyright@packtpub.com` with a link to the suspected pirated material.

We appreciate your help in protecting our authors, and our ability to bring you valuable content.

Questions

You can contact us at `questions@packtpub.com` if you are having a problem with any aspect of the book, and we will do our best to address it.

1
Installation, Deployment, and Configuration

The recipes in this chapter will help users learn the following:

- Deploying and configuring a standalone agent manually
- Deploying JEE ODI Agent
- Configuring a standalone agent with OPMN
- Deploying JDBC drivers with JEE ODI Agent

Introduction

Installation, deployment, and configuration are key to every successful software implementation. Oracle Data Integrator is no different; thoroughly understanding the different installation and deployment options will help in planning the overall topology for ODI.

This chapter provides quick-start recipes for installation, deployment, and configuration. For detailed information on each topic, please review the Oracle Fusion Middleware Installation Guide for Oracle Data Integrator at `http://docs.oracle.com/cd/E23943_01/core.1111/e16453/toc.htm`, as well as the Fusion Middleware Developers Guide for Oracle Data Integrator located at `http://docs.oracle.com/cd/E23943_01/integrate.1111/e12643/toc.htm`.

Understanding the ODI Installation

Before jumping into the recipes, some background is needed on the ODI components:

- **ODI repositories**: It consists of Master and Work repositories in which ODI metadata and data is stored
- **ODI Studio**: It is used to develop ETL mappings as well as to administer and monitor the ODI
- **ODI standalone agent**: The ODI runtime process that orchestrates ETL flows
- **JEE components**:
  - **Enterprise manager fusion middleware control plugin for ODI**: It is used to monitor ODI from a web browser
  - **Public web services**: They are used to start and monitor scenarios through the JEE or a standalone agent
  - **ODI console**: It is used to execute and monitor ODI jobs as well as browse ODI metadata from a web browser
  - **JEE agent**: JEE enabled ODI agent that allows the ODI agent to inherently take advantage of the application server's enterprise features, such as high availability, connection pooling, and so on.

Each component can be installed and configured with the Oracle Universal Installer, which is delivered in the installation bundle that was downloaded from `Oracle.com`. The ODI Oracle Universal Installer has three choices for installing ODI. Each option is not exclusive; one option or all three options may be selected.

The first option is **Developer Installation**; this installation will install and configure ODI Studio and the ODI SDK. As you might guess, any ODI developer will need this installation type.

The ODI Studio agent can be manually installed from the ODI Companion CD.

The second option is **Standalone Installation**; this installation installs and configures the standalone agent.

The ODI standalone agent can be manually installed from the ODI Companion CD.

The third option is **Java EE Installation**. This option will install the ODI JEE files in an existing Oracle Middleware home. Each JEE component is configured during another process using the FMW configuration utility.

The ODI installation process has been extensively documented. Each enterprise deployment of ODI will vary, depending on many of the variables. The Oracle Universal Installer automates virtually every aspect of the ODI installation and guides the user through the installation process and configuration process. Additional configuration tasks are needed for the JEE components. Please refer to the ODI Installation guide for more information.

Although the Oracle Universal Installer does automate most ODI installation and configuration tasks, there are use cases when it is not feasible to use the Oracle Universal Installer, such as when the server where the ODI component is installed does not have graphical capabilities or if there is no platform specific installation for an OS. For this type of installation, many of the ODI components can be deployed manually. Deploying the ODI standalone agent is outlined in the next recipe.

Deploying and configuring a standalone agent manually

Performing a manual installation is required when the server on which you would like to set up your ODI standalone agent does not possess the graphical capabilities required to run the Oracle Universal Installer for Oracle Data Integrator, or when there is no installer available for the operating system platform you are working with. Manually installing a standalone agent should be done only when necessary, as bypassing the installer will not allow the application of patches, so proceed with caution.

Getting ready

In this recipe, we will be using files included in the ODI Companion CD. At the time of writing, it can be downloaded at `http://www.oracle.com/technetwork/middleware/data-integrator/downloads/index.html` from the Oracle Technology Network. You can follow the instructions using your own repository. No other prerequisites are required.

How to do it...

1. Unzip the content of the ODI Companion CD and then open up the `/agent_standalone` folder. Unzip the `oracledi-agent-standalone.zip` file to the location in which you would like to deploy your standalone agent.
2. Go to the directory in which you extracted the files required to run your standalone agent, then navigate to the `oracledi/agent/bin` directory, and open up the `odiparams.sh` or `odiparams.bat` file using your favorite text editor.

3. We will now modify some of the parameters included in the `odiparams` file starting with the Master repository information. Edit the file so that `ODI_MASTER_DRIVER` has the correct JDBC driver class name and the `ODI_MASTER_URL` value is a valid JDBC URL for the database hosting your Master repository. Finally, complete the Master repository configuration by providing the database username and its password using the `ODI_MASTER_USER` and `ODI_MASTER_ENCODED_PASS` parameters. We use the following values in this recipe:

```
REM #
REM # Repository Connection Information
REM #
set ODI_MASTER_DRIVER=oracle.jdbc.OracleDriver
set ODI_MASTER_URL=jdbc:oracle:thin:@localhost:1521:orcl
set ODI_MASTER_USER=ODI_REPO_11G
set ODI_MASTER_ENCODED_PASS=dpfHbipjYbBAfm7P,Dt69kPBV
```

4. Next we need to provide the name of the ODI Supervisor user along with its encoded password using the `ODI_SUPERVISOR` and `ODI_SUPERVISOR_ENCODED_PASS` variables.

```
REM #
REM # User credentials for agent startup program
REM #
set ODI_SUPERVISOR=SUPERVISOR
set ODI_SUPERVISOR_ENCODED_PASS=d,yXMMv0Rk6rgNVKEnBb1xE.E
```

The encoded passwords such as `ODI_MASTER_ENCODED_PASS` or `ODI_SUPERVISOR_ENCODED_PASS` can be obtained using the `encode.bat` or `encode.sh` command provided in the `agent/bin` directory.

5. Subsequently, we set the value of `ODI_SECU_WORK_REP` to the name of the Work repository that will be used by this standalone agent. The Work repository is named `WORKREP` in this recipe.

```
REM #
REM # Work Repository Name
REM #
set ODI_SECU_WORK_REP=WORKREP
```

6. Optionally we can also change the Java Virtual Machine settings for this agent using the `ODI_INIT_HEAP and ODI_MAX_HEAP` parameters. Out of the box, the JVM settings are quite low, so it is a good idea to increase their values; the values below are not example settings:

```
REM #
REM # Other Parameters
```

```
REM #
set ODI_INIT_HEAP=256m
set ODI_MAX_HEAP=1024m
```

The `ODI_INIT_HEAP` and `ODI_MAX_HEAP` are recommended settings for this exercise. The required settings for each parameter depend on the actual aggregate memory requirements for all the integrations run on an agent.

7. Now save the `odiparams.sh` or `odiparams.bat` file and close it.
8. Open up ODI Studio and go to **Topology Navigator**.
9. In **Physical Architecture**, right-click on the **Agents** node and select **New Agent**.

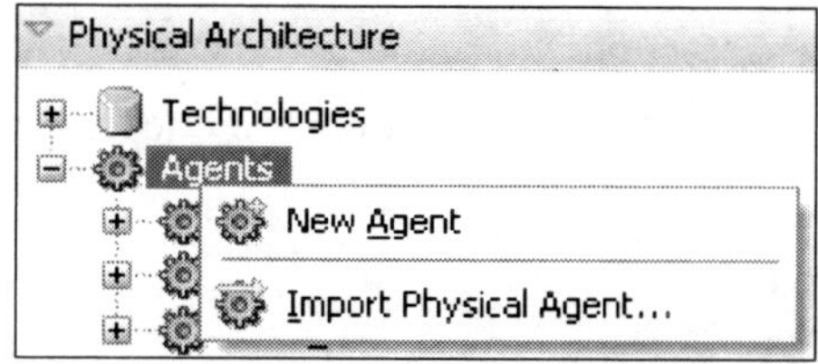

10. In the **Agent** panel, specify the agent's name along with the machine hostname and its port. Save the settings.

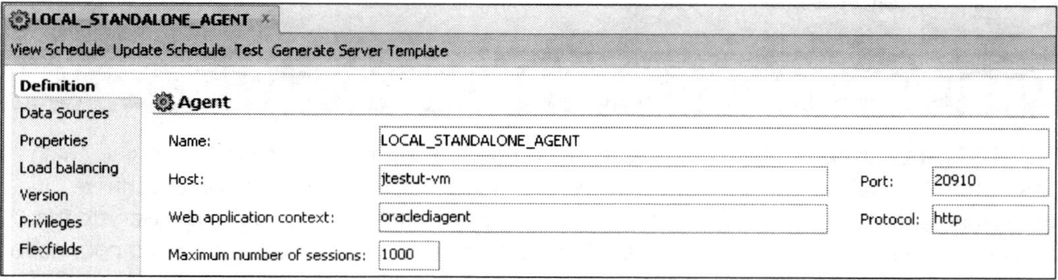

11. Open up a terminal and navigate to your agent's installation `/bin` directory.
12. Start your standalone agent using the `agent.sh` or `agent.bat` script and by providing its name (same as the one specified in Topology) and its port. In this recipe we use the following command:

    ```
    agent.bat -NAME=LOCAL_STANDALONE_AGENT -PORT=20910
    ```

13. Go back to Topology, open up your newly created Physical Agent, and click on **Test** to verify if all the parameters were entered correctly.

How it works...

The `odiparams.sh or odiparams.bat` file contains all the parameters required for a standalone agent to connect to an existing pair of Master and Work repositories. We will now highlight some of the parameters included in the file that were used in this recipe:

- `ODI_MASTER_DRIVER` stores the class name of the JDBC driver used to access the Master repository database
- `ODI_MASTER_URL` holds the JDBC URL utilized to connect to the Master repository database
- `ODI_MASTER_USER` is the name of the database account for your Master repository
- `ODI_MASTER_ENCODED_PASS` contains the encoded password of your Master repository database account
- `ODI_SUPERVISOR` represents the name of the ODI Supervisor user
- `ODI_SUPERVISOR_ENCODED_PASS` stores the encoded password of the ODI Supervisor user

There's more...

It is also possible to install a standalone agent using the Oracle Universal Installer for an ODI if you select the **Standalone Installation** option. The Oracle Data Integrator Installer has the capability to deploy a standalone agent and configure it automatically for a given Master and Work repositories pair.

Deploying a JEE ODI Agent

The ODI Agent can be deployed as a Java EE component within an application server. This installation type allows the ODI agent to take advantage of the benefits of an enterprise application server. When the ODI JEE Agent is deployed within Oracle WebLogic Server, the ODI JEE Agent can leverage the WebLogic's enterprise features, such as clustering and connection pooling for high availability and enterprise scalability. This Java EE Agent exposes an interface enabling lifecycle operation (start/stop) from the application server console and metrics that can be used by the application server console to monitor the agent activity and health.

The ODI 11g Java EE Agent can be deployed to an existing domain or deployed automatically when creating a new domain.

Weblogic Server 10.1.3.6.0 is required for this recipe. Please review the latest Oracle Data Integrator Certification Matrix for the latest version compatibility.

This recipe will create a new WebLogic domain by deploying the Java EE Agent template.

The standard ODI Java EE Agent template will be used to deploy our Java EE Agent. A template for any agent can also be generated from within ODI Studio and then used to deploy this agent.

How to do it...

1. The Java EE Agent must exist in the ODI topology before the WLS domain server is started for the agent. Connect to ODI Studio, expand ODI **Agents** within the topology, and add an agent with the name `OracleDIAgent` and with the port `8001`.

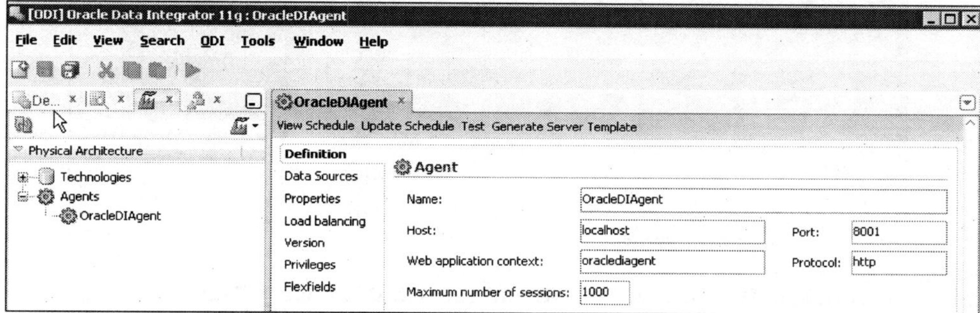

2. To deploy and configure domains with WLS, execute `config.bat` or `config.sh` from within the ODI Home Install at `Middleware_HOME\ODI_HOME\common\bin`.

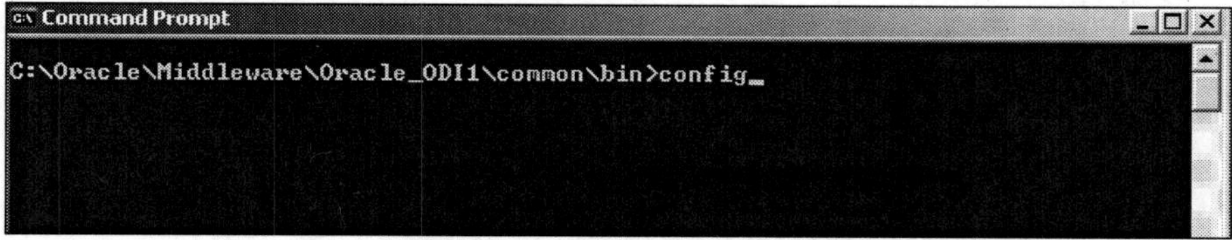

Downloading the example code

You can download the example code files for all Packt books you have purchased from your account at `http://www.packtpub.com`. If you purchased this book elsewhere, you can visit `http://www.packtpub.com/support` and register to have the files e-mailed directly to you.

3. Select the **Create a new Weblogic domain** option and click on **Next**.

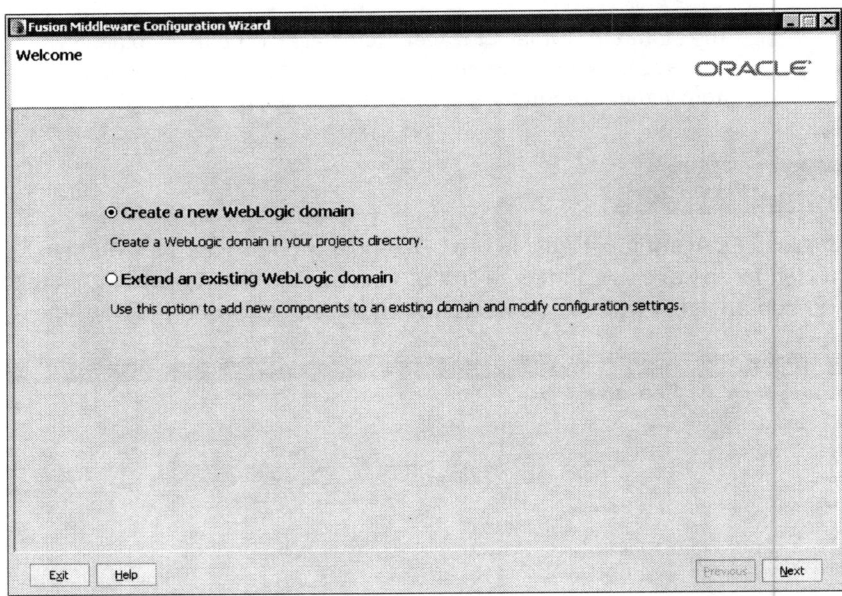

4. Select **Oracle Data Integrator - Agent - 11.1.1.0 [Oracle_ODI1]**, which will additionally select the two options as shown in the following screenshot, and click on **Next**:

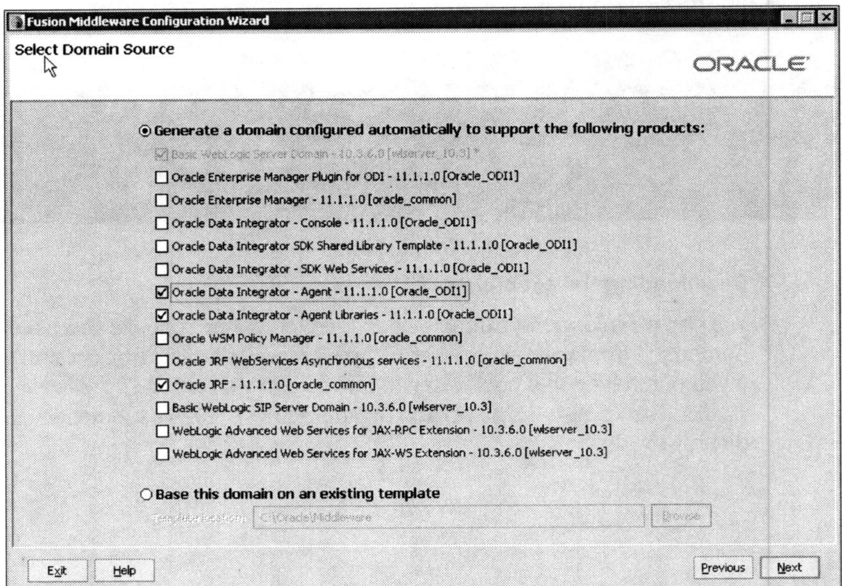

5. For this recipe, accept the defaults and click on **Next**.

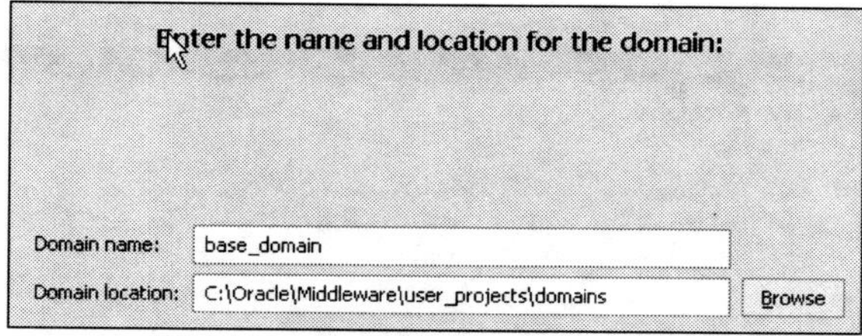

6. Accept the default name as `weblogic`, set the password as `weblogic1`, and click on **Next**.

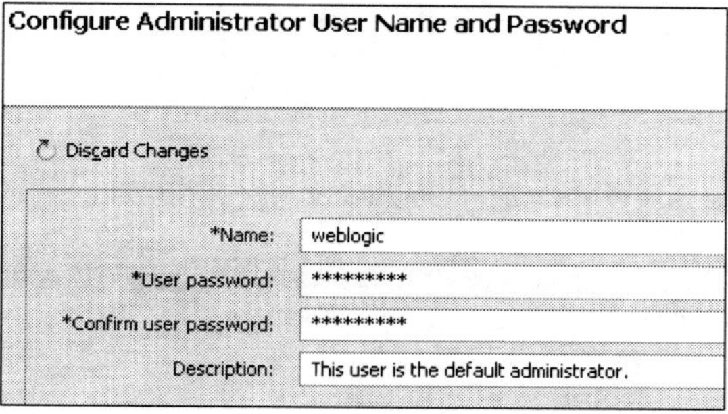

7. Select **SUN JDK** and click on **Next**.

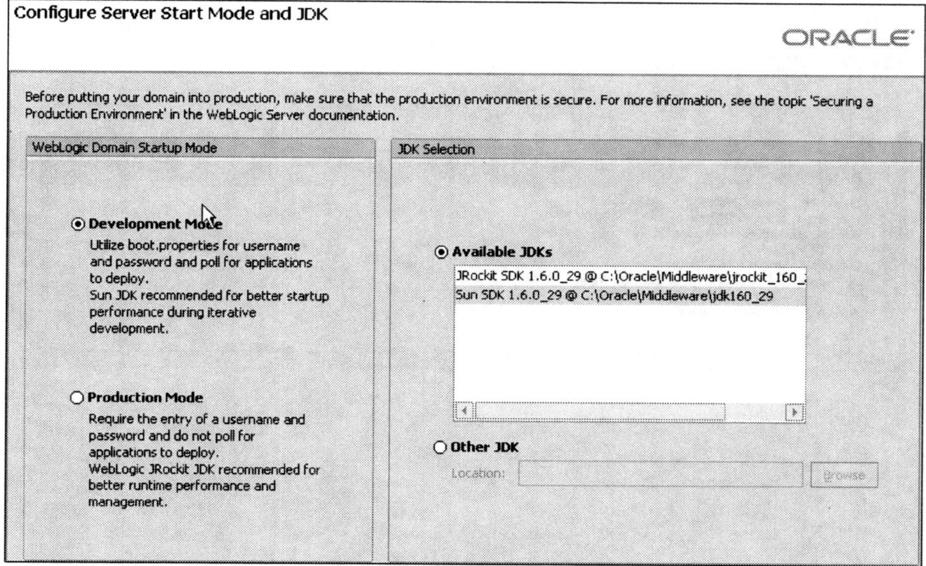

8. Enter the appropriate connection information to connect to the Master repository and click on **Next**.

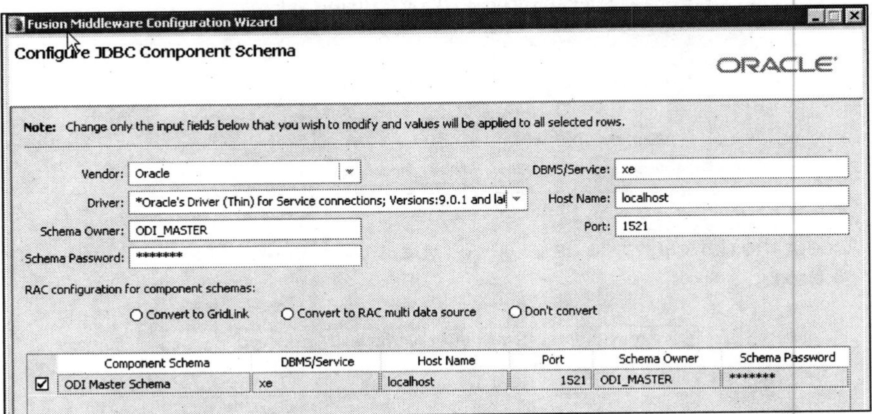

9. Ensure that the test connection was successful and click on **Next**.

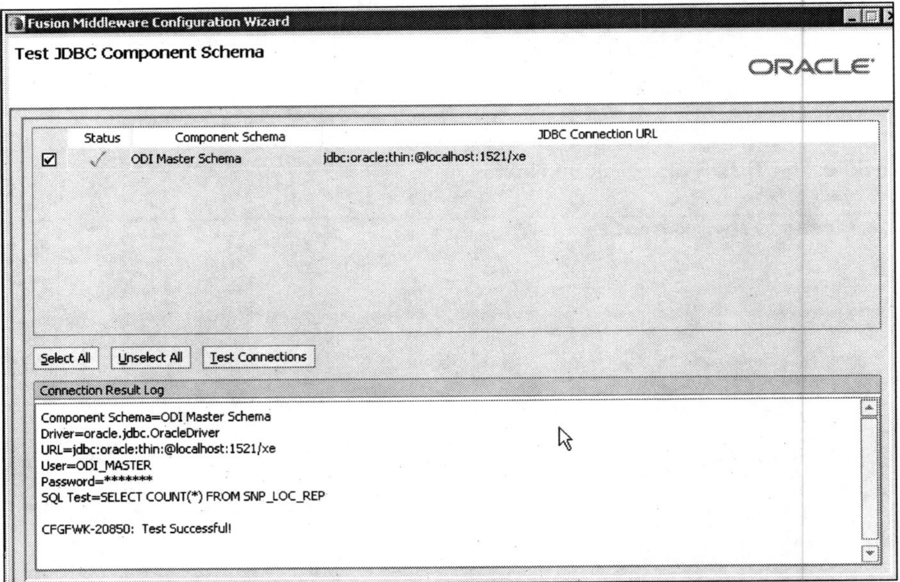

10. Check the **Managed Servers, Clusters and Machines** option and click on **Next**.

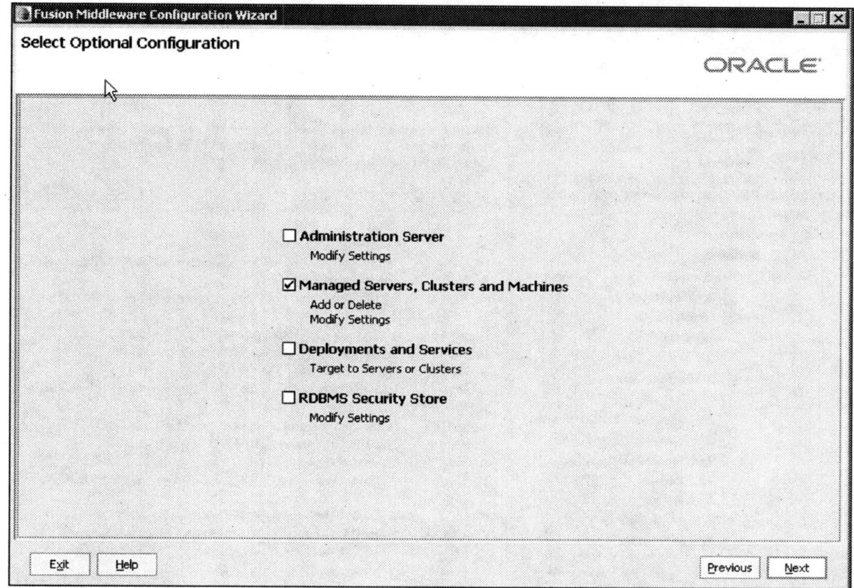

11. Set the port to `8001`, accept the defaults, and click on **Next**.

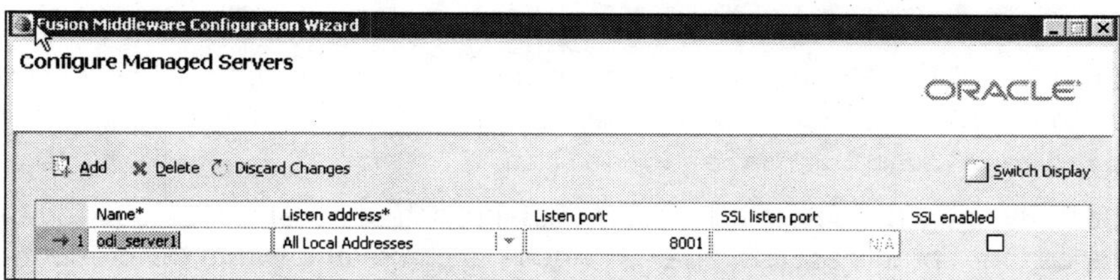

12. Click on the **Next** button on the **Configure Clusters** screen.
13. Accept the defaults and click on **Next** on the **Configure Machines** screen.
14. Click on **Next** on the **Assign Servers to Machines** screen.

15. Review the **Configuration Summary** screen and click on **Create**.

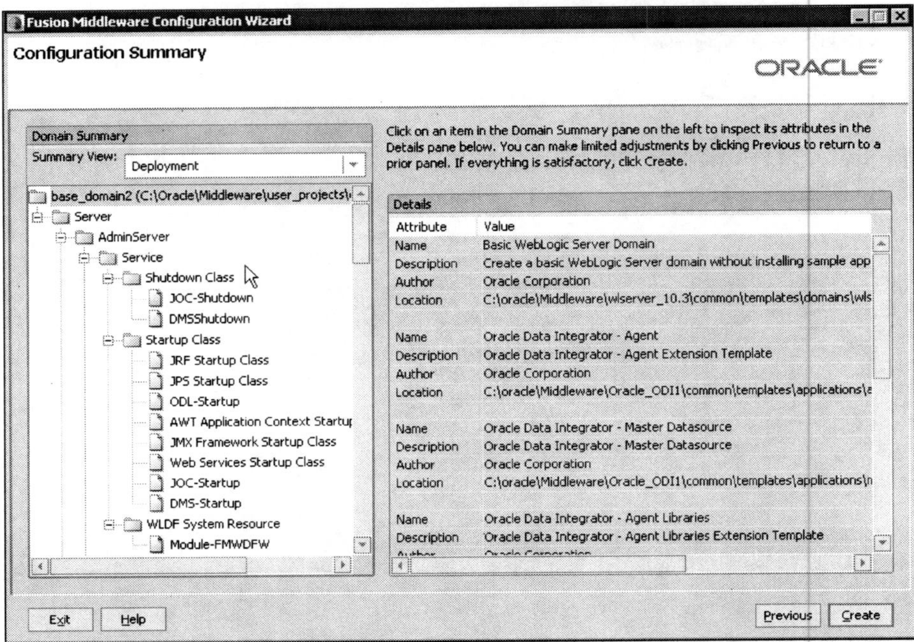

16. Do not click on the **Start Admin Server** check box. Then, click on **Done**.
17. Start the ODI WLS admin server for this domain from the command shell. Execute `startweblogic.cmd` or `startweblogic.sh` from `Middlware_Home\user_projects\domains\base_doman\bin`.
18. Security has to be set up for the JAVA EE application to have access to the ODI repository. For this access, an entry needs to be created within the credential store that will allow the JAVA EE Agent to authenticate itself and consume the resources that are needed. This user must already be set up in the ODI Security. To do this, we will do the following:
    1. Execute WLST, connect to our running admin server, and add the credential store.
    2. Start WLST from a command shell and change the directory to `Middleware_home\odi_home\oracle_common\common\bin`.

3. Execute WLST.

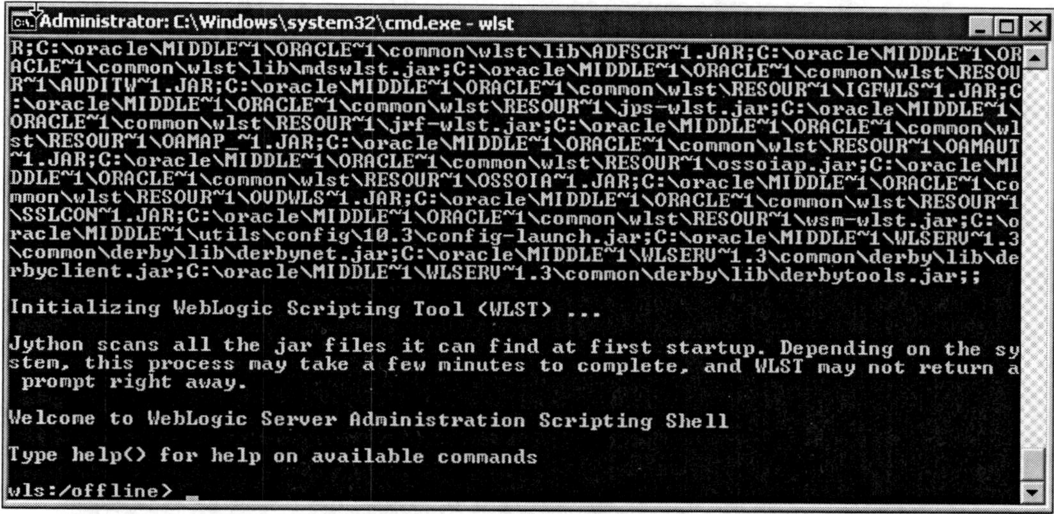

19. Execute the following command to connect to the running admin server:

```
connect ('weblogic','weblogic1','t3://localhost:7001').
```

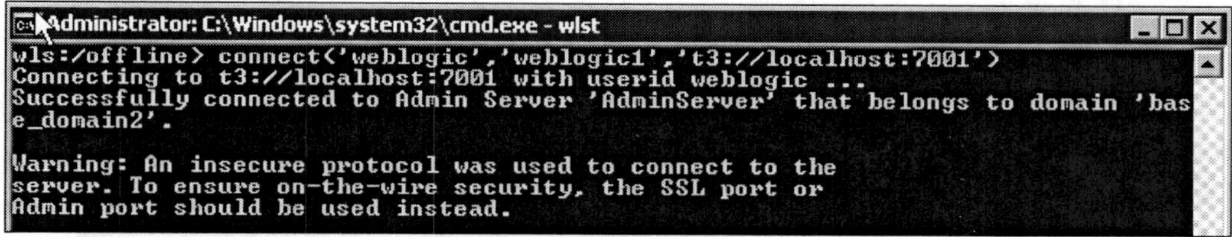

20. Execute the following command to add the correct credential store for ODI Supervisor:

```
createCred(map="oracle.odi.credmap", key="SUPERVISOR",
user="SUPERVISOR", password="SUNOPSIS", desc="ODI SUPERVISOR
Crendential")
```

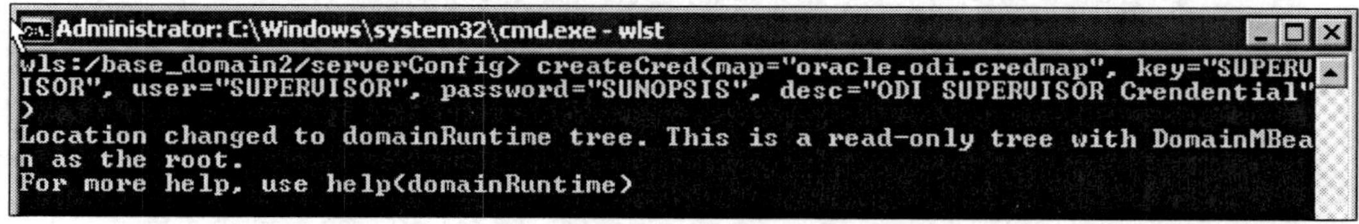

During runtime, the JAVA EE Agent will access this credential store to authenticate itself.

1. Type `exit()` to close WLST.
2. Start a command shell and change the directory to the `user_projects` directory of the Middleware_Home - `Middleware_HOME\user_projects\domains\base_domain\bin`.
3. Execute `StartManagedWeblogic odi_server1`.

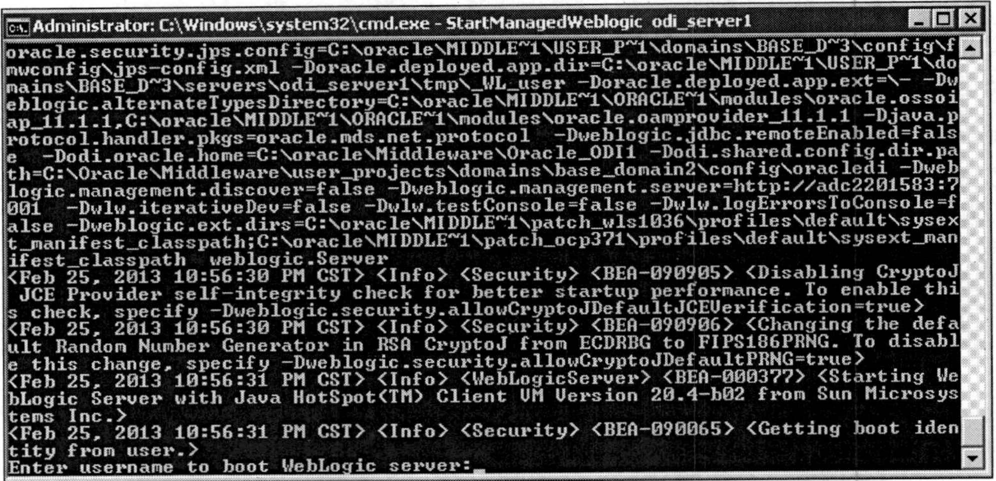

21. Enter `weblogic` as the username and `weblogic1` as the password.

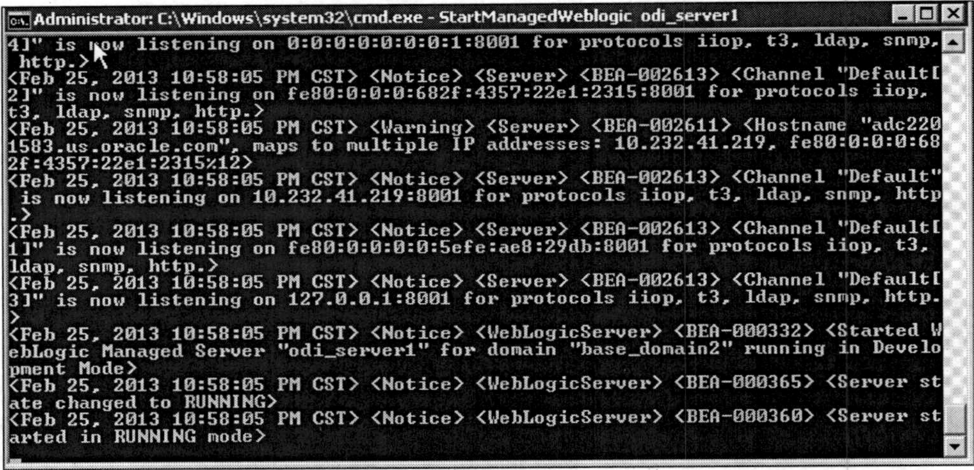

22. Verify `base_domain` is in the running mode and that there are no stack trace errors.

23. Verify connectivity to Java EE Agent through ODI Studio Topology.

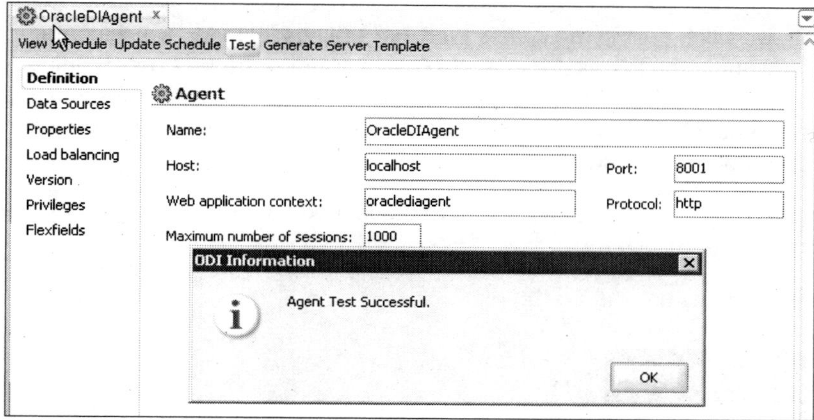

How it works...

Oracle has documented the overall process of installation and configuring the ODI JEE Agent. However, installation and deployment are broken into different sections of the documentation. This recipe gives a quick walk-through of the steps needed to easily install the JEE ODI Agent and also the steps necessary to configure the agent on the WebLogic server as well as the updates required within the ODI repository.

There's more...

The ODI JEE Agent can easily take advantage of the enterprise scalability features of Weblogic Server. Setting up clustering with the ODI JEE Agent is straightforward and follows the same setup as above. However, two agents would be created and then clustered. This is outlined in the Fusion Middleware High Availability Guide at `http://docs.oracle.com/cd/E14571_01/core.1111/e10106/odi.htm`.

There are also many more exciting ODI JEE components that are also easily installed and deployed, including the ODI Console, the ODI Admin Plug-in for the FMW EM Control, and the SDK Web Services, which are outlined at `http://docs.oracle.com/cd/E21764_01/core.1111/e16453/configure.htm#autoId9`.

Configuring a standalone agent with OPMN

Oracle Process Manager and Notification Server (**OPMN**) provides the ability to manage the lifecycle of ODI standalone agents. Using OPMN Oracle Data Integrator, users can control and monitor the status of standalone agents in Oracle Enterprise Manager. In addition, OPMN can automatically restart ODI standalone agents in case of failures.

Getting ready

In this recipe, we will be using the Oracle Web Tier Utilities installer, which contains OPMN. At the time of writing, the installer for Oracle Fusion Middleware Web Tier Utilities 11g can be downloaded from the Oracle Software Delivery Cloud (`https://edelivery.oracle.com/`) as part of the 'Oracle Fusion Middleware 11g Media Pack'. Make sure to download the right version for your operating system.

An agent named `ODI_OPMN_AGENT` needs to be defined as a Physical Agent in your ODI Topology.

No other prerequisites are required.

How to do it...

1. Start the Oracle Fusion Middleware Web Tier Utilities 11g installer from its installation directory.
2. In the **Install and Configure** section, select **Install and Configure** and click on **Next**.

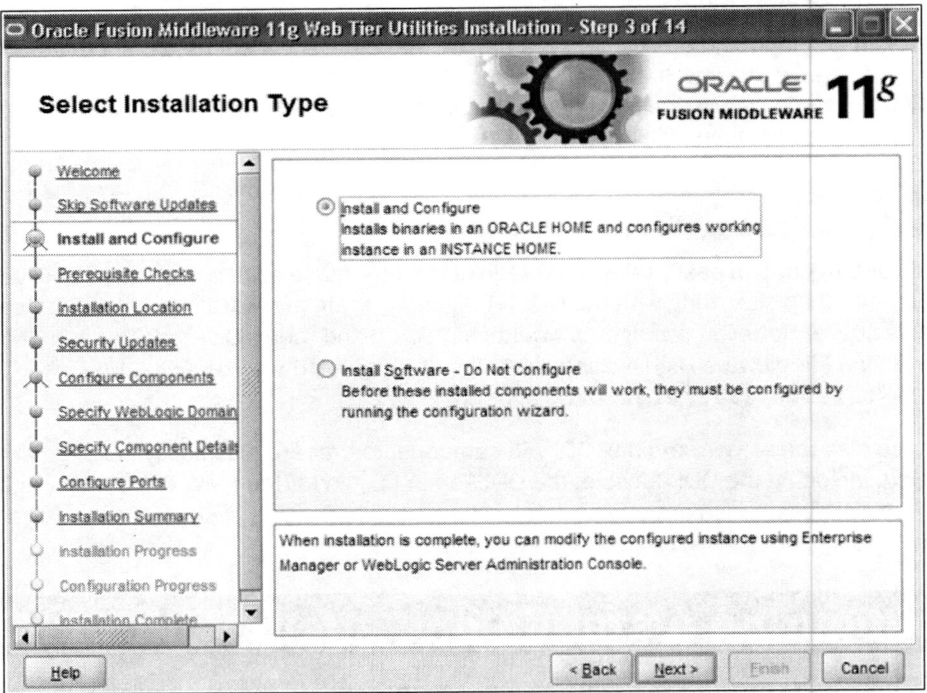

3. In the **Configure Components** part of the installer, check the **Oracle HTTP Server** and **Oracle Web Cache** checkboxes and then click on **Next**.

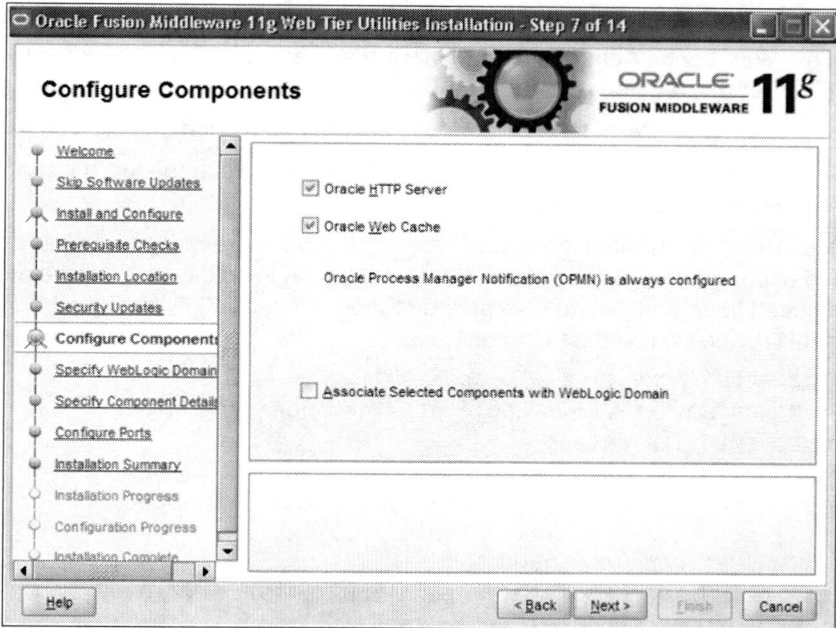

4. In the **Specify Component Details** step, we use the default installation setting for the **Instance Home Location**, **Instance Name**, **OHS Component Name**, and **Web Cache Component Name** options:

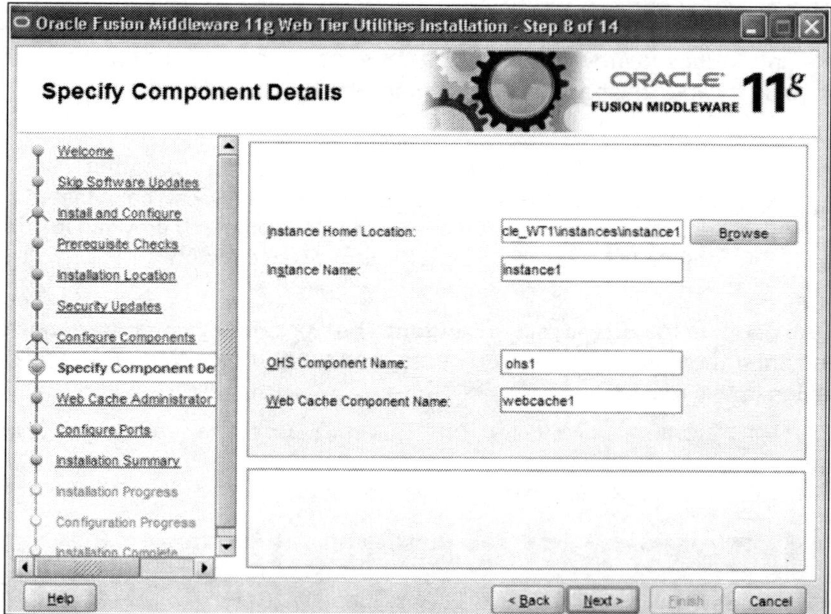

5. Click on **Next** to go to the next installer screen.
6. In the **Web Cache Administrator Password** screen, enter the password of your choice. In this recipe, we use `welcome1` and click on **Next**.
7. In the **Configure Ports** step, select **Auto Port Configuration** and click on **Next.**
8. Finally, click on **Install** in the **Installation Summary** screen to start the Oracle Web Tier Utilities installation process.
9. Once OPMN is installed, go to your `ODI_HOME/oracledi/agent/bin/` directory and open up the `agentcreate.properties` file to edit it. The parameters in this file need to be modified to correspond to your ODI and OPMN configuration settings. In this recipe we use the following values:

```
ORACLE_ODI_HOME=C:/fmw/Oracle_ODI_1
INSTANCE_HOME=C:/fmw/Oracle_WT1/instances/instance1
COMPONENT_TYPE=odiagent
COMPONENT_NAME=ODI_OPMN_AGENT
ODI_MASTER_DRIVER=oracle.jdbc.OracleDriver ODI_MASTER_
URL=jdbc:oracle:thin:@localhost:1521:orcl
ODI_MASTER_USER=ODI_REPO_11G
ODI_MASTER_ENCODED_PASS=dpfHbipjYbBAfm7P,Dt69kPBV
ODI_SECU_WORK_REPO=ODI_11G_WREP
ODI_SUPERVISOR_ENCODED_PASS=d,yXMMv0Rk6rgNVKEnBb1xE.E
PORTNO=20920
JAVA_HOME=C:/Java/jdk1.6.0_24
ORACLE_OPMN_HOME=C:/fmw/Oracle_WT1
JMXPORTNO=21920
```

The path values to provide such as `ORACLE_ODI_HOME` or `INSTANCE_HOME` must be by using forward slashes ('/') and not backward slashes ('\').

The encoded passwords, such as `ODI_MASTER_ENCODED_PASS` or `ODI_SUPERVISOR_ENCODED_PASS`, can be obtained using the `encode.bat` or `encode.sh` command provided in the `ODI_HOME/oracledi/agent/bin` directory.

10. Next, open up the `odi_opmn_addagent.bat` or `odi_opmn_addagent.sh` script and enter the path values for `ODI_HOME` and `OPMN_HOME`. We use the following values in this recipe:

```
if "%ODI_HOME%" == "" set ODI_HOME=C:/fmw/Oracle_ODI_1/oracledi/
agent
REM call "%ODI_HOME%\bin\odiparams.bat"

if "%OPMN_HOME%" == "" set OPMN_HOME=C:/fmw/Oracle_WT1
if "%INSTANCE_HOME%" == "" set INSTANCE_HOME=C:/fmw/Oracle_WT1/
instances/instance1
```

11. Go to `OPMN_HOME/instances/INSTANCE_NAME/bin`, in which `INSTANCE_NAME` needs to be replaced by the OPMN instance name created earlier with the Web Tier Utilities installer (`instance1` in our recipe).
12. Then run the following command to start OPMN:

    opmnctl.bat start

13. Once OPMN is started, navigate to `ODI_HOME/oracledi/agent/bin/` in your command prompt and run the following command to add a standalone agent to OPMN:

    odi_opmn_addagent.bat

14. Subsequently, go back to `OPMN_HOME/instances/INSTANCE_NAME/bin` and enter the following command to verify that the ODI standalone agent named `ODI_OPMN_AGENT` is started:

    opmnctl.bat status

```
C:\fmw\Oracle_WT1\instances\instance1\bin>opmnctl status

Processes in Instance: instance1
---------------------------------+--------------------+---------+---------
ias-component                    | process-type       |     pid | status
---------------------------------+--------------------+---------+---------
ODI_OPMN_AGENT                   | odiagent           |    4208 | Alive
```

15. The agent `ODI_OPMN_AGENT` has now been successfully started and is now managed by OPMN. You can test the connection to the agent from **Topology Navigator** in ODI Studio.

How it works...

The `agentcreate.properties` file contains all the required information for OPMN to manage a standalone agent. We'll take a look at some of those parameters:

- `ORACLE_ODI_HOME` represents the path to the ODI installation directory
- `INSTANCE_HOME` points to the OPMN instance home directory
- `COMPONENT_NAME` is the name of the Physical Agent that will be managed through OPMN
- `ODI_MASTER_DRIVER` and `ODI_MASTER_URL` respectively represent the class name of the JDBC driver and the JDBC URL used to connect to the Master repository
- `ODI_MASTER_USER` and `ODI_MASTER_ENCODED_PASS` are the database username and encoded password required to access the Master repository
- `ODI_SECU_WORK` contains the name of the Work Repository
- `ODI_SUPERVISOR_ENCODED_PASS` stores the encoded ODI Supervisor user password

- `PORTNO` corresponds to the port number the agent will be listening to
- `JMX_PORTNO` is the **Java Management Extensions** (**JMX**) port number the agent will be using. JMX is used to propagate events from the agent to monitoring applications such as Oracle Enterprise Manager.

There's more...

The `odi_opmn_deleteagent` command allows users to remove agents that were previously added to the OPMN configuration settings. It is also possible to stop and restart the ODI agents' processes using the `opmnctl` command.

Deploying JDBC drivers with a JEE ODI Agent

In this recipe, we will be looking at how to deploy additional JDBC drivers to a JEE ODI Agent. ODI is delivered out of the box with support for many relational databases, however there are times when additional data sources may be needed. The ODI generic knowledge modules support virtually any Type 4 JDBC drivers. If the new source does have a Type 4 JDBC driver, this driver can be used to extract data from the source and can also be used to load to a target.

In this recipe, we will use a JDBC driver that is not shipped out of the box with ODI. Microsoft SQL Server 2012 was released after ODI 11.1.1.6.0 was released. Although there is no specific support listed in the ODI Certification Matrix for ODI 11.1.1.6.0 and SQL Server 2012, the new JDBC driver can be deployed to ODI Studio. Once the driver is deployed to the ODI Studio and the ODI JEE Agent, a SQL Server 2012 data server can be set up in the ODI topology and then used within an integration.

Getting ready

This recipe we will use the Microsoft SQL Server 2012 JDBC driver as an example. This file can be downloaded from `Microsoft.com` and deployed to ODI as outlined in the following section. No other prerequisites are required.

How to do it...

1. Download the Microsoft JDBC Driver SQL 4.0 with SQL Server 2012 support from `Microsoft.com`.
2. First, make sure to exit all ODI processes on the machine where the driver will be deployed.

3. Copy the `.jar` file to the `odi\oracledi\userlib` path, which is located in the `appdate` environment variable. For example, on Windows 2008 Server the directory is `C:\Users\dsgray\AppData\Roaming\odi\oracledi\userlib\`.
4. Restart ODI Studio, go to topology, and add a new data sever to Microsoft SQL Server Technology.

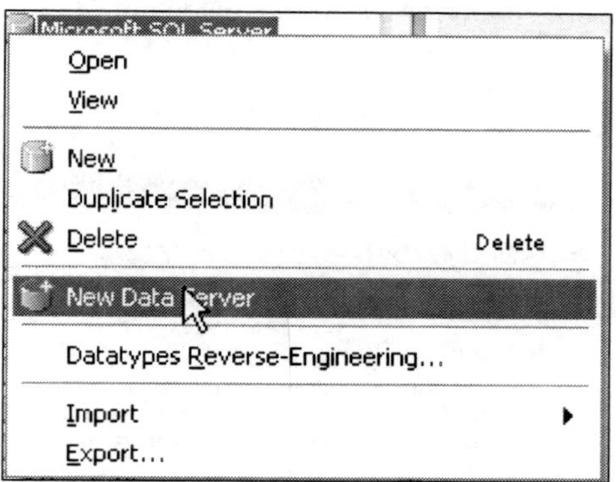

5. Set **Name**, **User**, and **Password** to match your SQL 2012 Server settings.

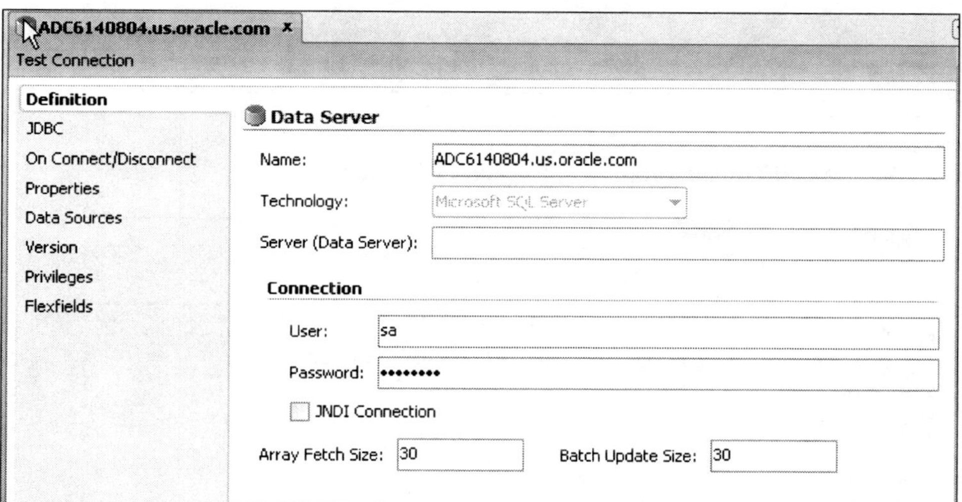

6. On the **JDBC** tab, click the search icon to get the list of JDBC drivers. Notice that the new driver now shows in the list **Microsoft SQL Server 2005 Driver for JDBC**. Select this driver and click on **OK**.

This driver shows SQL Sever 2005, however this is from the description embedded in the driver, not ODI.

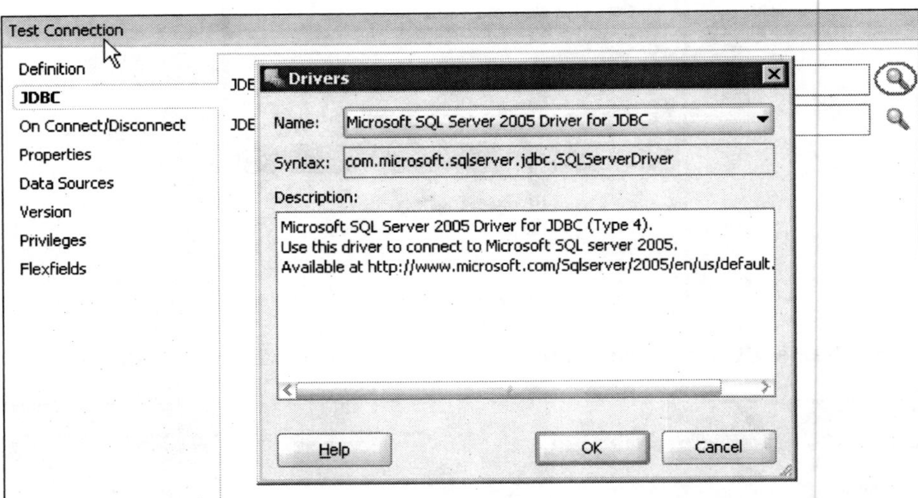

7. Set the JDBC URL appropriately for your SQL 2012 Server.

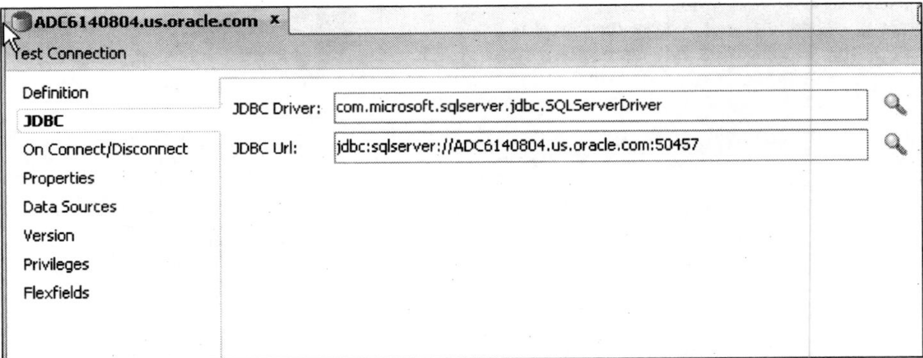

8. Click on the **Test Connection** button.

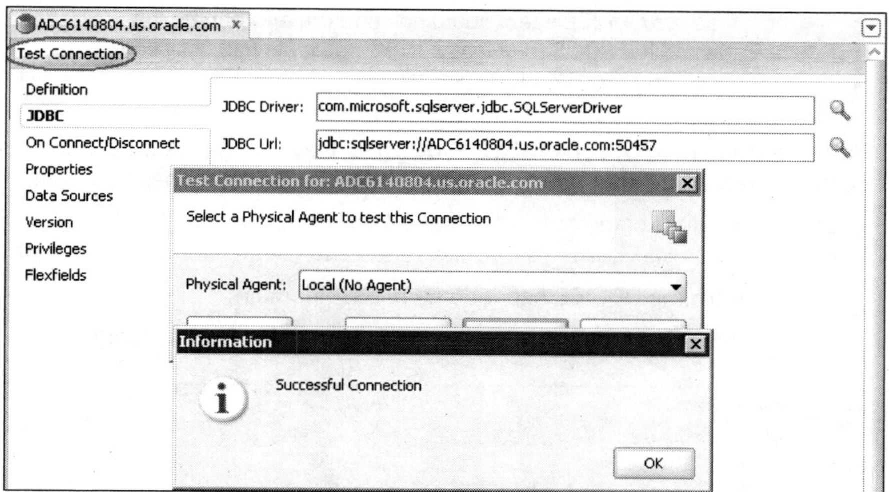

9. We have now successfully tested the new driver within ODI Studio. However, we can also test the ODI JEE agent here by selecting **OracleDIAgent** that was setup in the previous *Deploying a JEE ODI Agent* recipe.

10. Click on the **Test Connection** button.

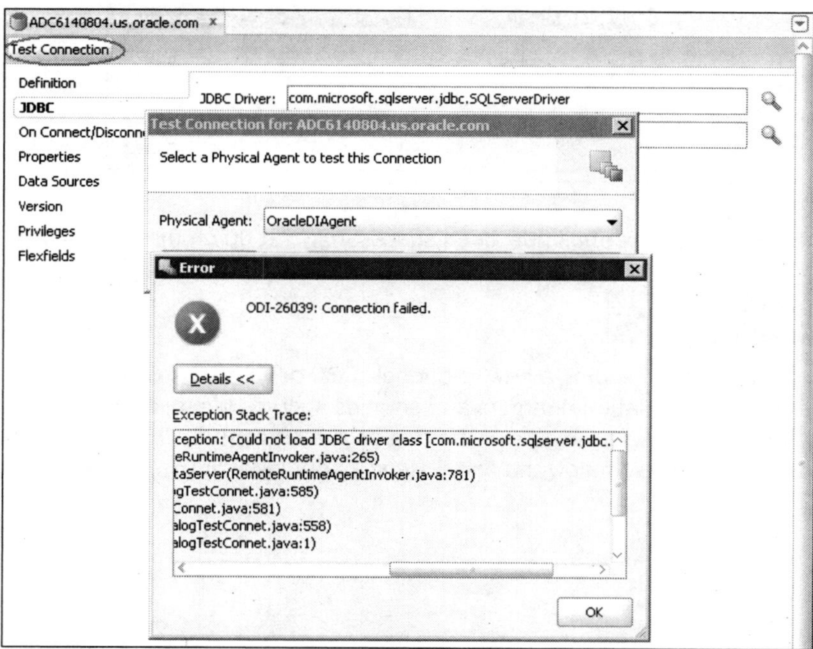

Notice there was an error during this test. This was expected as the ODI JEE Agent could not load the appropriate class since the SQL Server 2012 JDBC `.jar` file has not been copied to the WebLogic server.

11. Before copying the SQLServer2012 JDBC `.jar` file to the Weblogic server, the ODI domain needs to be shut down. Shut down the ODI JEE Agent base domain.
12. Once the domain is completely shut down, copy the SQLServer2012 JDBC jar to the `Middleware_Home\user_projects\domains\base_domain\lib` path.
    1. Restart the ODI JEE Agent domain, base domain.
    2. Within ODI Studio, click on the **Test Connection** button again.

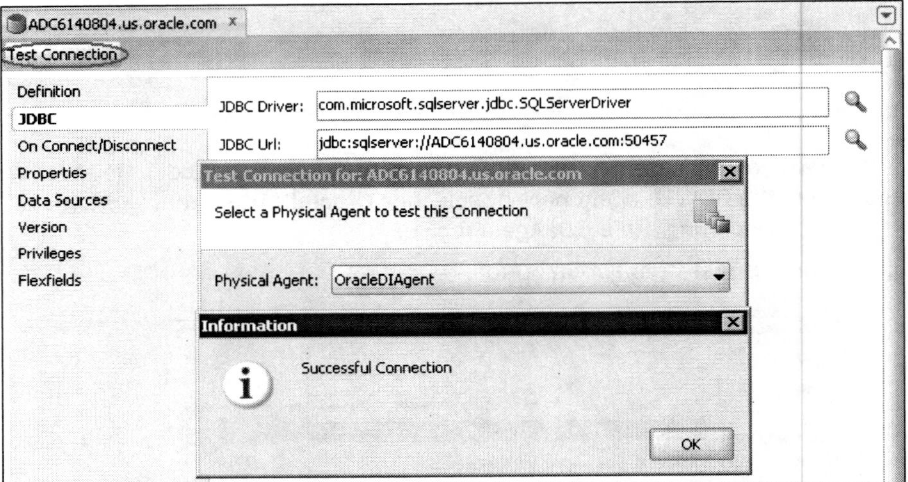

13. The new JDBC driver has now been successfully set up on the ODI JEE Agent.

There's more...

This recipe demonstrated adding a new relational JDBC driver to the ODI JEE Agent. JDBC drivers do exist for non-relational targets and sources such as Microsoft Excel, or also for applications such as `SalesForce.com`. Setting up the additional JDBC drivers for these types of technologies would follow the same steps as outlined for the SQL Server 2012 driver.

2

Defining the Oracle Data Integrator Security

The recipes in this chapter will help users understand and learn how to:

- Setting up LDAP security for Oracle Data Integrator
- Setting external authentication with Oracle Data Integrator
- Creating users using generic profiles
- Creating users using non-generic profiles
- Creating new custom profiles in the Security navigator

Introduction

Oracle Data Integrator provides, out of the box, a comprehensive security framework allowing administrators to manage users, assign pre-defined security profiles, or grant access to particular objects in a specific repository. ODI also offers the ability to integrate with external authentication mechanisms to authenticate users accessing ODI itself or the source and target systems.

It is recommended to familiarize yourself with the ODI security concepts prior to following this chapter's recipes. You can refer to the *Managing the Security in Oracle Data Integrator* chapter in the ODI documentation, which at the date of this publication could be found at `http://docs.oracle.com/cd/E23943_01/integrate.1111/e12643/security.htm#CDDIFFCB`.

Setting up LDAP security for Oracle Data Integrator

By default, ODI authenticates users as well as user privileges against the security information stored in the ODI master repository. Beginning with the ODI 11.1.1.3 release, ODI can utilize OPSS to authenticate users against a variety of identity stores. This architecture allows ODI users to be authenticated outside of ODI, however ODI's internal security still provides the user's authorization to the ODI objects. ODI users and their privileges must be created in ODI's internal security. The ODI users are mapped to the identity store and, during authentication, the ODI user is authenticated against the identity store, and once authenticated, ODI's internal security provides the authorization of the user to ODI objects.

OPSS works with a variety of identity stores; more information on OPSS can be found here at `http://docs.oracle.com/cd/E23943_01/core.1111/e10043/underjps.htm#CIHFHJCC`.

This recipe will utilize the LDAP Server, which is embedded with Oracle WebLogic Server. The Oracle WebLogic Embedded LDAP Server is documented at `http://docs.oracle.com/cd/E17904_01/web.1111/e13707/ldap.htm`. This recipe walks you through the steps of enabling the WebLogic Embedded LDAP Server on Oracle WebLogic 10.1.3.6.0 as well as configuring the users needed for ODI's external authentication.

How to do it...

1. Navigate to the Oracle WebLogic Administration Console, for example `http://localhost:7001/console/`, and log in with the WebLogic administrator user.
2. Enable the Oracle WebLogic Embedded LDAP Server by setting the Embedded LDAP Server Credential:
    - Click on the name domain, for example `ODI_AGENT. C`, click on the **Security** tab in the main panel.

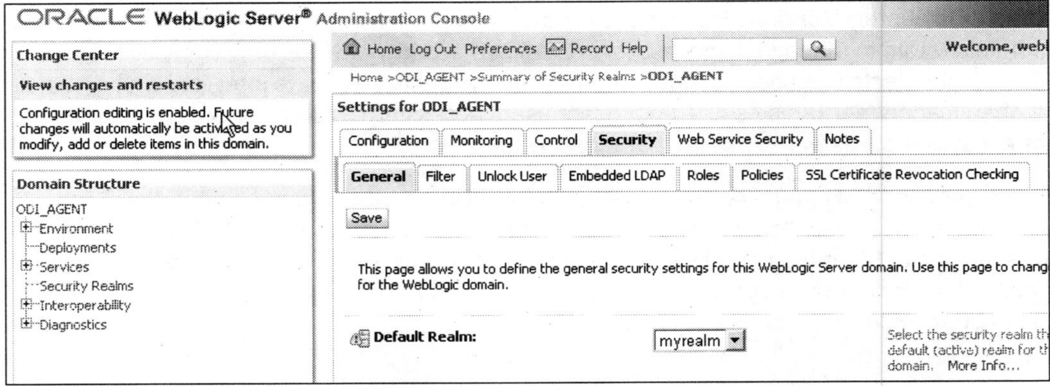

- Click on the **Embedded LDAP** tab to show the **Credential**; set the **Credential** to `weblogic1` and click on **Save**.
- This will set the default password for the WLS Embedded LDAP Server and enable the LDAP Server if not already enabled.

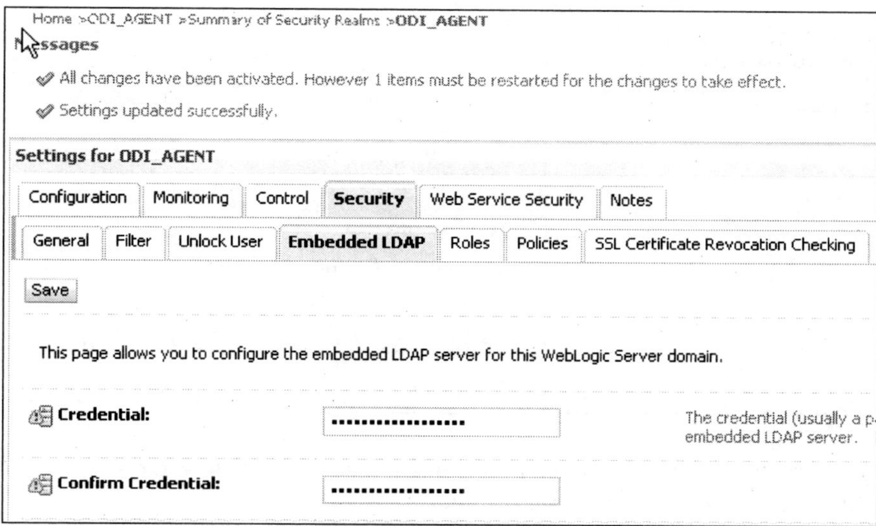

- Notice the message that the server must be restarted for the credential change to take effect. Restart the Oracle WebLogic Server.

3. Once the Oracle WebLogic Server has been restarted, the ODI users must be created in the Oracle WebLogic LDAP Server. These are the users that will be used to log in to ODI Studio as well as used within the ODI agent processes.
4. Navigate to the Oracle WebLogic Administration Console, for instance, `http://localhost:7001/console/`, and log in with the WebLogic administrator user.

5. Click on **Security Realms** in the **Domain Structure** tree.

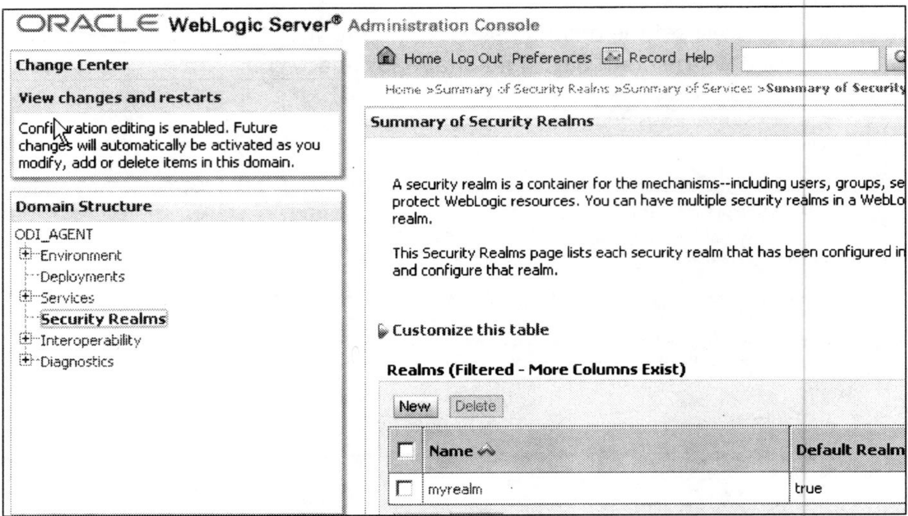

6. Click on **myrealm**, then **Users and Groups**, then click on **New** to create a new user that will be used to login to ODI Studio.

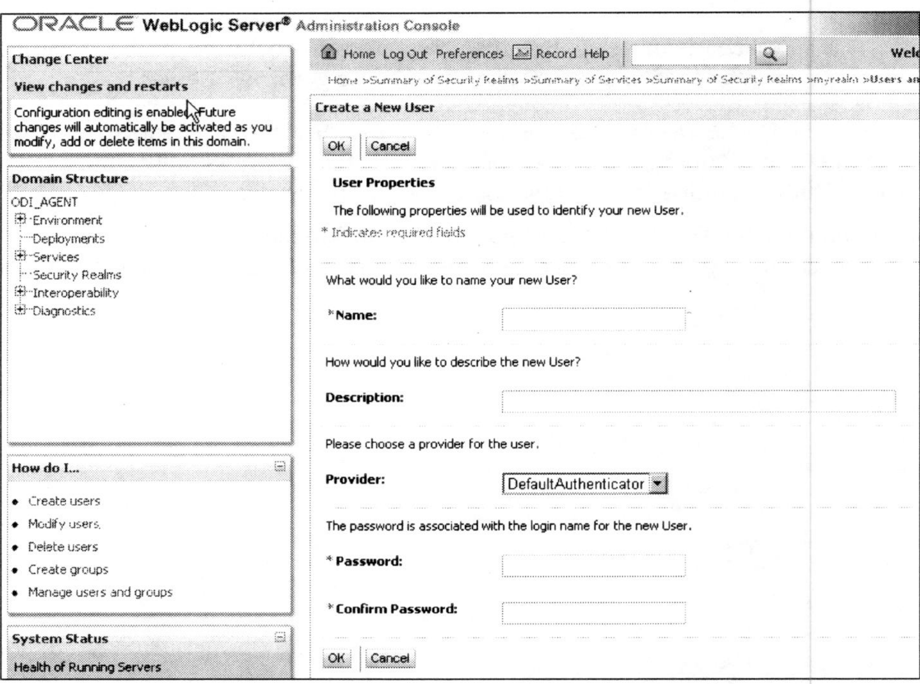

7. Set the **Name** to `SUPERVISOR`, **Description** to `ODI Supervisor` and **Password** to `weblogic1`. Leave **Provider** as **DefaultAuthenticator**. Click on **OK** to create.

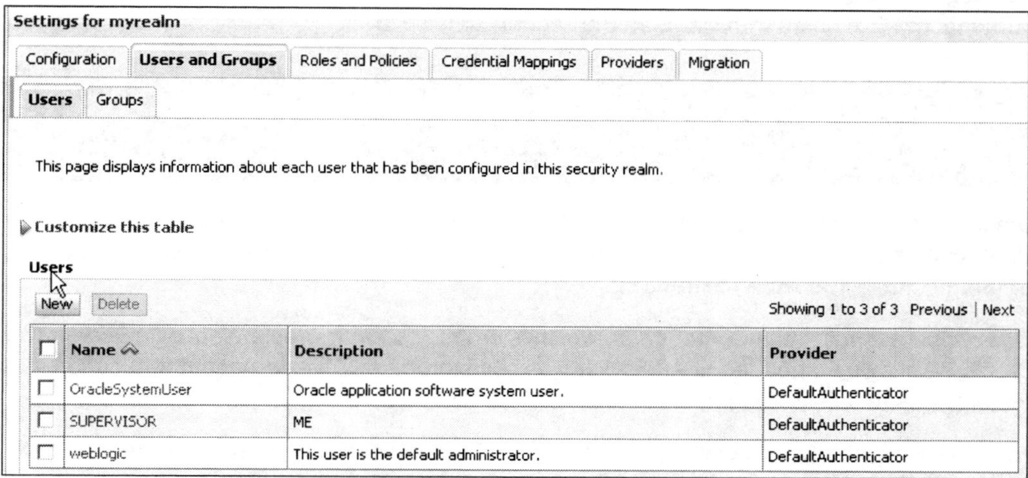

The Oracle WebLogic Embedded LDAP Server has now been setup. Two users will be used during the ODI external authentication setup. The default administrator for the WebLogic LDAP Server is `Admin` with the credential weblogic1, which was set in step 3, and the LDAP `SUPERVISOR` user with the password `weblogic1`, which was setup in the step 6.

Once the Oracle WebLogic Embedded LDAP Server and the LDAP users are created and configured, the ODI External Authentication must be configured. The first step is to configure the OPSS `jps-config.xml`, which is used by ODI to connect to the Oracle WebLogic Embedded LDAP Server using OPSS. A default `jps-config.xml` file named `odi-jps-config-jse.xml` is delivered with the installation of ODI Studio and located within the `ODI_HOME\oracledi\client\odi\bin` directory. This configuration is performed in the recipe *Setting up external authentication with Oracle Data Integrator*.

How it works...

By default, ODI security information is stored within the ODI Master repository. Beginning with ODI 11.1.3.0, administrators have the option to store the username and password in an external identity store and have ODI authenticate its users against this identity store. This allows enterprise level applications to use one central identity store for usernames and passwords, allowing for user passwords to only be stored in one location and administered outside of ODI. Within ODI, user authorization is still managed by ODI and privileges are stored in the ODI master repository.

ODI utilizes OPSS as the foundation for external authentication, allowing ODI to work with a variety of identity stores including the Oracle WebLogic Embedded LDAP Server. The Oracle WebLogic Embedded LDAP Server is simple to enable and can easily be configured to authenticate ODI users with OPSS as the security service layer.

Setting external authentication with Oracle Data Integrator

Oracle Platform Security Services works with a variety of identity stores; more information on OPSS can be found here at `http://docs.oracle.com/cd/E23943_01/core.1111/e10043/underjps.htm#CIHFHJCC`.

This recipe will utilize the LDAP Server, which is embedded with Oracle WebLogic Server. The Oracle WebLogic Embedded LDAP Server was configured for ODI external authentication in the previous recipe, *Setting up LDAP Security with ODI*.

For this recipe, the Oracle WebLogic Embedded LDAP Server will be used to authenticate ODI users with ODI Studio as well as the ODI Agent processes for both standalone and the JEE agents. Oracle WebLogic 10.1.3.6.0 was installed with the default settings. ODI was then installed in the same Oracle `Middleware_HOME` directory and an ODI JEE agent was then deployed to a managed server within this instance of Oracle WebLogic; the WebLogic domain is named `ODI_AGENT`.

Once the Oracle WebLogic Embedded LDAP Server has been set up and configured, ODI can be configured for external authentication to this LDAP Server. The default administrator for the WebLogic LDAP Server is `Admin` with the credential weblogic1. This was set up in the recipe *Setting up LDAP security for Oracle Data Integrator* in step 3, and the LDAP user `SUPERVISOR` with the password `weblogic1` was set up in step 6.

How to do it...

1. The first step is to configure the `jps-config.xml` file, which is used by ODI to connect to the Oracle WebLogic Embedded LDAP Server using OPSS. A default `jps-config.xml` file named `odi-jps-config-jse.xml` is delivered with the install of ODI Studio and located within the `ODI_HOME\oracledi\client\odi\bin` directory. Open this file.

Once opened, update the `serviceProviders` section to include the embedded LDAP Server store.

```
<serviceProviders>
    <serviceProvider type="CREDENTIAL_STORE" name="credstoressp" class="oracle.security.jps.internal.c
        <description>SecretStore-based CSF provider</description>
    </serviceProvider>

    <serviceProvider type="IDENTITY_STORE" name="idstore.xml.provider" class="oracle.security.jps.inte
        <description>XML-based IdStore Provider</description>
    </serviceProvider>

    <serviceProvider type="POLICY_STORE" name="policystore.xml.provider" class="oracle.security.jps.in
        <description>XML-based PolicyStore Provider</description>
    </serviceProvider>
```

```
<serviceProvider type="IDENTITY_STORE" name="idstore.ldap.
provider" class="oracle.security.jps.internal.idstore.ldap.
LdapIdentityStoreProvider">
            <description>LDAP-based IdentityStore Provider</
description>
</serviceProvider>
```

```
<serviceProviders>
    <serviceProvider type="CREDENTIAL_STORE" name="credstoressp" class="oracle.security.jps.internal.c
        <description>SecretStore-based CSF provider</description>
    </serviceProvider>

   <serviceProvider type="IDENTITY_STORE" name="idstore.ldap.provider" class="oracle.security.jps.inte
        <description>LDAP-based IdentityStore Provider</description>
    </serviceProvider>

    <serviceProvider type="IDENTITY_STORE" name="idstore.xml.provider" class="oracle.security.jps.inte
        <description>XML-based IdStore Provider</description>
    </serviceProvider>

    <serviceProvider type="POLICY_STORE" name="policystore.xml.provider" class="oracle.security.jps.in
        <description>XML-based PolicyStore Provider</description>
    </serviceProvider>
```

2. Update the `serviceInstances` section to include the following service instance, where `ldap.URL` is the url of the WebLogic Embedded LDAP Server, the `subscriber.name` is the name of the domain for the WebLogic Embedded LDAP Server, and `ou=myrealm,dc=ODI_AGENT`, and the `security.principal.alias` is the credential map to use `oracle.odi.credmap`.

```
<serviceInstances>
    <!--following instance define where is the cwallet.sso will be located program try to create one -->
    <serviceInstance name="credstore" provider="credstoressp" location="./">
        <description>File Based Credential Store Service Instance</description>
    </serviceInstance>

    <serviceInstance name="idstore.xml" provider="idstore.xml.provider" location="./system-jazn-data.xml">
        <description>File Based Identity Store Service Instance</description>
        <property name="subscriber.name" value="jazn.com"/>
    </serviceInstance>

    <serviceInstance name="policystore.xml" provider="policystore.xml.provider" location="./system-jazn-data.xml">
        <description>File Based Policy Store Service Instance</description>
    </serviceInstance>

    <serviceInstance name="idstore.loginmodule" provider="jaas.login.provider">
        <description>Identity Store Login Module</description>
        <property name="loginModuleClassName" value="oracle.security.jps.internal.jaas.module.idstore.IdStoreLoginModule"/>
        <property name="jaas.login.controlFlag" value="REQUIRED"/>
    </serviceInstance>
```

Here is the screenshot of the code after adding the preceding code:

```
<serviceInstances>
    <!--following instance define where is the cwallet.sso will be located program try to create one -
     <serviceInstance name="idstore.wlsovd" provider="idstore.ldap.provider">
                <property name="idstore.type" value="WLS_OVD"/>
                <property name="ldap.url" value="ldap://localhost:7001"/>
                <property name="subscriber.name" value="ou=myrealm,dc=ODI_AGENT"/>
                <property name="security.principal.key" value="ODI_AGENT"/>
                <property name="security.principal.alias" value="oracle.odi.credmap"/>
                <extendedproperty>
                    <name>user.search.bases</name>
                    <values>
                       <value>ou=people,ou=myrealm,dc=ODI_AGENT</value>
                    </values>
                </extendedproperty>
                <extendedproperty>
                    <name>group.search.bases</name>
                    <values>
                      <value>ou=people,ou=myrealm,dc=ODI_AGENT</value>
                    </values>
                </extendedproperty>
                <property name="username.attr" value="uid"/>
                <property name="groupname.attr" value="cn"/>
  </serviceInstance>
    <serviceInstance name="credstore" provider="credstoressp" location="./">
        <description>File Based Credential Store Service Instance</description>
    </serviceInstance>
```

3. Update the JPS Contexts section to the following for the default `jpsContext` for the embedded LDAP store:

```
<jpsContexts default="default">
    <!-- This is the default JPS context. All the mendatory services and Login Modules must be configu
    <jpsContext name="default">
        <serviceInstanceRef ref="credstore"/>
        <!--serviceInstanceRef ref="keystore"/-->
        <!--serviceInstanceRef ref="idstore.xml"/-->
        <!--serviceInstanceRef ref="policystore.xml"/-->
        <!--serviceInstanceRef ref="idstore.loginmodule"/-->
    <!--serviceInstanceRef ref="audit"/-->
    </jpsContext>

    <jpsContext name="bootstrap_credstore_context">
        <serviceInstanceRef ref="bootstrap.credstore"/>
    </jpsContext>
```

```
</jpsContext>
```

```
<jpsContexts default="default">
    <!-- This is the default JPS context. All the mendatory services and Login Modules must be configu
   <jpsContext name="default">
        <serviceInstanceRef ref="credstore"/>
        <serviceInstanceRef ref="keystore"/>
        <serviceInstanceRef ref="idstore.wlsovd"/>
        <serviceInstanceRef ref="idstore.loginmodule"/>

    </jpsContext>
```

Save the file as `jps-config.xml` within the same directory.

4. Once the OPSS config file `jps-config.xml` is configured appropriately, the next step is to set up a credential store for the LDAP Server in the ODI wallet. This is performed on Linux using the `odi_credtool.sh`. No such command line tool exists for Windows. The following command, executed from the command line within the `ODI_HOME\ oracledi\client\odi\bin` directory within a middleware home, will perform the same as the Linux script:

java -classpath ..\..\.

.\..\oracledi.common\odi\lib\odi-core.jar;..\..\..\..\modules\ oracle.jps_11.1.1/

jps-manifest.jar -Doracle.security.jps.config=.\jps-config.xml oracle.odi.core.security.JPSContextCredTool

5. Executing this command will prompt for the following:

```
Administrator: C:\Windows\system32\cmd.exe - java -classpath ..\..\..\oracledi.common\odi\lib\o...

C:\oracle\Middleware\Oracle_ODI1\oracledi\client\odi\bin>java -classpath ..\..\.
.\..\oracledi.common\odi\lib\odi-core.jar;..\..\..\..\modules\oracle.jps_11.1.1/
jps-manifest.jar -Doracle.security.jps.config=.\jps-config.xml oracle.odi.core.s
ecurity.JPSContextCredTool
[input] Map:_
```

Enter the following:

```
Map: oracle.odi.credmap
Key:ODI_AGENT
User_Name:CN=Admin
Password:weblogic1
```

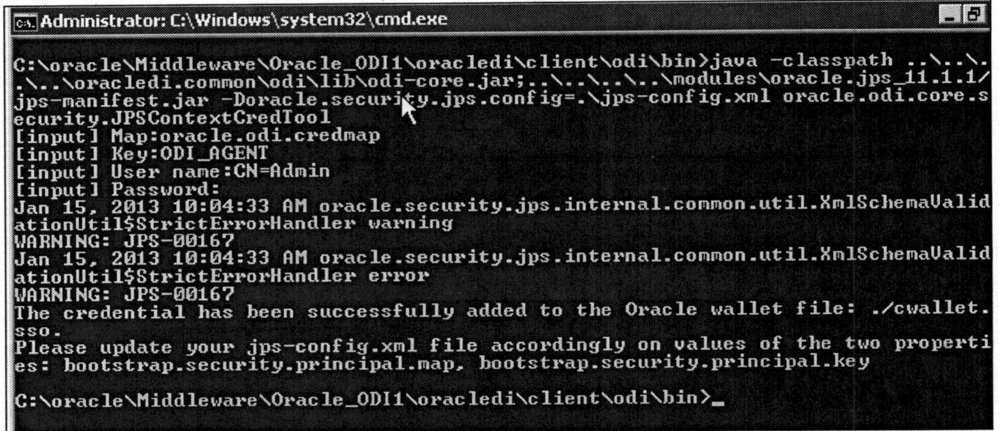
```
Administrator: C:\Windows\system32\cmd.exe

C:\oracle\Middleware\Oracle_ODI1\oracledi\client\odi\bin>java -classpath ..\..\.
.\..\oracledi.common\odi\lib\odi-core.jar;..\..\..\..\modules\oracle.jps_11.1.1/
jps-manifest.jar -Doracle.security.jps.config=.\jps-config.xml oracle.odi.core.s
ecurity.JPSContextCredTool
[input] Map:oracle.odi.credmap
[input] Key:ODI_AGENT
[input] User name:CN=Admin
[input] Password:
Jan 15, 2013 10:04:33 AM oracle.security.jps.internal.common.util.XmlSchemaValid
ationUtil$StrictErrorHandler warning
WARNING: JPS-00167
Jan 15, 2013 10:04:33 AM oracle.security.jps.internal.common.util.XmlSchemaValid
ationUtil$StrictErrorHandler error
WARNING: JPS-00167
The credential has been successfully added to the Oracle wallet file: ./cwallet.
sso.
Please update your jps-config.xml file accordingly on values of the two properti
es: bootstrap.security.principal.map, bootstrap.security.principal.key

C:\oracle\Middleware\Oracle_ODI1\oracledi\client\odi\bin>_
```

There is an XML validation warning here, however you should see that the credential was successfully added to the Oracle wallet file.

Once successful, the credential is then stored in the Oracle wallet and will be used to connect and authenticate to the Oracle WebLogic Embedded LDAP Server.

6. Now that the Oracle WebLogic Embedded LDAP Server and ODI External Authentication have been set up, a new repository can be created and set up within ODI Studio.

An existing repository can also be used. Using ODI, a repository can be switched from external authentication to ODI internal and visa versa.

7. Create a new schema for the ODI repository; the following are the sample scripts used for this recipe:

```
-- USER SQL
CREATE USER ODI_EXT_AUTH IDENTIFIED BY weblogic1
DEFAULT TABLESPACE "USERS"
TEMPORARY TABLESPACE "TEMP";

-- ROLES
GRANT "DBA" TO ODI_EXT_AUTH ;
```

8. Open ODI Studio, making sure ODI Studio was started from the same location where the `jps-config.xml` file was configured and saved.

   Select **File** then **New** from the menu:

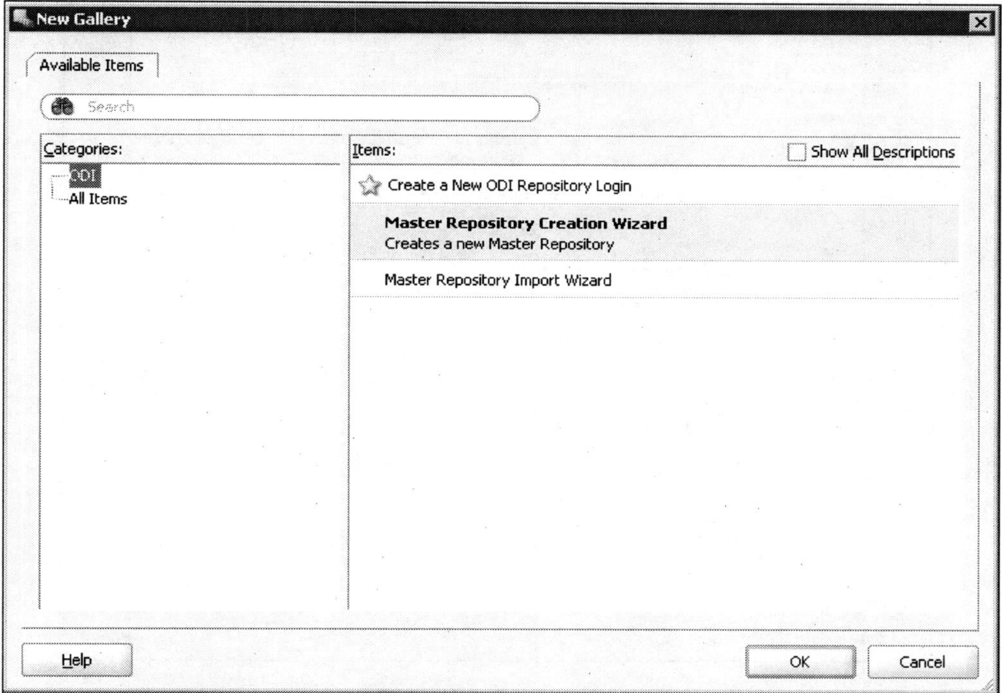

9. Select **Master Repository Creation Wizard** and click on **OK**.

   Enter the following:

   JDBC Driver: `oracle.jdbc.OracleDriver`

   JDBC Url: `jdbc:oracle:thin:@localhost:1521:xe`

   User: `ODI_EXT_AUTH`

   Password: `weblogic1`

   DBA User: `sys as sysdba`

   DBA Password: `DBA Password`

   Id: `111`

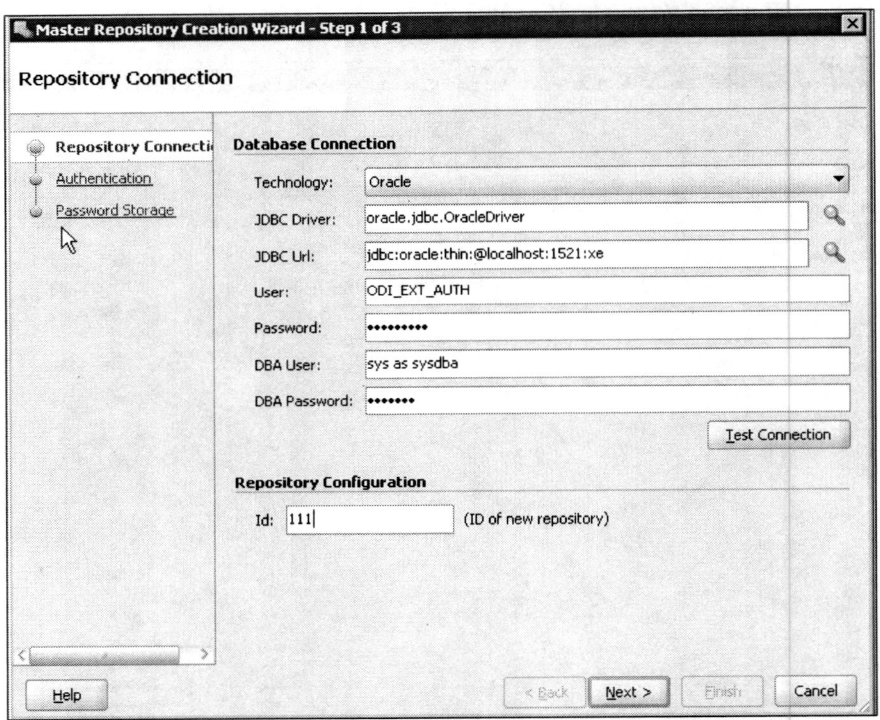

10. Test the connection to make sure there is connectivity to the database schema and then click on **Next**. Select **Use External Authentication** and set the **User** as `SUPERVISOR` and **Password** as `weblogic1`, then click on **Next >**.

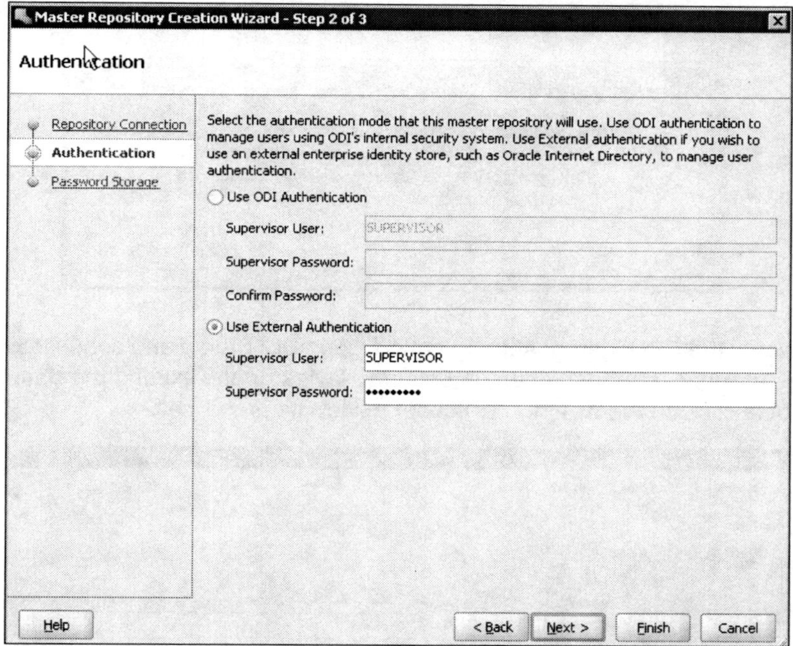

11. Select **Internal Password Storage** for this recipe and then click on **Finish**.

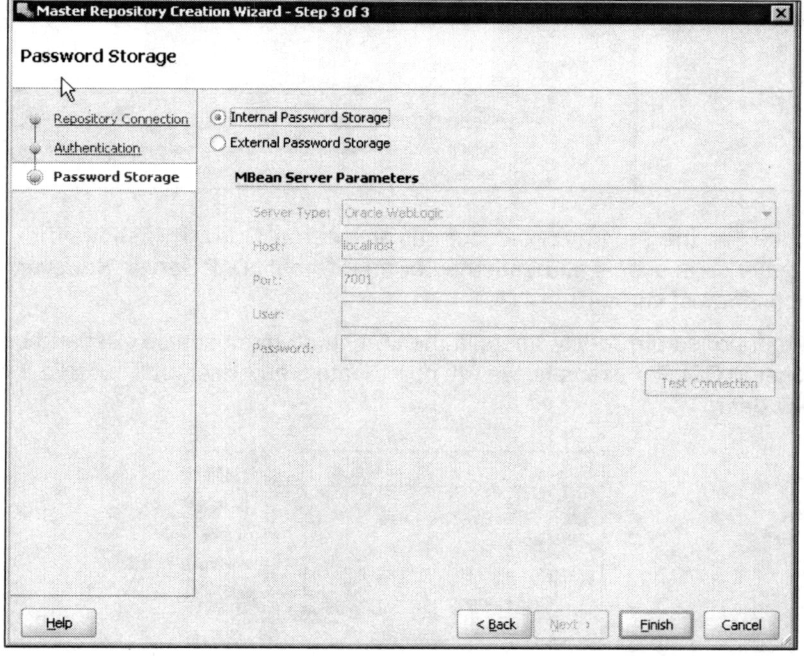

The repository will be created and the following message will appear when complete:

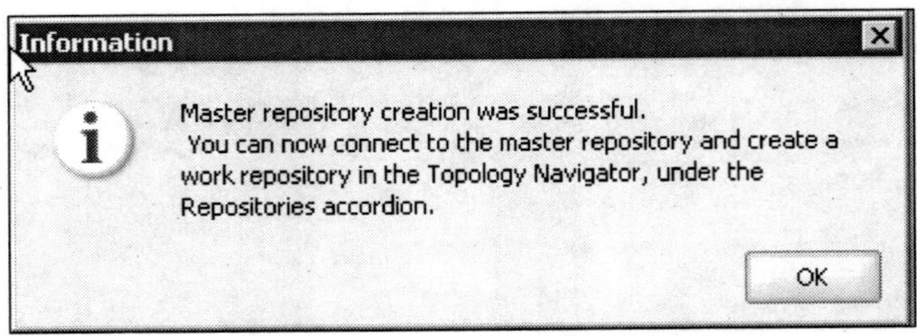

12. To verify the ODI External Authentication, open ODI Studio and connect to the new master repository. Then open up Security Navigator and expand the **User** accordion. Double-click on the `SUPERVISOR` user to view its properties.

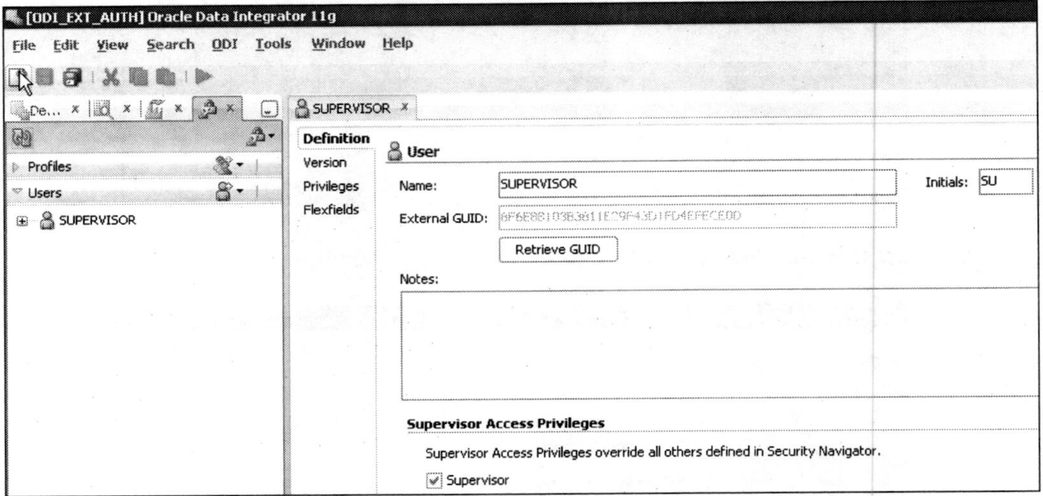

Notice that the `SUPERVISOR` user has an external GUID. This shows the `SUPERVISOR` user is authenticated by an external LDAP Server. However, the user must still exist in ODI.

13. As mentioned previously, users in the LDAP system must also exist and be mapped to a user in ODI. For example, we will now create a new user, `ODI_User1`, by clicking on **New User**:

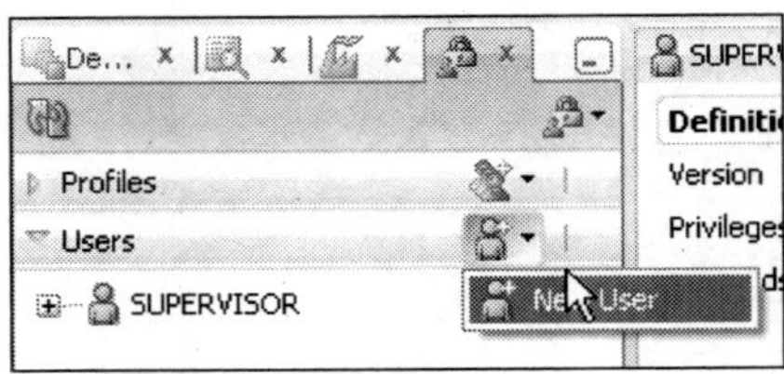

This user panel will now appear, allowing the new user to be created.

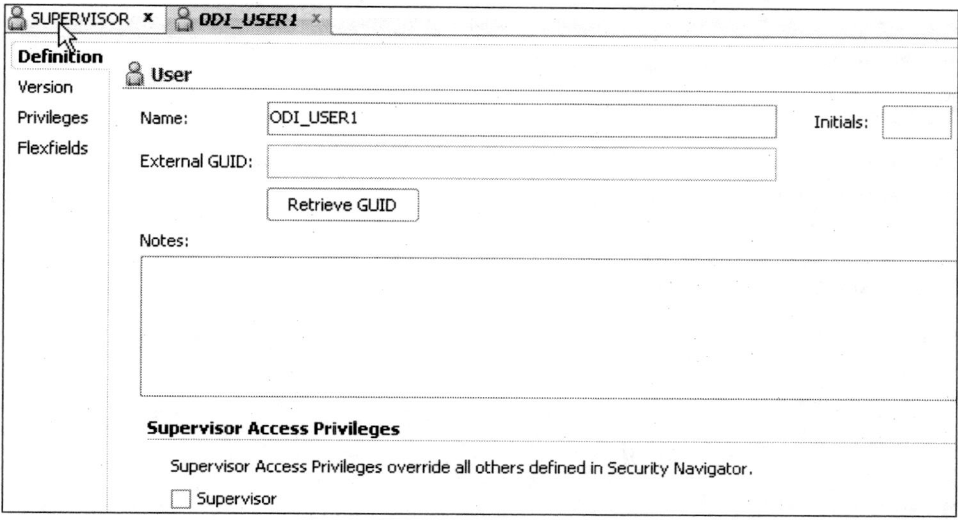

Click on **Save** and the following message appears:

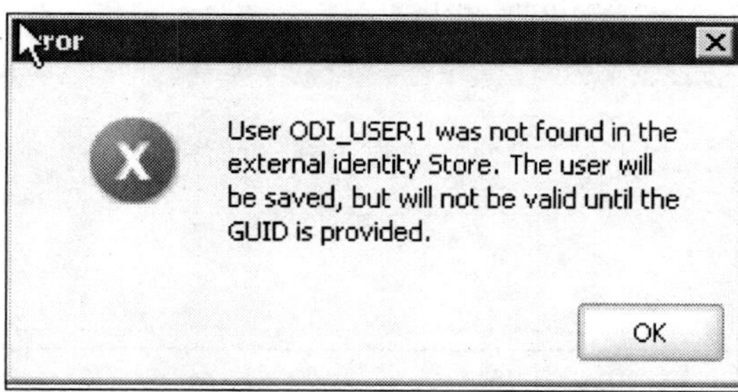

This user does not yet exist in the LDAP Server; create the user in the WebLogic Embedded Server and then retrieve the GUID.

14. Create `ODI_USER1` similarly to what was done in step 3 of the recipe *Set up LDAP security with Oracle Data Integrator*:

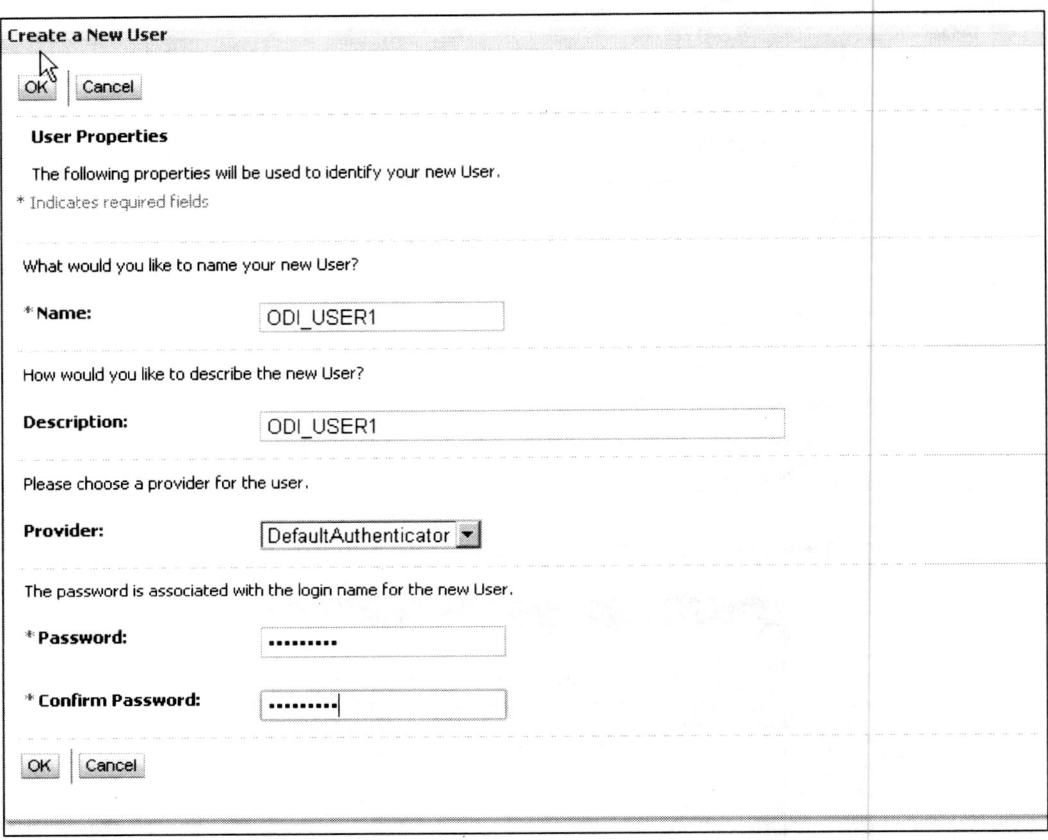

15. Within ODI, on the `ODI_USER1` screen, click on the **Retrieve GUID** button and the GUID will be retrieved from the LDAP Server:

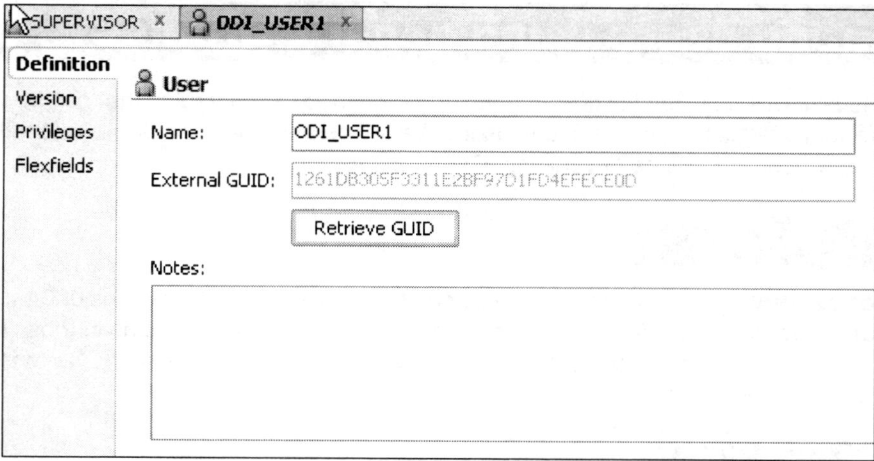

You have now successfully set up and tested external authentication with ODI and an LDAP Server. This same `jps-config.xml` OPSS file can be used with the ODI standalone agent as well as the ODI JEE Agent.

How it works...

ODI utilizes OPSS as the foundation for external authentication, allowing ODI to work with a variety of identity stores including the Oracle WebLogic Embedded LDAP Server. Once the identity store is configured (Oracle WebLogic Embedded LDAP Server for this recipe), the OPSS layer needs to be configured. OPSS configuration is accomplished by editing the `jps-config.xml` file; a template for this file is provided with the ODI installation. Once this configuration is complete and tested, a new master repository can be created in ODI with external authentication enabled. At any time, security authentication for ODI can be switched from using ODI's internal authentication to external authentication mode. The steps to perform this change in security are outlined in the ODI security documentation located here at `http://docs.oracle.com/cd/E17904_01/integrate.1111/e12643/security.htm#CHDIEAEJ`.

There's more...

Since ODI utilizes OPSS as the security service layer, the OPSS configuration only needs to be performed once, and the same `jps-config.xml` file can be used in any ODI process: ODI Studio, ODI Standalone Agent, or ODI JEE Agent.

Existing ODI repositories that currently use internal authentication can easily be switched to external authentication. Once OPSS and the identity store have been properly configured and tested, the authentication mode can easily be changed using the ODI Studio Switch Authentication Mode wizard.

Creating users using generic profiles

Out of the box, ODI provides **Profiles** containing predefined security rules that can be used to easily grant privileges to new or existing users. We will be utilizing some of those **Profiles** to create a new user who will be developing ETL mappings.

Getting ready

In this recipe, we will reuse the repositories and objects created in the recipes of *Chapter 10, Advanced Coding Techniques using the ODI SDK*. Follow the instructions in those recipes to create them. You can also follow the instructions using your own repository. No other prerequisites are required.

How to do it...

1. In ODI Studio, go to the ODI menu, then click on **Connect** and log into your repository using an ODI supervisor user.
2. Open up **Security navigator** and expand both the **Profiles** and **Users** accordions. You should see a structure similar to the following screenshot:

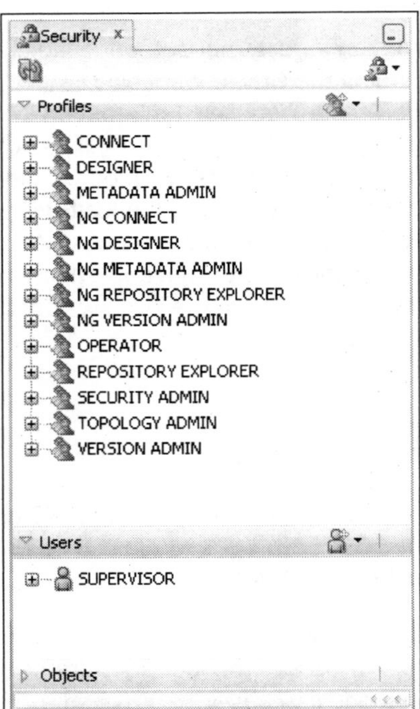

3. Click on the **New User** button in the **Users** accordion to open up the user creation wizard.

4. Next, specify a name in the **Name** field; we use `Cookbook Developer` in this example. The **User** creation panel should look like the following:

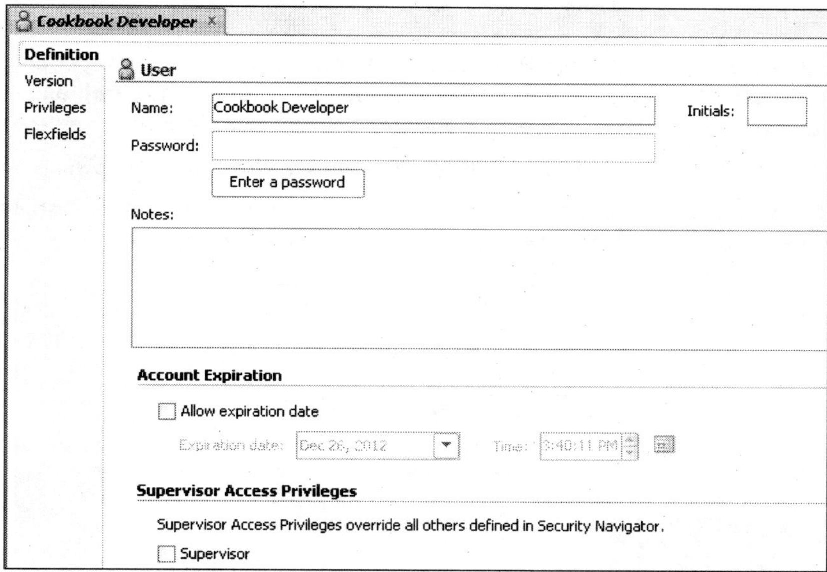

5. Then, click on the **Enter a password** button, specify a password, and optionally an expiration date for the password.

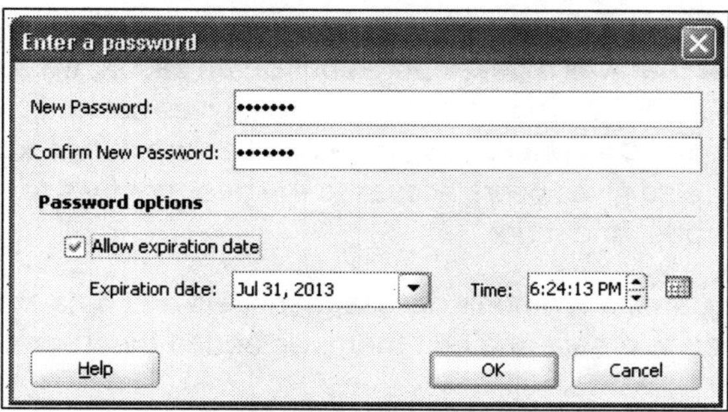

Then click on **OK** to close the pop-up window.

6. Optionally you can also define an expiration date for the user. Before you save the new user, make sure the `Supervisor` checkbox is not checked, unless you want to create a user with administrator privileges.
7. Click on the **Save** button in ODI Studio; you should now see a new user under the **User** accordion.

8. Finally, we will assign a few **Profiles** to that newly created user. Drag-and-drop the `CONNECT`, `DESIGNER`, and `METADATA ADMIN` profiles from the **Profiles** accordion into the newly created user. Those **Profiles** are typically required for a developer.
9. Click on **Yes** to confirm the profiles grant in the **Confirmation** windows.
10. Once you're done, expand the `Cookbook Developer` user and its **Profiles** node. You should see a list of three profiles as in the following screenshot:

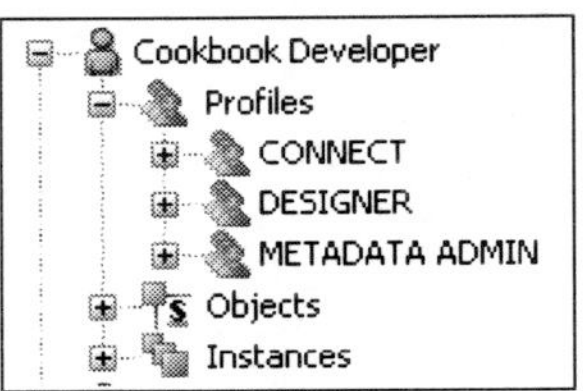

How it works...

We have used several built-in generic **Profiles** in this recipe. We started by assigning the `CONNECT` profile to our new user. The `CONNECT` profile only allows users to access the repositories; it is required for any user, but it doesn't grant access to any object stored in the repositories.

Since we created a user that was a developer in our organization, we also granted the `DESIGNER` profile to this person. The `DESIGNER` profile gives users the ability to access all the objects displayed in the **Designer** navigator as well as the option to create interfaces, packages, and so on. It also gives users access to the operator logs to review the execution details, the generated code, and more.

The `DESIGNER` profile grants a read-only access to models and data stores. Since a developer may also need to create and edit them, we added the `METADATA ADMIN` profile to our new user.

There's more...

We've used three of the built-in generic **Profiles** in this recipe, but there are more, such as `OPERATOR`, which allows access to all the objects found in the **Operator** navigator such as sessions. It is mostly used in production for users that will monitor the execution of ODI processes.

There are also the `TOPOLOGY ADMIN` and `SECURITY ADMIN` profiles, which can be granted to administrators along with the `CONNECT` profile to get full access to the connectivity and security settings of Oracle Data Integrator.

See also

You might also be interested in the recipe *Creating users using non-generic profiles*, which describes how to define more granular security settings when required.

Creating users using non-generic profiles

ODI offers the flexibility to specify security privileges at the object level, such as giving a user the ability to only access one project or one folder in a project. We will be utilizing a non-generic profile and providing access to one single interface to a user.

Getting ready

In this recipe, we will reuse the user named `Cookbook Developer` that we created in the previous recipe, *Creating users using generic profiles*. Follow the necessary steps of that recipe to create it. You can also follow the instructions using your own repository. No other prerequisites are required.

How to do it...

1. In ODI Studio, go to the ODI menu, then click on **Connect** and log into your repository using an ODI supervisor user.
2. In **Security** navigator, expand the `Cookbook Developer` user and its **Profiles** node, then right-click on the `DESIGNER` profile and select **Delete**.

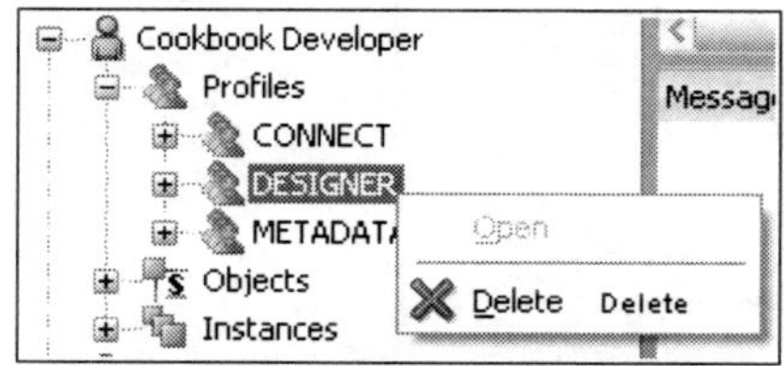

Click on **Yes** in the **Confirmation** window.

Next, drag-and-drop the `NG DESIGNER` profile to this user and click on **Yes** in the **Confirmation** window.

3. Click on the **ODI** menu in ODI Studio and select **Disconnect** to disconnect from your repository.
4. Next, click on the **Connect** button and connect to your repository using the newly edited `Cookbook Developer` user. Open up the **Designer** navigator and expand the **Interfaces** node in the `ODI SDK Project` and `SDK Folder`. No Interfaces are listed even though we know there is one in this folder, but this is expected since this user doesn't have access to any interfaces at this time thanks to the `NG DESIGNER` profile:

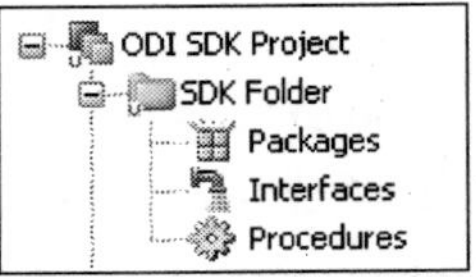

5. Now click again on the ODI menu in ODI Studio and select **Disconnect** to disconnect from your repository. Then click on the **Connect** button and connect to your repository using an ODI supervisor user.
6. Open up the **Designer** and **Security** navigators next to each other so you can drag-and-drop objects between them. Your panel layout should be similar to the one shown in the following screenshot:

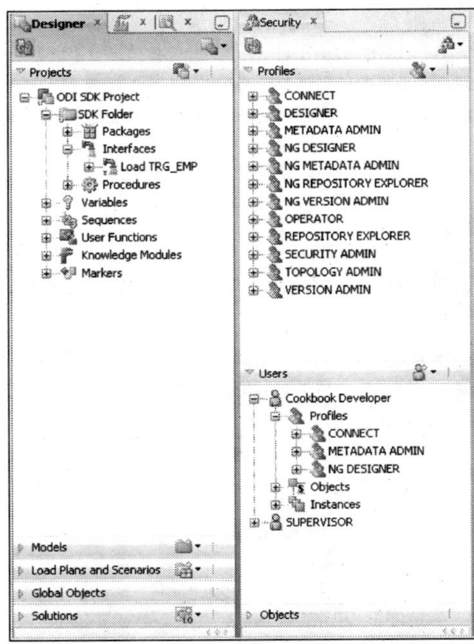

7. Drag-and-drop the `Load TRG_EMP` interface from the **Designer** navigator into the `Cookbook Developer` user. Click on **Yes** when asked in the **Confirmation** window.

8. Next, in the **Security** panel, click on the Allow all methods in all repositories button ( ) to allow access to all this interface's methods to the `Cookbook Developer` user in all repositories:

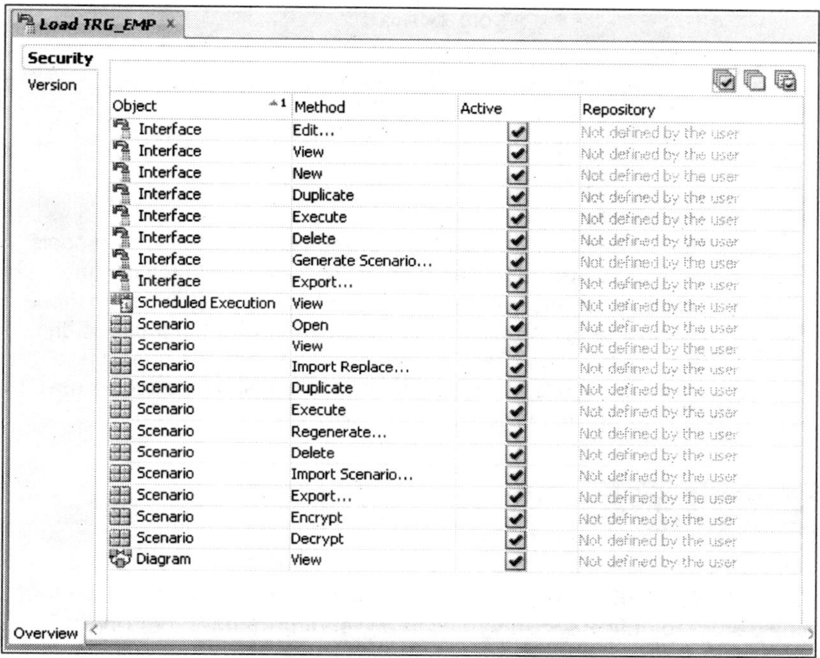

9. Click on **Save** and then expand the `Cookbook Developer` user, the **Instances**, and **Interfaces** nodes. You should now see the `Load TRG_EMP` interface listed there:

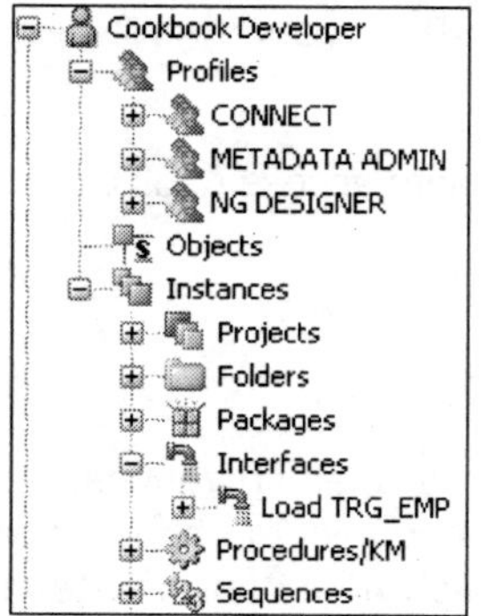

10. Finally, click on the ODI menu in ODI Studio and select **Disconnect** to disconnect from your repository. Then click on the **Connect** button and connect to your repository using the newly edited user, `Cookbook Developer`. Open up the **Designer** navigator and expand the **Interfaces** node in the `ODI SDK Project` and `SDK Folder`. You will now see the `Load TRG_EMP` interface listed:

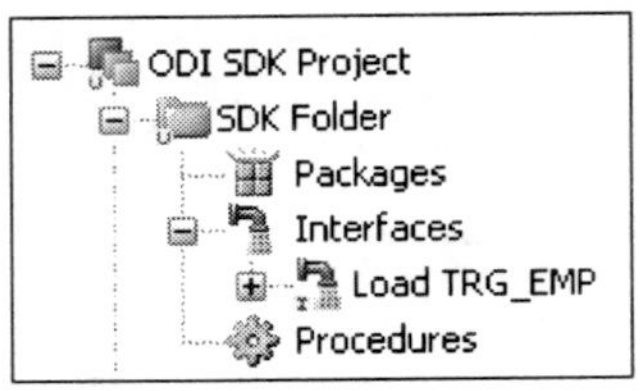

> The `METADATA ADMIN` profile provides full access to all models and data stores as well as read-only access to all projects and folders, which explains why we didn't have to drag-and-drop those objects into our `Cookbook Developer` user. If our user didn't have this profile, we would have needed to add the project and the folder storing the interface and the models and data stores used by the interface to our user.

How it works...

In this recipe, we assigned the `NG DESIGNER` profile to our `Cookbook Developer` user. This non-generic profile doesn't grant any access privileges on any object instance to a user, but it allows administrators to define security rules in a granular manner: per object, per repository, per user.

By default, non-generic profiles such as `NG DESIGNER` or `NG METADATA ADMIN` do not authorize users to access any object methods, for example, editing or viewing interfaces. Users to whom those profiles are assigned must be specifically authorized to use object methods for each object instances. This is done while dragging and dropping a specific instance of an object to a user.

In contrast, generic profiles grant users access to all object methods by default for all object instances.

There's more...

It is also possible to restrict access to object instances in specific repositories. This can be achieved when granting access to object methods; to do so, simply select the **Allow selected methods in selected repositories** button instead of the **Allow all methods in all repositories** button.

Creating new custom profiles in the Security navigator

ODI users have the ability to create their own security profiles in the **Security** navigator. In this recipe, we will be duplicating the `DESIGNER` profile and editing it to remove access to all CDC functionality.

Getting ready

In this recipe, we will reuse the user named `Cookbook Developer` that we created in the recipe *Creating users using generic profiles*. Follow the necessary steps of that recipe to create it. You can also follow the instructions using your own repository. No other prerequisites are required.

How to do it...

1. In ODI Studio, go to the ODI menu, then click on **Connect** and log into your repository using an ODI supervisor user.
2. In the **Security** navigator, open the **Profiles** accordion.
3. Right-click on the `DESIGNER` profile and select **Duplicate Selection:**

   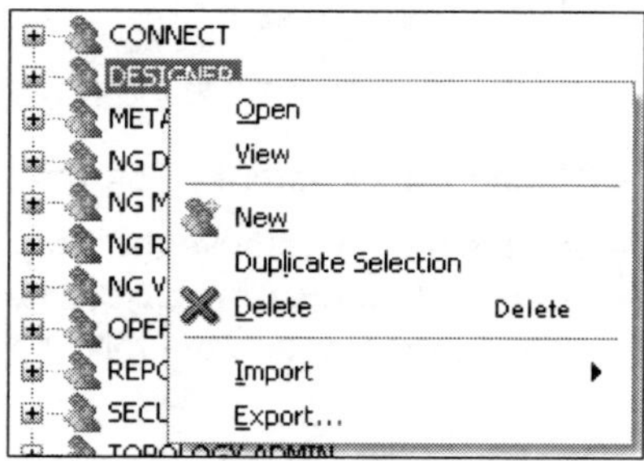

   Click on **Yes** to confirm the duplication.

4. Next, double-click on the copy of `DESIGNER` profile to open it and rename it to `NON-CDC DESIGNER`. Click on **Save** to save this new profile.

5. Then, expand the `NON-CDC DESIGNER` profile and expand the **Datastore** node to display all the methods available for this object:

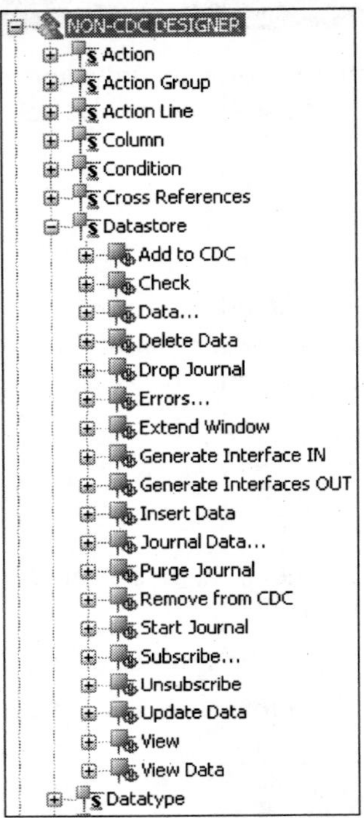

6. Right-click on **Add to CDC** and select **Delete**. Click **Yes** to confirm.
7. Similarly to what we've done in step 6, remove the **Drop Journal**, **Extend Window**, **Journal Data...**, **Purge Journal**, **Remove from CDC**, **Start Journal**, **Subscribe...**, and **Unsubscribe** methods. You should now see the following methods listed under the **Datastore** node:

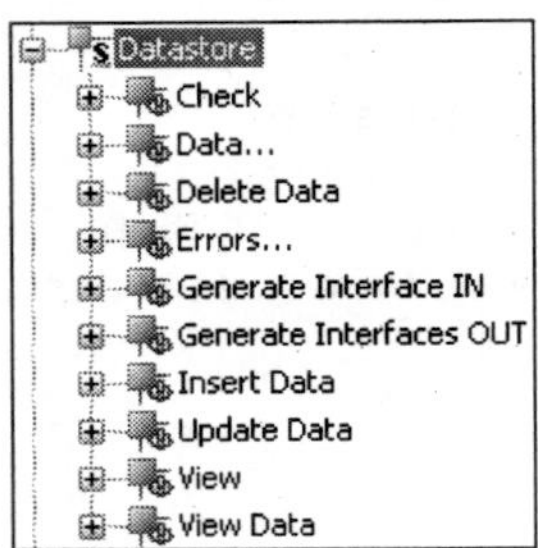

It is not possible to add access to new methods on an object, it is only possible to remove access to them.

8. Then, minimize the **Datastore** node and expand the **Model** node. Similarly to what we've done in the **Datastore** node, remove the **Add to CDC**, **Drop Journal**, **Extend Window**, **Lock Subscriber**, **Purge Journal**, **Remove from CDC**, **Start Journal**, **Subscribe**, **Unlock Subscriber**, and **Unsubscribe** methods. You should see the following methods listed under the **Model** node:

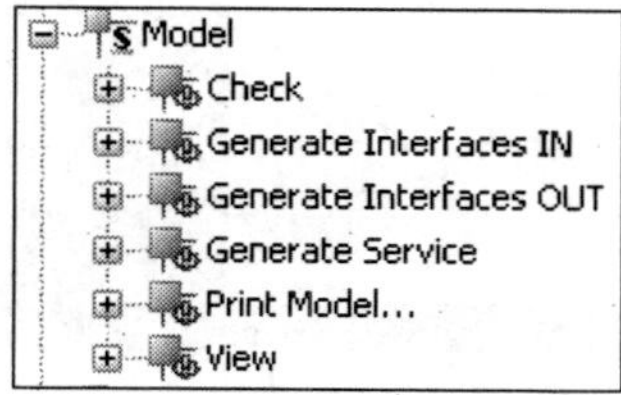

9. Finally, minimize the **Model** node and expand the sub-model node. Remove the **Add to CDC** and **Remove from CDC** methods.
10. We now have a profile that can be used to restrict access to the CDC methods in ODI. Expand the **Users** accordion, the `Cookbook Developer` user, and its **Profiles** node, then right-click on the **DESIGNER** profile and select **Delete**.
11. Click on **Yes** in the **Confirmation** window.
12. Subsequently, drag-and-drop the `NON-CDC DESIGNER` profile to this user and click on **Yes** in the **Confirmation** window.
13. Click on the ODI menu in ODI Studio and select **Disconnect** to disconnect from your repository.

14. Next, click on the **Connect** button and connect to your repository using our `Cookbook Developer` user. Open up the **Designer** navigator then the **Models** accordion. Right-click on **SRC_APP_ORACLE** and expand the **Changed Data Capture** menu as well as the **Subscriber** menu. All the methods are grayed out and unavailable to this user thanks to the `NON-CDC DESIGNER` profile:

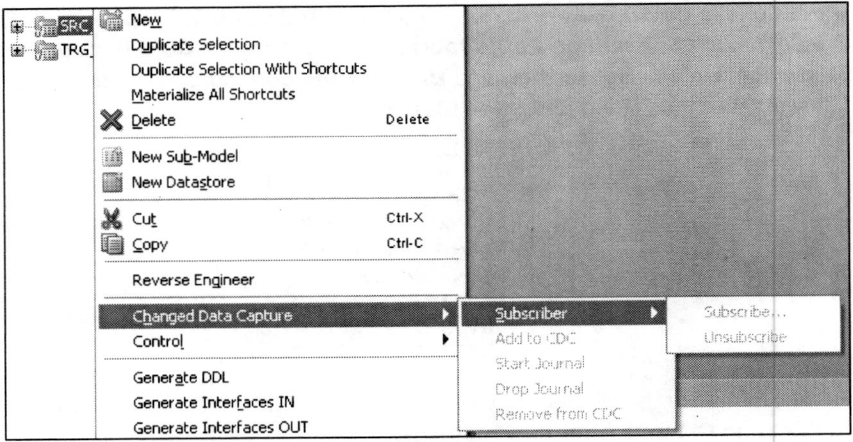

How it works...

Each object in Oracle Data Integrator comes with pre-defined methods, such as `New` or `View`, and the access to those methods is controlled by the security profiles assigned to users.

Each profile available in the **Security** navigator provides pre-defined access rules to every object method. Those methods are listed under each object name, such as **Model** under a **Profile** node, and can be removed to deny access to specific methods to specific users. This is what we did with all the CDC methods, such as `Add to CDC` in this recipe.

3

Advanced Topology

In this chapter, we will cover the following:

- Creating a new technology
- Modifying actions to get more from your diagrams
- Modifying and expanding datatypes
- Changing the case sensitivity for code generation
- Best practice – using the Staging Area User to access your target schema

Introduction

There is a lot more to ODI Topology than just defining server connectivity and listing schemas under these servers. In this chapter, we will experiment with customizations in ODI Topology to further expand the capabilities of the product.

The Topology navigator offers features that many people simply do not know about. With the proper ingredients, you can dramatically expand the way ODI works.

There are a few documents and links that are extremely helpful as you investigate these techniques, one of them is as follows:

Developer's Guide for Oracle Data Integrator (available at `http://docs.oracle.com/cd/E23943_01/integrate.1111/e12643/toc.htm`) explains all the generic concepts.

For more detailed explanations about specific options and fields, the ODI Studio online help (which comes with the product) will answer many questions. You can access this additional help from any screen inside the ODI studio, where it will provide contextual help on the different concepts you are looking at. To view this, press the *F1* key on your keyboard when you have the focus on the window you need help with.

Creating a new technology

ODI comes pre-packaged to cover dozens of technologies. However, there are cases where you want to connect to a less common technology. In this recipe, we will look into how to create a new technology—at least one that is new to ODI. Technologies are defined in the Topology navigator, so all you need to do to get started is to make sure that this navigator has been selected.

Getting ready

What we will do here is create a technology that we will arbitrarily name, `My New Database`. Obviously, to reproduce the steps described in this recipe, you will need to have enough privileges in ODI to access the Topology navigator.

In this particular case we will reuse the **Oracle** technology only because we already have the JDBC drivers in place for that. However, the technique would be the same for any other database as long as you can install the JDBC drivers to connect to these databases. We will review this in detail after the following step-by-step instructions.

How to do it...

1. First make sure that all the technologies are visible. There is a drop-down menu on the top-right corner of the Topology navigator where you have to make sure that the option **Hide Unused Technologies** is not selected.

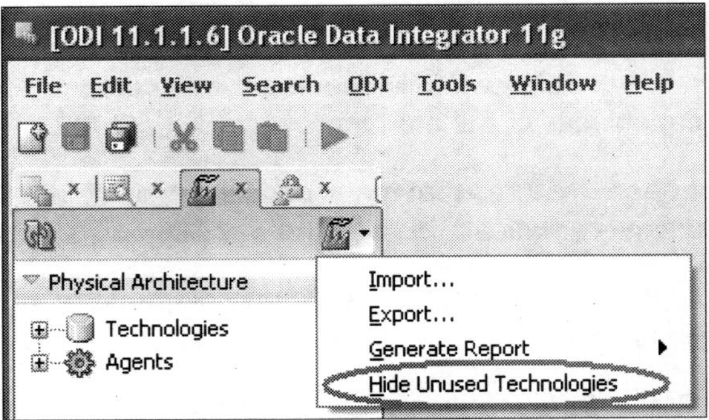

   Then expand **Technologies**, right-click on the **Oracle** technology, and select **Duplicate Selection**. ODI will create a new technology called `Copy of Oracle`. The duplication process may take some time because a lot of information has to be copied at one time.

2. Double-click on the new **Copy of Oracle** technology to modify the behavior so that it matches that of our new database technology as follows (note that these choices are not representative of any particular database best practices, since we are making up this new technology for illustration purposes):

   In the **Definition** tab, set the **Name** field to `My New Database`, set the **Code** field to `MY_NEW_DATABASE`, and uncheck the option **Not Ordered**.

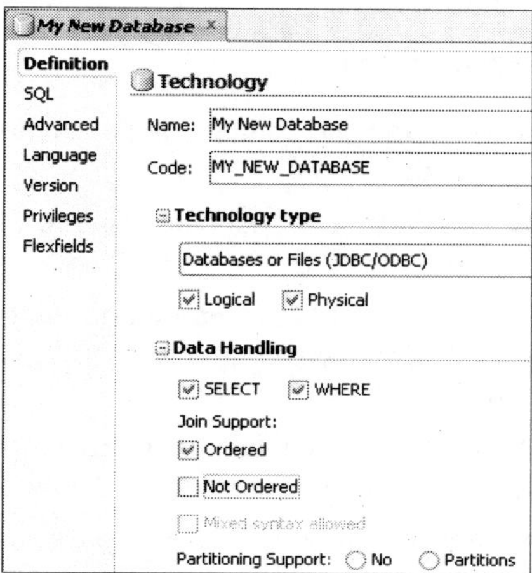

   Click on the **SQL** tab and review the content (we will make no changes here).

   Click on the **Advanced** tab and change all the **Default Table Prefixes** values to remove all dollar signs (as a result the new prefixes should be `E_`, `IX_`, and so on).

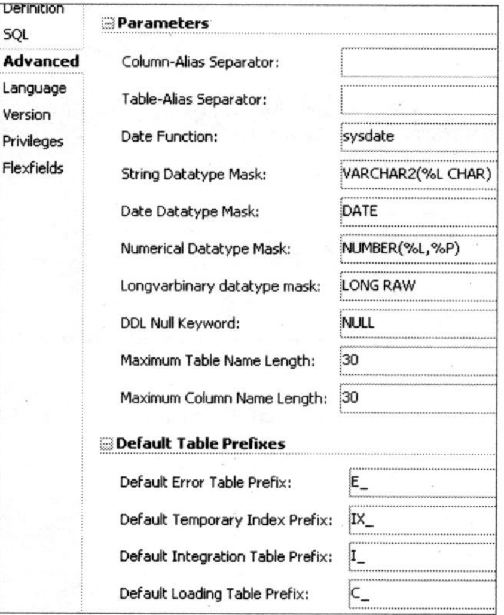

Click on the **Language** tab and remove the double quotes for the **Object Delimiter** option.

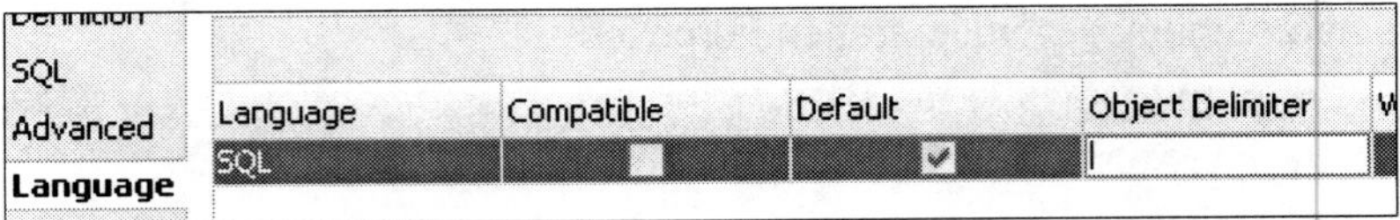

Save and acknowledge the warning.

3. Create a new data server with valid connection parameters to test that the JDBC driver works. Just follow these steps:

   Right-click on the **My New Database** technology in the **Technologies** tree and select **New Data Server**.

   Name that server and enter a valid **User name** and **Password** for your server (use one of your existing Oracle database connections for this as we are just simulating a new technology at this point).

   Select the proper **JDBC Driver** (again, use the Oracle driver for this example) and **JDBC Url** (again, use the necessary parameters to connect to your Oracle database).

   Click on the **Test Connection** button to make sure the connection is valid.

   Ignore the information window saying that you have to register a schema when you are prompted to save. Then click on the **Test** button when you are prompted by the following window:

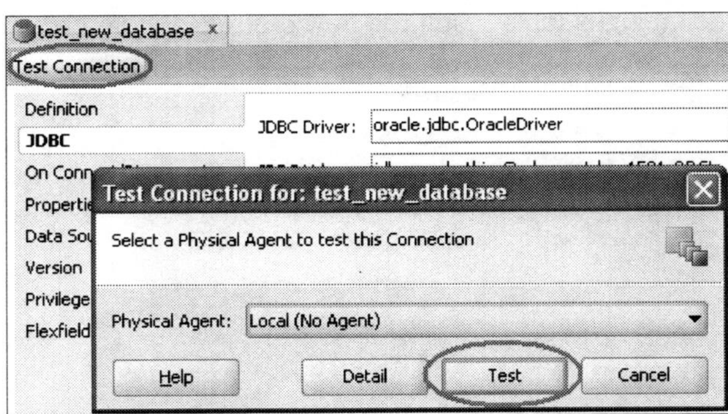

   If your connection fails, review the parameters you have just entered.

4. When your connection test is successful, click on the **Test Connection** button again. When prompted, select **Details** to confirm the version number of the JDBC driver and that of the database.

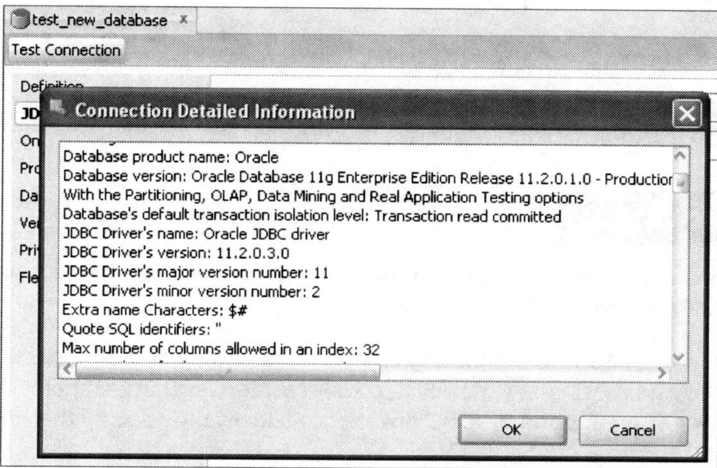

5. Close the **Connection Detailed Information** window. Then right-click on the technology **My New Database** and select **Datatypes Reverse-Engineering**. Then expand the **Datatypes** tree and compare the types listed with the datatypes that come with the default definition of the **Oracle** technology. Depending on the JDBC driver and database versions, there could be differences between the two technologies. In this case, with Oracle database Version 11.2.0.1.0 and the Version 11.2.0.3.0 of the JDBC driver, we have retrieved two new datatypes named `INTERVALDS` and `INTERVALYM`.

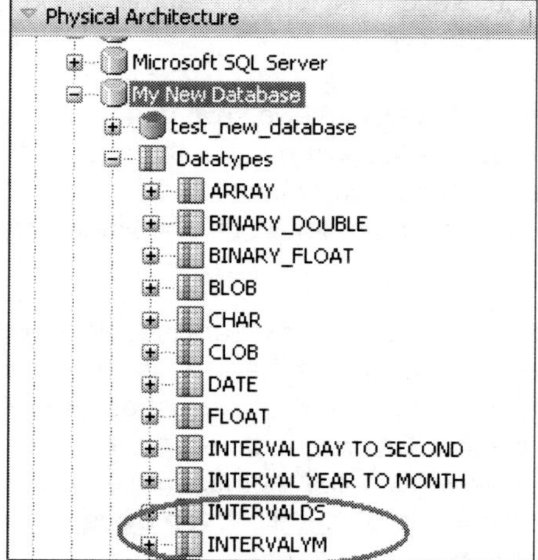

6. Double-click on the datatype VARCHAR2 of your new technology and make sure that the **Converted To** and **Converted From** mappings are correct (note that you can only edit the **Converted To** mapping, **Converted From** would have to be edited in the technology that defines the *from* datatype).

Note that since we copied this new technology from an existing technology, all the datatypes that existed in the original technology are already mapped for us. We only have to map the new datatypes!

How it works...

All technologies used by ODI are defined in the repository. This approach allows for a very flexible infrastructure and infinite expansions.

All that is needed to add a new technology is an understanding of the proper syntax for that technology (in most cases, how SQL code is written for that technology), along with a JDBC driver that supports it. JDBC drivers are usually provided by the vendors of the databases.

Note that one of the steps we skipped in this recipe was adding the JDBC driver. For ODI Studio to find the driver, we first need to add the proper files (`.jar`, `.dll`, and so on) into the following directory of ODI Studio:

```
C:\Documents and Settings\<username>\Application Data\odi\oracledi\userlib
```

After copying the required driver files, you will have to close and reopen ODI Studio to be able to access them.

The standalone agent will require that the drivers be in the agent's `/drivers` directory.

Once we have the proper drivers in place, all we have to do is to define the technology. Copying an existing technology takes care of most of the menial efforts of defining how SQL code is generated. The `where` clauses, outer joins, and the `from` statements do not vary much from one database vendor to the other. But if and when they do, we can control ODI's behavior right here.

Once the database behavior is defined, the next step is to declare the datatypes for the new technology. This can be a very tedious task if the JDBC protocol does not cover this for us. All we need is a connection to a database and then we just ask the JDBC driver to provide us with these datatypes. One thing we didn't do was to delete the old datatypes; we can always reuse existing definitions. But if the new technology comes with datatypes that are entirely different from the original ones, then we would be better off removing everything before importing the new datatypes. ODI does not remove the old ones for us.

The next step is the datatype mappings, and this is extremely important. The datatype mappings are what ODI needs to properly create the staging tables when extracting data from one system to another. Did you ever wonder how ODI knows that if you extract a numeric from SQL server it has to create a column as a number in Oracle? Well, this is where the information is coming from. For ODI to work properly, you have to define the conversions *to* and *from* in your new technology. If you want to have some fun with this, make some changes in the new technology, then reverse engineer a few tables and use them in your interfaces. Run the interfaces and check out the differences as the code gets generated!

New technologies may work fine with generic Knowledge Modules or may require their own specific Knowledge Modules. *Chapter 5, Knowledge Modules Internals*, and *Chapter 6, Inside Knowledge Modules: SCD and CDC*, both contain recipes that can be leveraged should you need to create your own Knowledge Modules.

There's more...

Real applications for this recipe are used more often than you may think. People regularly need to connect to non-mainstream technologies, or at least ones not shipped out of the box with ODI, and for this they define the technology themselves. There are two typical use cases: legacy technologies and extremely new technologies.

For **legacy** technologies, the best approach is to duplicate a very basic definition such as Dbase or Microsoft Excel, where the structure of SQL is simple and should be enough to let you do what you need on older systems, which were designed when SQL code was still quite limited. For instance, we sometimes see this for connections to ADABAS or Lotus Notes.

For new technologies, first try to see if the new database is an offspring of an existing database. Many appliances, for instance, start with a modified version of PostgresSQL, so simply duplicate that technology and apply the necessary changes. When you look at what ODI needs from a Topology perspective, chances are the only thing you will need to modify are the datatypes and their mapping into other technologies, and the JDBC driver provided by the vendor should take care of that for you!

Modifying actions to get more from your diagrams

Actions are defined in Topology so that you can alter the DDLs that are generated by ODI from the model / Generate DDL menu command. A good understanding of the ODI Common Format Designer will help you before diving into this recipe.

Getting ready

A good starting point is *Chapter 6, Working with Common Format Designer* in the ODI developer's guide, available at `http://docs.oracle.com/cd/E23943_01/integrate.1111/e12643/common_format.htm#CIHCBJJE`.

How to do it...

1. In the Topology navigator, under the **Physical Architecture** tab, expand the **Oracle** technology. Then expand the **Actions** entry.

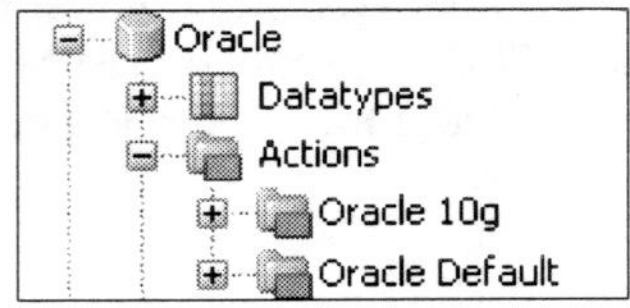

2. Right-click on **Actions** and select **New Actions Group**. Name the group `Oracle Cookbook`, save and close the **Group definition** window.
3. Right-click on the **Oracle Cookbook** group that you have just created and select **New Action**. Name the action `Create table with comment`, set the **Type** value to `Create Table`, then click on the **Details** tab. We will create two lines for this action. The first line will just be the template for the table creation, while the second will be to add a comment on the table:

   Add a line (click on the green plus sign on the top-right corner), name the line `Create Table`, and copy this code:

```
create table <%=odiRef.getTable("L","TARG_NAME","A")%>
(
  <%=odiRef.getColList("", "[COL_NAME]\t[DEST_CRE_DT] NULL",
",\n\t",
"",
"")%> )
```

   Add a second line, name it `Add Comment On Table`, and copy this code:

```
Comment on table <%=odiRef.getTable("L", "TARG_NAME", "A")%> is
'<%=odiRef.getTargetTable( "TABLE_DESC")%>'
```

Be careful to include the two single quotes that enclose the last substitution method. We need them to enclose the text of the comment on the table.

4. Go to the designer. If you have created the data models as described in the *Preface*, expand the model **DEMO_SRC** (if you haven't, you can do the same with any model of your choice as long as it is an Oracle model). Right-click on the model name and select **New Datastore**. Create this datastore and save it with the following modifications:

    - **Name**: `SRC_COST_CENTER`
    - **Description**: `Cost Center for employees' expenses`
    - **Columns**:

    ```
    CC_CODE          VARCHAR2(5)
    CC_NAME          VARCHAR2(50)
    CC_MANAGER_ID    NUMBER(4)
    ```

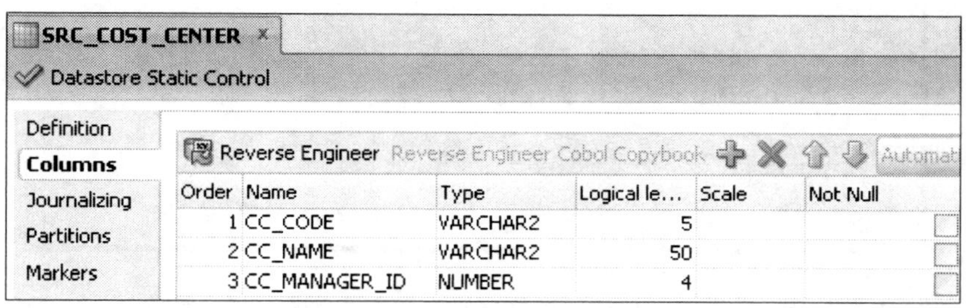

5. In the project of your choice, create a new folder named `DDL`. That folder is not required, but it will allow us to isolate the code that will be generated. Now go back to the model where you have just created the table, right-click on the model name, and select **Generate DDL**. When prompted, even whether you only want to process the tables in the ODI model, answer Yes, as we do not want to import ODI metadata for tables that would already be in the database.

6. On the next window, you can select the action group, the name of the ODI procedure that will contain the generated DDL, and you can also select the tables for which the DDL commands will be generated. Only the tables that have a different definition in ODI versus the database will be listed. The options allow you to restrict the list of tables for which the DDL code will be generated based on the differences you want to consider between the definition in the ODI metadata and the actual definition in the database. Make sure to select the following:

    - **Action Group**: `Oracle Cookbook`
    - **Procedure Name**: `DDL Cookbook 001`
    - **Generation Folder**: `<your project>.DDL`

- Click in the box next to the `SRC_COST_CENTER` table to synchronize the metadata for this table:

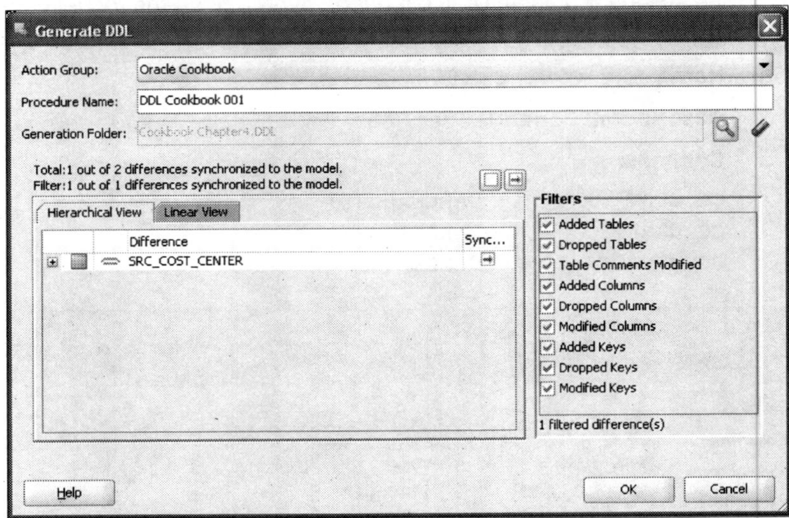

7. Click on **OK**. ODI will generate a procedure called `DDL Cookbook 001` and it will open it immediately. You can look at the content of the procedure in the following screenshot:

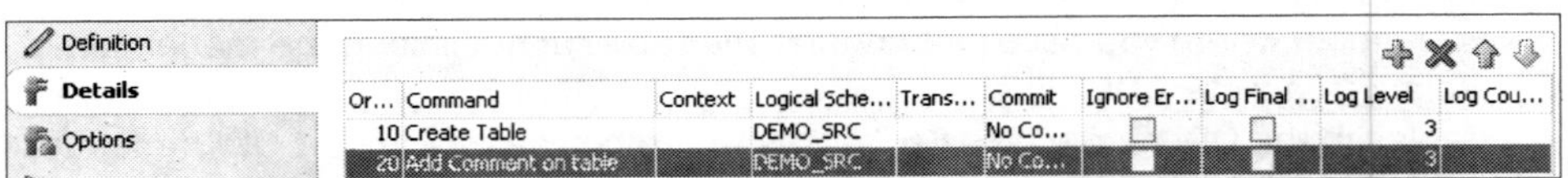

8. Now you can run the procedure.

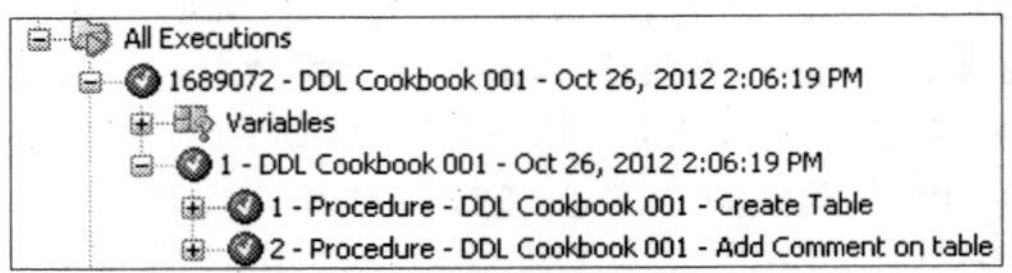

9. If you connect to the database with your favorite SQL tool (SQL Developer, Toad, and so on), you can run the following query to validate that the table was properly created with the expected comment:

```
select comments from user_tab_comments
where table_name = 'SRC_COST_CENTER'
SQL> /
COMMENTS
-----------------------------------
Cost Center for employees expenses
```

How it works...

The **Generate DDL** option on **Model** will use the default code generation rules unless you overwrite these rules in the action groups that you can define yourself. The purpose of the action groups is to define how to generate DDL statements when we want to alter the definition of tables and columns in the database. The wizard allows you to choose what types of differences you want to include, after which it generates a new procedure that contains the DDL statements needed to alter (or create, or drop) any of the tables within your model.

The way actions are created is very similar to that of Knowledge Modules, but they only focus on DDL code generation, and for this reason they are defined in the Topology navigator. But, they have no impact on the KM-generated SQL statements, that is, adding a `PURGE` clause to a `drop table` command within an action group will have no effect on how the IKM SQL-TO-SQL Knowledge Module behaves.

Note that because actions only focus on DDL generation, not all substitution methods will be available. Carefully check the Knowledge Modules documentation to make sure that the substitution method you want to use is actually available for actions.

A strong benefit of having these DDL statements generated as ODI procedures is that you can run them across all your contexts. Therefore, you can create the procedures in the development environment, validate that they work properly in your test environment, and run them against your production environment, guaranteeing that you have the exact same metadata definitions across the board. Beyond just the generation of DDL, this will get you ready for the automated generation of interfaces from the diagrams, a subject that we address in *Chapter 7, Advanced Coding Techniques*.

There's more...

To create your own actions and design your own DDL, it will be important to know which ODI substitution APIs can be used. The *Knowledge Module Reference Guide* (at the time of writing, available at `http://docs.oracle.com/cd/E23943_01/integrate.1111/e12645/toc.htm`) has a dedicated section that lists the substitution methods that can be used with actions in the *A.1.8 Actions* section.

Modifying and expanding datatypes

ODI is not limited to the datatypes that it knows out of the box. In this recipe, we will create an entirely new datatype and we will leverage it in an interface to see how it can be handled.

Getting ready

For this recipe, you will need a project where the following KMs have been imported:

- `LKM SQL to Oracle`
- `IKM SQL Control Append`

How to do it...

1. First we will create a new datatype in the database. You can do this with many databases; our example here is with Oracle. Use your favorite tool to connect to the database (SQL+, SQL Developer, Toad, and so on). If you re-created the environment described in the *Preface* of this book, log in as the owner of the source schema `DEMO_SRC` and enter the following commands:

```
create type FULL_SALARY AS OBJECT (BASE_SALARY number(8), BONUS_
SALARY number(8));

create table SRC_YEARLY_SALARY (
  EMP_ID number(4),
  YEAR  number(4),
  SALARY full_salary);
```

2. Go to ODI Topology. If you followed the first recipe of this chapter, you can modify the technology that you already created. Otherwise, just duplicate the **Oracle** technology, rename the new technology as `My New Database`, and create the new datatype under the new technology. To do this, in the **Physical Architecture** tab, expand the **My New Database** technology and expand the **Datatypes** entry. Right-click on **Datatypes** and select **New Datatype**.

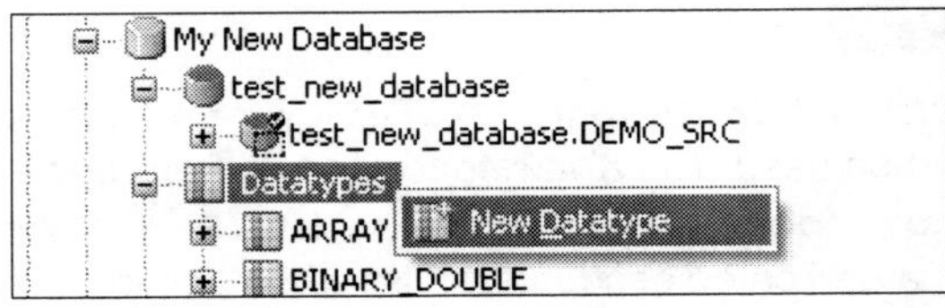

Enter the following to define the new datatype.

In the **Definition** tab, set the **Code**, **Name**, **Reversed Code**, **Create Table Syntax**, and **Writable Datatype Syntax** all to `FULL_SALARY`.

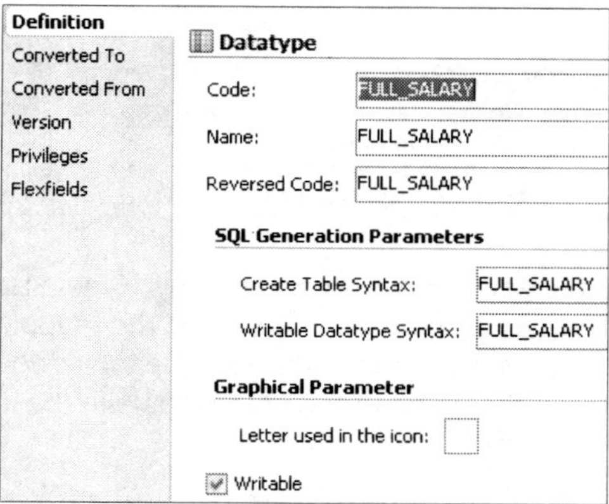

3. Click on the **Converted To** tab and define the conversion to the **Oracle** technology as `NUMBER` (you can define more conversions as you desire; a complete definition of a new datatype would require that you define all conversions):

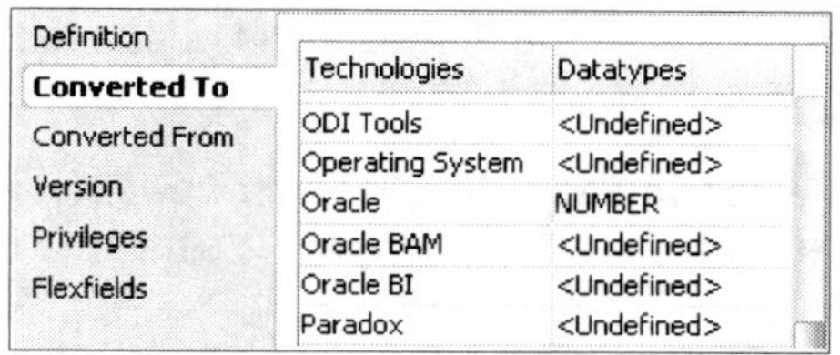

4. Now we will reverse engineer the table that was created in the database in Step 1 of this recipe. Make sure that you have a physical and logical schema defined for `DEMO_SRC` under the technology you have modified. If needed, you can call the logical schema as `NEW_DEMO_SRC` to differentiate this from the logical schema you may already have for the **Oracle** technology. In the Designer navigator, create a data model to point to the schema if you do not have one yet, and use the **Selective Reverse Engineer** option to reverse engineer the `SRC_YEARLY_SALARY` table.

After reverse engineering the table, edit the table from the object tree and see that the last column has the proper datatype. If the column has no datatype, make sure that that model points to the technology where you have defined the new datatype. Also, check for misspellings of the datatype.

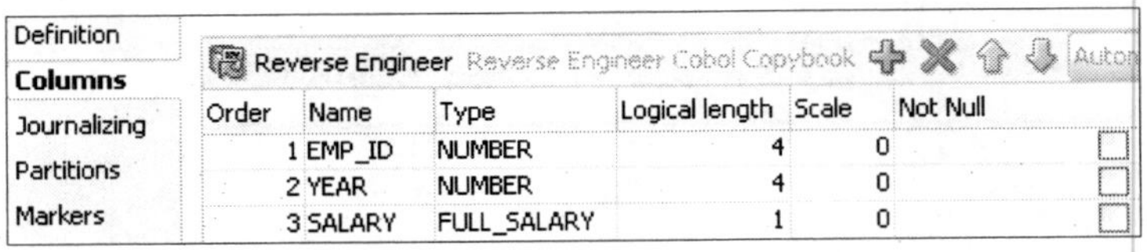

Order	Name	Type	Logical length	Scale	Not Null
1	EMP_ID	NUMBER	4	0	☐
2	YEAR	NUMBER	4	0	☐
3	SALARY	FULL_SALARY	1	0	☐

5. You can now use this new table in your mappings. Create an interface with this table as a source and the `TRG_EMP` table as a target. The mapping for the `SAL` column will be as follows (we changed the alias of the source table to `Y` for better readability; to replicate this, click on the name of the source table in the interface and replace the default alias with a shorter one):

```
Y.SALARY.BASE_SALARY + Y.SALARY.BONUS_SALARY
```

   Map the `EMP_ID` column to the `EMP_NO` column and make sure that the transformation for the `SAL` column occurs on the source where the new datatype is defined.

   Use the KMs that were imported for this interface (`LKM SQL to Oracle` and `IKM SQL Control Append`). Set the **Flow Control** option to `FALSE` for the `IKM SQL Control Append` KM.

6. Run the interface. When you go to the Operator navigator and expand the details for the session, you should see the code that is similar to the following in the **Load Data** task:

```
select
  Y.EMP_ID      C1_EMPNO,
  Y.SALARY.BASE_SALARY + Y.SALARY.BONUS_SALARY      C2_SAL
from  DEMO_SRC.SRC_YEARLY_SALARY    Y
where  (1=1)
```

How it works...

ODI is all about generating code that is understood by the database. As long as the data types are properly defined in ODI, they will be recognized when you reverse engineer the tables. If they are not defined however, they will be left blank.

When code is generated, the definition of the new datatypes will be important. There will arise questions such as how do you create a new column with this datatype? and how do you convert data from this type to other types in other databases? But as long as ODI knows what to use during code generation, the execution by the database will always be successful!

Changing the case sensitivity for code generation

Some databases are case sensitive while others are not. Some give you the flexibility to choose whether you want case sensitive table names and column names. Enclosing object names in quotes will ensure that the Oracle database, for one, enforces the case sensitivity. Since the Oracle database gives us this flexibility, we will use it to illustrate how ODI can also enforce case sensitivity by using double quotes around object names.

Getting ready

For this recipe, we will use the `DEMO_SRC` schema that is described in the *Preface* of this book. If you haven't done so in an earlier recipe, make sure to create a model in the designer that points to the database's `DEMO_SRC` schema.

How to do it...

1. Connect to the database using your favorite SQL tool (SQL+, SQL Developer, Toad, and so on) and create the `src_custs_lower` table in the `DEMO_SRC` schema as follows (be sure to use double quotes to force the table name into lowercase). We will also add a couple of records to make things more interesting:

```
create table "src_custs_lower" ("emp_no" number(4),
"emp_name" varchar2(10));

insert into "src_custs_lower" values (1, 'Jane Smith');
insert into "src_custs_lower" values (2, 'Bob Rivers');
commit;
```

2. Create a model that points to the `DEMO_SRC` schema if you do not have one yet. Selectively reverse engineer the `src_custs_lower` table.

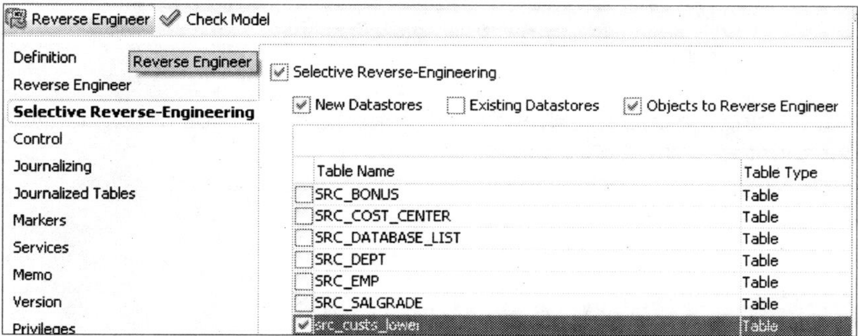

ODI will import the definition of the table and columns all in lowercase, exactly as they were created (this is the standard ODI behavior).

3. Right-click on the `src_custs_lower` table name in the object tree and select the data to read from the table; you will see the two records that we have created. Once you see the records, click on the top-left icon above the data as if you were about to create a new query; this will show you the query generated by ODI to retrieve the data. You will see that ODI properly enclosed the table name in double quotes to enforce case sensitivity:

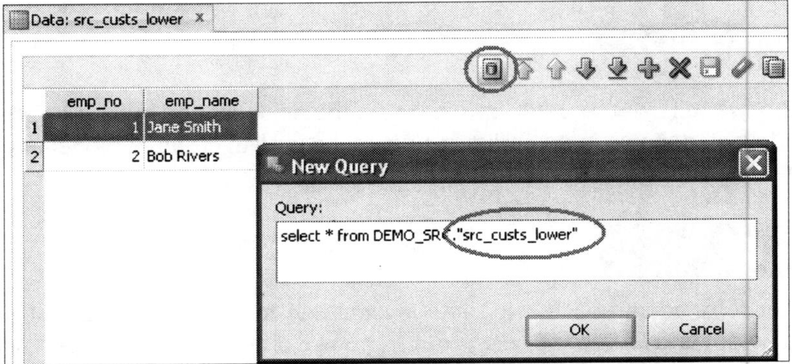

Close the query window and close the window that displays the data, as we will make some changes.

4. Now we will modify the behavior of ODI. Go into the Topology navigator and edit the **Oracle** technology. Select the **Language** tab, and under **Object Delimiter**, remove the double quotes, as shown in the following screenshot:

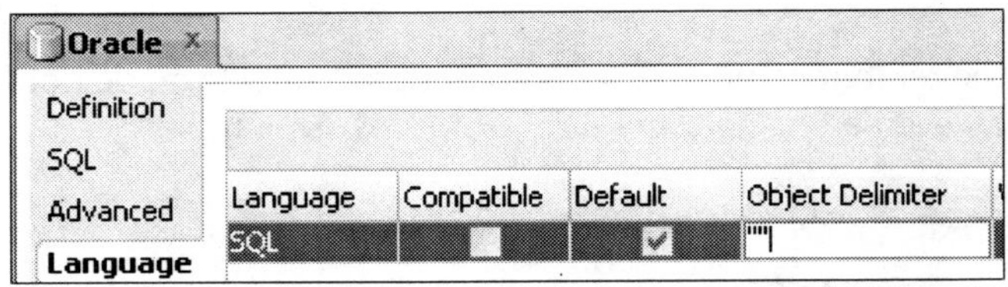

After erasing the quotes, advance to the next field (to validate the change) and save your changes to the technology.

5. Go back to the **Designer** navigator and right-click again on the `src_custs_lower` table name and select the data to be viewed. This time the database will reject your request with an error message indicating that the table does not exist. To get the actual database error message, click on the **Next** button on the first error window. Without the double quotes, Oracle converts the table name to `SRC_CUSTS_LOWER`, and there is no such table indeed.

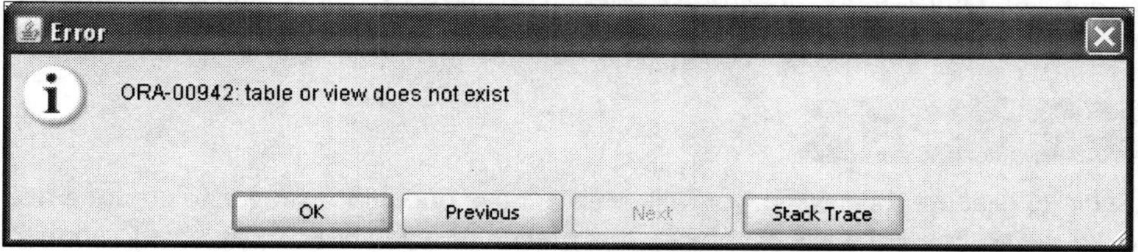

6. If you want to restore the technology to its original configuration, do not forget to go back into the Topology navigator to add the two double quotes that you have removed in this recipe.

How it works...

The mechanisms in play here are pretty simple. You can control a lot of the details on how code gets generated for the different databases. Case sensitivity is one of the aspects of code generation that can be quite tricky; there are cases where you absolutely want the generated code to be case sensitive, while there will be other cases where you will definitely not want the code to be case sensitive.

No matter what your needs are, you can make sure that ODI will behave exactly as you want in terms of case sensitivity.

There is more...

If you go back to the screen (in the **Oracle** technology, in the **Language** tab) where we removed the **Object Delimiter** double-quotes, you will notice that there are additional parameters that you can play with to define how code gets generated.

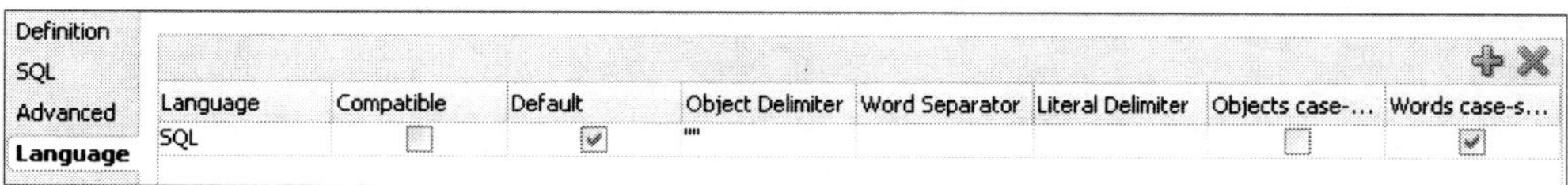

Directly from this window, you can press the *F1* key on your keyboard to gain access to the interactive help and to access more information on the subject.

Best practice – using the Staging Area User to access your target schema

Of all the parameters used to define how to connect to a database schema, the **Work Schema** parameter is probably the most crucial, even though many people do not understand the signification and importance of carefully selecting a proper schema. This is what we will focus on in this recipe.

Getting ready

To be able to execute this recipe, you will need to have enough privileges to create a new user in the database. For an Oracle database, this means that you need to be able to connect to the database with a user that has the `CREATE USER` and `ADMIN OPTION` privileges. If you are using a user that has the DBA privilege, you will have these privileges automatically.

How to do it...

1. In all databases where ODI is likely to stage data, it is a best practice to create a dedicated work schema (or catalog, or library) for this purpose. This work schema will be used by ODI as a staging area. In this recipe, connect to your database using your favorite SQL tool (SQL+, Toad, and so on) and create a new schema (also known as user) for use by ODI. Make sure to grant proper privileges to that user. For instance:

```
create user ODI_TMP  identified by ODI_TMP_PWD;
grant CONNECT, RESOURCE to ODI_TMP;
```

2. Edit the physical schemas that you have already created under that same data server in the Topology navigator and set the **Work Schema** value to `ODI_TMP`.

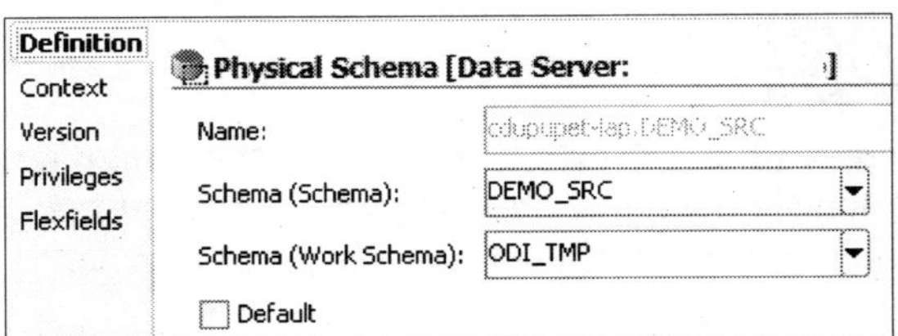

3. Edit the connection parameters for that data server and set `ODI_TMP` as the login user (set `ODI_TMP_PWD` as the password).

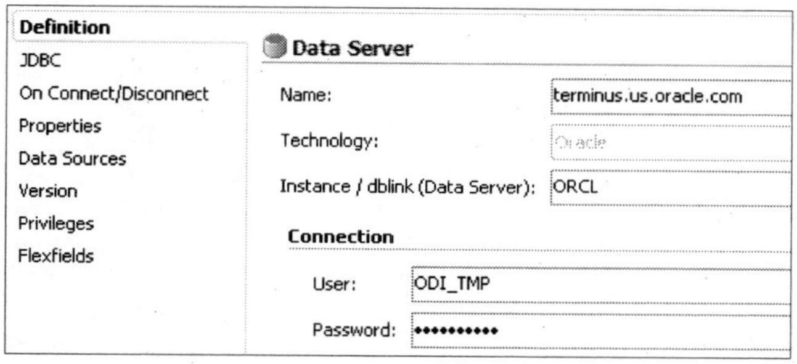

Definition
JDBC
On Connect/Disconnect
Properties
Data Sources
Version
Privileges
Flexfields

Data Server
Name: terminus.us.oracle.com
Technology: Oracle
Instance / dblink (Data Server): ORCL
Connection
User: ODI_TMP
Password: ••••••••••

How it works...

When ODI generates code, some of it will require the creation of staging tables. As your development evolves, so will the structure of the staging tables. As you map new columns, as you redesign your source and target tables by adding and removing columns, and as you add more source tables, ODI will automatically update the definition of these staging tables. To do so, ODI will simply drop the old definition and create new staging tables.

Furthermore, when a load fails, ODI doesn't know if it is because of the content of a staging table or because of an issue in the mappings. An easy solution is to drop the table with each new load, then re-create the table based on the current definition of the mappings.

The problem here is that if you start dropping tables in your production schemas, your DBAs generally will not be very happy, and to be absolutely honest, the last thing they want is for people to start dropping tables when they are responsible for the data to be available. As a result, they will almost never give you that privilege (nor should they).

But if you create a separate database schema, and if ODI logs in as the owner of that schema, you are free to create and drop anything you want in that schema because it is yours. And the DBAs shouldn't care about this one; they don't even have to back it up. After all, it will only contain transient data that will be removed when the load is completed. All you should need from your DBAs at this point is the necessary privileges to do the job assigned to you: Inserts and, updates (maybe deletes if that is required) in the tables that hold the production data. That should not be a problem!

Now that you have an ETL-dedicated schema, all other schemas on the same server can share the same login (and the same staging area). Single login to the database will ensure that all data movement within the database takes advantage of the set-based SQL optimizations that ODI is famous for.

4

Using Variables

The recipes in this chapter will deal with six situations that often arise while building **Extract-Load-Transform** (**ELT**) solutions using Oracle Data Integrator:

- Passing start-up parameters to a scenario using variables
- Using the table names that run in all contexts using `getObjectName`
- Using variables to filter data based on a timestamp
- Using variables in **Knowledge Module** (**KM**) options (and reusing the variables in an interface, package, and so on)
- Using variables in topology
- Using variables to control loops inside packages

Introduction

Whether you're an Oracle Data Integrator administrator or developer, there are frequently times when the best solution to a given problem may involve the use of variables. Knowing how to declare, set, refresh, and pass variables between the various ODI components will enable you to work through even the most complex design problems.

To read more about the details of variable usage within ODI, refer to *Chapter-12, Section-2* of the book *Developer's Guide for Oracle Data Integrator*, which at the time of writing could be found on the Oracle web site shown here:

`http://docs.oracle.com/cd/E23943_01/integrate.1111/e12643/toc.htm`

Another good resource to learn about ODI variables is in the note *Frequently Asked Questions Concerning ODI Variables [ID 471564.1]* on *My Oracle Support*.

Passing start-up parameters to a scenario using variables

One of the most popular methods of affecting the behavior of an ODI scenario is to pass in parameter values at execution time. Whether launching a scenario from the GUI, the command line, or from a web service, the use of parameter values is a simple yet effective way of controlling a scenario's activities. In this recipe, we will design a workflow to include a **start-up parameter** in order to pass in a specific value at execution time.

Getting ready

This recipe will create a simple interface that will require the following KM: `IKM - SQL Control Append`. Be sure to import this KM into your project. Also, be sure to reverse engineer the `DEMO_SRC` and `DEMO_TRG` data models.

How to do it...

1. Within your project, insert a new **Variable** called `PV_DATE_FILTER` (note that you may have already created this variable in a previous recipe).
    - Select the **Data type** option as `Alphanumeric`, since it will be easier for us to manipulate and pass the value around as a string rather than an actual date
    - Select the **Keep History** option as **Latest Value**

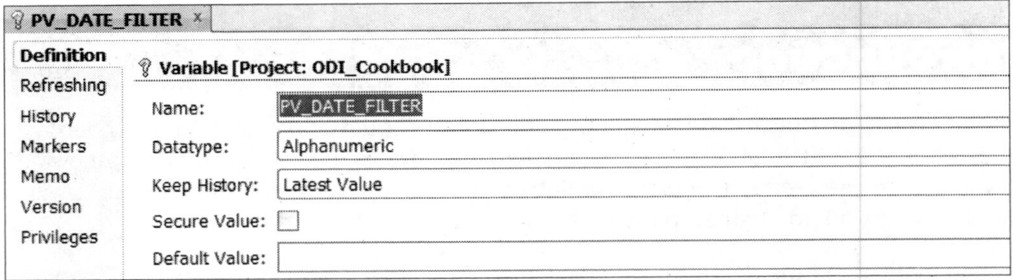

2. Within a folder of your choice, insert a new interface called `Int_Variable_Filter`.
    - For the source, drag and drop the `SRC_EMP` table onto the interface canvas.
    - For the target, drag and drop the `TRG_EMP` table onto the interface canvas. This particular table makes it easy to map all the columns from the data source.

- Place the mouse over the `HIREDATE` column in the `SRC_EMP` table, left-click on it, and drag that column onto the canvas in order to create a filter.
- Click on the filter and add the following implementation text:

```
SRC_EMP.HIREDATE <= TO_DATE('#PV_DATE_FILTER', 'YYYY-MM-DD')
```

- To give the interface something to do, modify one of the transformation mappings (in this example, we multiplied the salary by **1.10**).
- Click on the **Flow** tab and choose the KM `IKM - SQL Control Append`.

  Set **FLOW_CONTROL** to `False`

  Set **CREATE_TABLE** to `True`

  Set **TRUNCATE** to `True`

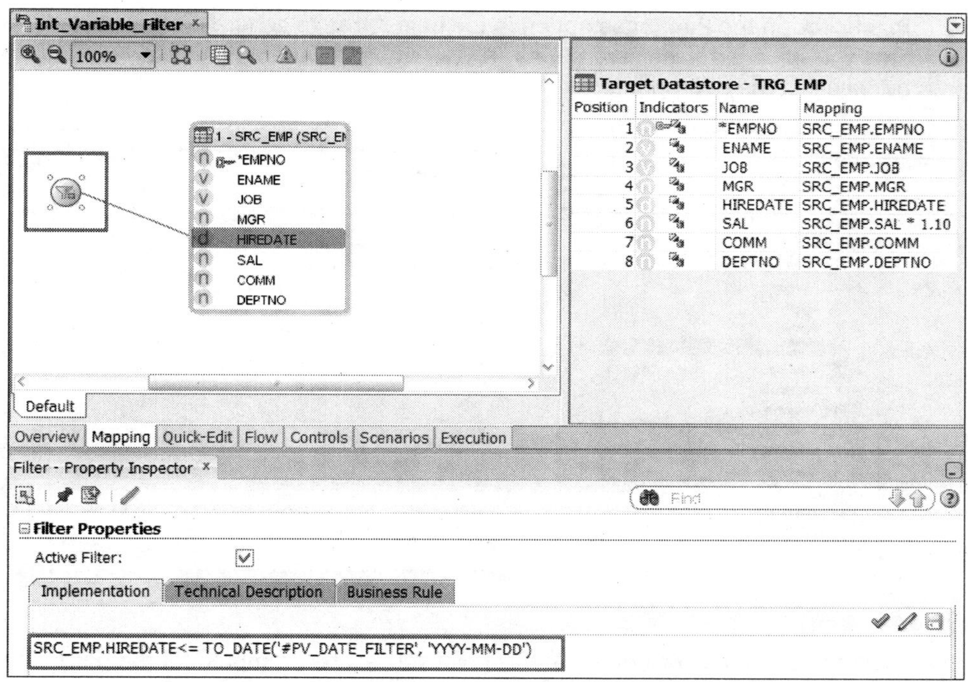

3. Within the same folder, insert a new **Package** called `Pkg_Variable_Parameter`
   - Drag the `PV_DATE_FILTER` variable onto the package diagram (note that this object will become the 'first step' in our flow)
   - Click on the variable icon
   - Within the **Properties panel**, select **Declare Variable** from the **Type** drop-down list

- Drag the `Int_Variable_Filter` interface onto the package diagram (after the variable) and connect the two icons; save the package

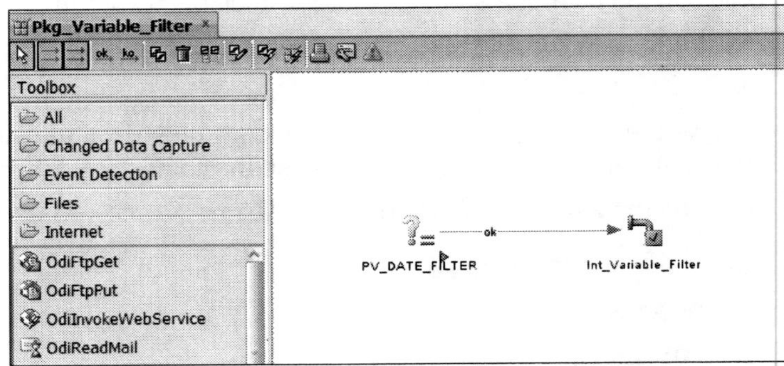

4. Right-click on the **Packages** option in the object tree to generate a scenario. This time you will need to declare the `PV_DATE_FILTER` variable as a start-up parameter by checking the appropriate box.

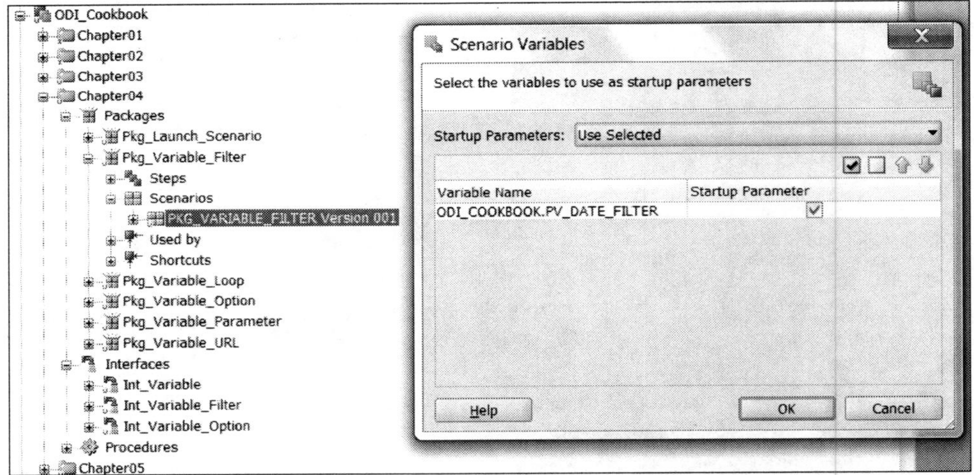

5. Execute the **Scenarios** option. At this point you will be prompted for the parameter value to be passed into the `PV_DATE_FILTER` variable. Unless the value from the last execution is to be reused, uncheck the **Last Value** box and enter the following date in the **Value** option: `1981-01-01`.

> The direct assignment of a parameter value is only one of several methods of passing parameters into a scenario; other methods include from the command line, from a web-service, or from another scenario. For more information on using variables as a means of passing parameters, refer to *Chapter-3* of the book *Getting Started with Oracle Data Integrator 11g – A Hands-on Tutorial, Peter C. Boyd-Bowman, Christophe Dupupet, Denis S. Gray, Julien Testut, David Hecksel, and Bernard Wheeler, Packt Publishing*.

6. Switch to the **Operator** tab, drill down to the most recent job log, and examine the results:
   - Within the `PV_DATE_FILTER` step, notice the statement: declare the `ODI_COOKBOOK.PV_DATE_FILTER` variable.
   - You will not see the variable value being set, since it was only passed into the package and interface as a parameter and not actually assigned within the module

How it works...

For every project or global variable found within an ODI package (no matter whether the variable is declared, set, evaluated, or refreshed), at the time of scenario generation, ODI will prompt the designer to declare if any of these variables are to be considered as a start-up parameter. At execution time, these parameter variables will be able to receive values from any external calling application, such as `STARTSCEN.BAT`, a web service, another scenario, or in this case, interactively through the GUI.

Using table names that run in all contexts using getObjectName

Since it's usually beneficial to avoid hard-coding fully qualified schema and object names (doing so can create issues when migrating code between environments), we will often want to employ a simple technique that uses one of the out of the box ODI substitution methods: `odiRef.getObjectName.odiRef.getObjectName`. This particular method can resolve and return the complete object name for a specified table depending on the context in which the application is currently running. In this recipe, we will examine some of the details of how ODI can resolve a complete database table name using only a base object name.

Getting ready

All references to tables in this recipe are taken from the data samples described in the *preface* of this book. Be sure to reverse engineer the `DEMO_SRC` and `DEMO_TRG` data models before beginning this recipe.

How to do it...

1. Within a folder of your choosing, insert a new variable called `PV_TABLE_CNT`.
   - Set the **Datatype** option to **Numeric**
   - Set the **Keep History** option as **Latest Value**

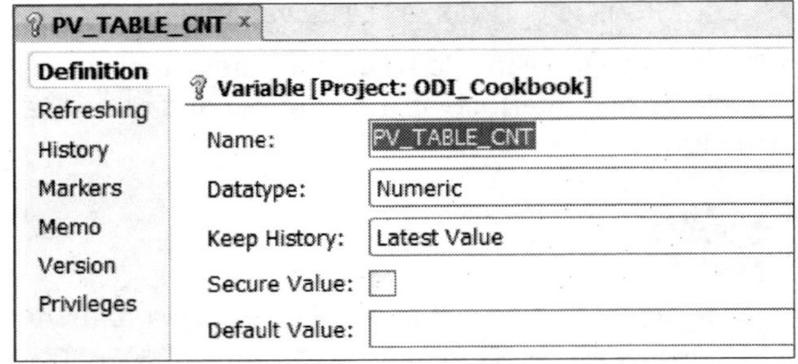

2. Click on the **Refreshing** subtab.
   - From the **Schema** drop-down list, select `DEMO_SRC`
   - In the **Select Query:** panel, enter the following SQL statement:

```
SELECT count(*) FROM  <%=odiRef.getObjectName("SRC_EMP")%>
```

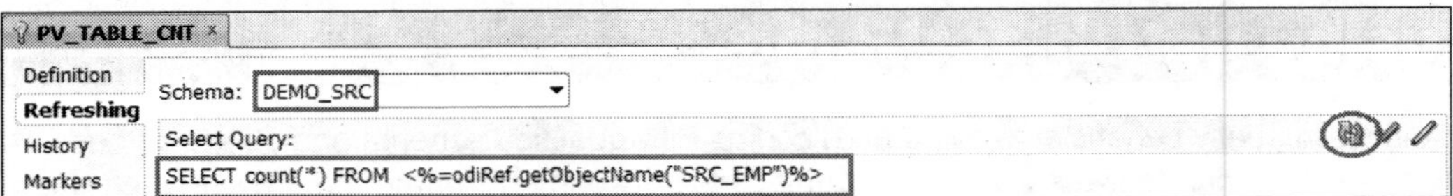

3. Test the variable refresh code by clicking on the Circular Arrow icon (you will be prompted to save your changes). To execute the variable refresh process:
   - Set the **Context** as **Global**
   - Set the **Logical Agent** as **Local (No Agent)**
   - Press **OK**

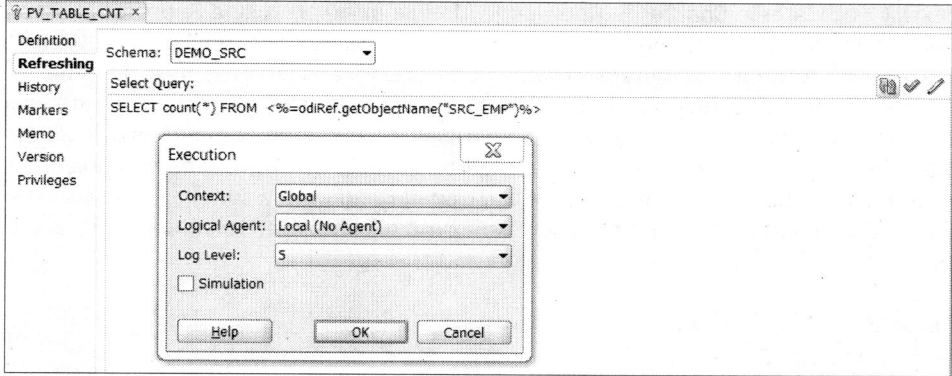

4. Verify the successful completion of the refresh variable action by clicking on the **History** subtab.
   - Click on the **Circular Arrow** icon.
   - You should see a row appear with a **Value** variable set to **14** (If you do not see this row appear, the refresh process encountered an error).

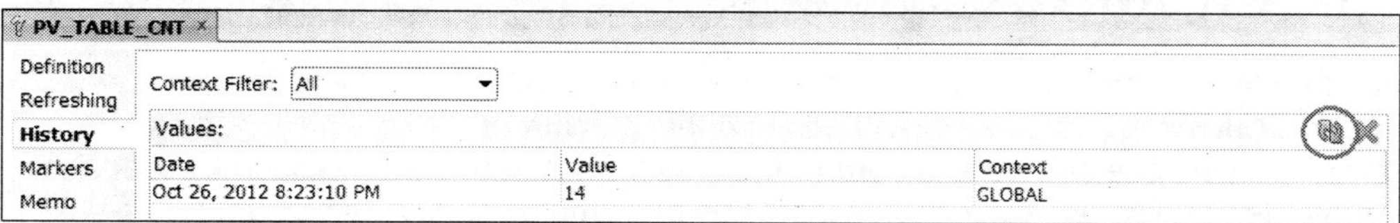

   - Go to the **Operator** tab and review the code from the most recent job log. Notice that the table name has been fully resolved to include the schema.

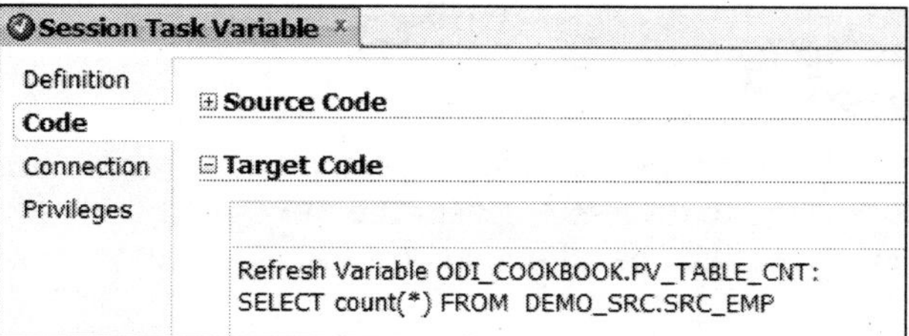

How it works...

There are many out of the box substitution methods provided by ODI and one of the most frequently used is `odiRef.getObjectName`. This particular method optionally uses up to five input arguments (refer to the *Oracledi_API_Reference.pdf* guide for complete details) to resolve and return the full name associated with the specified object based upon the current context. By using this method to provide the complete details for the specified object, developers can avoid hard-coding qualified object names within their applications.

As you will learn later in *Chapter 5, Knowledge Module Internals* (using Substitution Passes), ODI makes use of a Java interpreter to perform multiple passes over application objects. Whenever the interpreter recognizes any one of several tokens (such as <%= %>), the contents within those tokens are acted upon. In this exercise, the token contents that were used contained a reference to one of the numerous ODI substitution methods available: `odiRef.getObjectName`. This particular method accepted a partially named object and returned a complete resource name. Once the transformation was complete, the recipe's procedure submitted a SQL statement containing the fully resolved resource name to the target database for execution.

There's more...

This technique can be used in any SQL statement that is referenced within an ODI application. Instead of hard-coding the schema name (or catalog name, or library name, or whatever is required by the technology you are using), ODI will dynamically fill in the appropriate information.

Using variables to filter data based on a timestamp

One of the most frequent uses of variables is to apply a data filter to an ODI procedure or interface. Once a variable has been defined either globally or within a project, it can be populated using one of several different methods (that is, refreshed, assigned, passed as a parameter, and so on). Once the variable has acquired a value, it can be used as a filter condition within another project component. ODI currently supports four variable data types (`alphanumeric`, `numeric`, `text`, and `date`), any of which can be used as a data filter. In this recipe, we will discover how to use variables in order to filter data based on a timestamp.

Getting ready

All references to tables in this recipe are taken from the data samples described in the *Preface* of this book. Be sure to reverse engineer the `DEMO_SRC` and `DEMO_TRG` data models before beginning this recipe. Also, be sure to import the `IKM - SQL Control Append` KM.

How to do it...

1. Within your project, insert a new **Variable** called `PV_DATE_FILTER`.
   - Select the `Alphanumeric` data type, as it is often easier to manipulate and pass a string rather than `date`. In this fashion, we can handle date formatting through SQL functions rather than having to define a Java format.

Refer to the standard Oracle Data Integrator documentation for a complete list of variable data types and their usage.

   - Set the **Keep History** option as **Latest Value**.

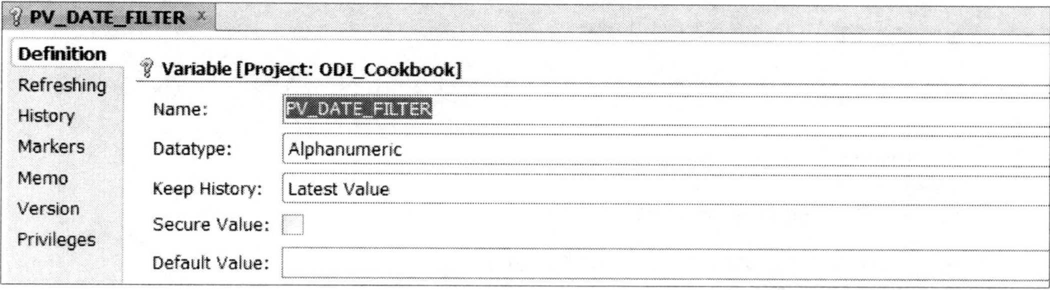

2. Within a folder of your choice, insert a new **Interface** called `Int_Variable_Filter`.
   - For the source, drag and drop the `SRC_EMP` table onto the interface canvas.
   - For the target, drag and drop the `TRG_EMP` table onto the interface canvas. This particular table makes it easy to map all the columns from the data source.
   - Place the mouse over the `HIREDATE` column in the source table, left-click on it, and drag that column onto the canvas in order to create a filter.
   - Click on the filter and add the following implementation text in the **Properties** window:

```
SRC_EMP.HIREDATE <= TO_DATE('#PV_DATE_FILTER', 'YYYY-MM-DD')
```

- To give the interface something useful to do, modify one of the transformation mappings (in this example, we multiplied the salary by **1.10**).

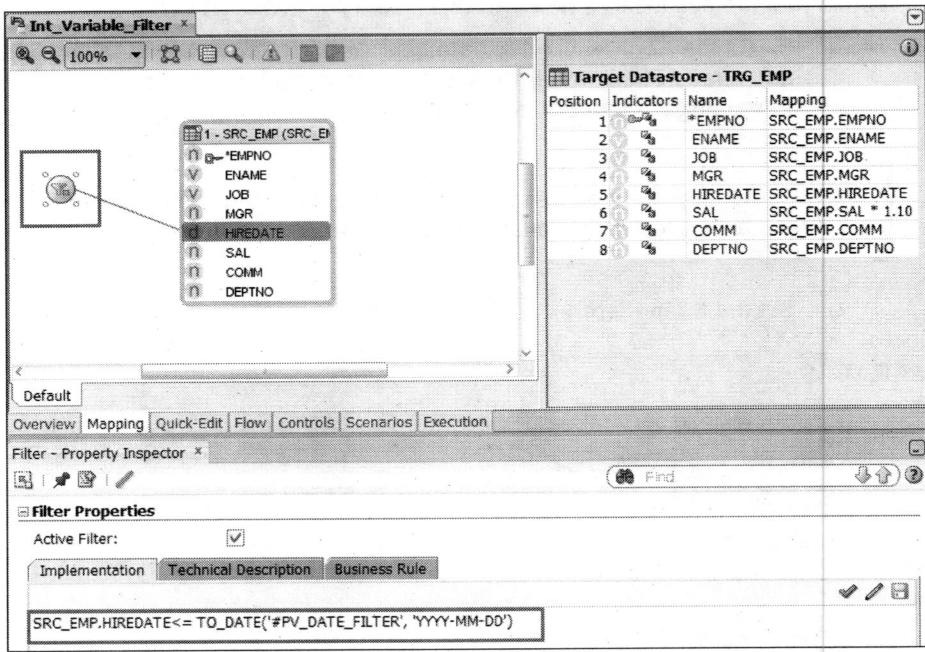

- Click on the Flow tab and choose the KM `IKM - SQL Control Append`:

  Set **FLOW_CONTROL** to **`False`**

  Set **CREATE_TABLE** to **`True`**

  Set **TRUNCATE** to **`True`**

3. Within the same folder, insert a new value in **Package** called `Pkg_Variable_Set`.
   - Drag the `PV_DATE_FILTER` variable onto the package diagram (note that this object will become the first step in the workflow).
   - Click on the variable icon, and within the properties panel, select **Set Variable** from the **Type** drop-down list. Within the **Value** box, insert a meaningful value for the variable. In our example, we will put `19810101`.

- Note that the date format is in YYYY-MM-DD order, which will match up with the `TO_DATE` format used by the interface filter.
- Drag the `Int_Variable_Filter` interface onto the package diagram (immediately after the variable) and connect the two icons.

4. Your package diagram should look something like this:

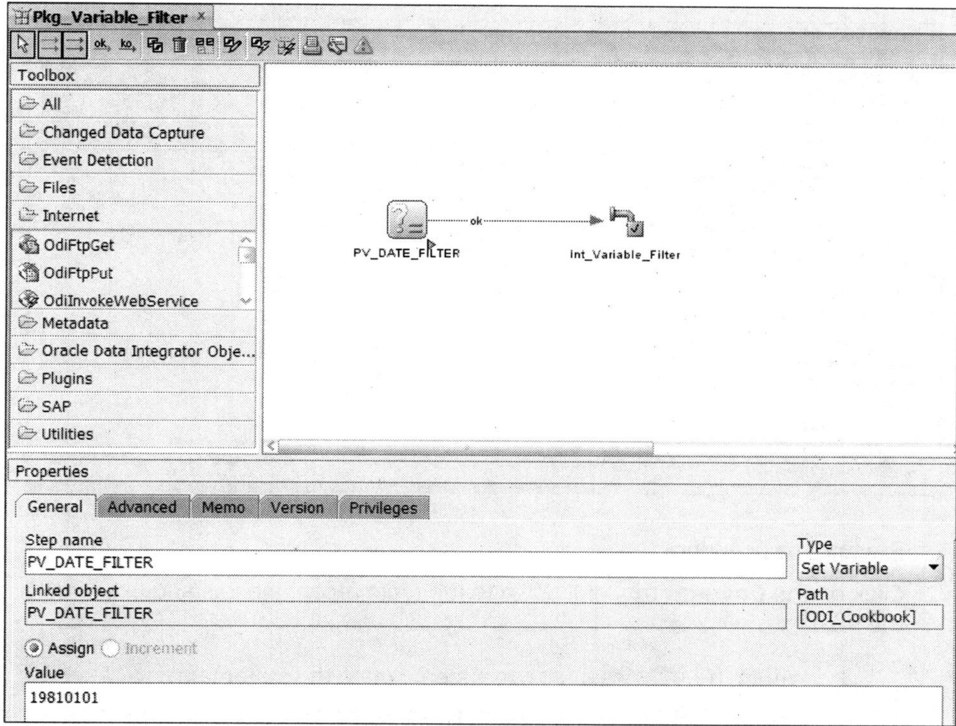

5. Right-click on the **Package** option in the object tree to generate a **scenario**.

> You will want to explicitly declare this package to use no start-up parameters by selecting **None** from the **Startup Parameters** drop-down list. Alternatively, you can simply uncheck the `PV_DATE_FILTER` variable.

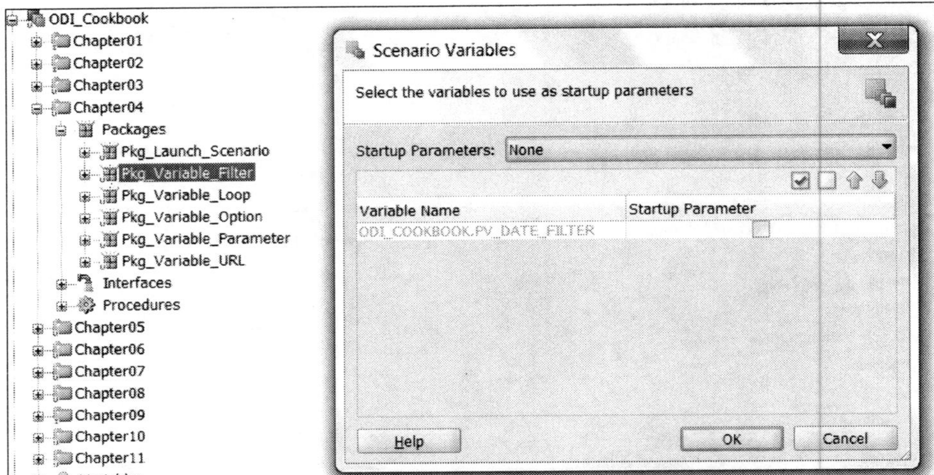

6. Execute the scenario.
7. Click on the **Operator** tab, drill down to the most recent job log, and examine the results:
   - Within the `PV_DATE_FILTER` step, notice the statement:

     ```
     Set Variable ODI_COOKBOOK.PV_DATE_FILTER. Set to 19810101
     ```

   - Within the Insert New Rows task of the interface step, notice the clause:

     ```
     Where(1=1)
     And (EMP.HIREDATE <= TO_DATE('#ODI_COOKBOOK.PV_DATE_FILTER',
     'YYYYMMDD'))
     ```

How it works...

ODI supports the use of several types of variables, either within a project or globally, and it can store the last value used or a complete history of all values. Once a variable has been set, its current value can be referenced in many different ways, such as within procedure steps, package steps, topology, mappings, and in this case, as a filter within an interface. When referencing a variable by another ODI component, proper syntax requires the use of a # symbol prefix, a `project code.` prefix, or a `GLOBAL.` prefix.

Projects are uniquely identified by their internal code. When referencing a variable in one project that was defined by another project, you should use the internal code of that project to prefix the variable. To find the code associated with a project, simply double-click on the project name in the designer tree; you will see both the name and the code.

Whenever ODI identifies the presence of a variable, its current value is acquired and inserted into the host code block during execution.

As you can see in the example provided previously, ODI only displays the variable name in the operator logs. If you want to see the value taken by the variable at execution time, you can run your scenario with the **Log Level** as `6` (since ODI 11.1.1.6). This log level uses more resources, but will allow you to view the actual variable values; a Toggle button on the top-right of the code will let you switch back and forth between the variable name and the variable value.

There's more...

Since a variable can have one of four possible data types, the use of a variable within any given code block may require modification to include a delimiter. For example, a reference to an `Alphanumeric` variable will require quote marks (`'`) in order to support the syntax requirements of the host language (as was the case in this example).

Using variables in KM options (and reusing the variables in an interface, package, and so on)

There are times when it is useful to insert a variable within a KM option and later access that variable's value within an interface or procedure. A typical use case might be to provide the primary directory path for a `log` file and then add a file name to the path definition from an interface. In this recipe, we will create a `log path` variable, embed it into a new option within a duplicated copy of an IKM, then create an interface that will amend the IKM option by adding a file name to the path.

How to do it...

1. Within your project, insert a new **Variable** called `PV_PATH_LOG`.
   - Select the data type as `Alphanumeric` (if the path were to be greater than 255 characters in length, we would need to use the `Text` data type)
   - Select the **Keep History** option as **No History**
2. Duplicate the `IKM SQL Control Append` KM and rename it to `IKM SQL Control Append - with logging`.
   - Insert a new option for the IKM called `DIRECTORY_FILE_PATH` as follows:

     Type: `Value`

     Description: `Directory/Path for status log files`

     Position: `900`

     Default Value: `#PV_PATH_LOG\FileName.log`

Knowledge Modules
Reverse-Engineering (RKM)
Loading (LKM)
Check (CKM)
Integration (IKM)
IKM SQL Control Append
IKM SQL Control Append - with logging
INSERT
COMMIT
FLOW_CONTROL
RECYCLE_ERRORS
STATIC_CONTROL
TRUNCATE
DELETE_ALL
CREATE_TARG_TABLE
DELETE_TEMPORARY_OBJECTS
DIRECTORY_FILE_PATH
Uses

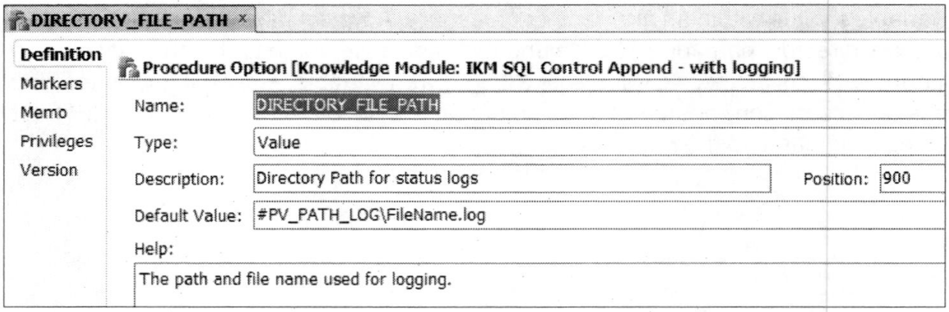

DIRECTORY_FILE_PATH ×

Definition
Markers
Memo
Privileges
Version

Procedure Option [Knowledge Module: IKM SQL Control Append - with logging]

Name: DIRECTORY_FILE_PATH

Type: Value

Description: Directory Path for status logs   Position: 900

Default Value: #PV_PATH_LOG\FileName.log

Help:

The path and file name used for logging.

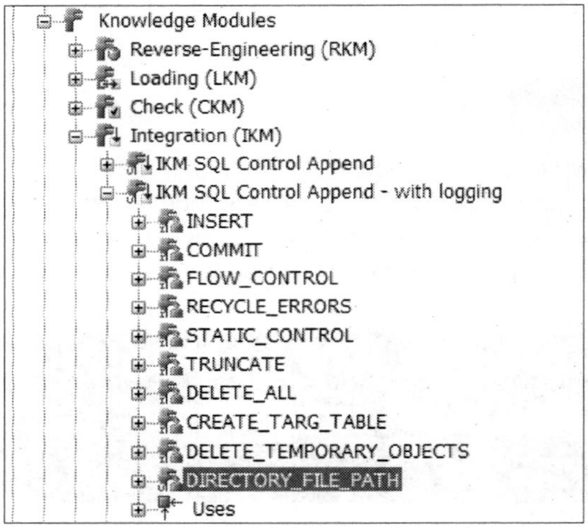

- Insert a new **Detail** called `Create Log File`

  Specify the **Technology** as **ODI Tools**

  Insert the following code in the **Command** field:

```
OdiOutFile "-FILE=<%=odiRef.getOption("DIRECTORY_FILE_
PATH")%>"
Successful integration
```

  Use the Up/Down arrows to move the new detail step immediately after **Insert New Rows**

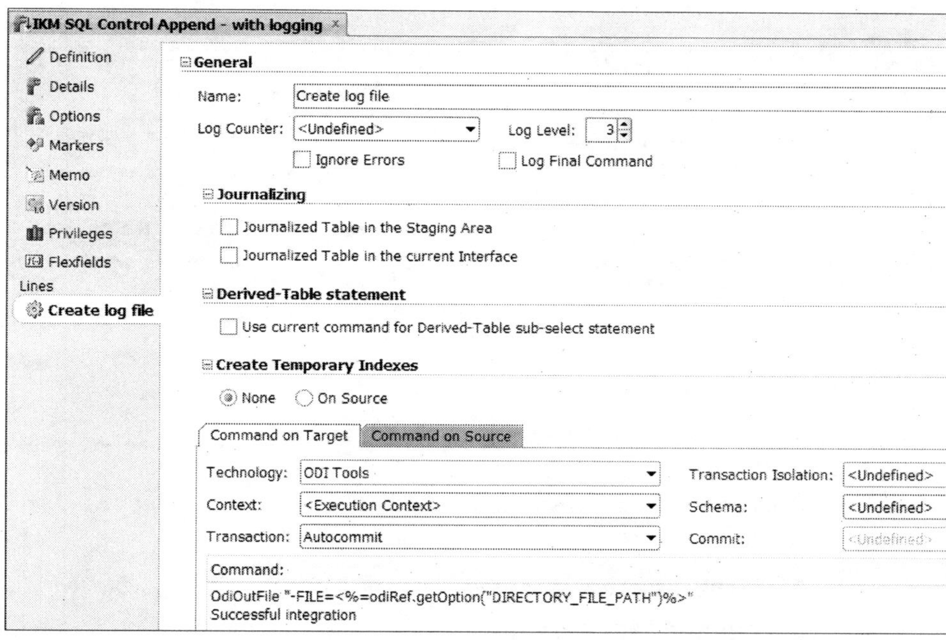

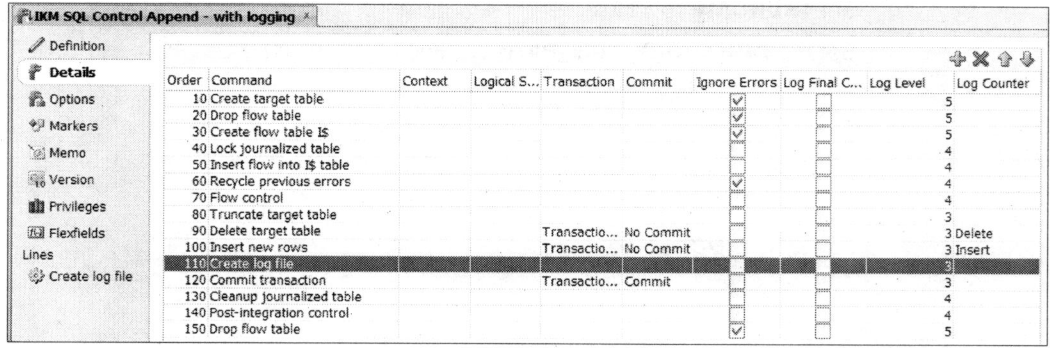

3. Within a folder of your choosing, insert a new **Interfaces** called `Int_Variable_Option`.
    - For the source, drag and drop the `SRC_EMP` table onto the **Interface** canvas.
    - For the target, drag and drop the `TRG_EMP` table onto the **Interface** canvas. This particular table makes it easy to map all the columns from the data source.
    - To give the interface something useful to do, modify one of the transformation mappings (in this example, we multiplied the salary by **1.10**)

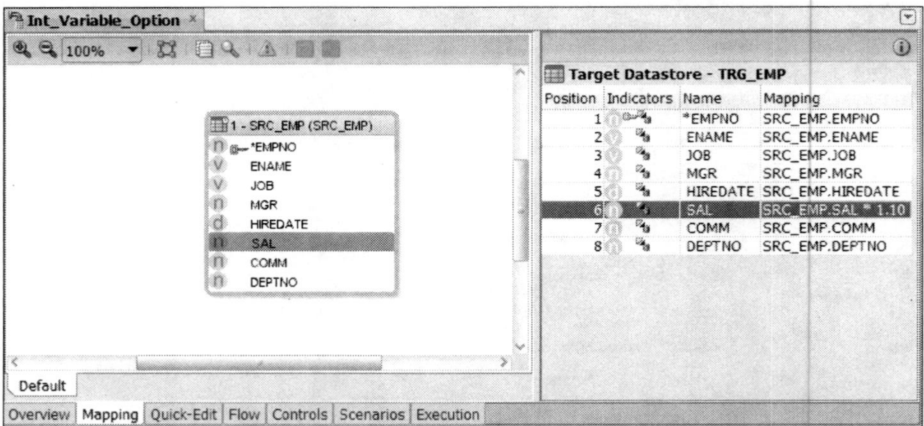

- Click on the **Flow** tab and choose the KM `IKM - SQL Control Append - with logging`:

  Set **FLOW_CONTROL** to `false`

  Set **CREATE_TABLE** to `true`

  Set **TRUNCATE** to `true`

  Set the **DIRECTORY_FILE_PATH** option to `#PV_PATH_LOG\Status.log`

When making changes to a KM option, remember to advance the cursor to the next field before saving your work in order to get ODI to register the change.

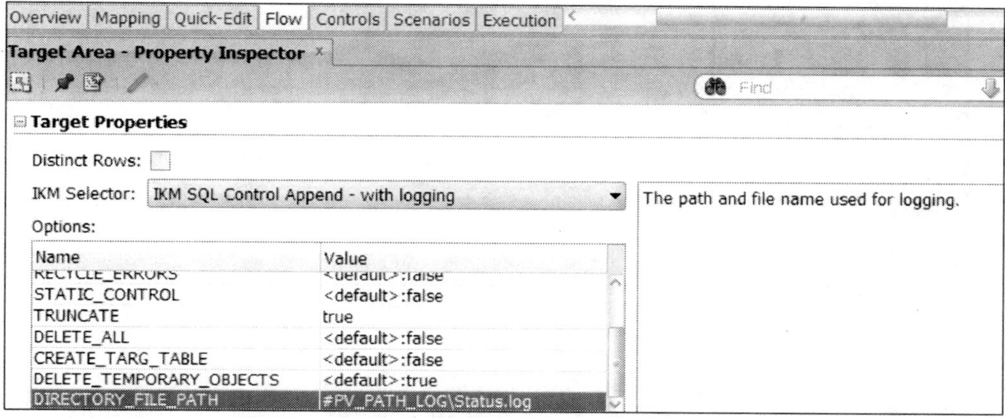

4. Within the same folder, create a new **Package** called: `Pkg_Variable_Option` and do the following:
   - Drag the `PV_PATH_LOG` variable onto the **Package** diagram
   - Click on the Variable icon, and within the properties panel, select **Set Variable** from the **Type** drop-down list and assign **Value** as `C:\temp`

In a more practical implementation of this technique, our variable would most likely acquire its value from an external source such as a database parameter table or as a scenario start-up parameter.

- Drag the `Ch1-Int_Variable_Option` interface onto the **Package** diagram and connect the two icons as follows:

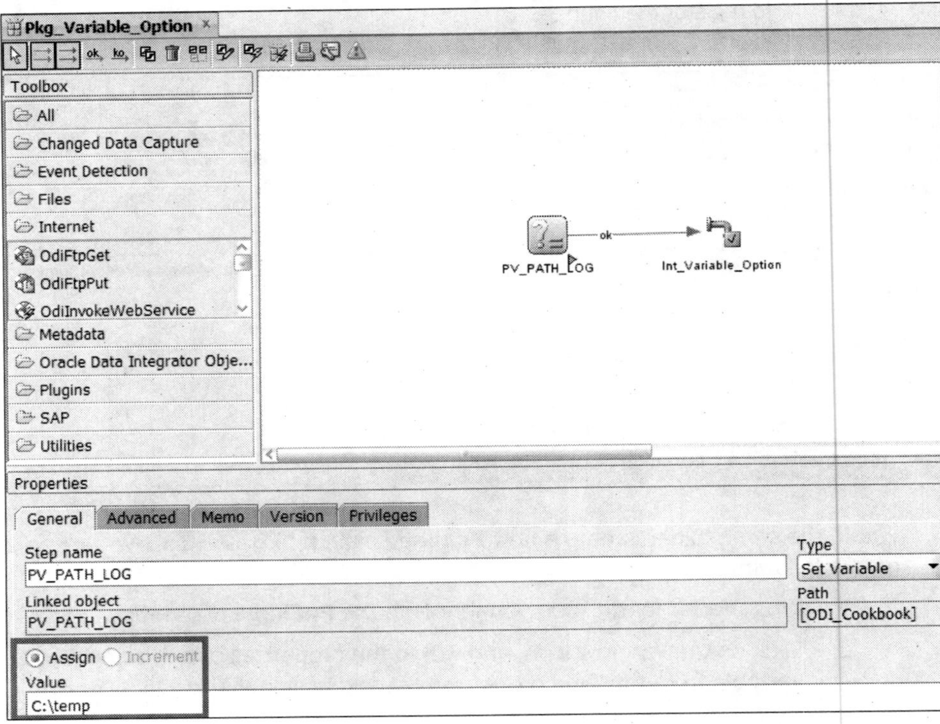

5. Right-click on the **Package** option in the object tree to generate a **scenario**.

> Instead of setting the value of the variable as we currently do, we could have just declared the variable in the package. In that case, we would have needed to define the variable as a **start-up parameter** and passed the selected value at start-up time.

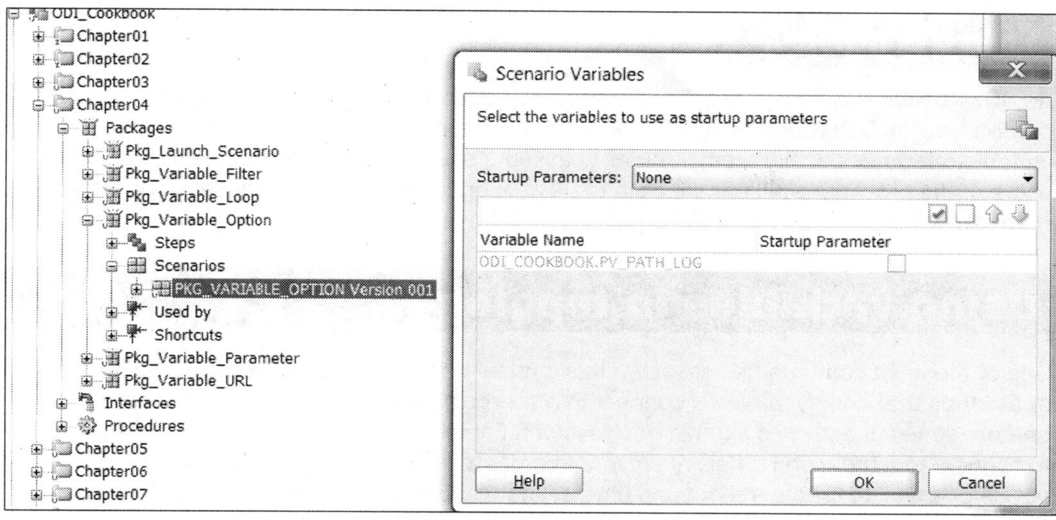

6. Execute the scenario.
7. Navigate to the `C:\temp` folder and verify that the `Status.log` file has been created.

How it works...

Just as ODI allows a developer to reference variables within interfaces, variables can also be referenced through the KM options. In this capacity, variables act somewhat like placeholders, and will assume whatever value the variable holds at execution time. Since KMs are referenced by interfaces, the developer can also extend and modify the KM option values as needed. In our example, we used a package to assign a specific directory path to the variable portion of a KM option and then later concatenated that value to a file name within the interface **Flow** tab. The combination of these two steps allowed us to provide a complete log file location and name into which the status of the interface could be captured. A more practical use case of this type would have the `PV_PATH_LOG` variable receive its value from a parameter table or a start-up parameter rather than a direct value assignment.

Whenever you are using variables in a KM, it is a good practice to expose these variables through the options of the KM, as this will let users of the KM know that they have to define this variable. If a variable is buried within the code of a KM, other users will lose time trying to understand why their interfaces do not run, simply because they did not know that more was expected from them: set a value, refresh the variable, or declare it so that the value can be passed as a parameter.

There's more...

An ODI procedure is similar in many ways to a KM because it also can use options as a means of modifying its behavior. And just like KM options, procedure options also allow the use of variable references within them in order to assume specific values at execution time. Other users of the procedure will benefit from the use of options for variables because it exposes them explicitly.

Using variables in topology

One of the most common use cases for this capability is to allow a developer to build an application that can dynamically connect to a source or target system in order to repeat a uniform series of activities against each system. For example, perhaps there is a requirement to connect to a thousand different servers in order to collect daily activity. Obviously it would not be practical to create a thousand physical data servers within the topology along with a thousand contexts, so instead we can create one data server and use a variable within it to direct subsequent activities towards each individual data server. In this recipe, we will examine the use of variables within the ODI topology.

A very important point to remember is that since ODI establishes all physical connections at session start-up time, embedded topology variables must be resolved before the connections are opened. Therefore, any application using this technique must be "launched" from an external point and have its requisite variables passed in as start-up parameters.

How to do it...

1. Create a **Variable** called `PV_DB_URL` and follow the given steps:
    - Select the **Data Type** as `Alphanumeric`
    - Select the **Keep History** option as **No History** (we do not need to remember each individual value)
2. Insert the `PV_DB_URL` variable into the topology:
    - Open the Oracle data server that corresponds to the **COOKBOOK_SRC** schema
    - Click on the **JDBC** tab

- Replace the `host:port:database` string with the `PV_DB_URL` variable

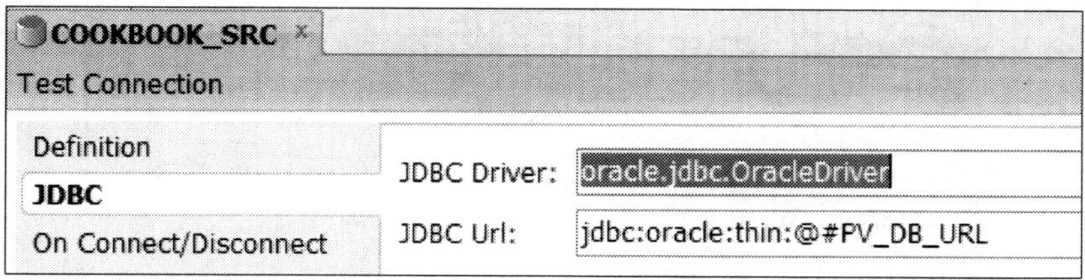

3. Within a folder of your choice, insert a new **Interface** called `Int_Variable`:
   - For the source, drag-and-drop the `SRC_EMP` database table
   - For the target, drag-and-drop the `TRG_EMP` table
   - Map all of the target columns from the corresponding source columns (or engage automapping)
   - To give the interface something useful to do, modify one of the transformation mappings (in this example, we can multiply the salary by **1.10**)
   - Click on the **Flow** tab and choose the `IKM - SQL Control Append` KM:

     Set **FLOW_CONTROL** to **`false`**

     Set **CREATE_TABLE** to **`true`**

     Set **TRUNCATE** to **`true`**

4. Within the same folder, create a new **Package** called `Pkg_Variable_URL`:
   - Drag the `PV_DB_URL` variable onto the **Package** diagram (note that this object will become the 'first step' in our flow)
   - Click on the Variable icon
   - Within the properties panel, select **Declare Variable** from the **Type** drop-down list

- Drag and drop the **`Int_Variable`** interface onto the package diagram (after the variable) and connect the icons

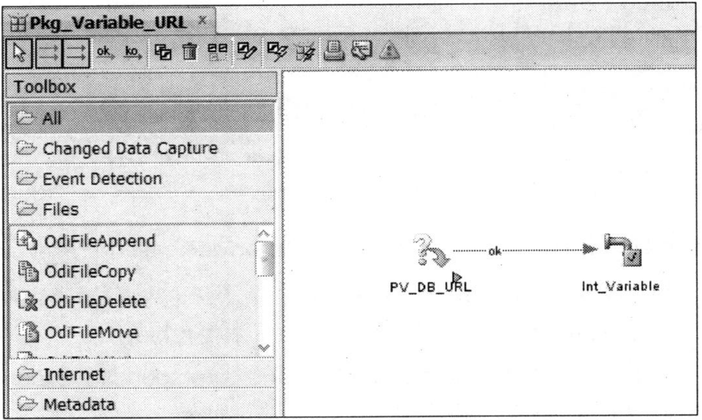

5. Generate a scenario for the package. You will want to declare the `PV_DB_URL` variable as a start-up parameter by checking the appropriate box.

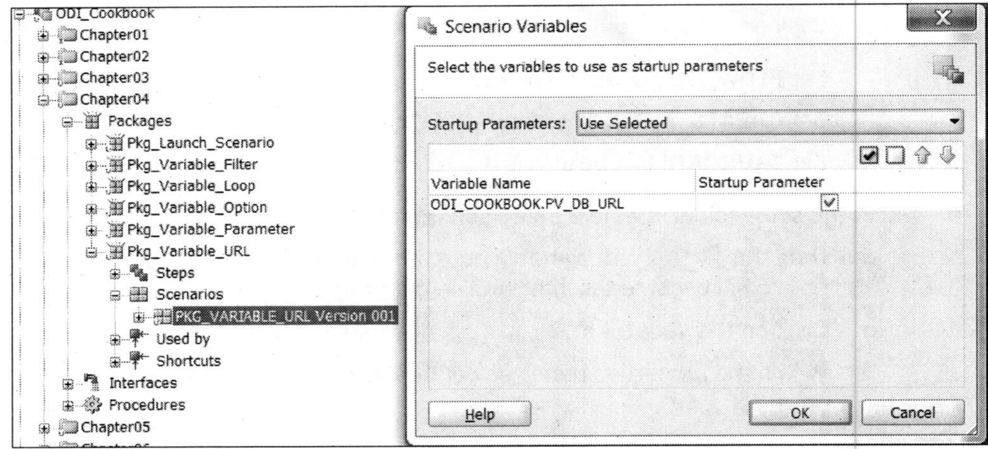

6. Next we will need to create a procedure to simulate a looping mechanism in order to drive our scenario.
   - Within the same folder, create a procedure called `Prc_Variable_URL`
   - Insert a step called `Launch Scenario`
7. Click on the **Command on Source** tab and enter the following:
   - **Technology:** `Oracle`
   - **Schema:** `DEMO_TRG`

- **Command:** `SELECT DATABASE_URL FROM DATABASE_LIST ORDER BY 1`

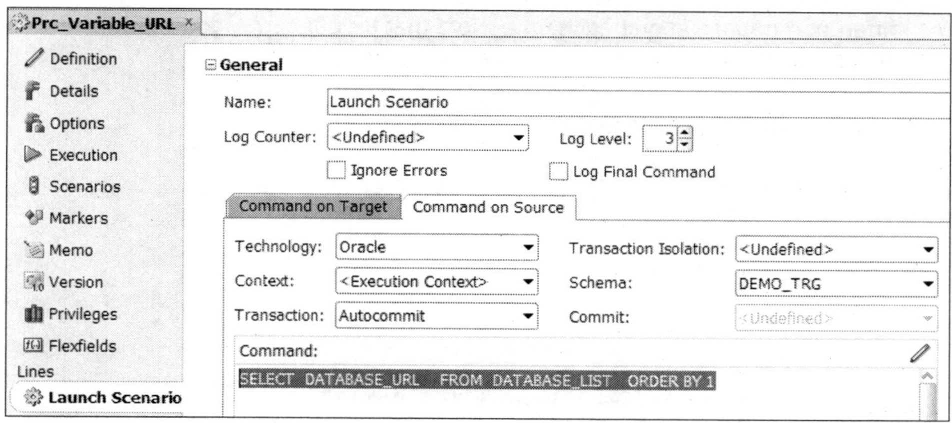

8. Click on the **Command on Target** tab and enter the following:
   - **Technology:** `ODI Tools`
   - **Command:** `OdiStartScen "-SCEN_NAME=PKG_VARIABLE_URL" "-SCEN_VERSION=001" "-ODI_COOKBOOK.PV_DB_URL=#DATABASE_URL"`

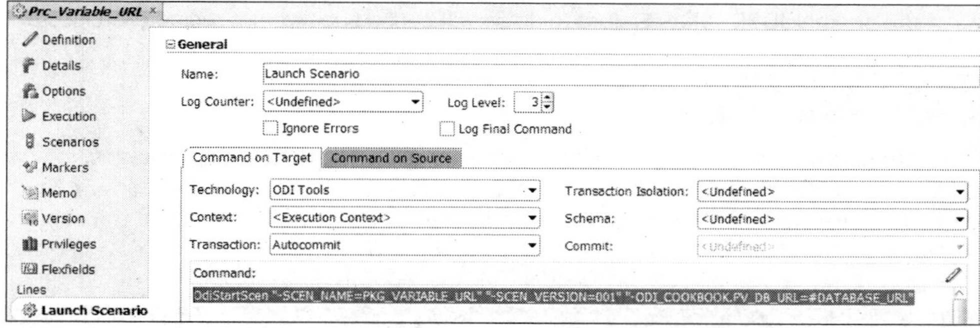

9. Save the completed procedure.
10. Execute the procedure `Prc_Variable_URL`.

11. Review the results from the **Operator** tab. Notice that the procedure looped the `Database_List` table and executed the `Pkg_Variable_URL` scenario three times by passing the JDBC URL as a parameter, which allowed the scenario to connect to a different database server each time. Note that for our simulation we used the same URL information for all three database connections.

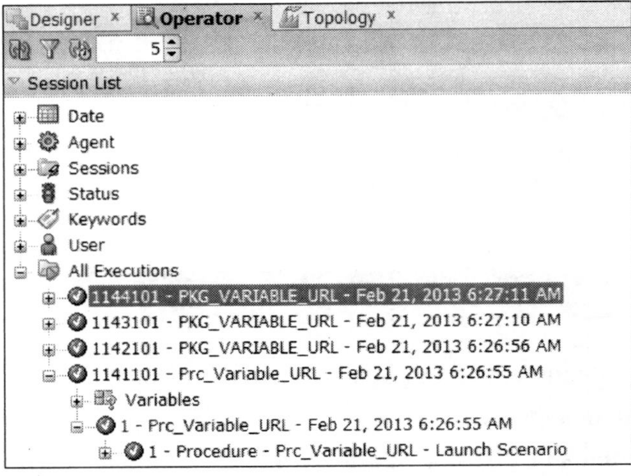

12. Once you have satisfactorily completed this exercise, be sure to change the `DEMO_SRC` connection information by replacing the variable used in this recipe with the original JDBC value. Failure to do so will cause subsequent recipe exercises to fail.

How it works...

Just as variables can be used to modify the behavior of ODI applications (packages, procedures, and interfaces), variables can also modify the behavior of the underlying topology. By embedding variables within the physical architecture, we can affect many of the connection details such as the JDBC URL, the User, and the Password.

Using variables to control loops inside packages

Process control looping is a commonly used technique in many forms of software development and the need for such methods is no different in ODI. There are many use cases where managing the exact number of process cycles is a functional requirement. By using separate steps to initialize, increment, and evaluate the value of a designated loop-control variable, an ODI developer is able to tightly manage the process cycles needed to satisfy those requirements. In this recipe, we will develop a package that executes an interface a specific number of times before terminating.

Getting ready...

In order to give our package something to do, we will reuse the `Int_Variable` interface created earlier in the previous *Using variables in topology* exercise.

How to do it...

1. Create a variable called `PV_LOOP_CNTRL`.
2. Select the **Data Type** as `Numeric`.
3. Select the **Keep History** option as **No History**.
4. Create a package called `Pkg_Variable_Loop`.
5. On the diagram panel of the package editor, drag the `PV_LOOP_CNTRL` variable onto the canvas three times:
   - Click on the first occurrence of the variable, then set the **Step name** option to `Initialize CNTRL`, the **Type** option to **Set Variable**, select the **Assign** option, and set the **Value** to `0`

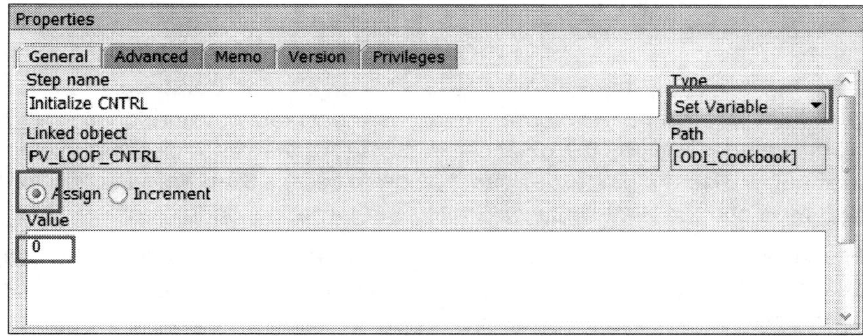

   - Click on the first occurrence of the variable and set the **Step name** to `Increment CNTRL`, the **Type** to `Set Variable`, select the `Increment` option, and set the **Value** to `1`

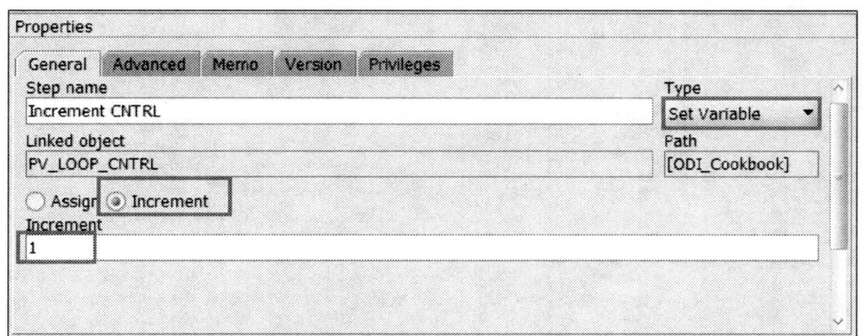

- Click on the first occurrence of the variable and set the **Step Name** option to `Is CNTRL > 4`, the **Type** value to **Evaluate Variable**, **Operator** to **>**, and the **Value** option to `4`

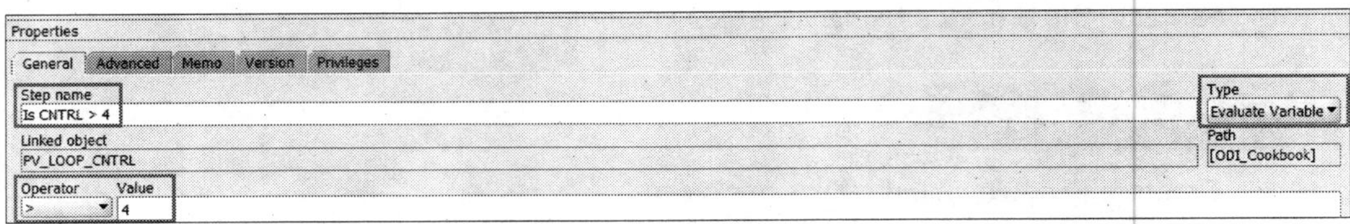

6. Drag the `Int_Variable` interface onto the canvas after the third variable occurrence.
7. Connect the four icons together using the **OK** option between the first three and **`false`** between the last two icons.

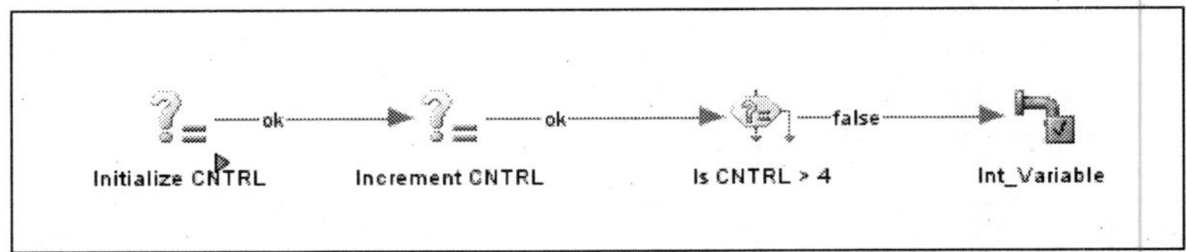

8. Open the `Toolbox Event Detection` folder, click on **OdiSleep**, then insert the wait utility by locating the cross-hairs above the variable evaluation icon and clicking on the canvas. Click on the object selector/arrow; then click on the odiSleep icon on the canvas. Use the properties panel below to set the **Step Name** option to `Wait 15 seconds` and the **Wait Delay** option to `15000` (milliseconds).
9. Open the `Toolbox Utilties` folder, click on **OdiBeep**, then insert the beep utility by locating the cross-hairs below the variable evaluation icon and clicking on the canvas.
10. Connect these last two icons to the other icons as shown in the following diagram (note how the Interface icon connects to the OdiSleep icon then back to the Increment Variable icon):

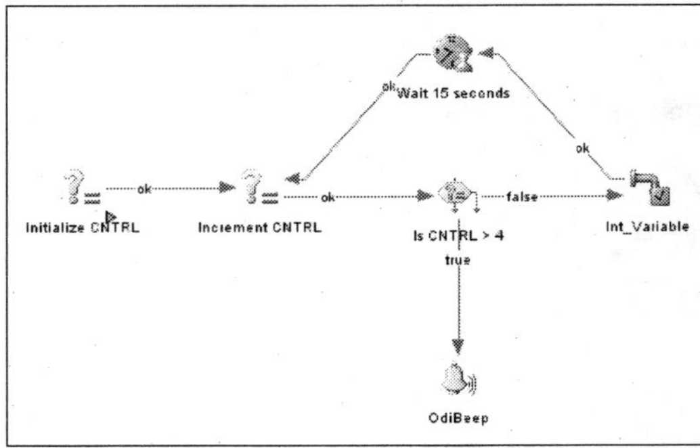

11. Save and execute the `Pkg_Variable_Loop` package. Upon completion, observe the operator log details noting that the interface has been executed four times with a fifteen second delay between each execution.

How it works...

Our package began with the initialization of the numeric loop control variable using a value of zero. The primary loop commenced by incrementing the loop variable using a value of one. The next step was the evaluation of the variable to determine if the maximum threshold had been reached. This evaluation step had two possible outcomes: if the variable was > 4 (true), the package branched to the ending step (**odiBeep**); if the variable was <= 4 (false), the package branched to the interface and **odiSleep** steps before returning to the beginning of the loop and incrementing the loop variable again.

There's more...

The value(s) that are used to set, increment, or evaluate a loop variable are not limited to constants, but in fact can reference other variables. This capability allows a developer to dynamically control the behavior of the loop control mechanism.

5
Knowledge Module Internals

In this chapter, we will cover:

- Using the substitution passes
- Using Java variables in KMs
- Using Java for condition code generation
- Invoking Java from the KMs
- Using substitution methods in Java
- Combining substitution methods in a Knowledge Module

Introduction

Advanced developers can easily get started with KMs by copying existing ones and altering the existing code. The recipes in this chapter will cover concepts that are little known or little understood, but will allow for further extensions in the KMs.

To get past the basic cut, paste, and modify methods used to alter KMs, you need to know more about how ODI leverages the code of the KMs to generate scripts, commands, and SQL code. A good understanding of the mechanisms in place to generate the code that will eventually be generated is key to the mastery of KMs. In this chapter, we will try to keep our examples as simple as possible, while exposing as much as possible about how all the elements are put together by ODI.

Before we look at the details of some advanced techniques in the design of KMs, there is one document that you really must have in hand: *Knowledge Module Developer's Guide for Oracle Data Integrator*. At the time of writing, it can be found on the Oracle website listed here: `http://docs.oracle.com/cd/E23943_01/integrate.1111/e12645/toc.htm`

This document describes in detail all the substitution APIs that can be used within the ODI KMs. It is the absolute reference guide to understanding and modifying KMs.

Using the substitution passes

We will look here at some of the details of how ODI uses multiple substitution rounds to replace some of the code within KMs with the actual code that will be ultimately executed by the databases and scripts.

Getting ready

To follow along with the examples listed here, you will need an ODI project with at least the following KMs: `LKM File to SQL (SQLLDR)` and `IKM SQL Control Append`. From a resource perspective, you will need a `Flat File` model with at least one file defined and an Oracle model with at least one table.

How to do it...

1. In your project, rename the `LKM File to Oracle (SQLLDR)` KM, to `LKM File to Oracle (SQLLDR) with substitutions`.
2. Edit the `LKM File to Oracle (SQLLDR) with substitutions` KM and within the step identified as `Call sqlldr`, insert the following code immediately after the different import statements:

```
# Loading table: <%=odiRef.getTargetTable("TABLE_NAME")%>
# Full table name: <%=odiRef.getTable("L", "TARG_NAME", "A")%>
# Loading server: <?=odiRef.getInfo("DEST_CON_NAME")?>
# Loading server: <@=odiRef.getInfo("DEST_CON_NAME")@>
```

3. We will use these new lines of code to better understand how the code generation works.
4. Create an interface using a `flat` file as your source and an Oracle table for the target. Select the modified `LKM File to Oracle (SQLLDR) with substitutions` KM to load data into the database, and the standard `IKM SQL Control Append` KM for the final integration in the target table. If you want to keep things simple, deactivate **FLOW_CONTROL** in the IKM. Save the interface.

5. In the code extracts provided later in this recipe, we are using a source file called `SALES.txt`. You can use any file of your choice. When we designed this recipe, we used a fixed-length file. Note that the choice of the IKM has no impact in this recipe.
6. Then right-click on the interface to generate a scenario.
7. Expand the interface in the object tree on the left until you see the name of the scenario you have just generated. Right-click on the name of the scenario to export it as an XML file.
8. Execute the scenario from the Studio; at this point we do not really care whether the scenario is successful or not, all we really want to do is to look into the code that gets generated.
9. Now edit the `LKM File to Oracle (SQLLDR) with substitutions` and look at the source code for the `Call sqlldr` step. You will see (among other elements) the following:

```
# Loading table: <%=odiRef.getTargetTable("TABLE_NAME")%>
# Full table name: <%=odiRef.getTable("L", "TARG_NAME", "A")%>
# Loading server: <?=odiRef.getInfo("DEST_CON_NAME")?>
# Loading server: <@=odiRef.getInfo("DEST_CON_NAME")@>
```

10. Now open in a text editor the XML file that was created in step 5 as a result of the export of the scenario, and you will see that only part of the substitution has been completed:

```
# Loading table: TRG_CUSTOMER
# Full table name: <?=snpRef.getObjectName("L", "TRG_CUSTOMER",
"ORA_SALES_DWH", "", "D") ?>
# Loading server: <?=odiRef.getInfo("DEST_CON_NAME")?>
# Loading server: <@=odiRef.getInfo("DEST_CON_NAME")@>
```

11. Finally, look at the generated code and you will see that all the elements were properly substituted similar to what follows, except for the code within the `<@ @>` brackets, which still has to be substituted:

```
# Loading table: TRG_CUSTOMER
# Full table name: SALES_DWH.TRG_CUSTOMER
# Loading server: DWH_ORACLE_DEV
# Loading server:<@=odiRef.getInfo("DEST_CON_NAME")@>
```

How it works...

There are actually four passes of substitution within ODI. When you generate a scenario, all substitution APIs encapsulated with `<%=... %>` are processed so that everything that is not dependent on Topology information is resolved; that is, table names, column names, and mappings are retrieved from the repository and included within the code. However, the information that is topology dependent (schema name, server name, user name, and password to connected to the databases) is not substituted yet. The same is true with variables that would be included in the code. ODI variables will only be assigned a value at execution time.

> When you execute a process directly from the ODI Studio without generating a scenario, the first thing ODI does is to go through this generation phase, then it can behave the same way it would with a scenario. Without a scenario, this generation happens with each new execution. A key benefit of the scenario is that the code is pre-generated and you do not have to go through this generation phase with each execution of the code.

When you execute a scenario, the agent will complete the code substitutions with current information from the `Master Repository`, that is, the context used for execution will define which user name and password must be used to access the database, which actual physical schemas host the tables, and which OS folders contain the flat files. For this last minute substitution to be possible, the ODI Studio retrieves only the information that will be the same from environment to environment: tables and column names, mappings, joins, lookups, and so on. It then replaces the original substitution APIs encapsulated within the `<%=...%>` brackets with another set of substitution APIs encapsulated within the `<?=... ?>` brackets whenever additional substitutions are needed. In our example, we can see that the `<%=odiRef.getTargetTable(...)%>` bracket is fully substituted, but the `<%=odiRef.getTable()%>` bracket is replaced initially with a call to another substitution API: `<?=odiRef.getObjectName(...)%>`, with the proper logical schema name and table name.

Now when you ask the agent to execute your scenario, you have to specify the execution context; this is part of the execution parameters to start the scenario. The agent can now complete the code substitution and write the finalized code into the operator tables, where that code can then be used for execution. One last detail however are the substitutions encapsulated with `<@=... @>`. These elements will never be substituted when the code is written into the `operator` tables; they will only be substituted when the agent sends the code to the databases and writes scripts. This is usually reserved for passwords, so that clear text passwords won't appear in the ODI operator logs.

The following figure represents these three rounds of substitution along with the components that are in charge of these substitutions and the location where you can see what is actually happening:

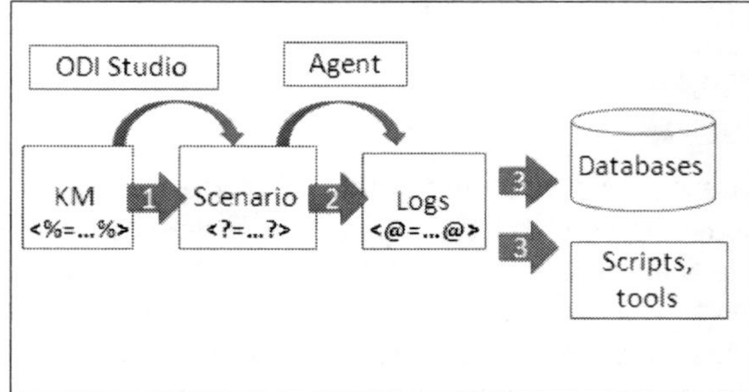

We started by saying that there were four substitution rounds, but we've only talked about three of them so far. So what about the fourth one? Remember, the other element that is only substituted at runtime is the value of ODI variables. What if you want your code to be dependent on the value of these variables? This is where you can use the last one of the substitution syntaxes: `<$=...$>`. At this point though, the substitution APIs have already been processed by ODI; you will still be able to use Java code within these brackets, but you cannot rely on substitution APIs anymore. We will see more later in this chapter on how to use Java code within the brackets.

What is important here is that you too can take advantage of all four passes in order to delay some operations. For instance, suppose that you want to work with the actual name of the target table. By delaying the operation to the second round of substitutions, using the `<?=...?>`convention, you can guarantee that your code is operating on the substituted table name, not on the API anymore. The same will stand true with column names.

Now when working with substitution APIs, one thing to remember is that not all APIs can be used immediately after the first round of substitution: APIs that retrieve table names and column names are only processed in the first round with `<%=...%>`. For instance, `<%=odiRef.getTable(...)%>` gets translated into `<?=getObjectName(...)%>`, as we have seen in our example. But with a little bit of practice, you will be able to implement these functions at a completely different level.

You will notice when you edit existing code that there are two identical classes for the substitution functions: `odiRef` and `snpRef`. Best practice is to always use `odiRef` in your own code, as `snpRef` is only maintained for backwards compatibility.

There's more...

You are not limited to using substitution APIs in these brackets, and as we will see later, you can use the same techniques to embed Java code to condition, alter, or control code generation.

Code generation is not limited to these substitution APIs and a lot more is done by ODI when the code is finally put together. Oracle support has a detailed note for these operations, compiled in the note *#753818.1* available at `http://support.oracle.com`.

Using Java variables in KMs

For this recipe, we will make a very simple modification to the `IKM SQL Control Append` KM using a Java variable. Then we will use this KMs in a series of interfaces to see how ODI handles the variable.

Getting ready

You will need to have a project available where the `IKM SQL Control Append` KM has already been imported. You must also have a few tables that can be used as target tables using this IKM (think of 3 or 4 tables).

How to do it...

1. Rename the `IKM SQL Control Append` to `IKM SQL Control Append with Variable`.
2. Right-click on the `IKM SQL Control Append with Variable` KM and add **New option**. Call this option `Reset Java Variable`. Set the type to Check Box and the default value to `FALSE`.
3. Edit the KM `IKM SQL Control Append with variable` and add a step. Name the step `Reset Java Variable` and write the following code in that step:

```
<%=my_var=0%>
```

   Because this step will not end up generating any code to be executed by a database or external tool, leave the technology as `<Undefined>`, as you can see on this screenshot:

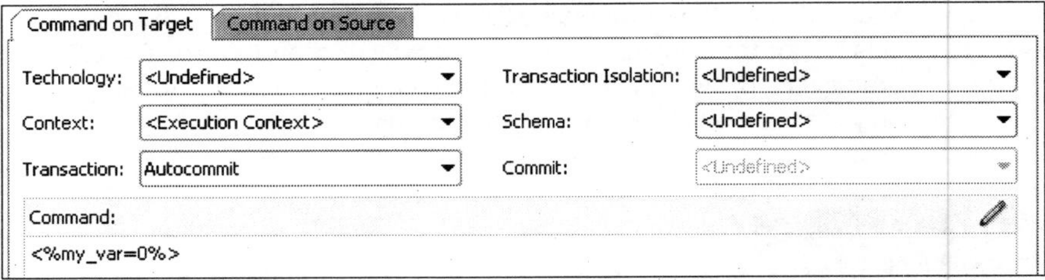

4. Scroll to the very bottom of the definition of the step, where you will find an entry for **Options**. Expand this entry, and make sure that the option `Reset Java Variable` is the only one that is selected.
5. Create another step called `Execution Count` and write the following code in that step:

```
/*
<%my_var=my_var+1;
out.print("This KM has been executed " + my_var + " time(s)");%>
*/
```

6. Move both steps to the very beginning of the KM. Go back to the **Details** tab of the KM, highlight the steps, and move them using the Up arrow available in the toolbar on top of the window, as you can see here:

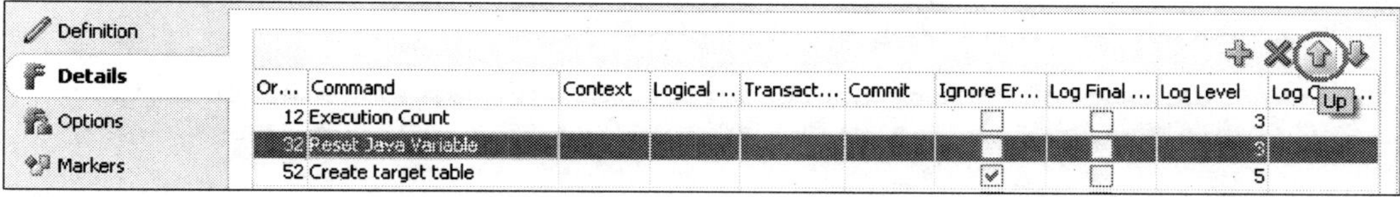

7. Next, create a series of interfaces that use the `IKM SQL Control Append with Variable` KM. The first interface that you will execute must have the `Reset Java Variable` option set to **YES**. The remaining ones must have this option set to **NO**.
8. Create a package for the sequencing of your interfaces (make sure that the interface that resets the Java variable is executed first or the other interfaces will all fail). For each interface executed by the package, examine the generated code in the operator, and focus on the details of the `Execution Count` step. You will see that the value of the variable is incremented for each interface in the package.

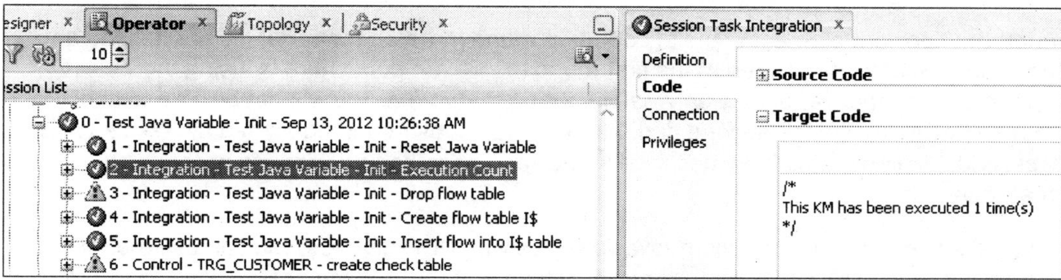

This will only be true if you execute the interfaces from a package where the variable has been initialized: this is what we are doing here with the `reset` step.

How it works...

The generation of the code is performed by a Java interpreter, which can process Java code and in particular handle Java variables.

The Java variables that we are creating here have a scope that matches that of the session that is being executed. As long as you are in the same session, you are using the same variables.

To confirm this, execute one of the interfaces that do not set the Java variable outside of the package: select the interface and execute just that interface. We will encounter an error because we are trying to increment a variable that has never been declared. This will literally prevent the generation of the code and instead of the expected code, you will see an error message that contain the following (among more details):

```
BeanShell script error: Sourced file: [...] illegal use of undefined
variable, class, or 'void' literal
```

The error message reported by ODI in the **Definition** tab of the **Operator** job log may vary; it will depend on which technology you have selected for this step in the KM. In all cases, the error message reported by ODI when trying to execute the code is not relevant since there is no code to be executed; the **Code** tab only contains the printout of the error that prevented the code generation.

This shows that we want to be careful when using Java code in the KMs (such as variables declaration and variables use); errors and inconsistencies will prevent the generation of the code, so these portions must be thoroughly tested.

Another important element is the substitution round in which the variables are defined and used. If a variable is declared in the first round (as we are doing here by using the `<%=...%>` symbols), then that variable is only visible during that round. You will not be able to see that same variable in the second and third round of substitution (identified by `<?=...?>` and `<@=...@>`). Likewise, a variable declared in the `<?=...?>` substitution round is only visible in that round.

If you are interested in combining Java variables with ODI variables, you can use the refresh statement of the ODI variables to retrieve the value of the Java variable as long as the refresh operation is done in the package where the Java variable is being declared. For instance, if we have access to an Oracle database, we can leverage the following refresh statement when we define the ODI variable (remember to use a valid logical schema name in the variable **Refresh** tab for the code to run against your database):

```
select <%out.print(my_var);%> from dual
```

Note that the reverse is more difficult: Java variables are substituted with a value when the code is generated. ODI variables are substituted with a value when the code is executed. If you were to assign the value of an ODI variable to a Java variable, you would have to process the Java code in the `<$...$>` substitution pass, where the substitution APIs are not available anymore

There's more...

As long as the variables are used in the same package, they can be used in other ODI objects. One approach that can be used is to create an ODI procedure to define (or reset) the Java variable. One benefit is that you would not have to worry about changing the value of the KM option to reset the variable or not. You would simply start the package with the ODI procedure then simply use the variables in the KMs as we have done here. This can be particularly useful if you keep inserting interfaces in your sequence of execution. One down side is that you are now using a variable in the KM that relies on an external component. If you share the KM with other developers, you must make sure that you also share the initialization procedure.

Using Java for condition code generation

If we really want code generation to be flexible, we need to have the ability to choose what code is generated based on external elements. This means that at code generation time, we need to have the ability to chose among different portions of code. If we were to write pure Java code, an `If` statement would give us exactly what we are looking for. So our approach will be just this: take advantage of the fact that we can execute Java code to control code generation and always generate the proper code as needed.

Getting ready

For this recipe, we will reuse the KM that was created in the previous recipe. If you did not follow the necessary steps to create the KM, you will need to perform steps 1 through 6 of the previous recipe: *Using Java Variables in KMs*.

How to do it...

1. Right-click on the `IKM SQL Control Append with Variable KM` to duplicate it. Then rename the copy of `IKM SQL Control Append with Variable` KM to `IKM SQL Control Append with Variable and Java Conditions`.
2. Edit the step `Execution Count` and modify the code so that we now write proper English, such as `once`, `twice`, `3 times`:

```
/*
<%my_var=my_var+1;
out.print("This KM has been executed ");%>
<%if (my_var==1){%>
once<%} else if (my_var==2){%>
twice<% } else {
out.print(my_var + " times");
}%>
*/
```

3. Create several interfaces that use the new `IKM SQL Control Append with Variable and Java Conditions` KM. Add these interfaces in a package, and make sure that the option `Reset Java Variable` is set to `TRUE` for the first interface of the package, and only for that interface.
4. Look at the generated code in the operator of ODI Studio. For the first interface, the `Execution Count` command will read:

   ```
   This KM has been executed
   Once
   ```

   For the second interface, the `Execution Count` command will read:

   ```
   This KM has been executed
   Twice
   ```

   For the third interface, the `Execution Count` command will read:

   ```
   This KM has been executed
   3 times
   ```

   Additional interfaces will only see an increment of the count of executions.

How it works...

When we use the java tags (`<%`, `<=` ,`<@` and, `<$`), we are altering the code generation with our own Java code. When it encounters a condition in Java, the module that handles the code substitution will evaluate the Java conditions and only generate the code that matches the conditions that are true. If we look at the following code extract:

```
<%if (my_var==1){%>
once<%}%>
```

The code generation engine will evaluate the `my_var` variable. It will compare it with the value `1`, and if the value is indeed one, it will print the code (or process the necessary substitutions) included before the end of the conditional code block. The conditional code block is enclosed in curved brackets, as you would normally do in Java: `{}`.

If the condition is not satisfied, we can test other conditions using the same syntax:

```
<%if (my_var==1){%>
once<%}else if(my_var==2){%>
twice<%}%>
```

An alternative approach was used for the final case, where instead of encapsulating the code to print within Java conditions, printing itself is executed as Java code:

```
<% } else {
out.print(my_var + " times");
}%>
```

This technique is already used by standard KMs. The `IKM SQL Control Append` KM has always had to know whether or not to create an `I$_` table or not. The challenge is that if that table is not created, the step that writes data into the target table will read from the source (the `C$_` table or actual source table) rather than from the `I$_` table. Since the creation of the `I$_` table depends on the need to control data quality (if the **FLOW_CONTROL** option is set to `True`), a simple test in Java will guarantee that the proper table name is always used. If you look at the step `Insert New Rows` in the standard `IKM SQL Control Append` KM, you will see the following:

```
<%if( odiRef.getUserExit("FLOW_CONTROL").equals("1") ){ %>
Insert […]
from<%=odiRef.getTable("L","INT_NAME","A")%>
<% } else { %>
Insert […]
FROM ….
<%}%>
```

> As you can see here, there is not even a Java variable in use; the `If` statement directly evaluates the value of the **FLOW_CONTROL** KM option set by the developer.

A few important points when you start using Java in the code of your KMs:

- Lines of code must finish with a semi-colon: `;` without this character, the code cannot be properly interpreted
- Blocks of code (especially the `for` loops and, `if - else` blocks) must be enclosed in brackets: { }
- And of course, you code must be valid Java code

As long as you respect these rules, you can put together all the code you want.

There's more...

Since the version 11g of ODI introduced the notion of data sets, you may now have more than one source data set. More Java code was added to the KMs to parse all the data sets and properly put the code together. For instance, in the previous example, the `from` clause when we read from the source has to loop over all the data sets. To do so, it will use a `for` loop in Java:

```
<%for (int i=odiRef.getDataSetMin(); i <= odiRef.getDataSetMax(); i++)
{%>
<%=odiRef.getDataSet(i, "Operator")%>
Select ([More code here])
```

Invoking Java from the KMs

So far in this chapter we have used Java to alter the code that is generated by ODI when we use KMs. But there may be cases where you want to generate Java code and actually run that code as part of the execution of the ODI processes. In this example, we will use Java code to write additional information to a file as we run an interface. There are two **technologies** that can be used in ODI to write Java code, namely **Jython** and **Groovy**. We will use **Groovy** here as it is closer to true Java code, but the use of one technology versus the other is mostly a matter of personal preference.

Getting ready

For this recipe, we will modify the `IKM SQL Control Append` KM, so make sure to import this KM into your project before getting started.

How to do it...

1. Rename the `IKM SQL Control Append` KM to `IKM SQL Control Append with Java Code`.
2. Right-click on the `IKM SQL Control Append with Java Code` and add **New option**. Call this option `Audit File Name`. Set the type to `Value` and the default value to `c:/temp/ODI.log`.

> Make sure to use a path that exists in your environment (you can replace `c:/temp` as needed). We are using forward slashes here as ODI will handle them properly on Unix, Linux, and Windows systems. In cases where ODI has to share this information with external tools, make sure to use the proper slashes (backslashes or forward slashes) for these tools given the operating system on which they run.

3. Edit the `IKM SQL Control Append with Java Code` KM and add a step. Name the step `Write Audit Data to Log File`, set the **Technology** to **Groovy**, and write the following code in that step:

```
auditFile=new File('<%=odiRef.getOption("Audit File Name")%>')
auditFile.write('<%=odiRef.getSession("SESS_NAME")%> was
executed by <%=odiRef.getSession("ODI_USER_NAME")%> on <%=odiRef.
getSysDate("MMM d, yyyy")%> at <%=odiRef.getSysDate("hh:mm a")%>')
```

4. Move this step to the very beginning of the KM: go back to the **Details** tab of the KM, highlight the step, and move it up the same way we did it in step 6 of *Using Java variables in KMs*.

5. Save your new KM.
6. Create a new interface (all you will need is a target table to try out the code execution, no source tables are needed at this point). In the **Flow** tab of the interface, select the `IKM SQL Control Append with Java Code`. Set the **FLOW_CONTROL** option of the KM to `false` to make sure that the interface does not fail.

> Even if the execution of the interface fails, the log file will be generated. When reproducing these steps, focus on the file generation. The successful execution of the interface is nice to have, but not required!

7. Save and execute the interface.
8. If you look under your `c:\temp` folder, you should now have a `ODI.log` file that contains something similar to this (here, the name of the interface was `JAVA_CODE_TEST` and the ODI user is `DEVELOPER_1`):

```
JAVA_CODE_TEST was executed by DEVELOPER_1 on Sep 19, 2012 at
11:22 PM
```

How it works...

The **Groovy** technology is actually an in-line Java interpreter. We can use this language in the KMs to generate and execute any kind of code we want. Since the different steps of a KM do not have to be all using the same technology, we can alternate between SQL code and other technologies (**Groovy**, **Jython**) to perform operations that we want to happen outside of the database.

What is important here is that this Java code is now interpreted at execution time. If we look at the generated code, we have mostly plain Java this time:

```
auditFile=new File('c:/temp/ODI.log')
auditFile.write('test java code was executed by SUPERVISOR on
<@=odiRef.getSysDate("MMM d, yyyy") @> at <@=odiRef.getSysDate("hh:mm
a") @>')
```

In all the recipes we have seen so far in this chapter, the Java code never appeared in the generated code. This time, the Java code is generated and executed at runtime.

There's more...

You can also take advantage of the Groovy technology to import external Java classes. This is actually how you can leverage your own Java classes or even the ODI SDK APIs: import the proper Java class, and then use the methods and functions available in your class. The following code would be used to take advantage of the ODI SDK (Java classes to build ODI code using APIs instead of the graphical interface) to connect to the ODI agent:

```
importoracle.odi.runtime.agent.invocation.RemoteRuntimeAgentInvoker
[more code here]
agent = new RemoteRuntimeAgentInvoker("http://localhost:20910/
oraclediagent", "SUPERVISOR", "SUNOPSIS".toCharArray())
...
```

For ODI Studio to find your own Java classes, they must be copied to the folder `C:\Documents and Settings\<username>\Application Data\odi\oracledi\userlib`, or you can edit the `additional_path.txt` file found in that directory to point to a separate directory.

The ODI standalone agent will look for additional Java classes in the `<ODI_HOME>\agent\lib` folder.

You can find more information on the Groovy language on the Groovy web site at: `http://groovy.codehaus.org`

You can find more details on the Jython language on the Jython web site available at `http://www.jython.org`.

Using substitution methods in Java

For this recipe, we will make a very simple modification to the `IKM SQL Control Append` by combining a Java variable and a substitution API. Then we will use this KM in an interface to see how the code gets generated.

Getting ready

You will need to have a project ready where the `IKM SQL Control Append` KM has been imported. You must also have a table that can be used as a target table using this IKM in an interface.

How to do it...

1. Rename the `IKM SQL Control Append KM` to `IKM SQL Control Append with Variable and Substitution`.
2. Add a step. Name the step `Retrieve Session Number` and write the following code in that step:

```
<%v_sess=odiRef.getSession("SESS_NO")%>
```

> There is no need to set the technology for this step: as you will see when we use the KM, no code will actually be generated for the agent to run.

3. Move this step up to make sure that it is the very first step in the KM, the same way we did it in step 6 of *Using Java variables in KMs*.
4. Edit the step `Create Flow Table I$` and insert the name of the variable that we use for the session name after the name of the table that is created (do not alter the rest of this step, as we still need to retrieve the column names):

```
create table <%=odiRef.getTable("L", "INT_NAME", "A")%><%=v_sess%>
```

> Note that there is no space in the code that we are adding `%><%=v_sess%>`. We want to concatenate the value of the variable to the table name. A space would render the code invalid.

5. Similarly, edit the steps **Insert flow into I$ table**, **Insert new rows**, and **Drop flow table**. Also, each time you see a reference to:

```
<%=odiRef.getTable("L", "INT_NAME", "A")%>
```

6. Replace it with:

```
<%=odiRef.getTable("L", "INT_NAME", "A")%><%=v_sess%>
```

7. Save the New KM.
8. Use the KM in an interface where you do have a source and a target table. Make sure that you leave the **FLOW_CONTROL** option to `True` so that the `I$` table is created.

> If you want the interface to run successfully, you will also have to modify the CKM used in the interface (as found in the interface **Controls** tab) the same way we have modified the IKM: always adding `<%=v_sess%>` to all references to the `I$` table. Otherwise, the CKM will point to a table name that does not exist. If you only want to look at the generated code, then use the default CKM, but keep in mind that the interface will fail!

9. Run the interface.
10. Look at the generated code for the first step, `Retrieve Session Number`, where you should see no generated code. This is Java code that ODI uses for code generation.
11. Look at any of the steps where you have altered the name of the `I$_` table: the table name should now include the session number. It should look something like this (with a different session number of course):

    ```
    create table ODI_TMP.I$_TRG_CUSTOMER1684072
    (
    [...]
    ```

12. If you check the session number for the process that created the table, you will notice that the IDs are indeed the same:

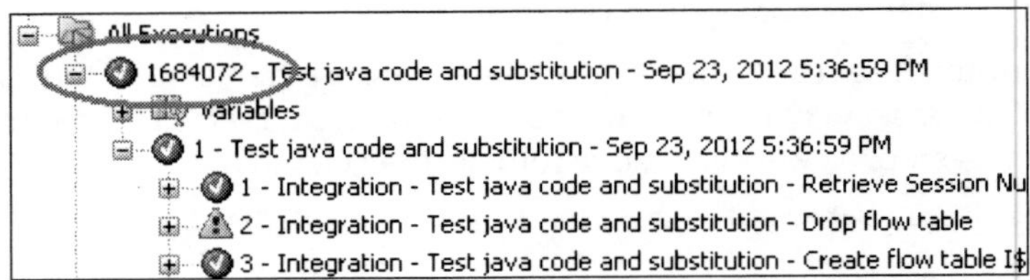

How it works...

The mechanisms at play here are actually quite simple. As long as you are not trying to reference substituted values before they are computed, you are free to use the substitution methods as much as you want, wherever you want.

Notice that when we use substitution functions within Java code, we do not have to enclose them with the brackets (`<%....%>`), since the entire code is already enclosed.

This behavior is actually already used in the original `IKM SQL Control Append` KM that we have seen in the recipe *Using Java for condition code generation*. If you set the **FLOW_CONTROL** option to `False`, there is no need for the KM to create an `I$_` table. The consequence is that when ODI goes to generate the code needed to insert the records in the target table, it will either have to read from the source or from the `I$_` table. To know where to read from, ODI uses Java code after checking out the value of the **FLOW_CONTROL** option:

```
<%if ( odiRef.getOption("FLOW_CONTROL").equals("1") ) { %>
[...]
select [...]
from <%=odiRef.getTable("L","INT_NAME","A")%>
<% } else { %>
select [...]
from <%=odiRef.getFrom()%>
<% } %>
```

There's more...

One downside of the example we have used here is that there is now a risk that we generate table names that are longer than what is allowed for any given technology. ODI can control this, but we would have to make sure that we let ODI put the entire name together, instead of adding characters ourselves at the end of the table name.

To achieve this, we can use Java variables to impact the code generation even further. The bloggers at ODI Experts (`http://odiexperts.com/interface-parallel-execution-a-new-solution/`) have a very good description of this. When you edit any of your data servers in Topology, ODI lets you modify the syntax used to generate the temporary tables: `I$`, `E$`, and `C$`. You can use Java variables to alter the default and make it `I$<?v_sess?>`, `E$<?v_sess?>`, and `C$<?v_sess?>`. Then use Java code in your KMs to retrieve the ID of the current session, as we have done it in this recipe. Note that only the modification described in step 2 is required with this approach; all other table name modifications would be inherited from **Topology**. From then on, all staging tables will have a name that is unique to the session they belong to. Also note that for this approach to work, you need the substitution to happen after the very first round. Remember: the `odiRef,getTable()` API is only replaced with another API in the initial substitution round. Nonetheless, this approach is is very useful when running concurrent iterations of the same interface.

> If you use this technique, make sure that all KMs used in any given interface (LKM, IKM, CKM) use the same approach. You cannot have KMs creating and referencing tables with a specific naming convention and then have other KMs using a different convention. Case in point: the example used here can only run successfully if the IKM and CKM are modified together.

Combining substitution methods in a KM

There are times where we need to use more than one substitution method to obtain what we need. We may need to concatenate the results of two methods, or to use one method to get the parameters for another. For such cases, the typical question is where and how to use the enclosing brackets. We will show some of this here.

Getting ready

For this recipe, we will make a very simple modification to the `IKM SQL Control Append` KM by combining several substitution methods. Then we will use this KM in an interface to see how the code gets generated. You will need to have a project ready where the original `IKM SQL Control Append` KM has been imported. You must also have a table that can be used as a target table using this IKM in an interface.

How to do it...

1. Rename the `IKM SQL Control Append` KM to `IKM SQL Control Append With Combined Substitution APIs`.
2. Edit the step `Create Flow Table I$` and alter the `Create Flow Table I$` portion of the code as follows:

   ```
   create table<%=odiRef.getTable("L", "INT_NAME", "A")+odiRef.
   getSession("SESS_NO")%>
   ```

3. Similarly, edit the steps `Insert flow into I$ table`, `Insert new rows` and `Drop flow table`. Each time you see a reference to:

   ```
   <%=odiRef.getTable("L", "INT_NAME", "A")%>
   ```

4. Replace it with:

   ```
   create table <%=odiRef.getTable("L", "INT_NAME", "A")+odiRef.
   getSession("SESS_NO")%>
   ```

5. Save the new KM.
6. Use the KM in an interface where you do have a source and a target table. Make sure that you leave the option **FLOW_CONTROL** to `True` to make sure that the `I$` table is created.

> If you want the interface to run, you will also have to modify the CKM used in the interface (as found in the interface **Controls** tab) the same way we have modified the IKM; always adding `odiRef.getSession("SESS_NO")` to all references to the I$ table. Otherwise, the CKM will point to a table name that does not exist!

7. Run the interface.
8. Look at any of the steps where you have altered the name of the `I$_` table: the table name should now include the session number. It should look something like this (with a different session number of course):

   ```
   create table ODI_TMP.I$_TRG_CUSTOMER1685074
   (
   [...]
   ```

9. If you check the session number for the process that created the table, you will notice that the IDs are indeed the same:

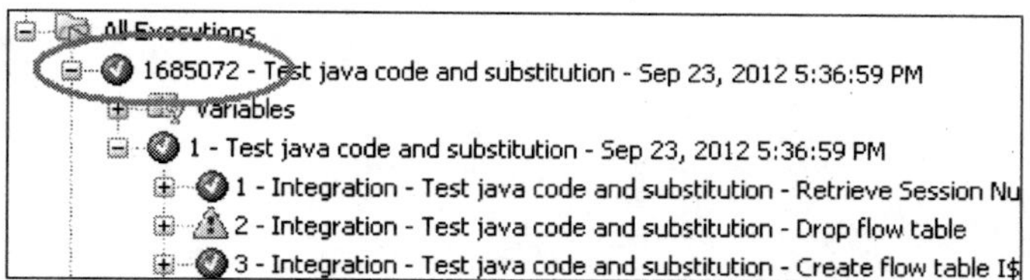

How it works...

What is important here is that we only open the enclosing brackets once. Then we can combine the substitution APIs as needed. All these substitution methods do in the end is to generate the proper code based on the context in which they are used. By concatenating the output, we simply generate more code.

The original `IKM SQL Control Append` KM takes advantage of this technique to create the `I$_ staging` table. Since the KM is generic (it must run on any database that supports SQL), it has to account for differences between these databases. When columns are null able, shall the `NULL` keyword be uppercase or lowercase? Or should it use a different keyword than `NULL`? Luckily, this information is available with the definition of the different technologies in the ODI topology, and that information can be retrieved with the API.

```
odiRef.getInfo("DEST_DDL_NULL")
```

We can now create a table with all the necessary columns and append the matching `NULL` keyword for the underlying technology:

```
<%=odiRef.getColList("", "[COL_NAME]\t[DEST_WRI_DT] " + odiRef.
getInfo("DEST_DDL_NULL"), ",\n\t", "", "INS")%>
```

There's more...

There are many examples where substitution APIs are combined, both in existing KMs and in sample code available on the Internet.

The following blog entries discuss some of these possibilities:

`http://www.business-intelligence-quotient.com/?p=812`

`http://www.business-intelligence-quotient.com/?p=954`

6

Inside Knowledge Modules – SCD and CDC

In this chapter, we will cover the following topics:

- Implementing Slowly Changing Dimensions (SCD) using ODI
- Modifying an Slowly Changing Dimensions KM to allow undefined behaviors
- Using Changed Data Capture (CDC) - simple
- Using Changed Data Capture(CDC) - consistent set
- Using a single interface to load changes that occur in any dimension

Introduction

Since ODI is frequently used during data warehouse load operations, it is only natural that the functional requirements of **Slowly Changing Dimensions** (**SCD**) and **Changed Data Capture** (**CDC**) be addressed as part of its core functionality. By encapsulating the complexities of these two methodologies within the delivered set of KMs, ODI allows the developer to focus on answering the questions of what, when, and where, while leaving the seemingly complex issue of how to be managed by the KMs.

Although unrelated to each other, SCD and CDC KMs are both integral parts of many ETL/ELT solutions. Unfortunately, the techniques these processes employ are not often well known or understood. So in order to understand how these advanced topics may be addressed by ODI, we begin by defining these terms:

- SCD is a name for a process that loads data into dimension tables, where the data changes slowly rather than changing on a time-based or regular schedule. The dimension tables are structured in a way that they can retain a history of changes to their data, thus providing a basis for analysis.

- CDC is a process used to identify/capture enterprise source data that has changed, then applying those changes to a target database. CDC minimizes the resources required for ETL operations because it only processes data that has changed. The ultimate goal of CDC is to ensure data synchronicity between systems.

In this chapter, we will go beyond the basics of the ODI documentation to study these two types of KMs in order to gain a better understanding of their internals.

Implementing Slowly Changing Dimensions (SCD) using ODI

If the reader is familiar with the fundamentals of data warehouse design, there should already be an understanding of three basic forms of dimension management:

- Type-I: No historical data (new record data replaces the old data)
- Type-II: Complete historical data (with start and end date bracketing)
- Type-III: Limited historical data (only the most recent data is kept)

> There are other SCD methods (that is history tables, hybrids, and so on) not mentioned, but due to the infrequency of their use or lack of support by ODI, they have been omitted from this discussion. It is not within the scope of this book to discuss the advantages, disadvantages, and reasons for using any of these SCD formats, rather, we will simply describe which of these types have been addressed by ODI.
>
> To read more about some of the less frequently used types of SCD methods, please refer to the following link:
>
> `http://www.kimballgroup.com/2013/02/05/design-tip-152-slowly-changing-dimension-types-0-4-5-6-7/`
>
> To read more about the fundamentals of slowly changing dimensions, please refer to the following website:
>
> `http://en.wikipedia.org/wiki/Slowly_changing_dimension`

The Type-I SCD format is provided out of the box by using one of the ODI Incremental Update IKMs.

The Type-II SCD format is the most commonly used method for managing dimension tables, and it is for this reason that ODI has provided a powerful IKM implementation.

The Type-III SCD format is rarely ever used and it is not currently delivered by ODI (although a custom KM could easily be developed).

Getting ready

In this recipe, we will demonstrate SCD management by developing a simple Type-II SCD interface using Oracle Data Integrator. To get started, it will be necessary to first list the major components and behaviors of the Type-II methodology:

- **Surrogate Key**: This column will be the primary key of the target table. The surrogate key is usually populated with a dynamically generated value.
- **Natural Key**: These column(s) usually define the original primary key of the source table. Because dimension keys will be duplicated to keep the history of changes, these columns cannot be the primary key of the target table. Nevertheless, the natural key columns are required to match incoming records with the existing ones in the target table.
- **Slowly Changing Attributes** (trigger fields): Any changes to these columns will result in the generation of a new record to keep a history of those changes.
- **Updatable attributes**: These columns will be updated without spawning a historical record.

Only the current record will be updated; historical records will not be affected.

- **Current Record Flag**: The column that identifies active records versus historical records.
- **Starting Timestamp**: The date and time when the new information went into effect.
- **Ending Timestamp**: The date and time when the information became inactive.

Using ODI, a developer must define the SCD behavior for every column of a target table by making the appropriate selection on the **Description** tab of the corresponding data store. As each behavior type is assigned, ODI will set a reserved `Boolean` flag corresponding to that behavior, thus allowing various KMs to manage their activities accordingly.

The following table lists the seven SCD-related `Boolean` flags:

`SCD_SK`	**Surrogate Key** in the data model definition.
`SCD_NK`	**Natural Key** in the data model definition.
`SCD_UPD`	**Overwrite on Change** in the data model definition.
`SCD_INS`	**Add Row on Change** in the data model definition.
`SCD_FLAG`	**Current Record Flag** in the data model definition.
`SCD_START`	**Starting Timestamp** in the data model definition.
`SCD_END`	**Ending Timestamp** in the data model definition.

All data store columns must have an assigned behavior and each of the seven SCD components must be assigned to at least one column.

How to do it...

1. Import the `IKM Oracle Slowly Changing Dimension` KM.
2. If you have not already done so, take this time to reverse engineer the `TRG_EMPLOYEE` table into the `DEMO_TRG` data model. Verify that any PK and FK constraint information is also captured by ODI during the reverse engineering process.
3. Open up the `DEMO_TRG` data model and expand the `TRG_EMPLOYEE` data store. Double-click each column, click on the **Description** tab, and select the appropriate attribute from the **Slowly Changing Dimension behavior** drop-down list. Assign an SCD behavior for each and every column in the table using the following information:
    - **Surrogate Key**: `EMP_ID`
    - **Natural Key**: `EMPNO`
    - **Current Record Flag**: `ACTIVE_FLAG`
    - **Starting Timestamp**: `EFF_BEG_DT`
    - **Ending Timestamp**: `EFF_END_DT`
    - **Add Row on Change**: `ENAME`, `JOB`
    - **Overwrite on Change**: All other columns

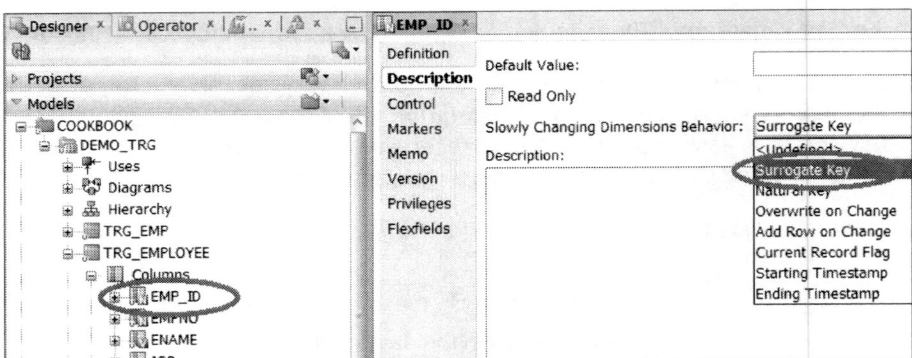

In this example, we have chosen to track history only when changes are made to the "trigger fields": `employee name` and `employee job`.

4. In your `Projects` folder, create a new **Interface** called `Int_Employee_SCD`
   - Drag the `SRC_EMP` and `SRC_DEPT` data stores onto the source area of the designer canvas (observe the creation of an automatic join condition based upon the foreign key relationship captured during the reverse engineering of the `DEMO_SRC` data model).
   - Drag the `TRG_EMPLOYEE` data store onto the target area of the designer canvas. Most of the columns will receive automatic mappings based on their names. Note that all columns not mapped will be ignored by the KM.
   - Set the `EMP_ID` column to execute on the target system as follows:

```
<%=odiRef.getObjectName("L", "TRG_EMPLOYEE_SEQ", "D")%>.
nextval
```

Always a good practice, in this example we use the `getObjectName` API to avoid hard-coding the schema name. For more information on this API, refer to the *Using table names that run in all contexts using getObjectName* recipe in *Chapter 4, Using Variables*.

Since the **Surrogate Key** option must always be mapped on the target side, uncheck the **Check Not Null** box of the `EMP_ID` column to ensure that ODI does not try to enforce this constraint. When **FLOW_CONTROL** is used, the primary key uniqueness constraint must also be "turned off" by un-checking the appropriate box on the **Controls** or **CKM** tab.

   - Set the remaining SCD columns to execute on the target system as follows:

```
ACTIVE_FLAG: 1
EFF_BEG_DT: SYSDATE
EFF_END_DT: TO_DATE('01-JAN-2400','DD-MON-YYYY')
```

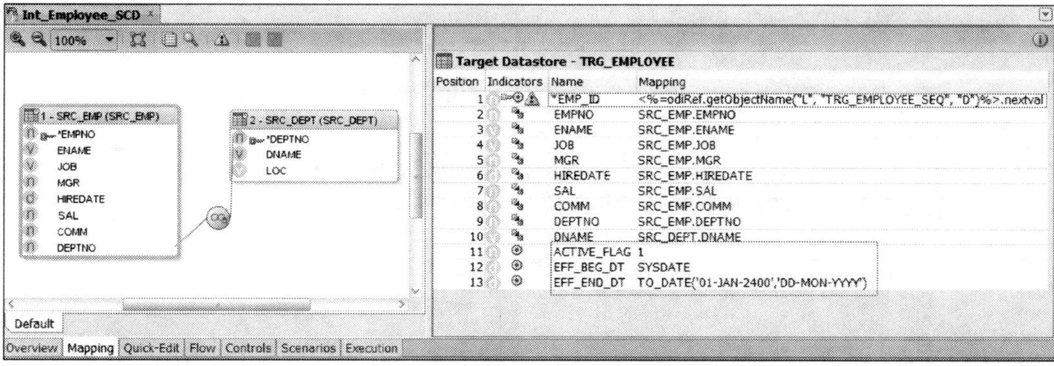

Even though the KM will automatically set the appropriate value during processing, the "active flag" column (denoting current or historical records) must always be mapped within the interface; set this field to the `Boolean` value of either `0` or `1` (it is necessary to map these critical columns within in an interface, because not doing so would cause ODI to omit them from the generated code).

Unless you modify the KM accordingly, the end date column should be set to `January 1st, 2400` in order to match the KM default value.

- Click on the **Flow** tab:

  Select the **LOADING** KM: `LKM SQL to Oracle`

  Select the **INTEGRATION** KM: `IKM Oracle Slowly Changing Dimension`

  Set **FLOW_CONTROL** to `False`

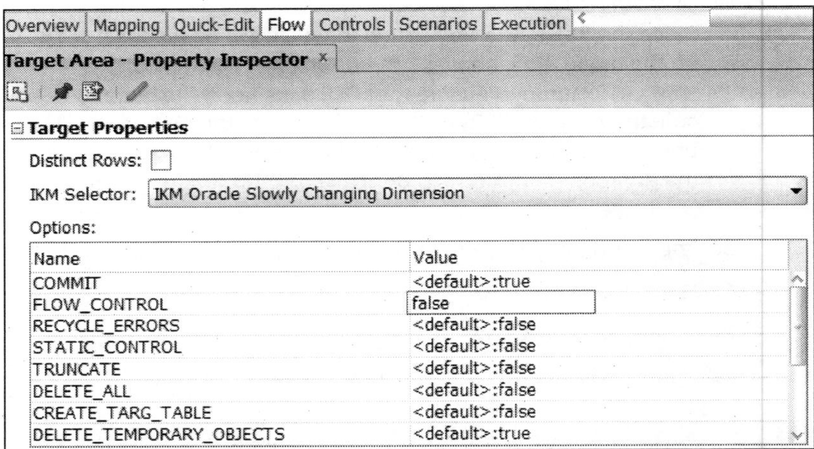

5. **Save** and execute the interface without closing the tab.

Ignore any warnings that the **Check Null** condition has been disabled for the **EMP_ID** field, this is to be expected.

6. Now let's first see what happens when we update columns that are not trigger fields, such as the `SAL` or `DEPTNO` columns. With the `Int_Employee_SCD` interface still open, right-click on the `SRC_EMP` data store, select `Data` from the drop-down menu, and change the following rows:

   `EMPNO 7369`: change the `DEPTNO` option from `20` to `30`

   `EMPNO 7839`: change the `SAL` option from `5000` to `6000`

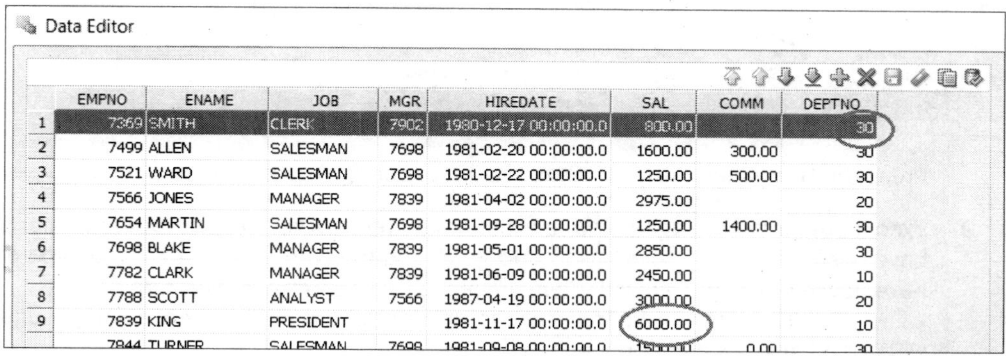

Data Editor

	EMPNO	ENAME	JOB	MGR	HIREDATE	SAL	COMM	DEPTNO
1	7369	SMITH	CLERK	7902	1980-12-17 00:00:00.0	800.00		30
2	7499	ALLEN	SALESMAN	7698	1981-02-20 00:00:00.0	1600.00	300.00	30
3	7521	WARD	SALESMAN	7698	1981-02-22 00:00:00.0	1250.00	500.00	30
4	7566	JONES	MANAGER	7839	1981-04-02 00:00:00.0	2975.00		20
5	7654	MARTIN	SALESMAN	7698	1981-09-28 00:00:00.0	1250.00	1400.00	30
6	7698	BLAKE	MANAGER	7839	1981-05-01 00:00:00.0	2850.00		30
7	7782	CLARK	MANAGER	7839	1981-06-09 00:00:00.0	2450.00		10
8	7788	SCOTT	ANALYST	7566	1987-04-19 00:00:00.0	3000.00		20
9	7839	KING	PRESIDENT		1981-11-17 00:00:00.0	6000.00		10
	7844	TURNER	SALESMAN	7698	1981-09-08 00:00:00.0	1500.00	0.00	30

   Press the Save Changes icon located in the upper-right corner of the data editor.

7. Execute the interface again and re-examine the results. Notice that no new records have been added; only the changes made to the "non-trigger" fields are evident.

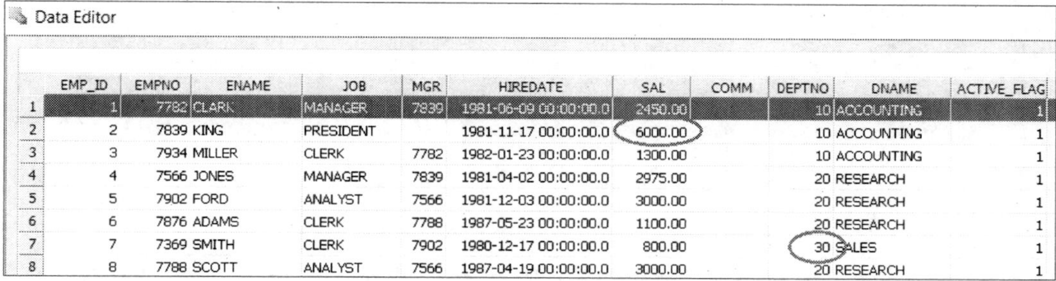

Data Editor

	EMP_ID	EMPNO	ENAME	JOB	MGR	HIREDATE	SAL	COMM	DEPTNO	DNAME	ACTIVE_FLAG
1	1	7782	CLARK	MANAGER	7839	1981-06-09 00:00:00.0	2450.00		10	ACCOUNTING	1
2	2	7839	KING	PRESIDENT		1981-11-17 00:00:00.0	6000.00		10	ACCOUNTING	1
3	3	7934	MILLER	CLERK	7782	1982-01-23 00:00:00.0	1300.00		10	ACCOUNTING	1
4	4	7566	JONES	MANAGER	7839	1981-04-02 00:00:00.0	2975.00		20	RESEARCH	1
5	5	7902	FORD	ANALYST	7566	1981-12-03 00:00:00.0	3000.00		20	RESEARCH	1
6	6	7876	ADAMS	CLERK	7788	1987-05-23 00:00:00.0	1100.00		20	RESEARCH	1
7	7	7369	SMITH	CLERK	7902	1980-12-17 00:00:00.0	800.00		30	SALES	1
8	8	7788	SCOTT	ANALYST	7566	1987-04-19 00:00:00.0	3000.00		20	RESEARCH	1

8. Now let's see what happens when we update columns, which do include a trigger field, such as the `ENAME` or `JOB` columns. With the `Int_Employee_SCD` interface still open, right-click on the `SRC_EMP` data store, select `Data` from the drop-down menu, and change the following rows:

   `EMPNO 7934`: change the `ENAME` field from `MILLER` to `JOHNSON`

   `EMPNO 7900`: change the `JOB` field from `CLERK` to `ANALYST`

EMPNO 7839: change the SAL field from 6000 to 7000 (a "non-trigger" field change)

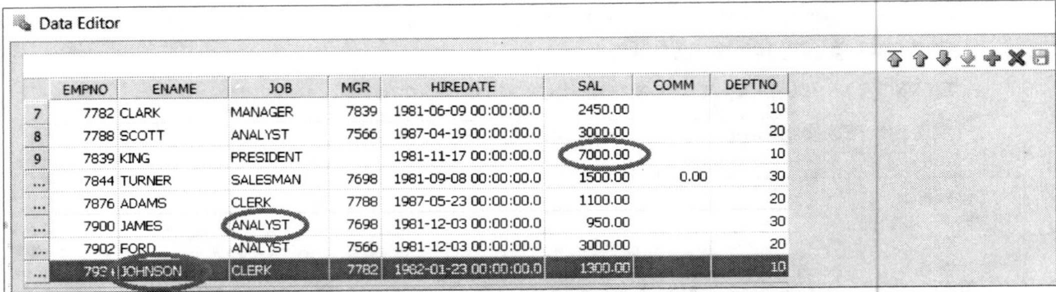

Data Editor

	EMPNO	ENAME	JOB	MGR	HIREDATE	SAL	COMM	DEPTNO
7	7782	CLARK	MANAGER	7839	1981-06-09 00:00:00.0	2450.00		10
8	7788	SCOTT	ANALYST	7566	1987-04-19 00:00:00.0	3000.00		20
9	7839	KING	PRESIDENT		1981-11-17 00:00:00.0	7000.00		10
...	7844	TURNER	SALESMAN	7698	1981-09-08 00:00:00.0	1500.00	0.00	30
...	7876	ADAMS	CLERK	7788	1987-05-23 00:00:00.0	1100.00		20
...	7900	JAMES	ANALYST	7698	1981-12-03 00:00:00.0	950.00		30
...	7902	FORD	ANALYST	7566	1981-12-03 00:00:00.0	3000.00		20
...	793[illegible]	JOHNSON	CLERK	7782	1982-01-23 00:00:00.0	1300.00		10

Press the Save Changes icon located in the upper-right corner of the data editor.

9. Execute the interface again and re-examine the results. Notice that two new records have been added for EMPNO 7934 and 7900 and the corresponding original records have now been historized with an ACTIVE_FLAG value of 0 and an EFF_END_DT value of today. Notice also that the SAL column for EMPNO 7839 has changed again without adding any additional records.

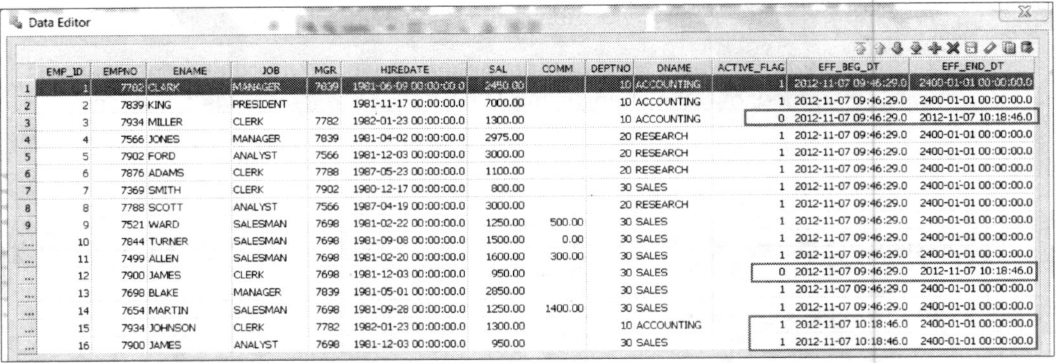

Data Editor

	EMP_ID	EMPNO	ENAME	JOB	MGR	HIREDATE	SAL	COMM	DEPTNO	DNAME	ACTIVE_FLAG	EFF_BEG_DT	EFF_END_DT
1	1	7782	CLARK	MANAGER	7839	1981-06-09 00:00:00.0	2450.00		10	ACCOUNTING	1	2012-11-07 09:46:29.0	2400-01-01 00:00:00.0
2	2	7839	KING	PRESIDENT		1981-11-17 00:00:00.0	7000.00		10	ACCOUNTING	1	2012-11-07 09:46:29.0	2400-01-01 00:00:00.0
3	3	7934	MILLER	CLERK	7782	1982-01-23 00:00:00.0	1300.00		10	ACCOUNTING	0	2012-11-07 09:46:29.0	2012-11-07 10:18:46.0
4	4	7566	JONES	MANAGER	7839	1981-04-02 00:00:00.0	2975.00		20	RESEARCH	1	2012-11-07 09:46:29.0	2400-01-01 00:00:00.0
5	5	7902	FORD	ANALYST	7566	1981-12-03 00:00:00.0	3000.00		20	RESEARCH	1	2012-11-07 09:46:29.0	2400-01-01 00:00:00.0
6	6	7876	ADAMS	CLERK	7788	1987-05-23 00:00:00.0	1100.00		20	RESEARCH	1	2012-11-07 09:46:29.0	2400-01-01 00:00:00.0
7	7	7369	SMITH	CLERK	7902	1980-12-17 00:00:00.0	800.00		30	SALES	1	2012-11-07 09:46:29.0	2400-01-01 00:00:00.0
8	8	7788	SCOTT	ANALYST	7566	1987-04-19 00:00:00.0	3000.00		20	RESEARCH	1	2012-11-07 09:46:29.0	2400-01-01 00:00:00.0
9	9	7521	WARD	SALESMAN	7698	1981-02-22 00:00:00.0	1250.00	500.00	30	SALES	1	2012-11-07 09:46:29.0	2400-01-01 00:00:00.0
...	10	7844	TURNER	SALESMAN	7698	1981-09-08 00:00:00.0	1500.00	0.00	30	SALES	1	2012-11-07 09:46:29.0	2400-01-01 00:00:00.0
...	11	7499	ALLEN	SALESMAN	7698	1981-02-20 00:00:00.0	1600.00	300.00	30	SALES	1	2012-11-07 09:46:29.0	2400-01-01 00:00:00.0
...	12	7900	JAMES	CLERK	7698	1981-12-03 00:00:00.0	950.00		30	SALES	0	2012-11-07 09:46:29.0	2012-11-07 10:18:46.0
...	13	7698	BLAKE	MANAGER	7839	1981-05-01 00:00:00.0	2850.00		30	SALES	1	2012-11-07 09:46:29.0	2400-01-01 00:00:00.0
...	14	7654	MARTIN	SALESMAN	7698	1981-09-28 00:00:00.0	1250.00	1400.00	30	SALES	1	2012-11-07 09:46:29.0	2400-01-01 00:00:00.0
...	15	7934	JOHNSON	CLERK	7782	1982-01-23 00:00:00.0	1300.00		10	ACCOUNTING	1	2012-11-07 10:18:46.0	2400-01-01 00:00:00.0
...	16	7900	JAMES	ANALYST	7698	1981-12-03 00:00:00.0	950.00		30	SALES	1	2012-11-07 10:18:46.0	2400-01-01 00:00:00.0

10. As a final step, click on the **Operator Navigator** tab and fully expand the job log for the most recent execution of your interface. Notice the record count statistics for steps 12-14 and how those numbers reflect what we expect based upon the changes we made.

How it works...

The ODI software comes delivered with a extensive set of out of the box KMs, including several for managing slowly-changing-dimensions (based on the technology being used). By leveraging the column-level SCD attributes assigned by the user, each of the SCD IKMs can construct and execute the SQL commands needed to perform the three essential steps of SCD processing:

- `Update existing rows`: When the natural key matches incoming records but where no data changes were made to any of the "trigger" fields
- `Historize old rows`: When the natural key matches incoming records and data changes have been detected in one or more "trigger" fields (sets the active indicator to `False` and updates the ending date for records)
- `Insert changing and new dimensions`: When the natural key matches incoming records and data changes have been detected in one or more "trigger" fields, or where no natural key matches are found

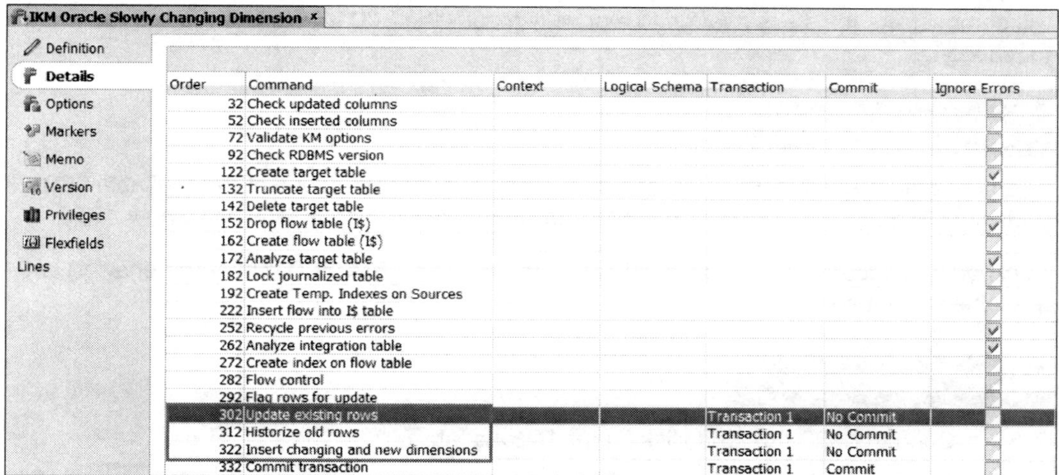

As seen in this previous image, all the three critical steps have been addressed by the SCD knowledge module. Observe how all three steps were grouped together within the same `Transaction` ID in order to isolate and commit their activities as a single transaction.

Modifying a Slowly Changing Dimension KM to allow undefined behaviors

When working with a slowly changing dimension, you may sometimes encounter a dimension table that has dozens (or perhaps hundreds) of attributes, making the task of setting the SCD behavior for each column very tiresome. There may also be occasions when business requirements dictate that all activity on a specific dimension table be captured historically, that is, all columns are considered to be the "trigger" fields.

In order to address these two situations, a few simple modifications can be made to the SCD IKM to allow the developer to avoid having to set the SCD behavior for every column. By making these simple modifications, the developer will only need to set the behaviors for the **Surrogate Key**, the **Natural Key**, the **Active Flag**, and **The Starting and Ending date** columns; all other columns will be implicitly managed as trigger fields by automatically setting the **Add Row on Change** condition.

Although it's certainly possible to script this process using an SDK application, this recipe will demonstrate the steps needed to manually modify the SCD IKM to achieve the desired functionality.

Getting ready

If you have already worked through the first recipe in this chapter, one of the available SCD IKMs should have already been imported into your project; if not, please do so now.

To expedite the learning process, a version of the modified IKM (SCD IKM Auto Behavior) is available for upload.

How to do it...

1. Open the SCD IKM and click on the **Details** tab.
2. Click on the **Insert Flow into I$ table** step and replace the appropriate sections of code as follows:

   ```
   (((SCD_NK or SCD_INS or SCD_UPD) and !TRG) and REW)
   ```

   is replaced by:

   ```
   (((SCD_NK or SCD_INS or SCD_UPD or (!SCD_SK and !SCD_NK and !SCD_
   UPD and !SCD_INS and !SCD_FLAG and !SCD_START and !SCD_END)) and
   !TRG) and REW)
   ```

The `Boolean` attributes `!TRG` and `REW` specify that the associated action only applies to columns that are not processed on the target system and whose read-only flag was not selected.

By adding and evaluating a new series of ODI `Boolean` conditions, we can also determine if no individual behavioral attributes were set.

There are two places where this code substitution must occur: in the `INSERT` statement and in the `SELECT` statement.

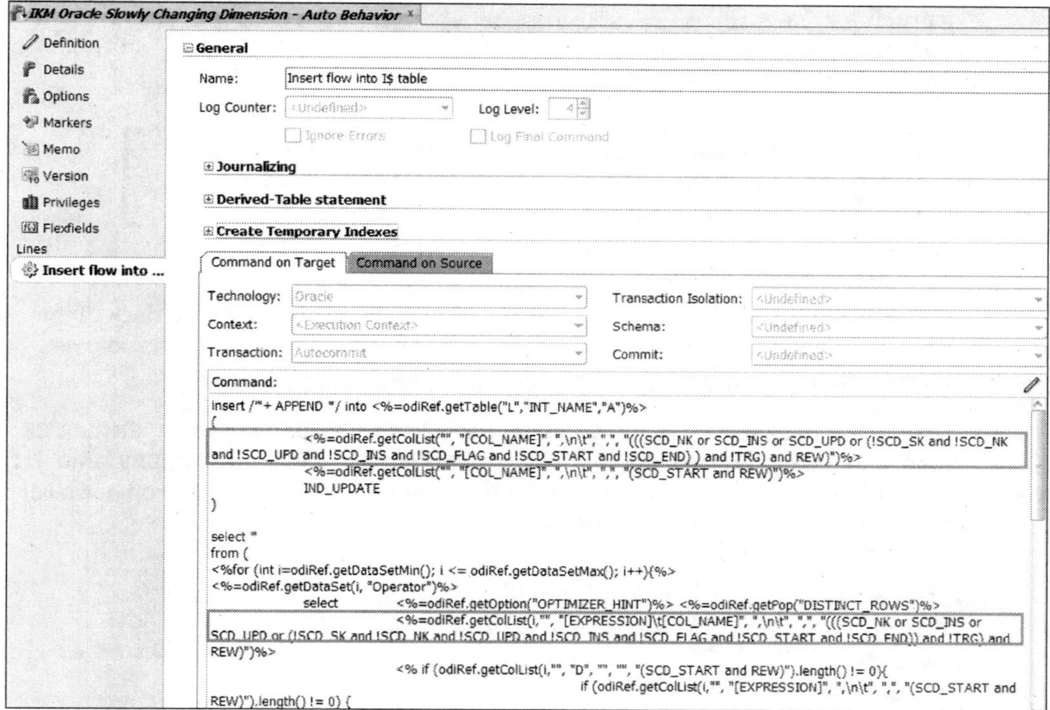

3. Click on the **Flag** rows for the **Update** step and replace the appropriate sections of code as follows:

```
SCD_INS and !TRG
```

is replaced by:

```
(SCD_INS or (!SCD_SK and !SCD_NK and !SCD_UPD and !SCD_INS and
!SCD_FLAG and !SCD_START and !SCD_END)) and !TRG
```

To force ODI to evaluate the `or` condition before the outer `and` condition, be sure to insert an extra parenthesis before the `SCD_INS` and after the `SCD_END` variables.

4. Click on the **Insert Changes** step and then the **New Dimensions** step and replace the appropriate sections of code as follows:

```
(((SCD_SK or SCD_NK or SCD_INS or SCD_UPD) and !TRG) and REW)
```

   changes to:

```
(((SCD_SK or SCD_NK or SCD_INS or SCD_UPD or (!SCD_SK and !SCD_NK
and !SCD_UPD and !SCD_INS and !SCD_FLAG and !SCD_START and !SCD_
END)) and !TRG) and REW)
```

There are four places where this code substitution must occur: two in the `INSERT` statement and two in the `SELECT` statement.

5. Save and close the SCD IKM.

   Before we can properly test our new IKM functionality, we must first go back to the `TRG_EMPLOYEE` data store and change the SCD behavior for most of the columns back to `Undefined`.

6. Open the **Model** section of the **Designer** navigator and expand the `TRG_EMPLOYEE` data store column list. Except for the `EMP_ID`, `EMPNO`, `ACTIVE_FLAG`, `EFF_BEG_DT`, and `EFF_END_DT` columns, click on the **Description** tab and use the drop-down list to set the **Slowly Changing Dimensions Behavior** to `<Undefined>`.

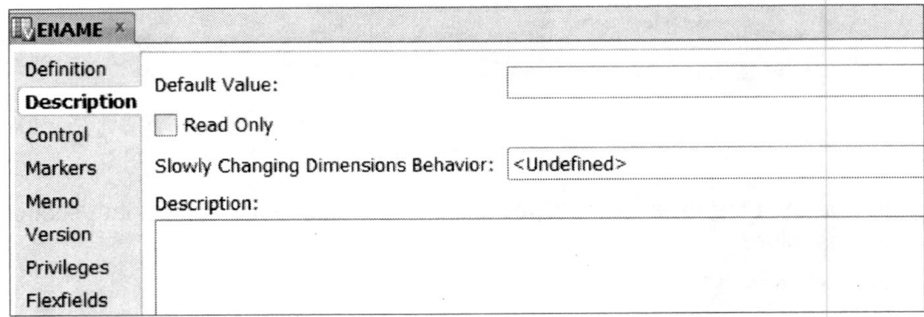

7. Open the `Int_Employee_SCD` interface (see the recipe, *Implementing Slowly Changing Dimensions (SCD) using ODI* of this chapter), click on the **Mapping** tab, right-click on the `SRC_EMP` source table, select **Data**, and change the `SAL` amount for `SMITH` to `900`. Save your changes by pressing the Save Changes icon located in the upper-right corner of the data editor.

8. Execute the `Int_Employee_SCD` interface and review the results by right-clicking on the target data store and selecting **Data**. Notice that the previous record for employee **SMITH** was historized and a new active record was created, despite the fact that many of the table columns had an undefined SCD behavior.

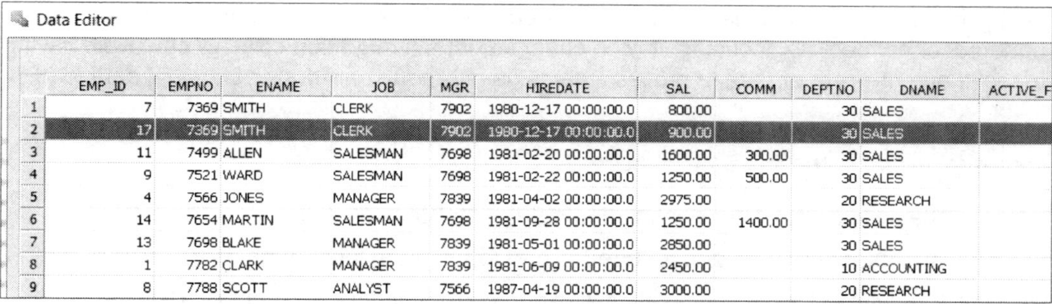

	EMP_ID	EMPNO	ENAME	JOB	MGR	HIREDATE	SAL	COMM	DEPTNO	DNAME	ACTIVE_F
1	7	7369	SMITH	CLERK	7902	1980-12-17 00:00:00.0	800.00		30	SALES	
2	17	7369	SMITH	CLERK	7902	1980-12-17 00:00:00.0	900.00		30	SALES	
3	11	7499	ALLEN	SALESMAN	7698	1981-02-20 00:00:00.0	1600.00	300.00	30	SALES	
4	9	7521	WARD	SALESMAN	7698	1981-02-22 00:00:00.0	1250.00	500.00	30	SALES	
5	4	7566	JONES	MANAGER	7839	1981-04-02 00:00:00.0	2975.00		20	RESEARCH	
6	14	7654	MARTIN	SALESMAN	7698	1981-09-28 00:00:00.0	1250.00	1400.00	30	SALES	
7	13	7698	BLAKE	MANAGER	7839	1981-05-01 00:00:00.0	2850.00		30	SALES	
8	1	7782	CLARK	MANAGER	7839	1981-06-09 00:00:00.0	2450.00		10	ACCOUNTING	
9	8	7788	SCOTT	ANALYST	7566	1987-04-19 00:00:00.0	3000.00		20	RESEARCH	

9. Click on the **Operator** navigator and click on the most recent interface execution. By drilling into a few of the more critical steps, you should notice that each one performed the same as before except for the **Update Existing Rows** step; here, the **Code** tab is entirely blank since the IKM has been modified to consider that any change is a historical change.

How it works...

As you probably already knew, much of the power of ODI comes through the use of KMs. However, there is no magic here, rather a KM is simply a set of logically arranged steps designed to produce a specific result. And since many of the KM steps are written in a format that looks similar to SQL, they are usually quite easy to understand. The tricky part comes when those KM steps also include one of the many substitution APIs (for more information on KM internals, refer to Oracle's *Knowledge Module Developer's Guide for Oracle Data Integrator*).

In this recipe, the SCD IKM KM was originally designed to execute a series of steps to prepare a temporary integration table (`I$_`) from which it would make several passes in order to collect the information needed to affect the specified target table in the proper manner. What we did in this exercise was to modify three of those KM steps to treat an undefined SCD behavior as if it had been set to **Add Row on Change**. To achieve this result, we leveraged the seven internal SCD-related Boolean variables (that is `SCD_SK`, `SCD_NK`, `SCD_INS`, and so on) and looked to see if all seven were undefined. By changing some of the API parameters to include a set of not conditions, we were able to modify the knowledge module to treat the absence of a SCD behavior as if the `SCD_INS` variable had been set to `True`.

Using Changed Data Capture (CDC) - simple

As mentioned during the introduction of this chapter, one of the more commonly used ETL/ELT methodologies is CDC. This generic term refers to the means by which a data migration design can identify source data, which has been altered in some way (that is, inserted, updated, or deleted). By focusing only on changed data, a migration strategy can avoid having to move an entire set of data, a process that is usually done only during an initial data load.

When determining which ODI KMs and CDC methods to use, a developer/architect should consider several of the following points:

- The availability of pre-existing timestamp attributes on source systems tables
- The database privileges required to create table triggers on the source system
- The availability of database log files and corresponding internal CDC delivery mechanisms (that is, Oracle Logminer, Oracle Streams, and so on)
- The availability of Oracle Golden Gate for specific technologies

Oracle Data Integrator delivers a comprehensive set of CDC offerings ranging from basic trigger-based journaling to log-based journaling to the non-intrusive Golden Gate journaling method. Since each of these methods involves some degree of additional setup, administration, and potential licensing costs, careful thought should be given before deciding which approach will provide the best solution.

To learn more about how Oracle GoldenGate functions, please refer to the following link at `http://www.oracle.com/webfolder/technetwork/tutorials/obe/fmw/odi/odi_11g/odi_gg_integration/odi_gg_integration.htm`.

Chapter 7, *Working With Changed Data Capture* of the *Developer's Guide for Oracle Data Integrator* provides basic information on CDC:

`http://docs.oracle.com/cd/E23943_01/integrate.1111/e12643/toc.htm`

Another good source of information on this subject can be found on the following blog:

`http://odiexperts.com/changed-data-capture-cdc/`

Getting ready

In this recipe, we will begin by demonstrating one of the most basic forms of CDC within the ODI arsenal: simple trigger-based journalizing. You can prepare for this recipe by importing into your project the ODI **Journalizing Knowledge Module** (**JKM**) that best matches your source system technology, which in this example should be Oracle. Therefore, the JKM you will import is the JKM Oracle Simple KM.

To avoid tying a data model to any specific project, consider importing JKMs, RKMs, and CKMs as global KMs.

Since this CDC method involves the introduction of triggers into a source system, the reader should be aware that there will be some impact on transactional performance.

There will also be a small footprint within the work schema on the source system, which includes ODI journal tables, triggers, and views. It is quite possible that a source system DBA may take issue with installing these objects as being in violation of certain corporate security policies.

How to do it...

1. Modify the source data model to specify the journal method that we will employ:
   - Expand the Models section within the navigator and open the source data model by double-clicking on `DEMO_SRC`
   - Click on the Journalizing option from the left-side sub-menu and set the following options:

     Journalizing Mode: Simple

     Knowledge Module: `JKM Oracle Simple.ODI_Cookbook`
   - Close and save the `DEMO_SRC` data model

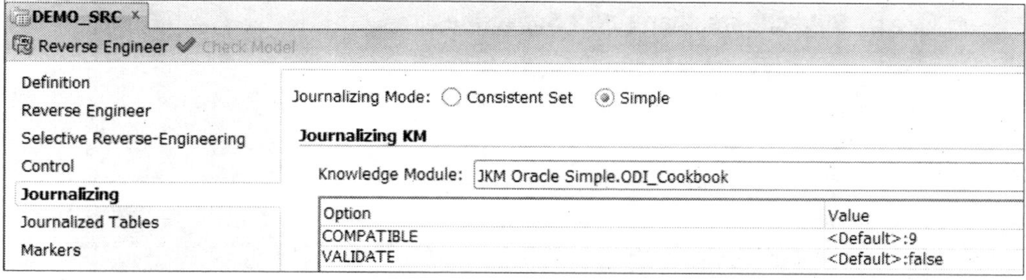

2. In this exercise, we will only set up CDC on a single source table: `SRC_EMP`. Right-click on the `SRC_EMP` data store, select **Changed Data Capture**, then select **Add to CDC**.

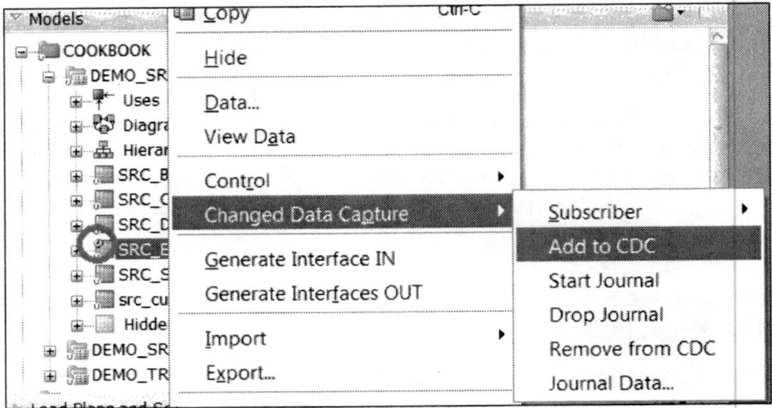

Notice the addition of a yellow clock within the data store icon. This indicates that **Journalization** has been marked as active in the model, but that no appropriate **Journalization** infrastructure has been detected yet on the source system.

3. Add a subscriber to the data store:
   - Right-click on the `SRC_EMP` data store, select **Changed Data Capture**, select **Subscribers**, then select **Subscribe...**.

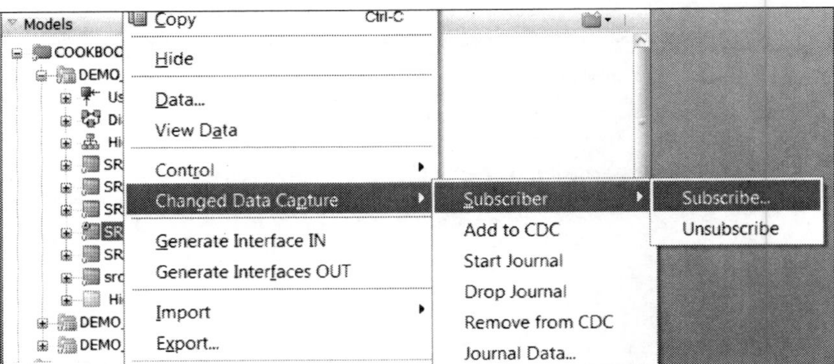

- Enter the name of a subscriber: `SUB-A`. Press the **+** sign to add the name to the list of subscribers that will be able to consume the journalized data. Press **OK**.

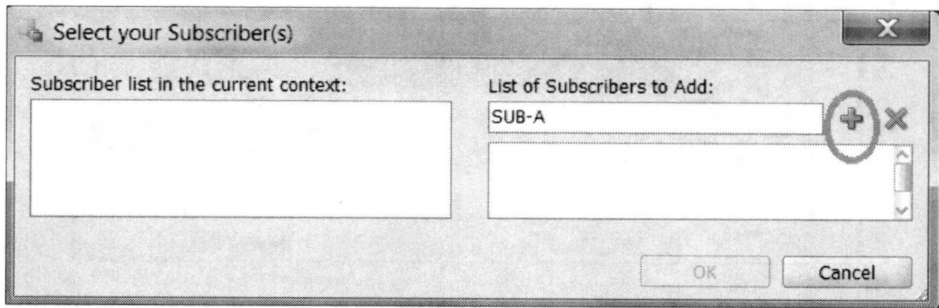

- Since this step will require the JKM to install specific infrastructural components onto the source system, we must submit this job for execution. Proceed to the **Execution** screen, choose an appropriate context and agent, and press **OK** to submit the job for execution.

  As mentioned earlier, the use of a trigger-based journaling method will require installing tables, triggers, and views on the source system. Be sure that the DBA has issued the appropriate grants to the source system connection user (that is, Create table, Create trigger, and so on).

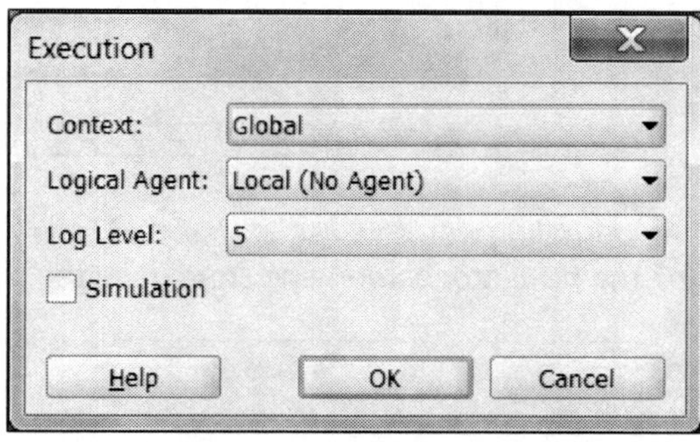

- Check the **Operator** tab to ensure that the job completed successfully.

4. Now it's time to start the journaling:

   - Right-click on the `SRC_EMP` data store once more, select **Changed Data Capture**, then select **Start Journal**.

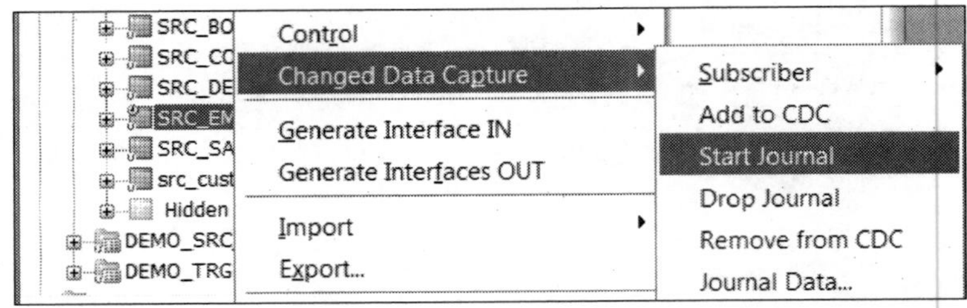

   - Since this step will require the JKM to install specific infrastructural components onto the source system, we must submit this job for execution. Proceed to the **Execution** screen, choose an appropriate context and agent, and press **OK** to submit the job for execution.

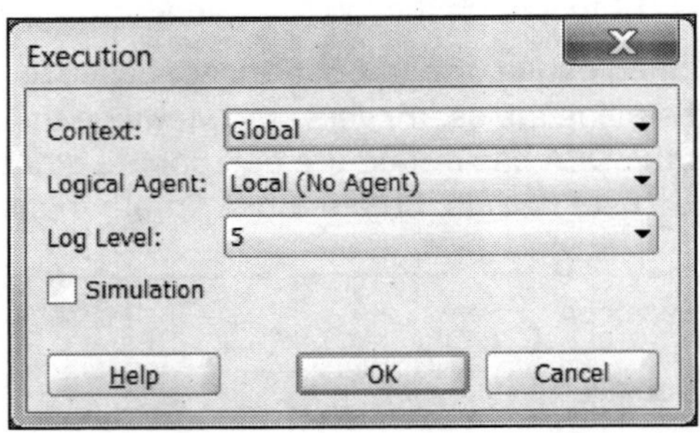

   - Verify that journaling was successfully started by reviewing the job logs or by refreshing the navigator screen and examining the data model.

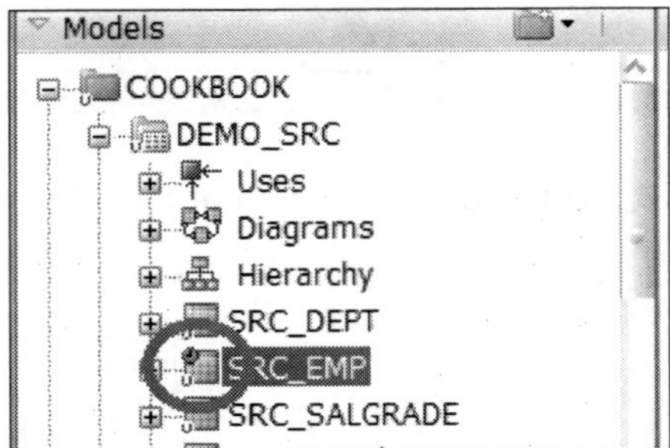

[The clock within the data store icon has changed color from yellow to green. This indicates that the journalizing infrastructure for this data store is now in place and transaction journalization is fully active.]

- Once journalizing of the `SRC_EMP` data store has been started, we can observe how CDC influences an interface and see what happens when subsequent transactions are made to the `SRC_EMP` table.

5. In your project folder, create a new interface called: `Int_CDC_Simple_Emp`:
   - Drag the `SRC_EMP` and `SRC_DEPT` data stores onto the source area of the designer canvas (the creation of an automatic `join` condition based upon the foreign key relationship captured during the reverse engineering of the `DEMO_SRC` data model).
   - Drag the `TRG_EMP` data store onto the target area of the designer canvas (most of the columns should receive automatic mappings based upon their names).
   - Click on the **Flow** tab. Select the IKM as `IKM Oracle Incremental Update` KM. Set **FLOW_CONTROL** to `False`.

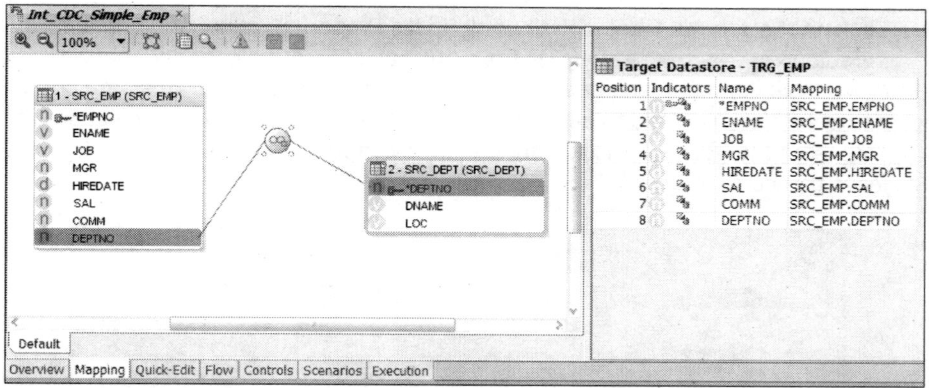

6. Save (without closing) and execute the interface as currently implemented. This action will serve as an initial data load and will ensure that all 14 source records are loaded into the `TRG_EMP` table.
7. Click back again on the **Mapping** tab and right-click on the `SRC_EMP` source table; select **Data** from the drop-down menu. Notice that there are 14 records visible:
   - Change the salary for `SMITH` to `901`
   - Change the department number for `ALLEN` to `20`

- Click on the Save Changes icon in the upper-right corner of the editor

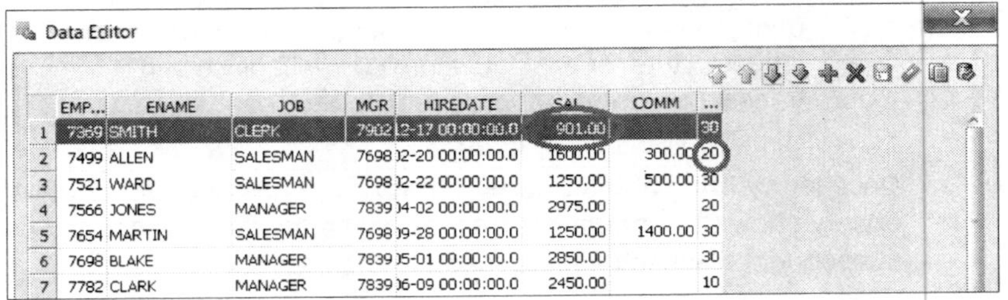

8. Click on the caption of the `SRC_EMP` table to activate the properties panel. In the **Source Properties** panel, click on the **Journalized Data Only** checkbox. Notice that a new filter has been added to the diagram.

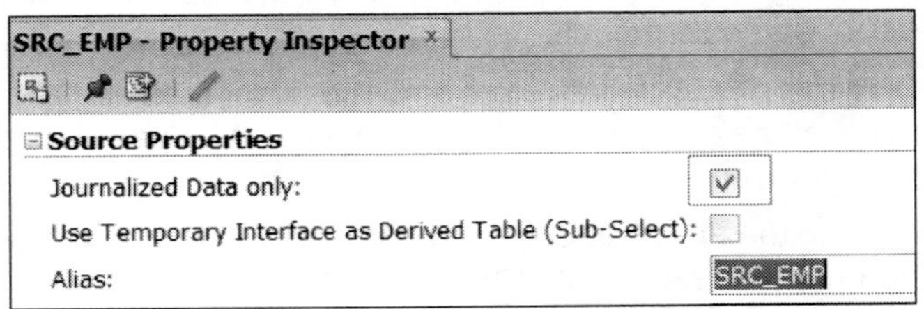

9. Click on the Journal Filter icon to bring up it's Properties panel and change the default `JRN_SUBSCRIBER` value from `SUNOPSIS` to `SUB-A` (notice that an optional `JRN_DATE` condition has been suggested but commented out. This date condition can potentially be used to eliminate "future-dated" transactions in the case where the source and target systems are not using a synchronized date. However, it is okay to leave this code as is).

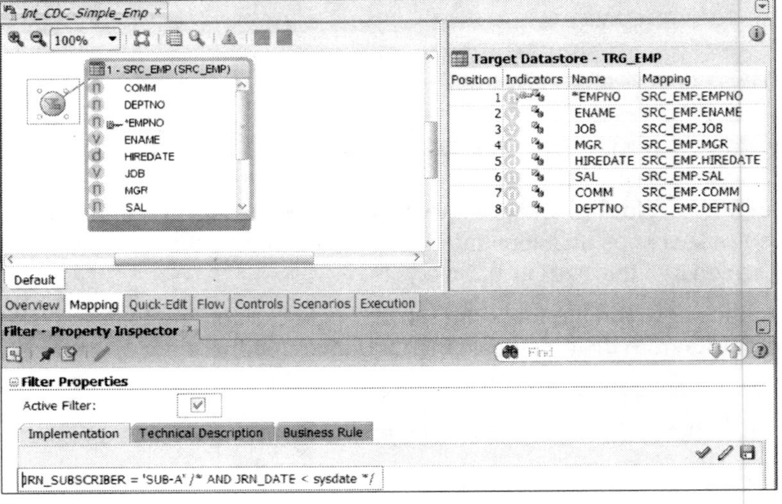

10. Right-click on the `SRC_EMP` source table again and observe that this time there are only two records showing. This is because the `SRC_EMP` object has now been directed to the underlying CDC view, so only new transactions have been made available for the `SUB-A` subscriber to see.

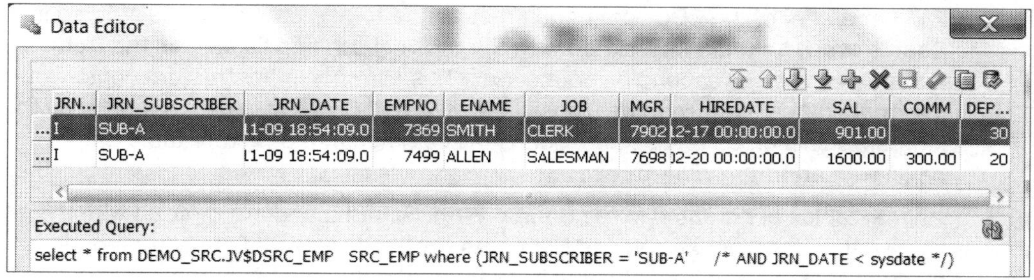

Data Editor

	JRN...	JRN_SUBSCRIBER	JRN_DATE	EMPNO	ENAME	JOB	MGR	HIREDATE	SAL	COMM	DEP...
...	I	SUB-A	11-09 18:54:09.0	7369	SMITH	CLERK	7902	12-17 00:00:00.0	901.00		30
...	I	SUB-A	11-09 18:54:09.0	7499	ALLEN	SALESMAN	7698	02-20 00:00:00.0	1600.00	300.00	20

Executed Query:

select * from DEMO_SRC.JV$DSRC_EMP SRC_EMP where (JRN_SUBSCRIBER = 'SUB-A' /* AND JRN_DATE < sysdate */)

Notice the three extra columns in the table view: `JRN_FLAG`, `JRN_DATE`, and `JRN_SUBSCRIBER`. These are infrastructure fields that were added by the JKM KM when it created the `JV$DSRC_EMP` view.

11. Save (without closing) and execute the interface. Right-click on the `SRC_EMP` table again and select **Data** from the drop-down menu. Notice this time there are no records available for display, since all previous transactions were consumed during the execution of the interface and the corresponding journal table has since been purged.

12. Review the results of the interface execution by examining both of the job logs on the **Operator** tab. Notice that the number of records updated was two.

How it works...

The ODI developer begins by associating the JKM Oracle Simple KM to a data model. The developer then tags each data store that is to participate in the CDC process, after which one or more subscribers are created and assigned to each selected data store. The final step in the CDC set-up process is to start the CDC journals.

When the CDC journals are first started, the journalizing infrastructure within the database schemas (if not already installed) is deployed or updated in the following locations:

- Triggers are created on the tables in the **Source Data Schema**. The journalizing trigger names are prefixed with the value specified in the **Journalizing Elements Prefixes** section for the associated physical schema (the default value for this prefix is `T$`).

When using non trigger-based JKMs such as GoldenGate, triggers will not be needed and therefore will not be created during the infrastructure build process.

- The remainder of the CDC common infrastructure for the data server is created in the **Source Work Schema** associated with the physical schema flagged as the **Default Schema** for the corresponding data server. This common infrastructure contains information about subscribers, consistent sets, and CDC-registered tables for all the journalized schemas on this data server. All common infrastructure table names begin with an `SNP_CDC_ prefix`.
- Journal tables are created in the **Source Work Schema** and are prefixed with the value defined in the **Journalizing Elements Prefixes** section of the corresponding physical schema (the default value is `J$` for a journal table). A journal table is used to capture the timestamp, mode (insert/update/delete), and the primary key information for each record.
- Journal views are created in the **Source Work Schema** and are prefixed with the value defined in the **Journalizing Elements Prefixes** section of the corresponding physical schema. The default value is **JV$** for a journal view. A journal view effectively establishes a time window over the associated journal table data relative to what a given subscriber needs to see for the current processing cycle.

Once the common infrastructure components are all in place and the individual components for each CDC-participating table have been created, subsequent transactional activity against the source tables is captured in the corresponding journal tables and exposed to the consuming applications (interfaces) using a pair of corresponding journal views. These views, coupled with the journal filters, which have been added to the interfaces, present only those transactions that have not previously been consumed by the named subscriber.

After all the subscribers have consumed each journal record (it's possible that more than one subscriber is assigned to a given data store), the JKM will purge the journal record.

There's more...

From a change detection perspective, we are not limited to triggers. ODI can also leverage other products (such as Oracle GoldenGate) and ships the appropriate KMs to generate the necessary configuration files for these technologies. For simplicity's sake, we chose to use KMs based on triggers to illustrate the concepts described within this chapter, but if the intrusiveness of triggers is not acceptable to you, ODI definitely supports other products that can also be leveraged for CDC.

To learn more about ODI CDC functionality, please refer to:

Oracle® Fusion Middleware Developer's Guide for Oracle Data Integrator

(*Chapter 7, Working with Changed Data Capture*).

This reference can be found at:

`http://docs.oracle.com/cd/E23943_01/integrate.1111/e12643/data_capture.htm#CFHFHIA`

Nevertheless, the use of the simple trigger-based CDC JKM means that each data store is managed independently from every other data store that has been flagged to participate in CDC. Unfortunately, this approach ignores the fact that some target tables may have referential integrity relationships, which may be violated if child records are processed before the corresponding parent records have arrived (this concept is relevant only in systems where referential integrity is being enforced. If there are known data quality issues or known situations of late-arriving parent data, referential integrity constraints are often disabled). In the next recipe, the use of consistent set CDC will be explored.

Using Changed Data Capture (CDC) - consistent set

Unlike the simple CDC method demonstrated in the previous section, the use of consistent set CDC does address the problem of how to coordinate the flow of data into a target system when there are explicitly defined foreign key relationships between one or more target tables. One possible problem with simple CDC is that while you are processing changes for the parent records, more data can arrive, possibly including both parent and child records. In this case, once you are done processing the parents, you want to make sure that the children records that you will process belong only to these parents, and that the children that have arrived in the middle of your processing will only be processed with the next round of processing. The KMs for consistent CDC will solve this problem by allowing us to mark all the records that are ready for processing before we start processing any of them through a windowing strategy. The essence of consistent set CDC is that it establishes a windowing strategy from which ODI can guarantee no child records are moved from source to target without the corresponding parent records, provided that the table data is consumed in the proper order.

Getting ready

In this recipe, we will demonstrate the second basic form of CDC: consistent set trigger-based journalization. We will develop two interfaces and a driver package used to coordinate the data flow by managing the CDC window. In this scenario, ODI will automatically determine for a given subscriber the time period between the previous ETL processing cycle and the current ETL processing cycle. Only the journalized transactions that fall within this CDC window will be exposed to the executing applications.

You can prepare for this recipe by importing into your project the ODI JKM that best matches your source system technology, which in this example should be Oracle. Therefore, the JKM you will import is the `JKM Oracle Consistent KM`.

How to do it...

1. Modify the source data model to specify the journal method that we will employ:
   - Expand the **Models** section within the navigator and open the source data model by double-clicking on `DEMO_SRC`
   - Click on the **Journalizing** option from the left-side sub-menu and set the following options:

     Journalizing Mode: **Consistent**

     Knowledge Module: **JKM Oracle Consistent.ODI_Cookbook**
   - Close and save the `DEMO_SRC` data model

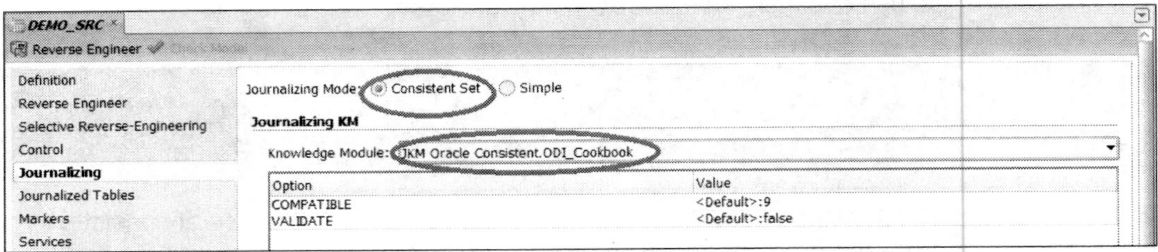

2. In this exercise, we will set up CDC on two source tables: `SRC_EMP` and `SRC_DEPT`. Right-click on both the `SRC_EMP` and `SRC_DEPT` data stores, select **Changed Data Capture**, then select **Add to CDC**.

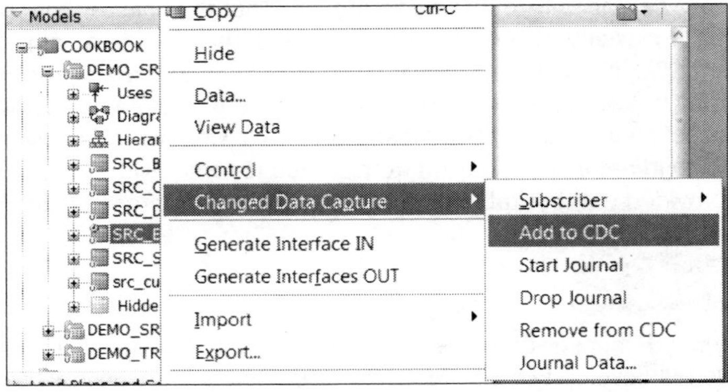

The addition of a yellow clock on each of the data store icons. This indicates that journalizing has been marked as active in the model, but that no appropriate journalizing infrastructure has been detected yet on the source system.

3. Add a subscriber to the data model:
   - Right-click on the `DEMO_SRC` data model, select **Changed Data Capture**, select **Subscribers**, then select **Subscribe**.

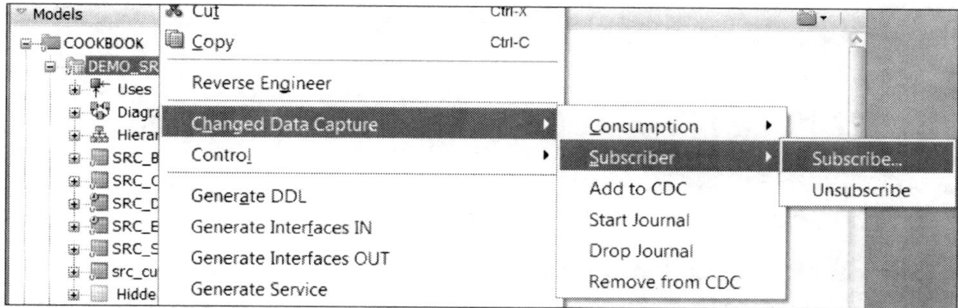

   - Enter the name of a subscriber: `SUB-A`. Press the **+** sign to add the name to the list of subscribers that will be able to consume the journalized data. Press **OK**.

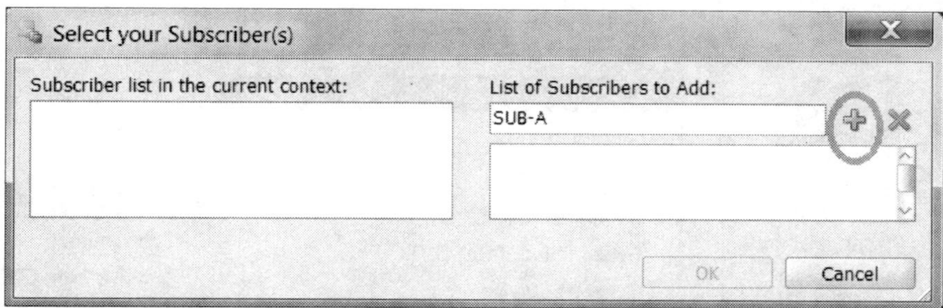

   - Proceed to the **Execution** screen, choose an appropriate context and agent, and press **OK** to submit the job for execution.
   - Check the **Operator** tab to ensure that the job completed successfully.

4. The next step when setting up consistent set CDC is to specify the order in which source tables changes are to be journaled:
   - Double-click to open the `DEMO_SRC` data model, then click on the **Journalized Tables** tab.

- Modify the **Order** number for each table and/or use the up and down arrows to set the desired order. In this example, we will set the **Order** number for the `SRC_DEPT` parent table to value lower than `SRC_EMP` child table.

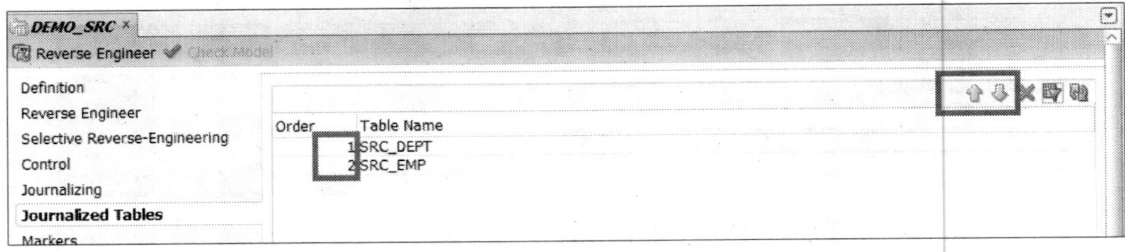

5. Now it's time to start the journaling:
   - Right-click on the `DEMO_SRC` data model once more, select **Changed Data Capture**, then select **Start Journal** (starting a journal for the entire data model is faster than starting a journal on each individual data store).

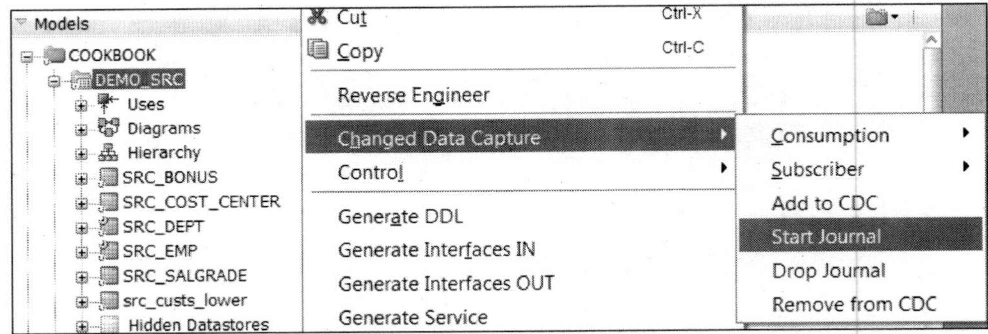

   - Proceed to the **Execution** screen, choose an appropriate context and agent, and press **OK** to submit the job for execution.

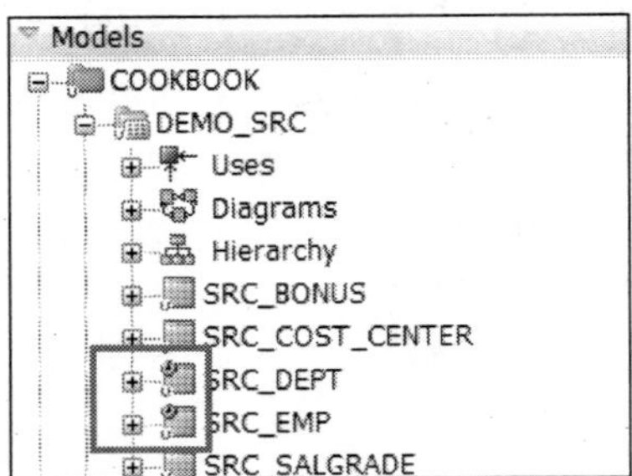

The clocks within the two data store icons have changed color from yellow to green. This indicates that the journalization infrastructure for these data stores are now in place and transaction journalization is fully active.

Once journalizing of the `DEMO_SRC` data model has been started, we can observe how CDC influences an interface and see what happens when subsequent transactions are made to the `SRC_EMP` and `SRC_DEPT` tables.

6. In your **Project** folder, create a new interface called `Int_CDC_Consistent_Emp`:
   - Drag the `SRC_EMP` data store onto the source area of the designer canvas.
   - Drag the `TRG_EMP` data store onto the target area of the designer canvas (most of the columns should receive automatic mappings based upon their names).
   - Click on the **Flow** tab. Select the IKM as `IKM Oracle Incremental Update`. Set **FLOW_CONTROL** to `False`.

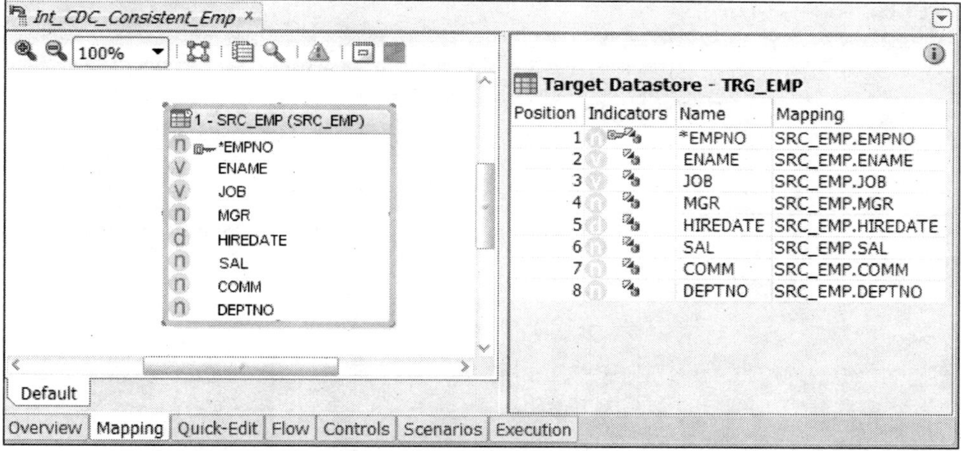

7. Save (without closing) and execute the interface as currently implemented. This action will serve as an initial data load and will ensure that all 14 source records are loaded into the `TRG_EMP` table.
8. Click on the **Mapping** tab and right-click on the `SRC_EMP` source table; select **Data** from the drop-down menu. Notice that there are 14 records visible.
   - Change the salary for `SMITH` to `902`
   - Change the department number for `ALLEN` to `30`

- Click on the Save Changes icon in the upper-right corner of the editor

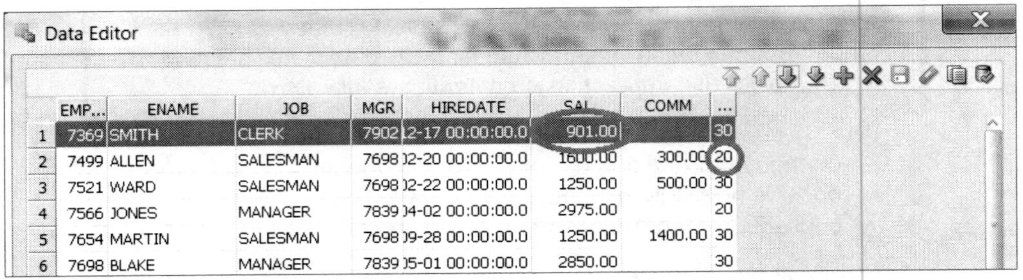

9. Click on the **Journalized Data Only** checkbox located on the **Source Properties** panel. Notice that a new filter has been added to the diagram.
10. Click on the Journal Filter icon to bring up it's Properties panel and change the default `JRN_SUBSCRIBER` value from `SUNOPSIS` to `SUB-A`. Notice that an optional `JRN_DATE` condition has been suggested but commented out. It is okay to leave this code as is.

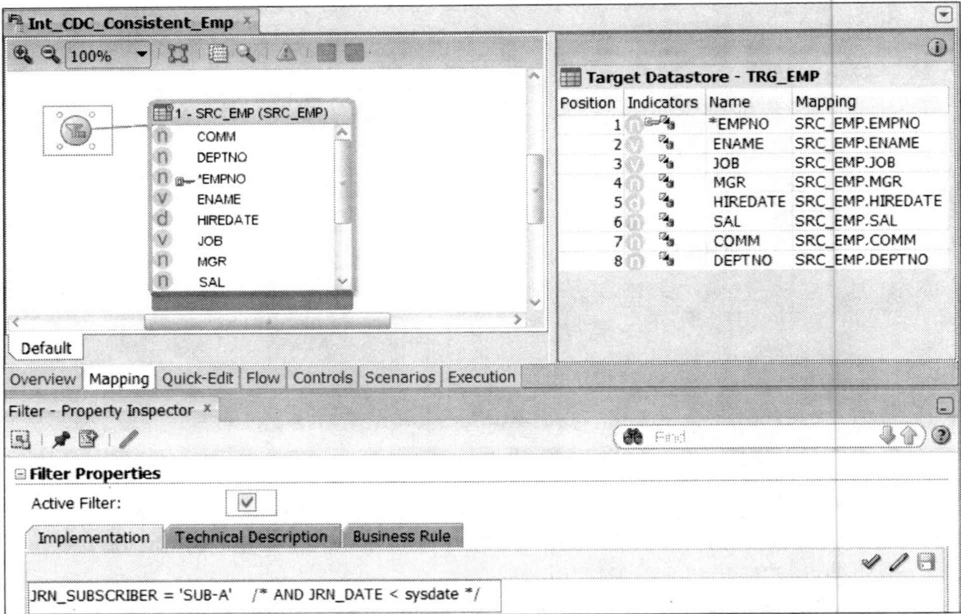

11. Right-click on the `SRC_EMP` source table again and observe that this time there are only two records showing. This is because the `SRC_EMP` object has now been directed to the underlying CDC view, so only new transactions have been made available for the `SUB-A` subscriber to see.

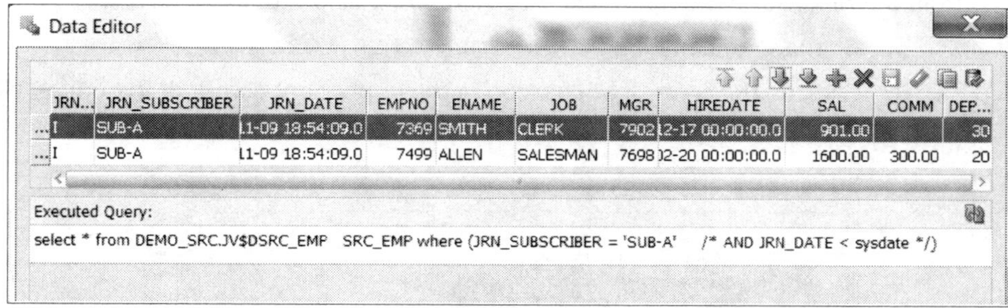

> There are three extra columns in the table view: `JRN_FLAG`, `JRN_DATE`, and `JRN_SUBSCRIBER`. These are infrastructure fields and were added by the JKM KM when it created the `JV$DSRC_EMP` view.

12. Save and close the interface, but do not execute it at this time.
13. Next we will create a second new interface called `Int_CDC_Consistent_Dept`:
    - Drag the `SRC_Dept` data store onto the source area of the designer canvas.
    - Drag the `TRG_Dept` data store onto the target area of the designer canvas (most of the columns should receive automatic mappings based upon their names).
    - Click on the **Flow** tab. Select the IKM as `IKM Oracle Incremental Update`. Set **FLOW_CONTROL** to `False`.

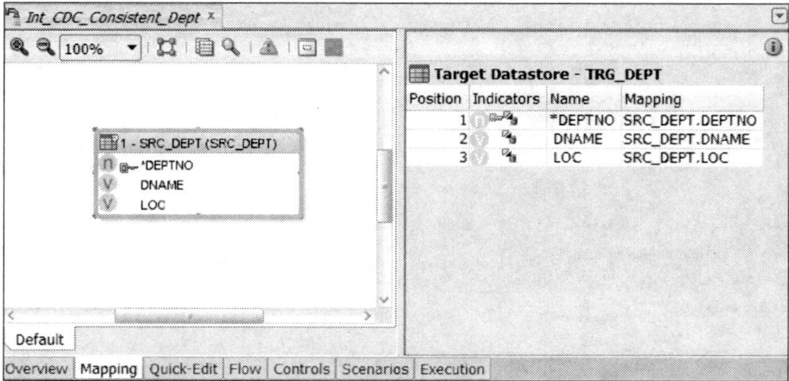

14. Save (without closing) and execute the interface as currently implemented. This action will serve as an initial data load and will ensure that all four source records are loaded into the `TRG_Dept` table.
15. Click on the **Mapping** tab and right-click on the `SRC_Dept` source table; select **Data** from the drop-down menu. Notice that there are still four records visible.
    - Change the Location for `NEW YORK` to `NEW YORK_CITY`
    - Click on the Save Changes icon in the upper-right corner of the editor; click on Close to terminate the editor

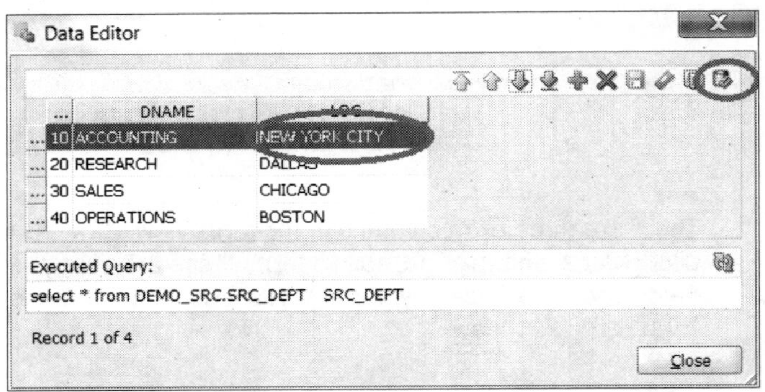

16. Click on the **Journalized Data Only** checkbox located on the **Source Properties** panel. Notice that a new filter has been added to the diagram.
17. Click on the Journal Filter icon to bring up it's Properties panel and change the default `JRN_SUBSCRIBER` value from `SUNOPSIS` to `SUB-A` (notice that an optional `JRN_DATE` condition has been suggested but commented out. It is okay to leave this code as is).

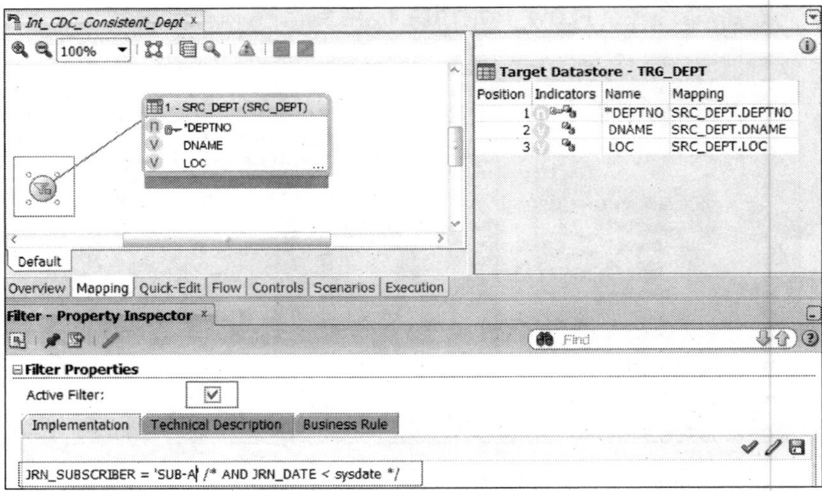

18. Right-click on the `SRC_DEPT` source table again and observe that this time there is only one record showing. This is because the `SRC_DEPT` object has now been directed to the underlying CDC view, so only new transactions have been made available for the `SUB-A` subscriber to see.

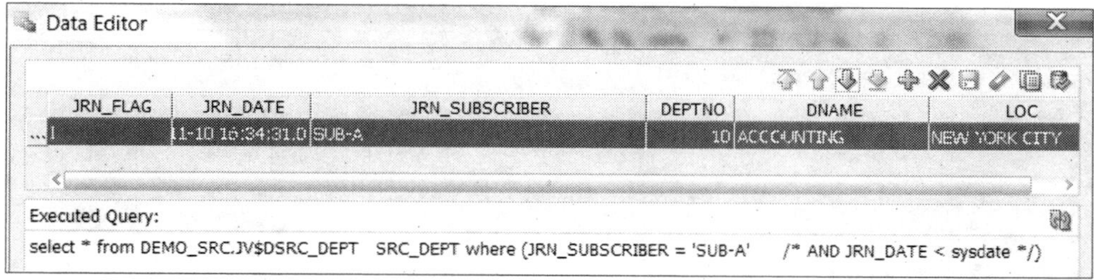

19. Click on Close to terminate the editor. Save and close the interface, but do not execute it at this time.

20. The final task when building our consistent set CDC data flow is to create a package to orchestrate the entire operation:

    - Create a new package called `Pkg_CDC`
    - Drag-and-drop the `DEMO_SRC` Data Model onto the canvas two times

    For both the data model icons, select **Journalizing Model** from the drop-down list within the **Properties** panel.

    Click the appropriate **Consumption** check-box for each model as follows:

    1st model icon: **Lock Subscribers** & **Extend Window**

    2nd model icon: **Purge Journal** & **Unlock Subscribers**

Change the step name to match the action being taken for each model icon.

- Drag-and-drop the two new Interfaces onto the canvas and arrange them between the second and third model icon. Apply the package step **Connectors** to all four icons.

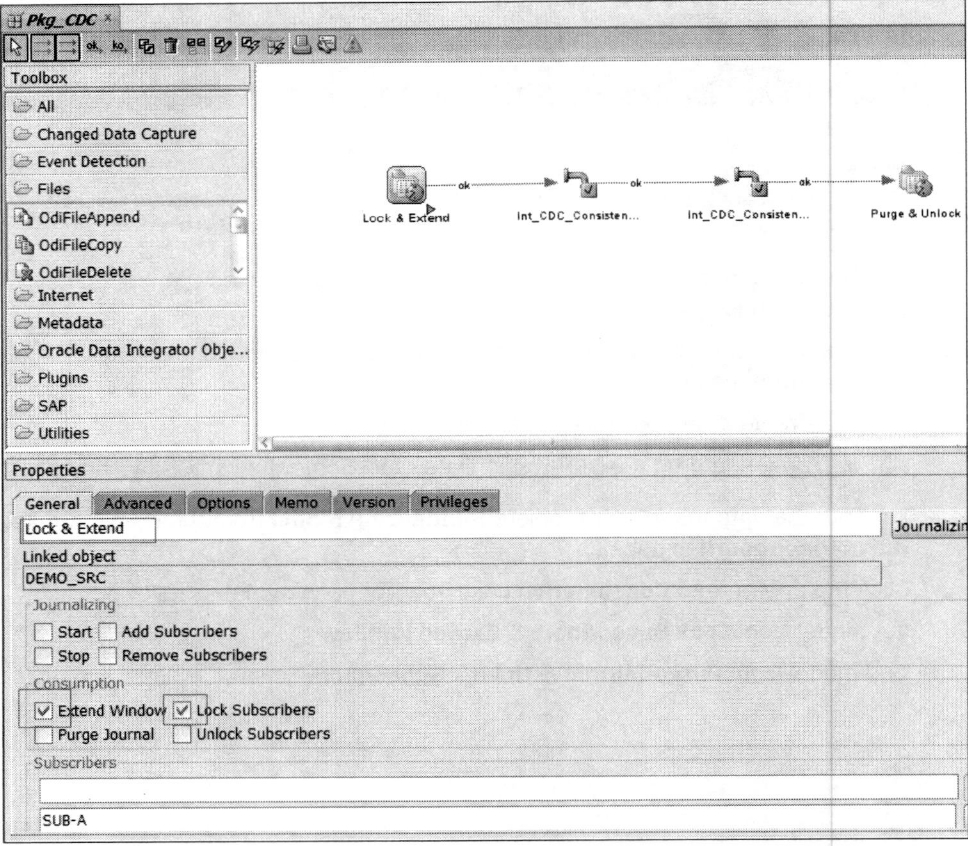

- Save the `Pkg_CDC` package and execute it.
- Click on the **Operator** tab; double-click to open the most recent job. The step summary should look similar to the following:

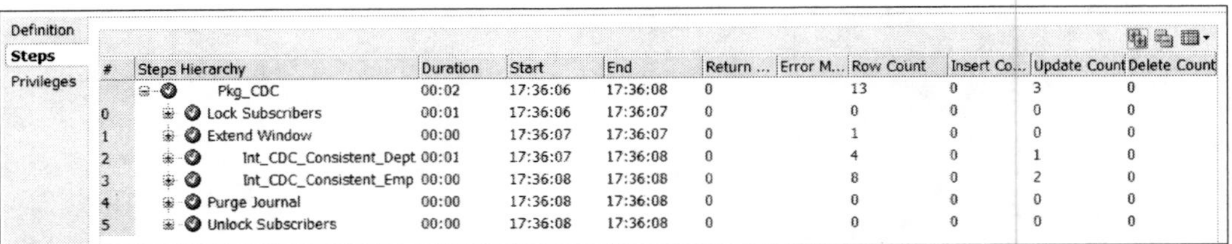

Definition
Steps
Privileges

#	Steps Hierarchy	Duration	Start	End	Return ...	Error M...	Row Count	Insert Co...	Update Count	Delete Count
	Pkg_CDC	00:02	17:36:06	17:36:08	0		13	0	3	0
0	Lock Subscribers	00:01	17:36:06	17:36:07	0		0	0	0	0
1	Extend Window	00:00	17:36:07	17:36:07	0		1	0	0	0
2	Int_CDC_Consistent_Dept	00:01	17:36:07	17:36:08	0		4	0	1	0
3	Int_CDC_Consistent_Emp	00:00	17:36:08	17:36:08	0		8	0	2	0
4	Purge Journal	00:00	17:36:08	17:36:08	0		0	0	0	0
5	Unlock Subscribers	00:00	17:36:08	17:36:08	0		0	0	0	0

How it works...

Consistent set CDC begins by associating the JKM Oracle Consistent KM to a specific data model. The developer tags data stores within that model to indicate which objects are to participate in the CDC process. The next step is to assign one or more subscribers to the data model, which when executed, will add the subscriber(s) to the `SNP_SUBSCRIBERS` table on the source system. The final step in the CDC set-up process is to start the CDC journalizing for the data model.

When the CDC journals are first started by clicking on Start Journal, the journalizing infrastructure (if not already installed) is deployed or updated in the following locations:

- Triggers created on the tables in the **Source Data Schema**. The journalizing trigger names are prefixed with the value specified in the **Journalizing Elements Prefixes** section for the associated physical schema (the default value for this prefix is `T$`).
- The remainder of the CDC common infrastructure for the data server is created in the **Source Work Schema** associated with the physical schema flagged as the **Default Schema** for the corresponding data server. This common infrastructure (that is, journalization control tables) contains information about subscribers, consistent sets, and CDC-registered tables for all the journalized schemas on this data server. All common infrastructure table names begin with an `SNP_CDC_` prefix.
- Journal tables are created in the **Source Work Schema** and are prefixed with the value defined in the **Journalizing Elements Prefixes** section of the corresponding physical schema (the default value is `J$` for a journal table). A journal table is used to capture the timestamp, mode (insert/update/delete), and the primary key information for each record.
- Journal views are created in the **Work Schema** and are prefixed with the value defined in the **Journalizing Elements Prefixes** section of the corresponding physical schema (the default value is `JV$` for a journal view). A journal view effectively establishes a time window over the associated journal table data relative to what a given subscriber needs to see for the current processing cycle.

Once the common infrastructure components are all in place and the individual components for each CDC table have been created, subsequent transactional activity against the source tables is captured into the corresponding journal tables and exposed to the consuming applications (interfaces) using two corresponding journal views. These two views, coupled with the journal filter added to the interfaces, will present only transactions not previously been seen by the named subscriber(s).

The main difference between consistent and simple CDC processing however is that, before and after any interfaces are executed, four extra CDC tasks are used by a package/scenario to establish a CDC window for a specific subscriber.

Before the first interface:

- **Extend Window**: The consistency window is a range of available changes in all the tables of the consistency set for which the insert/update/delete options are possible without violating referential integrity. The **Extend Window** operation re-computes this window to take into account any new changes captured since the previous **Extend Window** operation. This operation is implemented using a package step with the `Journalizing Model` type. This operation can be scheduled separately from other journalizing operations. This window applies to both children and parent records, so that a consistent set can be processed through the different interfaces that you will create to process each set of data.
- **Lock Subscribers**: Although the **Extend Window** is applied to the entire consistency set, subscribers can consume the changes at different intervals. The lock operation performs a subscriber(s) specific snapshot of current changes within the consistency window, including changes that have not yet been consumed by the subscriber(s). This operation is usually implemented using a package step with the `Journalizing Model` Type. It should be always performed before the first interface.

After the last interface:

- **Unlock Subscribers**: This operation commits the use of the changes that were locked during the **Lock Subscribers** operation for the subscribers. It should be processed only after all the changes for the specified subscribers have been processed. This operation is typically implemented using a package step with the `Journalizing Model` type. It should always be performed after the last interface. If any changes need to be processed again (for example, in case of an error), this operation should not be performed.
- **Purge CDC Journal**: After all the subscribers have consumed the changes they have subscribed to, the transaction entries still remain in the journalizing tables and should be deleted. This is performed by the **Purge Journal** operation. This operation is typically implemented using a package step with the `Journalizing Model` type. Although this particular step can be called at any time, the journal records will only be purged after all the current subscribers have consumed them.

There's more...

Although it is certainly possible to schedule a CDC scenario or execute a CDC scenario on demand, it is more common to put the inner workings of the CDC package inside a hybrid loop controlled by one of several ODI tools designed for event detection:

- `OdiWaitForData` waits for a number of rows in a table or a set of tables.
- `OdiWaitForLogData` waits for a certain number of modifications to occur on a journalized table or a list of journalized tables.

- `OdiRetrieveJournalData` retrieves the journalized events for a given table list or CDC set for a specified journalizing subscriber. Calling this tool is required if using database-specific processes to load journalizing tables.
- `OdiRefreshJournalCount` refreshes the number of rows to consume for a given table list of CDC set for a specified journalizing subscriber.

For more information on the ODI tools mentioned previously, please refer to *Appendix-A Oracle Data Integrator Tools Reference* in the *Oracle® Fusion Middleware Developer's Guide for Oracle Data Integrator* at:

`http://docs.oracle.com/cd/E23943_01/integrate.1111/e12643/data_capture.htm#CFHFHIA`

Using one single interface to load changes that occur in any dimensions

When data is de-normalized, data that is originally in multiple source tables often ends up in a single target table. From that perspective, changes that occur in any one of the source tables have to be reflected in the same target table.

One challenge here is that if you simply join the changes from the different source tables while loading the target table, you will only have data to load if all tables have changes: that is, if we simply join the changes from `SRC_EMP` to the changes from `SRC_DEPT`, we will only have target data to process when changes occur simultaneously in both tables. If one of the sets is empty, then we will have nothing to process.

For this reason, ODI will only accept one journalized table per data set, and the interface must be duplicated to process the changes of every single one of the source tables. This can be a daunting task if you have a lot of sources and complex mappings. With this recipe, we will limit the complexity of the mappings and the joins to a single interface and isolate the processing of the changes outside of that interface.

Getting ready

Before starting this recipe, we need to make sure that journals are already set up for the `SRC_EMP` and `SRC_DEPT` tables. You can follow steps 1 through 6 of the recipe *Using CDC – consistent set* to make sure that the tables are properly journalized.

How to do it...

1. First we will create a new table in the database to identify changes. Use your favorite tool to connect to the database (Sql*Plus, Toad, and so on). If you created the environment as described in the *Preface* of this book, you should already have this table defined in the `DEMO_SRC` data model; otherwise, log in as the owner of the source schema `DEMO_SRC` and enter the following code:

   ```
   create table CDC_EMP(EMPNO number(4),
   JRN_CONSUMED VARCHAR2(1),
   JRN_FLAG VARCHAR2(1)
   CONSTRAINT CDC_EMP_KEY PRIMARY KEY(EMPNO));
   ```

2. Reverse engineer the `CDC_EMP` table into the `DEMO_SRC` data model.
3. Create a new interface called `Int_EMP_Changes` to identify changes in the `SRC_EMP` table:
   - Drag-and-drop the `SRC_EMP` table in the source panel
   - Drag-and-drop the `CDC_EMP` table in the target panel
   - Click on the caption of the source table and select `Journalized data only`
   - Map the `CDC_EMP` columns as:

     `EMPNO: SRC_EMP.EMPNO`

     `JRN_CONSUMED: 0`

     `JRN_FLAG: SRC_EMP.JRN_FLAG`

Because the `JRN_FLAG` column comes from a journal view, it will not be directly accessible from the mapping editor. You can, however, simply type the column reference directly into the mapping area.

- Use the standard IKM Oracle Incremental Update to load the target table and set **FLOW_CONTROL** to `False`

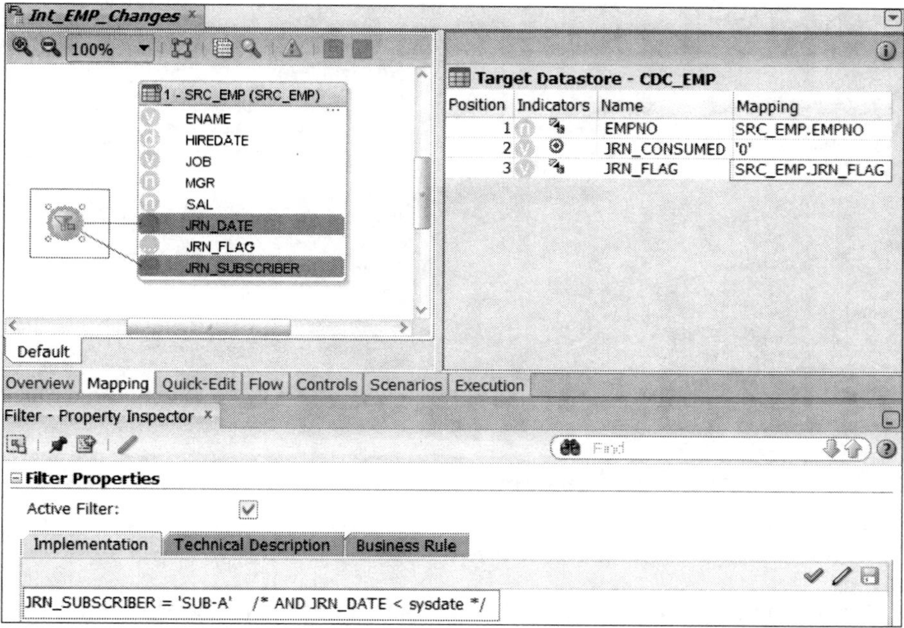

4. Create a second new interface called `Int_DEPT_Changes` to identity the changes in the `SRC_DEPT` table:
   - Drag-and-drop the `SRC_DEPT` table and the `SRC_EMP` table in the source panel
   - Drag-and-drop the `CDC_EMP` table in the target panel
   - Join `SRC_EMP` and `SRC_DEPT` on to the `DEPTNO` column
   - Click on the caption of the source `SRC_DEPT` and select **Journalized data only**
   - Map the `CDC_EMP` columns as:

     `EMPNO`: `SRC_EMP.EMPNO`

     `JRN_CONSUMED`: `0`

     `JRN_FLAG`: `SRC_DEPT.JRN_FLAG`

- Use the standard IKM Oracle Incremental Update to load the target table and set **FLOW_CONTROL** to `False`.

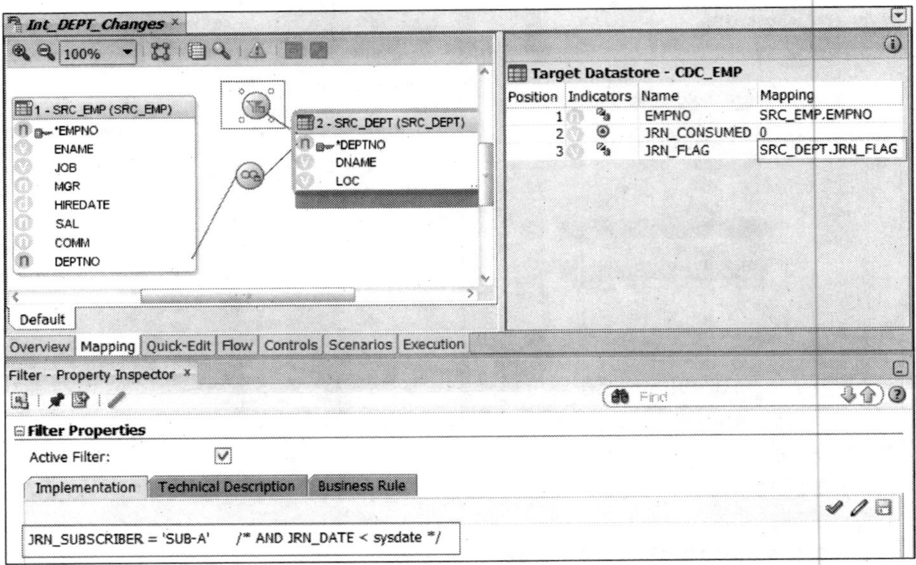

5. Create an ODI procedure called `Prc_Lock` that has the following code on the `Command on Target`:

   Name: Lock records

   Technology: Oracle

   Logical Schema: DEMO_SRC

   Command: `update <%=odiRef.getObjectName("L","CDC_EMP","D")%>`

   `set JRN_CONSUMED = 1`

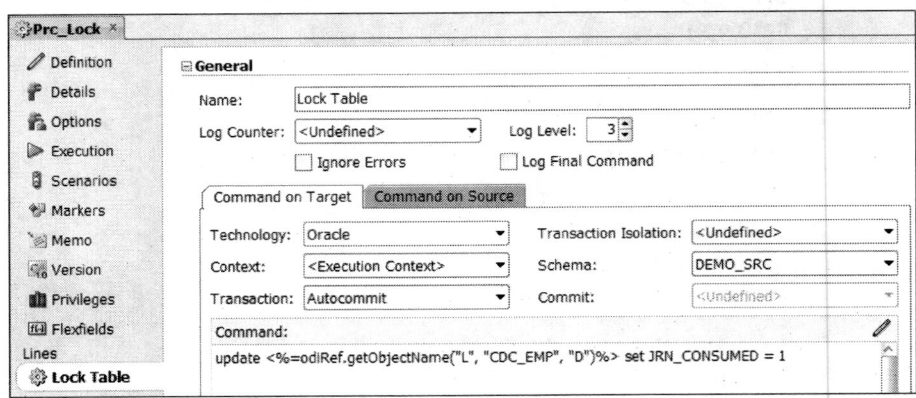

6. Create a new interface called `Int_ALL_Changes` to process all the changes:
    - The sources are `SRC_EMP`, `SRC_DEPT`, and `CDC_EMP`.
    - Join `SRC_EMP` and `SRC_DEPT` on to the `DEPTNO` column.
    - Join `SRC_EMP` and `CDC_EMP` on to the `EMPNO` column.
    - Create a filter on the `JRN_CONSUMED` column of the `CDC_EMP` table and use the following filter expression:

      ```
      JRN_CONSUMED = 1
      ```

    - The target table is `TRG_EMPDEPT` (which should already be in the `DEMO_TRG` data model). We are using auto-mappings.
    - Use the standard `IKM Control Append KM` to load the target table and set **FLOW_CONTROL** to `False`.

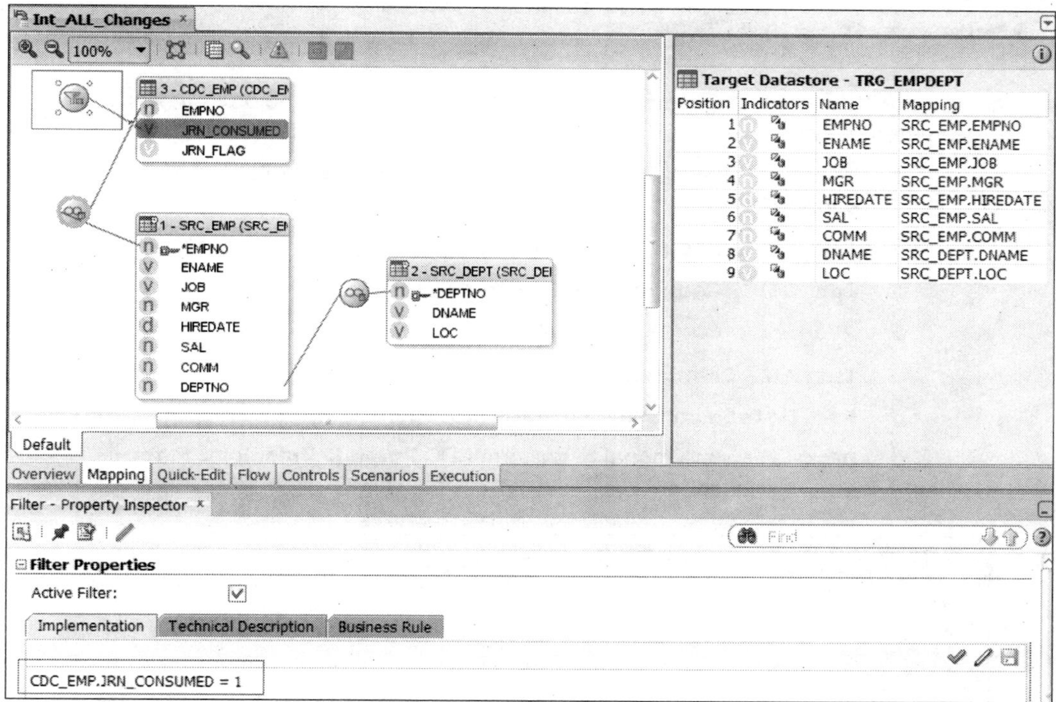

7. Create another ODI procedure, `Prc_Delete`, to remove consumed changes from the CDC table:
    - **Name**: `Remove consumed records`
    - **Technology**: `Oracle`
    - **Logical Schema**: `DEMO_SRC`

- **Command**: `Delete from <%=odiRef.getObjectName("L", "CDC_EMP", "D")%> where JRN_CONSUMED = 1`

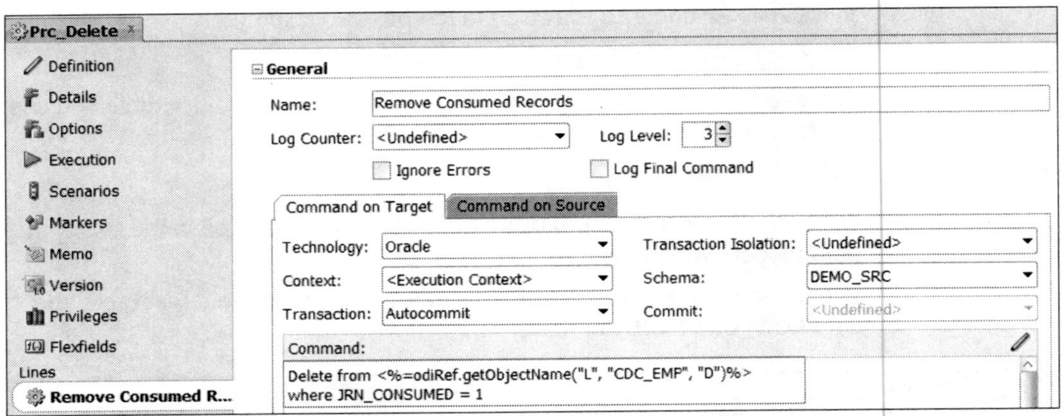

8. Create a package, `Pkg_Run_All`, that runs the objects in the order in which we created them:
    - `DEMO_SRC` data model to perform CDC **Lock & Extend** for the `SUB-A` subscriber
    - `Int_EMP_Changes` interface
    - `Int_DEPT_Changes` interface
    - `Prc_Lock` records procedure
    - `Int_ALL_Changes` interface
    - `Prc_Delete` consumed records procedure
    - `DEMO_SRC` data model to perform CDC **Purge & Unlock** for the `SUB-A` subscriber

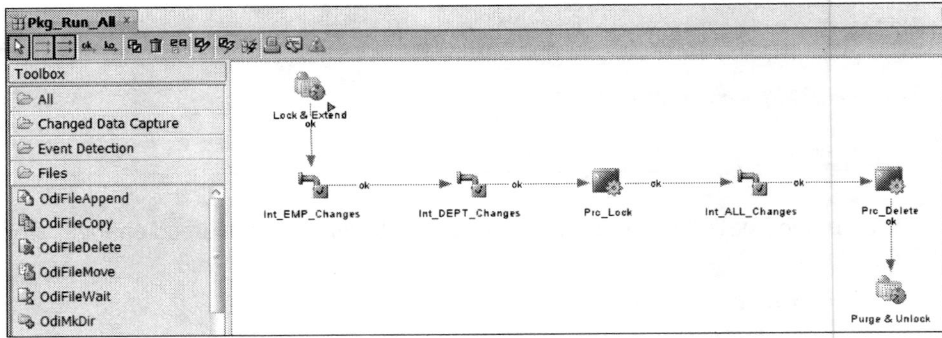

9. Using the data editor of your choice, make a few changes to both the SRC_EMP and SRC_DEPT tables:

```
set SRC_EMP.COMM = 35 where EMPNO = 7844
set SRC_DEPT.LOC = 'DALLAS AREA' where DEPTNO = 20
```

10. Execute the package. You will notice that:
    - The CDC_EMP table is empty after the changes have been committed to the target table
    - The data changes appear in the TRG_EMPDEPT target table

EMPNO	ENAME	JOB	MGR	HIREDATE	SAL	COMM	DNAME	LOC
7566	JONES	MANAGER	7839	1981/04/02	2975		RESEARCH	DALLAS AREA
7788	SCOTT	ANALYST	7566	1987/04/19	3000		RESEARCH	DALLAS AREA
7876	ADAMS	CLERK	7788	1987/05/23	1100		RESEARCH	DALLAS AREA
7902	FORD	ANALYST	7566	1981/12/03	3000		RESEARCH	DALLAS AREA
7566	JONES	MANAGER	7839	1981/04/02	2975		RESEARCH	DALLAS AREA
7788	SCOTT	ANALYST	7566	1987/04/19	3000		RESEARCH	DALLAS AREA
7876	ADAMS	CLERK	7788	1987/05/23	1100		RESEARCH	DALLAS AREA
7902	FORD	ANALYST	7566	1981/12/03	3000		RESEARCH	DALLAS AREA
7844	TURNER	SALESMAN	7698	1981/09/08	1500	35	SALES	CHICAGO

How it works...

The idea behind the setup proposed in this recipe is to expand the concepts found in the KMs beyond just the one table that they are supposed to handle.

Let's first look at the problem we are trying to solve. We want to process changes that can occur in either the SRC_EMP or SRC_DEPT table, and reflect those in the TRG_EMPDEPT table. We could create two identical interfaces, one with the journaling option turned on for the SRC_EMP table, the other on the SRC_DEPT table. But as the complexity of the interfaces increases, and as the number of source tables rises in that interface, maintenance will become a real nightmare.

The approach we are taking here is to identify the driving table in our source environment. It does not matter whether the change occurs in the SRC_EMP or in the SRC_DEPT table, all we really need to identify is all the employees we have to update the information for on the target side. All we need is the list of EMPNO to be processed. And it does not really matter what changed as long as we know that there is a change.

So our first interface identifies the changes for the SRC_EMP table and stores EMPNO in our own table (CDC_EMP).

The second interface retrieves `EMPNO` affected by the changes in the `SRC_DEPT` table and updates our table with the changes.

The only interface that needs to combine all the sources and process the complex transformation is our last interface. By joining it with the `CDC_EMP` table that we have created, we do not have to worry about activating journalizing on one table or the other; we are getting all the changes from all the tables (and imagine the benefit if you have 20 tables instead of the two that we have here).

The first two interfaces rely on standard journalizing processes, so all we need is to extend our window, lock the subscribers, then unlock and purge. But the table that we have created in the middle (our `CDC_EMP`) is not known to ODI as an element of the CDC infrastructure. As a consequence, we are in charge of the locking and unlocking in that table. This is what we achieve with the two procedures that we have added before and after the execution of the interface.

What we have done here is taken advantage of the fact that there has to be a driving table in the source environment. The only changes we are interested in are changes that impact the objects identified by the primary key of this driving table. As long as we can identify this driving primary key, it does not really matter what changed or in what table the change occurred; as long as we can retrieve the details associated with this PK (and our final interface does just that), we can apply the changes on the target side.

Using this approach, you can add as many source tables as you want and only maintain a single interface where all the dimensions come together.

There's more...

In this recipe, we have created two procedures to make a logical lock on the changed records and to purge the consumed records. One possible extension to this recipe would be to include these steps in other KMs and to control their execution with options.

7

Advanced Coding Techniques

This chapter covers:

- Using diagrams to develop and maintain models
- Generating DDL from data models
- Generating interfaces from data models or diagrams
- Creating a temporary interface (subquery)
- Loading data from a SQL query
- Performing a pivot
- Loading data using partition exchange

Introduction

A few of the lesser known features of Oracle Data Integrator involve the use of model diagrams. Having a comprehensive understanding of diagrams not only facilitates the development and maintenance of data models, but it enables developers to accelerate the development of basic interfaces.

The **Oracle Data Integrator Graphical User Interface** (**ODI GUI**) provides many features that enable a developer to quickly produce sophisticated solutions to complex problems. There is also a wealth of additional functionality available within the wide array of ODI Knowledge Modules. Unfortunately, many of these features are not as well known by the ODI community. The intent of this chapter is to demonstrate a few of the most overlooked features of the GUI and a few of the more interesting knowledge modules.

To read additional information about the ODI GUI, you should always refer to the following reference book: *Developer's Guide for Oracle Data Integrator*. At the time of writing, this reference manual could be found on the Oracle web site at `http://docs.oracle.com/cd/E23943_01/integrate.1111/e12643/toc.htm`.

The first three recipes in this chapter will examine how diagrams and data models can enhance the ODI experience. The next four will cover four additional use cases that occasionally arise when confronting some of the more advanced ELT requirements.

Using diagrams to develop and maintain models

During the course of application development, there are times when it may be necessary to migrate data from one system technology to another. In the simplest of cases, the structure of the given object may require only minimal changes such as data type conversions. Using ODI diagrams to perform these basic functions is an easy way to accomplish these tasks.

Getting ready

In order to follow this recipe, it is assumed that the reader has performed the preliminary installation steps outlined in the *Preface*. If these steps were done correctly, the reader should already have a `DEMO_FILE` data model containing two flat file data stores and a `DEMO_TRG` model that defines objects found in the `DEMO_TRG` database schema.

Now, let's suppose that we wish to quickly build an application that migrates data from a flat file into a database table. What we will do in this recipe is to use an ODI diagram to automatically construct a database data store based upon the file data store. In subsequent recipes, we will generate and populate this new database object using additional ODI diagram functionality.

How to do it...

1. Click and expand the **DEMO_TRG** data model:
    1. Right-click on the **Diagrams** option and select **New Diagram**.
    2. Enter the diagram name as `DEMO_TRG_DIAGRAM_1`.
    3. Click on the **Diagram** tab located at the bottom of the screen.
2. Click and expand the **DEMO_FILE** data model:
    1. Using the mouse left-click button, drag-and-drop the `SRC_SALES_PERSON` data store onto the diagram.
    2. Click **OK** when a confirmation message appears.

Although advantageous to copy data stores onto a model diagram, it is also permissible to copy and paste objects directly onto another model or submodel.

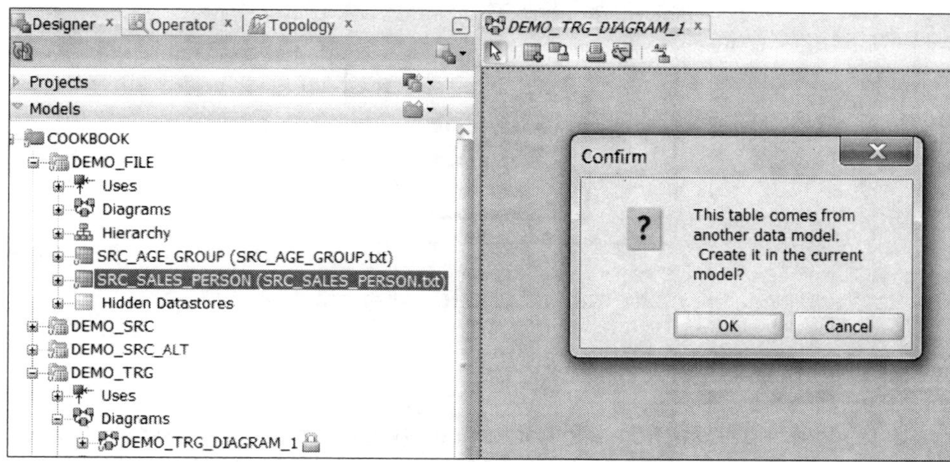

3. After ODI creates the new data store in the **DEMO_TRG** data model:
    1. Change the name of the data store to `TRG_SALES_PERSON`.
    2. Change the resource name to `TRG_SALES_PERSON` (without any `.TXT` suffix).
    3. Change the alias to `TSP`.
    4. Click on the **Columns** tab and take note of the modified data types.

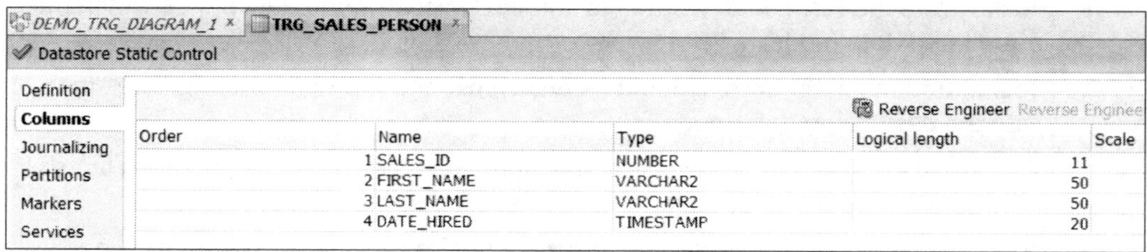

4. Save and close the `TRG_SALES_PERSON` data store.

5. Note that an icon for the new `TRG_SALES_PERSON` data store appears within the diagram.

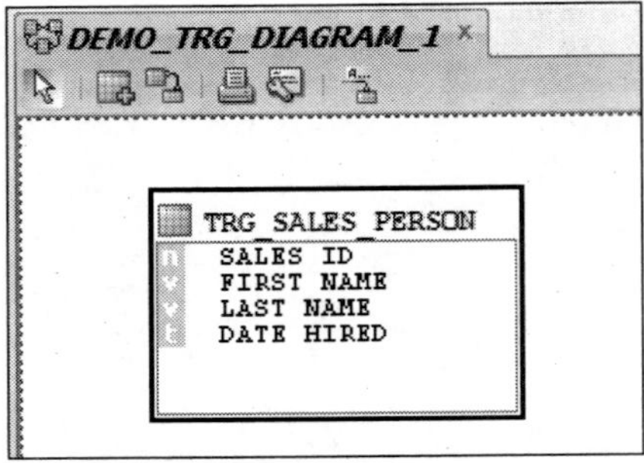

6. Save and close the `DEMO_TRG_DIAGRAM_1` diagram.

How it works...

When a data store originating from another technology is brought into a diagram, ODI applies a series of conversion rules to translate each column into an appropriate data type for the new technology. These conversion rules can be found within the data type definitions of the corresponding technologies maintained by the Topology Manager.

There's more...

Oracle Data Integrator developers can use diagrams for several reasons:

- To graphically illustrate the existence of **data stores** within the associated data model
- To illustrate the **relationships** (that is, foreign keys) between data stores within the associated data model
- To add and maintain **keys**, **columns**, **conditions**, and **filters** to existing data stores with the associated data model
- To provide a way for automatically converting data types when copying data stores from one technology to another (as demonstrated in this recipe)
- To provide a way of generating the **interface** needed to migrate data from the originating source schema to the target schema (if a diagram is not used, ODI can only place the source or the target data store within the generated interface, but not both)

Once a data store(s) has been represented in a diagram, it becomes possible to generate both DDL statements to create the objects and interfaces to populate them. The next two features of ODI will be demonstrated in the following recipes.

Generating DDL from data models

For each and every data store represented within a given data model, ODI has the ability to generate a procedure containing the **Data Definition Language** (**DDL**) statement needed by the associated technology to create that object. This feature provides an expedient and effective way to automatically create procedures that can be used within a package workflow to manage the creation of any data store object.

Getting ready

The purpose of this recipe is to demonstrate DDL generation. To follow along, you will only need to have imported the **DEMO_SRC** and **DEMO_TRG** data models as described in the *Preface*.

How to do it...

1. From the **Designer** tab, expand the **Models** section and right-click on the **DEMO_TRG** data model. Select the **Generate DDL** option.

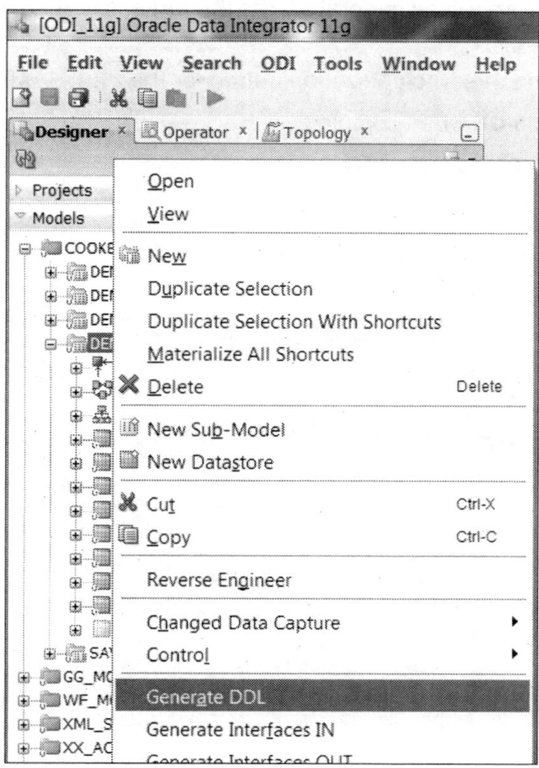

2. Depending on whether you wish to generate DDL statements for only those data stores defined in the data model or for data stores and tables located in the associated database schema, click on **Yes** or **No** in the following pop-up message. For our example, click on **Yes**.

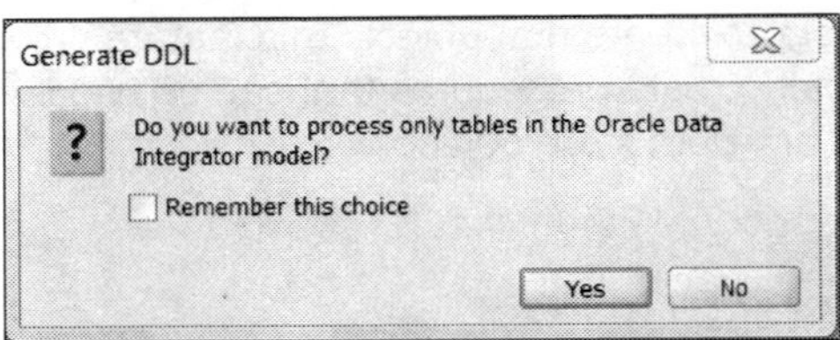

3. On the **Generate DDL** screen, ODI will display an entry for each object that either exists only in the data model (but not the database) or is determined to be different from the existing database object. Your screen should look something like what is shown in the following screenshot:
   1. Keep the auto-named **Procedure Name** as `DDL Demo_TRG 001`.
   2. Use the browse magnifying-glass to select the folder into which the procedure will be generated. Set the target folder as: `ODI_Cookbook.Chapter7`.
   3. Click on the synchronization button for the `TRG_SALES_PERSON` data store.
   4. Click on **OK** when complete.

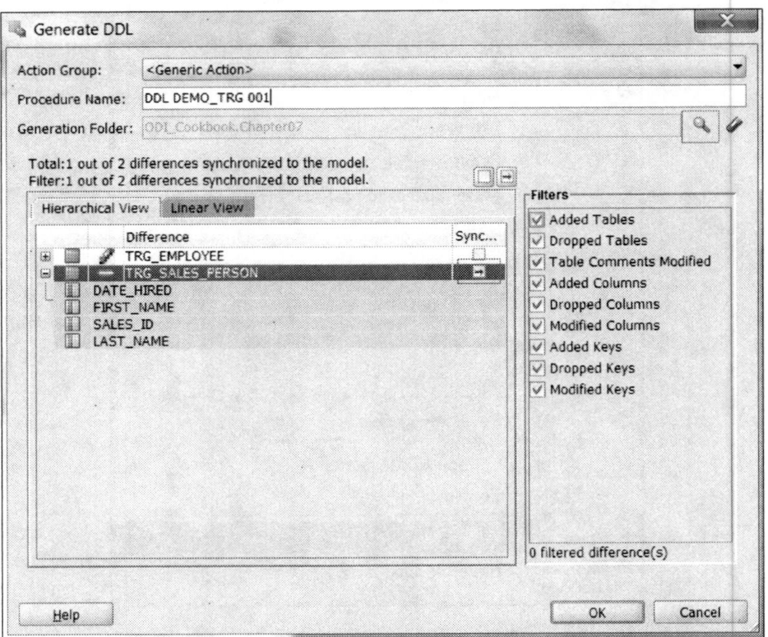

4. After ODI has finished generating the procedure, it will automatically open up a procedure editor in case there are further changes to be made. Click on the **Details** tab and notice the numerous steps generated after we left all of the previous checkboxes set on.

> Most of these steps will be empty since there were no constraints defined.

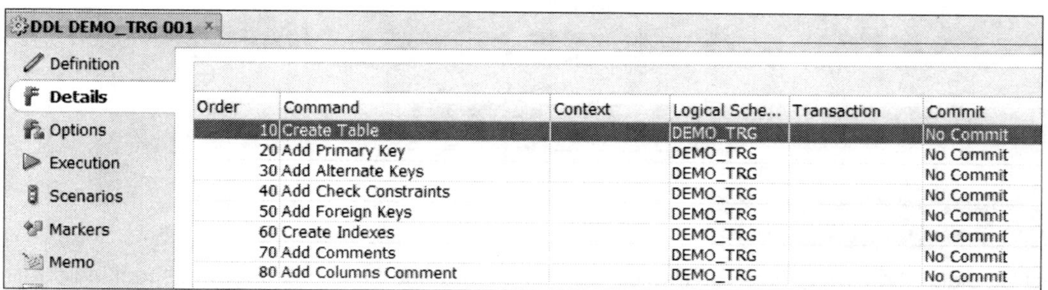

Order	Command	Context	Logical Sche...	Transaction	Commit
10	Create Table		DEMO_TRG		No Commit
20	Add Primary Key		DEMO_TRG		No Commit
30	Add Alternate Keys		DEMO_TRG		No Commit
40	Add Check Constraints		DEMO_TRG		No Commit
50	Add Foreign Keys		DEMO_TRG		No Commit
60	Create Indexes		DEMO_TRG		No Commit
70	Add Comments		DEMO_TRG		No Commit
80	Add Columns Comment		DEMO_TRG		No Commit

5. From the **Details** tab, double-click on the **Create Table** step. Review the DDL statement that was generated by ODI and notice the use of substitution APIs, which allow for the dynamic reference of certain details.

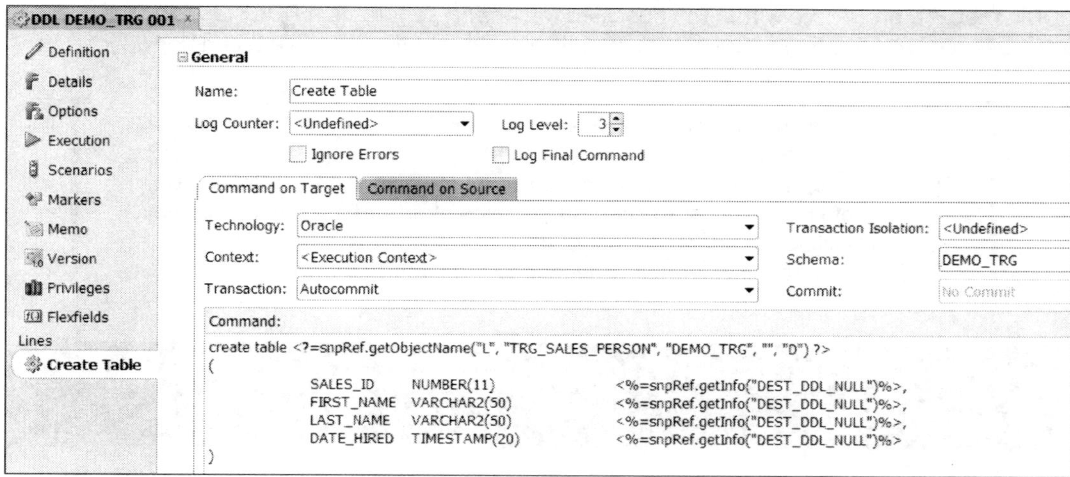


```
create table <?=snpRef.getObjectName("L", "TRG_SALES_PERSON", "DEMO_TRG", "", "D") ?>
(
        SALES_ID      NUMBER(11)         <%=snpRef.getInfo("DEST_DDL_NULL")%>,
        FIRST_NAME    VARCHAR2(50)       <%=snpRef.getInfo("DEST_DDL_NULL")%>,
        LAST_NAME     VARCHAR2(50)       <%=snpRef.getInfo("DEST_DDL_NULL")%>,
        DATE_HIRED    TIMESTAMP(20)      <%=snpRef.getInfo("DEST_DDL_NULL")%>
)
```

6. Close and save the procedure.

7. Using the Designer navigator, expand your project and folder and open up the **Procedures** container. Notice the new `DDL Demo_TRG 001` procedure.

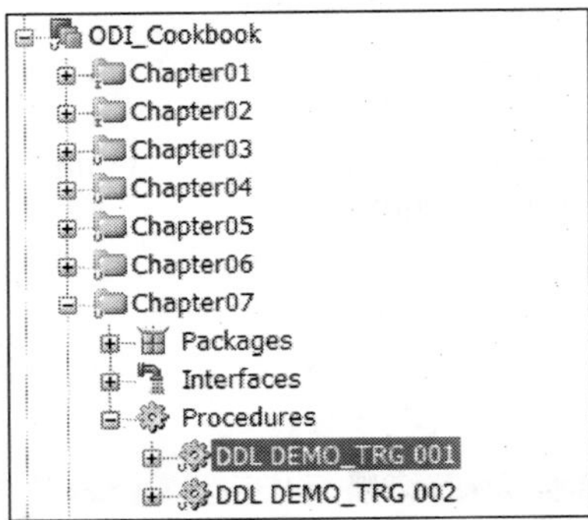

How it works...

ODI begins the DDL generation process by first comparing the contents of the specified data model to that of the corresponding database schema. Depending on which options the user specifies, ODI displays either a complete listing of the objects found in the target schema or only a list of deltas. The user then chooses which objects are to be processed, which secondary filters are to be applied (tables, comments, columns, keys, and so on), and the name and location of the procedure to be generated. Once all selections have been made, ODI creates a procedure within the specified folder and generates a DDL step for each process category selected that is syntactically appropriate for the given technology.

> Since not everyone has access to a modeling tool, this approach can allow a developer to quickly generate the code necessary to build or update a physical model. This method also has the advantage of knowing what the current contents of an ODI data model already include compared to that of the existing physical model, thereby generating only what is needed to synchronize the two.

Generating interfaces from data models or diagrams

Another often overlooked feature of ODI is its ability to generate interfaces from either data models or model diagrams. By selecting one or more data stores from a data model or diagram, ODI can create either an inbound or outbound interface capable of moving data in or out of the specified data store.

Getting ready

In this recipe, we will generate three such interfaces and compare the results. To follow along with the examples listed here, you will need an ODI project with at least the following KMs: **LKM SQL to SQL**, **IKM SQL Control Append**, and **IKM Oracle Incremental Update**. From a resource perspective, you will need to have imported the `DEMO_SRC` and `DEMO_TRG` data models as described in the *Preface*.

How to do it...

1. To create the first two examples, expand and right-click on the **DEMO_TRG** data model and select the **Generate Interfaces IN** option.

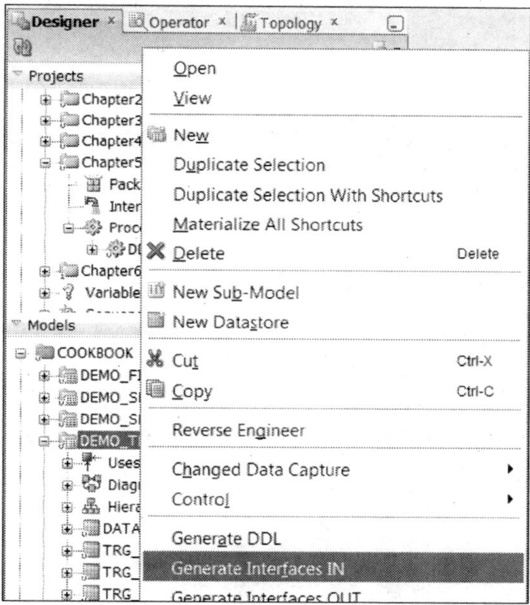

2. Use the browse magnifying-glass to select the folder into which the procedure will be generated. Set the target folder as `ODI_Cookbook.Chapter7`.

3. Discard all the suggested interfaces using the blank button on the right; instead select only the **TRG_EMP** and **TRG_SALES_PERSON** data stores.

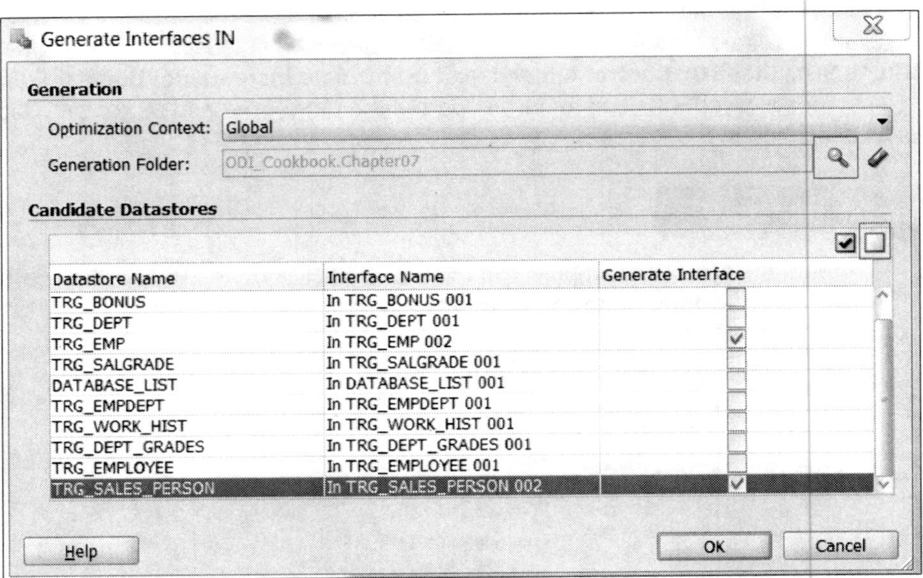

4. Click on **OK** to start the interface generation.
5. To create the third example, expand and right-click on the **DEMO_TRG** data model and select the **Generate Interfaces OUT** option.

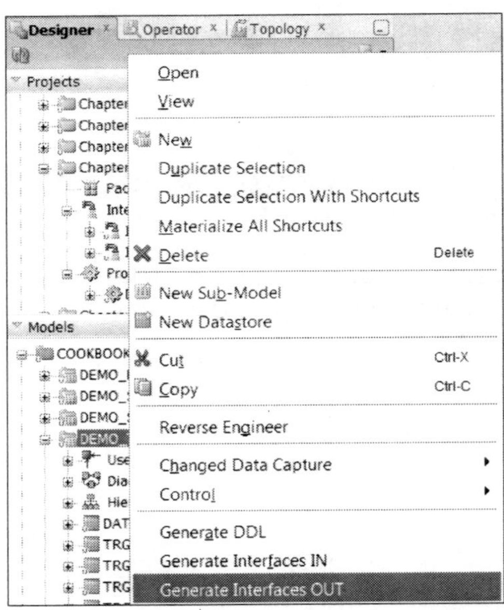

6. Use the browse magnifying-glass to select the folder into which the procedure will be generated. Set the target folder as `ODI_Cookbook.Chapter7`.
7. Discard all the suggested interfaces using the blank button on the right; instead select only the **TRG_SALES_PERSON** data store.
8. Click on **OK** to start the interface generation.

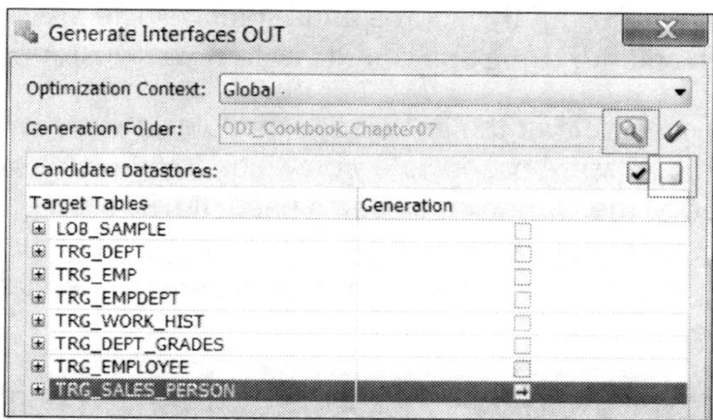

9. Open the project target folder `ODI_Cookbook.Chapter7`. Open and compare the three interfaces that were created.
   - Note that both a source and target are defined in the `In TRG_SALES_PERSON 001` and `Out TRG_SALES_PERSON 001` interfaces, because ODI remembered that the `TRG_SALES_PERSON` data store was originally based on the `SRC_SALES_PERSON` data store
   - Note the directionality of the source and target in the `In TRG_SALES_PERSON 001` and `Out TRG_SALES_PERSON 001` interfaces; in one case the `TRG_SALES_PERSON` data store is the target while in the other case the `TRG_SALES_PERSON` data store is the source
   - Note that `In TRG_EMP 001` has no source object defined since ODI had no prior knowledge of how the `TRG_EMP` data store was created

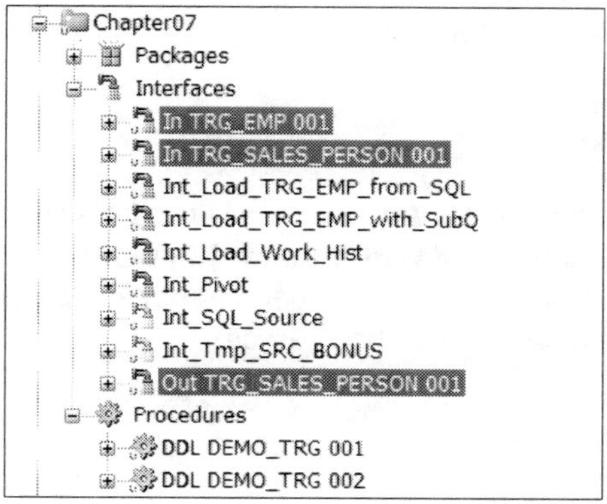

How it works...

ODI has the ability to generate a basic interface for every data store found within a data model or from an individual data store within a model diagram. These interfaces can be generated either as "In" or "Out" applications. If the specified data store was previously created from another data store, ODI will remember this and will use the original data store as the source object for the interface. When both the source and target objects are known, ODI will automatically map each column using appropriate data type transformations.

The developer should be aware that the knowledge modules chosen by ODI during the interface generation process were based solely on which KMs were available within the project and were related to the technologies being used. If there were multiple KMs that met the technology requirements, ODI may have chosen a module other than the one the developer had in mind, in which case, a KM modification should be made on the **Flow** tab of the interface designer.

Creating a temporary interface (subquery)

During normal application development, there may be times when the complexities of the functional requirements extend beyond the capabilities of a single ODI interface. To address these situations, and with the release of version 11g, ODI allowed temporary interfaces to be used as subqueries. Using a temporary interface allows developers to split up the complex logic into multiple interfaces. While a comprehensive list of use cases is impractical to mention here, this section will provide an example of one of the two basic types of temporary interfaces available:

- Temporary interfaces using persistent data stores (target tables that already exist or will be created within the designated target schema)
- Temporary interfaces using non-persistent data stores (target tables that are not instantiated but will be used to form a subquery within other interfaces)

In this recipe, we will demonstrate the implementation of a non-persistent temporary interface used as a subquery to a second interface.

Getting ready

To follow along with the examples listed here, you will need an ODI project with at least the following KMs: **LKM SQL to Oracle**, **IKM SQL Control Append**, and **IKM Oracle Incremental Update**. From a resource perspective, you will need to have imported the `DEMO_SRC` and `DEMO_TRG` data models as described in the *Preface*.

How to do it...

We begin by creating a temporary interface using a non-persistent data store.

1. Expand the **Cookbook** project folder and right-click on the **Interfaces** container; select **New Interface**.
2. On the interface **Definition** panel, do the following:
    1. Set the interface name as `Int_Tmp_SRC_BONUS`.
    2. Set the staging area as `DEMO_SRC`.

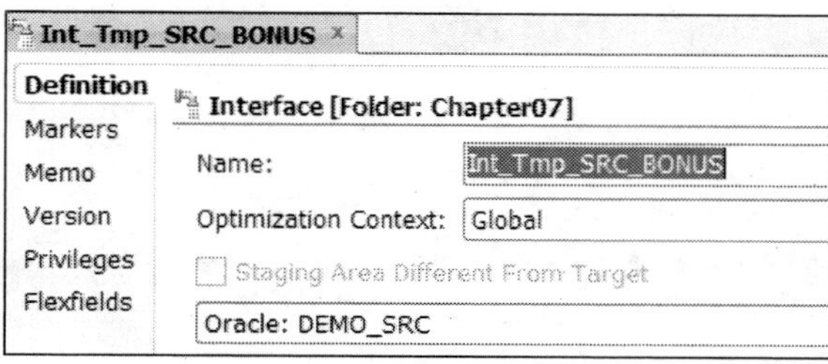

3. On the interface **Mapping** panel, do the following:
    1. Drag-and-drop the **SRC_BONUS** data store from the **DEMO_SRC** data model onto the source area.
    2. Click on the **Target Datastore** tab to display the **Temporary Target Properties** panel.
    3. Set the name as `Tmp_SRC_BONUS`.
    4. Right-click on the **ENAME** column of the source data store and drop it underneath the **Target Datastore** area.
    5. Right-click on the **COMM** column of the source data store and drop it underneath the **Target Datastore** area. Modify the transformation to perform the following aggregation function: `MAX(SRC_BONUS.COMM)`.

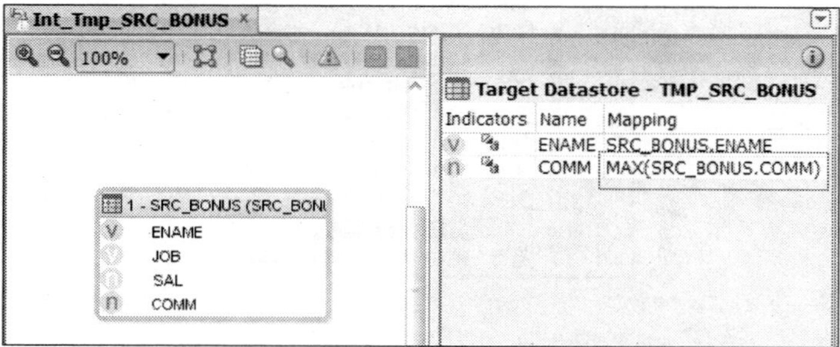

4. On the interface **Flow** panel, do the following:
    1. Choose the IKM as the **IKM SQL Control Append** option.
    2. Set the **FLOW_CONTROL** option to **false**.

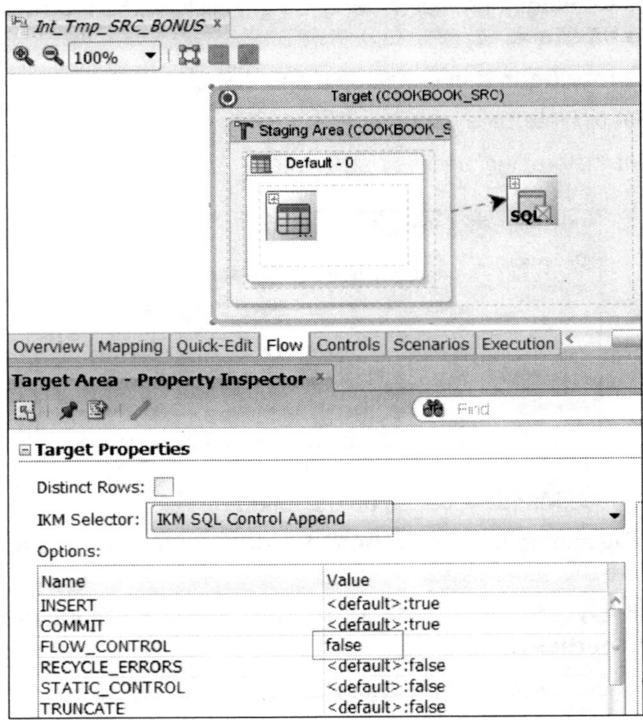

5. Save and close the **Int_Tmp_SRC_BONUS** interface. Note the display of a yellow interface icon denoting a temporary interface.

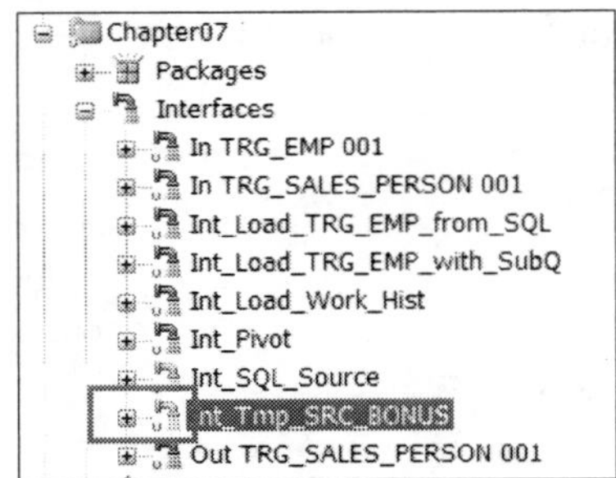

We will now create a regular interface that uses the temporary interface as one of its data sources.

1. Right-click on the **Interfaces** container; select **New Interface**.
2. On the interface **Definition** panel, set the interface name as `Int_Load_TRG_EMP_with_SubQ`.
3. On the interface **Mapping** panel, do the following:
    1. Drag-and-drop the **TRG_EMP** data store from the **DEMO_TRG** data model onto the **Target Datastore** area.
    2. Drag-and-drop the **SRC_EMP** data store from the **DEMO_SRC** data model onto the source area.
    3. Drag-and-drop the **Int_Tmp_SRC_BONUS** temporary interface onto the source area; modify the source properties by clicking on the **Use Temporary Table as Derived Table (Sub-Query)** box.
    4. Join the **SRC_EMP** datastore with the **Int_Tmp_SRC_BONUS** temporary interface where:

```
SRC_EMP.ENAME = TEMP_SQ.ENAME
AND
SRC_EMP.COMM >= TEMP_SQ.COMM
```

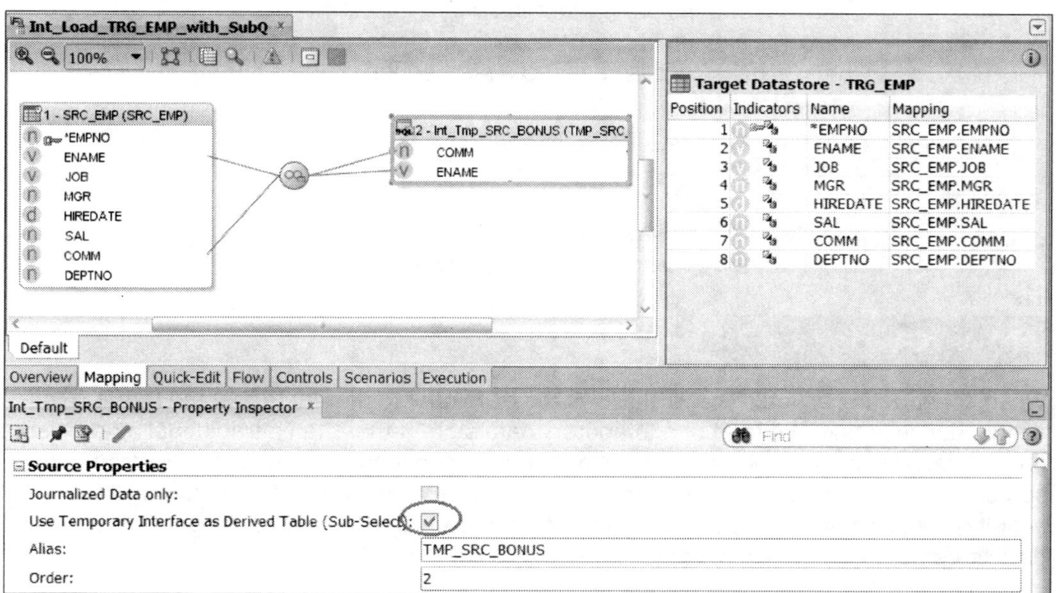

4. On the interface **Flow** panel, do the following:
    1. Set the LKM as **LKM SQL to Oracle**.
    2. Set the IKM as **IKM Oracle Incremental Update** (set **FLOW_CONTROL** as **false**).
5. Save and close the **Int_Load_TRG_EMP_with_SubQ** interface.
6. Execute the **Int_Load_TRG_EMP_with_SubQ** interface.
7. From the **Operator** tab, open the appropriate job log and review the **Load Data** step. Notice how the logic of the temporary interface was used as a subquery to the primary interface.

```
select
  SRC_EMP.EMPNO C1_EMPNO,
  SRC_EMP.ENAME C2_ENAME,
  SRC_EMP.JOB C3_JOB,
  SRC_EMP.MGR C4_MGR,
  SRC_EMP.HIREDATE C5_HIREDATE,
  SRC_EMP.SAL C6_SAL,
  SRC_EMP.COMM C7_COMM,
  SRC_EMP.DEPTNO C8_DEPTNO
    from DEMO_SRC.SRC_EMP SRC_EMP,
      (Select SRC_BONUS.ENAME ENAME,
        MAX(SRC_BONUS.COMM) COMM
        From DEMO_SRC.SRC_BONUS SRC_BONUS
        Where (1=1)
        Group by SRC_BONUS.ENAME
      ) TEMP_SQ
    Where (1=1)
      and (SRC_EMP.ENAME = TEMP_SQ.ENAME
      and SRC_EMP.COMM >= TEMP_SQ.COMM)
```

How it works...

When constructing an interface, ODI allows the developer to designate that the target destination is to take the form of a temporary data store rather than a traditional model-based data store. A temporary data store is defined by dragging individual columns over from the source area or by manually inserting additional columns directly into the temporary target definition. When defining a temporary data store, it is also necessary to assign a temporary data store name and schema location.

If the temporary interface is to be used as a subquery to another interface (as in this exercise), the temporary data store will not be persisted, so it will not necessary specify any IKM options.

Once a temporary interface has been created, it can be used as a source object to another interface. Temporary interfaces can be used in one of two ways. If you want to run the temporary interface, you can have it create the table that it loads. In this case, adding the temporary interface as a source in another interface amounts to adding the target table of the temporary interface as a source, except that you do not have to reverse engineer this table.

The second way to use the temporary interfaces is to use them as a subselect. In this case, there is no need to run the temporary interface at all; ODI will use the mappings of the temporary interface to generate a subquery that will be directly inserted in the `from` section of the code: *from (select ... from..)*. In this case, at a minimum, a temporary interface must be joined to at least one other source object using one or more common fields. When the temporary interface is to be used as a subquery (with a non-persisted temporary data store), the **Use Temporary Table as Derived Table (Sub-Query)** box must be checked in the properties window of that object when it is placed as a source in another interface; otherwise, the temporary interface must be executed prior to the second interface in order to populate the persisted temporary data store.

For a temporary interface to qualify as a subquery, it must be defined within the same logical schema as the other participating data stores in the sources portion of the interface.

There's more...

Using temporary interfaces and data stores will also help minimize the number of objects that must be defined in standard data models. By defining temporary data stores on the fly, developers can quickly put together a series of focused temporary interfaces one after another and then use them as needed to solve complex transformations, which can't be done using a single interface.

Loading data from an SQL query

With the release of ODI 11*g* came two very important new features: the ability to specify an inline query in the form of a temporary interface and the ability to specify the use of an inline query within a knowledge module. Together, these two new features can be combined to provide developers with the ability to use any SQL expression as a data source to an interface. It is the intent of this recipe to demonstrate a simple example of this powerful capability.

Getting ready

To follow along with the examples listed here, you will need an ODI project with the following KMs: **LKM SQL to Oracle**, **IKM SQL_as_Source** (this module can be downloaded from the Packt website), and **IKM Oracle Incremental Update**. From a resource perspective, you will need to have imported the `DEMO_SRC` and `DEMO_TRG` data models as described in the *Preface*.

How to do it...

We begin by creating a temporary interface using a projection (list of columns) based on an inline view definition and managed by a custom IKM.

1. Expand the **Cookbook** project folder and right-click on the **Interfaces** container; select **New Interface**.
2. On the interface **Definition** panel, do the following:
    1. Set the interface name as `Int_SQL_Source`.
    2. Set the staging area as `DEMO_SRC`.

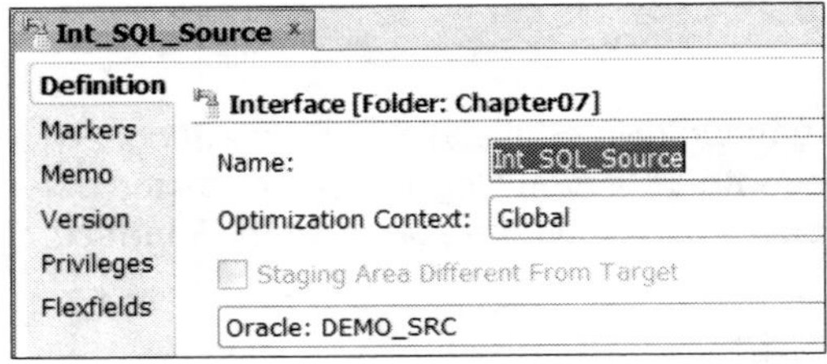

3. On the interface **Mapping** panel, do the following:
    1. Click on the **Target Datastore** tab and set the name to `EMP_QUERY`.
    2. Create a projection of target fields representing all of the columns that will be returned by the inline view (`EMPNO`, `ENAME`, `JOB`, `MGR`, `HIREDATE`, `SAL`, `COMM`, and `DEPTNO`). In the properties panel, set each column with a dummy transformation value of '--', which executes on the target.

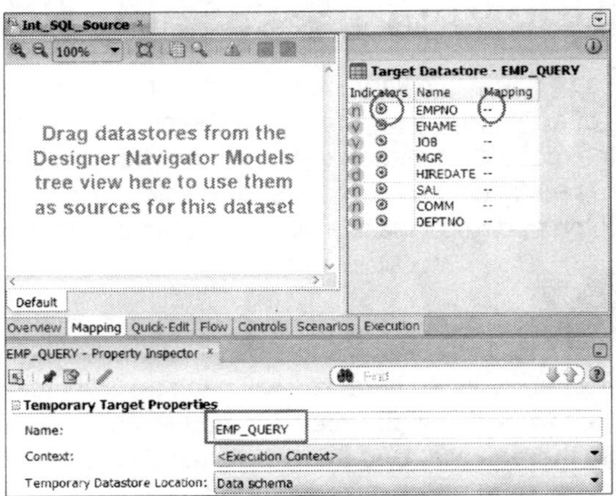

4. On the interface **Flow** panel, do the following:
    1. Set the IKM to **IKM SQL_as_Source**.
    2. Set the **VIEWQUERY** option to:

```
SELECT EMPNO, ENAME, JOB, MGR, HIREDATE, SAL, COMM, DEPTNO
  FROM <%=odiRef.getObjectName("L", "SRC_EMP", "DEMO_SRC",
  "D")%>
  WHERE SAL > 100
```

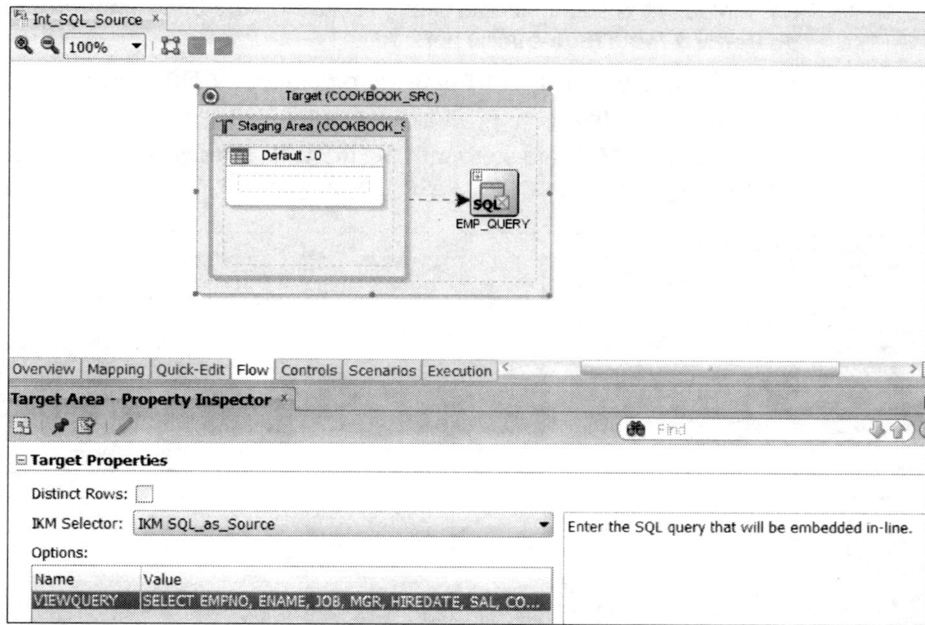

5. Save and close the **Int_SQL_Source** interface. Note the display of a yellow interface icon denoting a temporary interface.

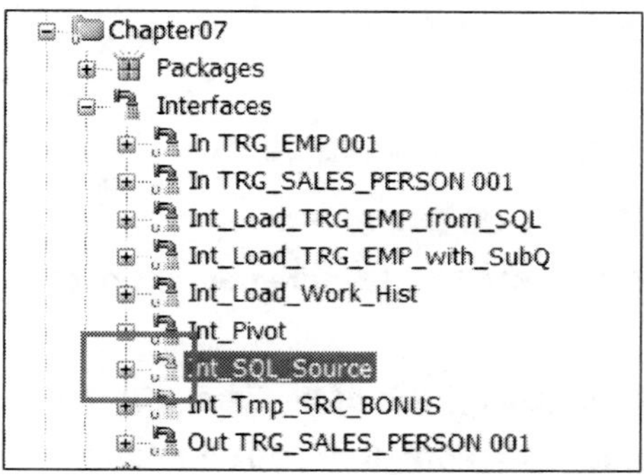

We will now create a regular interface that uses the temporary interface as one of its data sources.

1. Right-click on the **Interfaces** container; select **New Interface**.
2. On the interface **Definition** panel, set the interface name as `Int_Load_TRG_EMP_from_SQL`.
3. On the interface **Mapping** panel, do the following:
    1. Drag-and-drop the **Int_SQL_Source** temporary interface onto the source area. Modify the source properties by clicking on the **Use Temporary Table as Derived Table (Sub-Query)** box.
    2. Drag-and-drop the **SRC_DEPT** data store from the **DEMO_SRC** data model into the source area.
    3. Join the **SRC_DEPT** data store with the **Int_SQL_Source** temporary interface where `EMP_QUERY.DEPTNO = SRC_DEPT_.DEPTNO`.

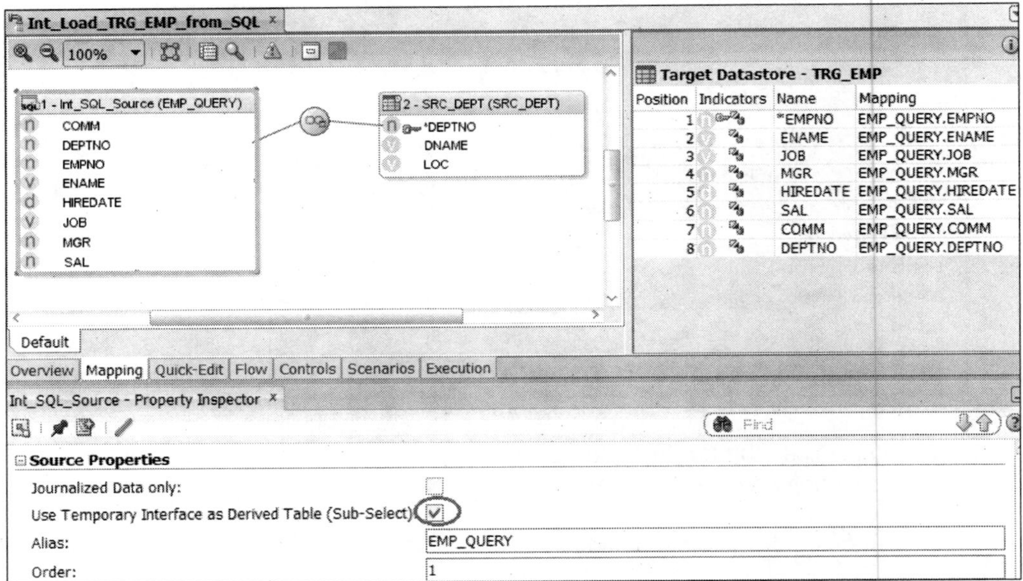

4. On the interface **Flow** panel, do the following:
    1. Set the LKM as **LKM SQL to Oracle**.
    2. Set the IKM as **IKM Oracle Incremental Update** (set **FLOW_CONTROL** as **false**).
5. Save and close the **Int_Load_TRG_EMP_from_SQL** interface.
6. Execute the **Int_Load_TRG_EMP_from_SQL** interface.

7. From the **Operator** tab, open the appropriate job log and review the **Load Data** step. Notice how the logic of the temporary interface was used as a subquery to the primary interface.

```
select
  EMP_QUERY.EMPNO C1_EMPNO,
  EMP_QUERY.ENAME C2_ENAME,
  EMP_QUERY.JOB C3_JOB,
  EMP_QUERY.MGR C4_MGR,
  EMP_QUERY.HIREDATE C5_HIREDATE,
  EMP_QUERY.SAL C6_SAL,
  EMP_QUERY.COMM C7_COMM,
  EMP_QUERY.DEPTNO C8_DEPTNO
   from(
    SELECT EMPNO, ENAME, JOB, MGR, HIREDATE, SAL, COMM,
    DEPTNO
    FROM DEMO_SRC.SRC_EMP
    WHERE SAL > 100
    ) EMP_QUERY,
    DEMO_SRC.SRC_DEPT SRC_DEPT
Where (1=1)
    and (EMP_QUERY.DEPTNO=SRC_DEPT.DEPTNO)
```

How it works...

Taking advantage of ODI's ability to process inline queries, very complex SQL statements can now be represented as simple inline views using a generic `SQL_as_Source` IKM knowledge module. This custom IKM effectively converts its **VIEWQUERY** option into a derived table (subquery), which when referenced by a temporary interface can project its query results into a temporary non-persistent data store.

Once a temporary interface has been created, it can then be used as a source object in another interface. Because the temporary interface is being used as a subquery, the **Use Temporary Table as Derived Table (Sub-Query)** box must be checked within the properties panel.

For a temporary interface to qualify as a subquery, it must be defined within the same logical schema as any other data stores that it may be joined with.

Performing a pivot

Pivoting data is a typical requirement for data warehousing. Let's say that we want to compare salary grades across departments. Based on the `SRC_EMP`, `SRC_DEPT`, and `SRC_SALGRADE` tables described in the *Preface* of this book, we can run the following query:

```
select SRC_DEPT.DEPTNO, grade, count(grade)
  from SRC_EMP, SRC_DEPT, SRC_SALGRADE
  where SRC_EMP.DEPTNO=SRC_DEPT.DEPTNO
  and (SRC_EMP.SAL between SRC_SALGRADE.LOSAL and
  SRC_SALGRADE.HISAL)
  group by SRC_DEPT.DEPTNO, grade
  order by 1,2;
```

The query gives us the result we want, but not something that helps much with the comparison of data:

```
    DEPTNO      GRADE COUNT(GRADE)
---------- ---------- ------------
        10          2            1
        10          4            1
        10          5            1
        20          1            2
        20          4            3
        30          1            1
        30          2            2
        30          3            2
        30          4            1
```

What we are really looking for is, for each grade, how many entries are found in each department.

A SQL construct with an Oracle database would look like the following:

```
select GRADE,ACCT_DEPT, RESEARCH_DEPT, SALES_DEPT from
(
select GRADE,
  DEPTNO as PV_DEPTNO, GRADE as PV_GRADE
  from DEMO_SRC.SRC_EMP SRC_EMP, DEMO_SRC.SRC_SALGRADE
  SRC_SALGRADE
  where (1=1) And (SRC_EMP.SAL between SRC_SALGRADE.LOSAL and
  SRC_SALGRADE.HISAL)
)
PIVOT(Count(PV_GRADE) for PV_DEPTNO in
(10 as ACCT_DEPT, 20 as RESEARCH_DEPT, 30 as SALES_DEPT))
```

This would give us a result like the following:

```
    GRADE   ACCOUNTING_DEPT   RESEARCH_DEPT   SALES_DEPT
---------- ---------------- -------------- ----------------
         1                0              2                1
         2                1              0                2
         4                1              3                1
         5                1              0                0
         3                0              0                2
```

Pivoting is the technique that will allow us to achieve this result.

Getting ready

For this recipe, we will need the `SRC_EMP`, `SRC_DEPT`, and `SRC_SALGRADE` tables on the source side of our interface (make sure these tables are reverse engineered in an ODI model).

We will need the following target table (make sure this table is reverse engineered in an ODI model):

```
create table TRG_DEPT_GRADES
  (GRADE NUMBER,
   ACCT_GRADE NUMBER,
   RESEARCH_GRADE NUMBER,
   SALES_GRADE NUMBER);
```

How to do it...

1. Create a new KM called `IKM Oracle Pivot`. In the `Definition` tab of the KM, make sure that you select the option **Multi-Technology**. Leave the source technology as `<Undefined>`, and select **Oracle** for the target technology.
2. Close the KM and add the following options:

Options	**Type**	**Default value**
TRUNCATE	Check Box	Yes
PIVOT_FOR_CLAUSE	Value	DEPTNO
PIVOT_AGGREGATE_COLUMN	Value	GRADE
PIVOT_AGGRGATE_FUNCTION	Value	Count(PV_GRADE)

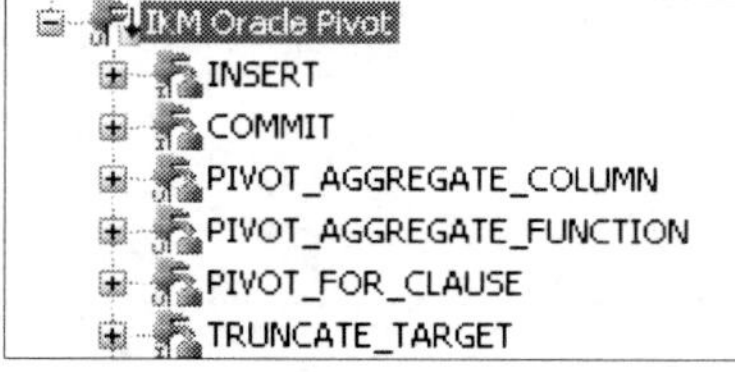

3. Open the `IKM Oracle Pivot` KM and create a first step called `Truncate Target`. Leave all the options as they are, and in the **Command on Target** area, copy the following code:

   ```
   truncate table <%=odiRef.getTable("L","TARG_NAME","A")%>.
   ```

   At the very bottom of the screen, expand **Options** to uncheck **Always Execute** and only select **TRUNCATE**.

4. Create a second step for the actual code for the pivot. Call this step `Insert new rows`. In the **Command on Target** area, set the **Log Counter** option to **Insert**, the **Transaction** option to **Transaction 1**, and the **Commit** option to **No Commit**. Copy the following code in the **Command** area:

   ```
   insert into <%=odiRef.getTable("L","TARG_NAME","A")%>
   (
     <%=odiRef.getColList("", "[COL_NAME]", ",\n\t", "", "INS
     and REW")%>
   )

   select <%=odiRef.getColList("", "[COL_NAME]", ",\n\t", "", "INS
   and REW")%> from
   (
     select <%=odiRef.getColList("", "[COL_NAME]", ",\n\t",
     "", "((INS and !TRG) and REW)")%>,
     <%=odiRef.getOption("PIVOT_FOR_CLAUSE")%> as
     PV_<%=odiRef.getOption("PIVOT_FOR_CLAUSE")%>,
     <%=odiRef.getOption("PIVOT_AGGREGATE_COLUMN")%> as
     PV_<%=odiRef.getOption("PIVOT_AGGREGATE_COLUMN")%>
   from <%=odiRef.getFrom()%>
   where (1=1) <%=odiRef.getJoin()%>
   <%=odiRef.getFilter()%>)
   PIVOT(<%=odiRef.getOption("PIVOT_AGGREGATE_FUNCTION")%>
   for PV_<%=odiRef.getOption("PIVOT_FOR_CLAUSE")%> in
   (<%=odiRef.getColList("", "[EXPRESSION] as [COL_NAME]",
   ",\n\t", "", "((INS and TRG) and REW)")%>))
   ```

5. Create a last step to commit. Call this step `Commit`. In the **Command on Target** area, set the **Transaction** option to **Transaction 1**, and the **Commit** option to **Commit**. There is no code in the **Command** area.

6. Save the KM and close it.

7. Create a new interface called `Int_Pivot` where you are using the tables `SRC_EMP` and `SRC_SALGRADE` on the source and the table `TRG_DEPT_GRADES` on the target. Once you have added the target table, go back to the **Overview** tab, select **Staging Area Different From Target**, and select the **DEMO_SRC** logical schema that points to source tables' location in the schema drop-down list.

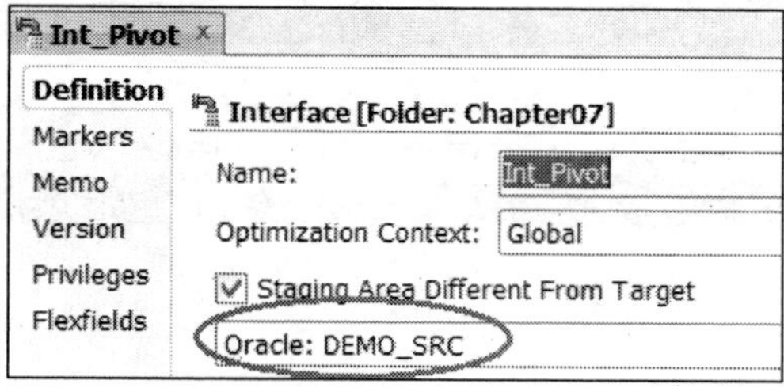

8. Add join `SRC_EMP.SAL` between the tables `SRC_SALGRADE.LOSAL` and `SRC_SALGRADE.HISAL`, then map the columns as follows:

Transformation location	Target columns	Mapping
Staging	9. `GRADE`	10. `SRC_SALGRADE.GRADE`
Target	11. `ACCT_GRADE`	12. `10`
Target	13. `RESEARCH_GRADE`	14. `20`
Target	15. `SALES_GRADE`	16. `30`

The interface should look similar to the following screenshot:

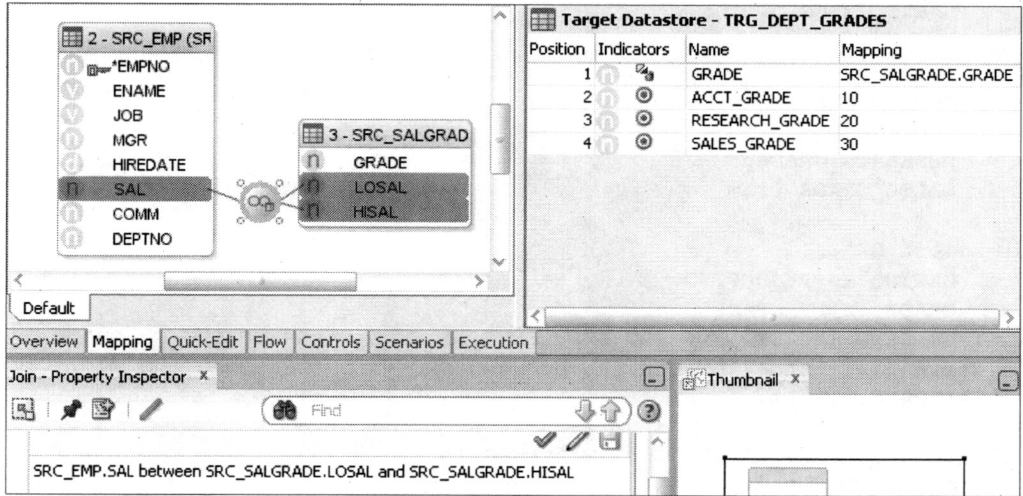

9. In the **Flow** tab, select **IKM Oracle Pivot** on the target schema.
10. Save and run the interface. Check in the **Operator** tab that the execution is successful. The insert step will report how many rows have been inserted. You can also right-click on the target table to see what data got inserted in the target table.

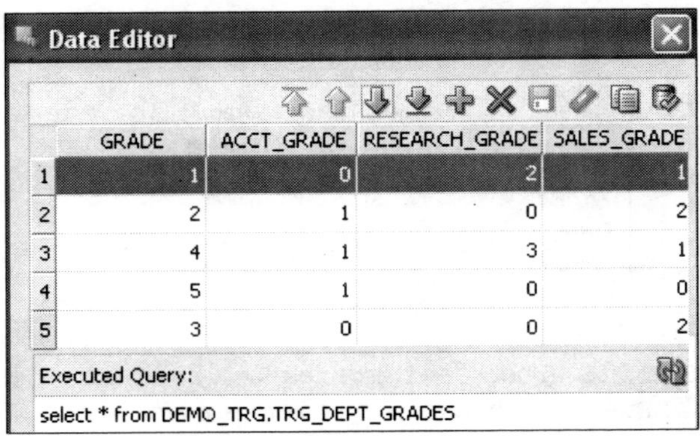

	GRADE	ACCT_GRADE	RESEARCH_GRADE	SALES_GRADE
1	1	0	2	1
2	2	1	0	2
3	4	1	3	1
4	5	1	0	0
5	3	0	0	2

How it works...

The entire objective of this exercise is to get ODI to generate the following code:

```
insert into DEMO_TRG.TRG_DEPT_GRADES
(
  GRADE,
  ACCT_GRADE,
  RESEARCH_GRADE,
  SALES_GRADE
)

select GRADE,
  ACCT_GRADE,
  RESEARCH_GRADE,
  SALES_GRADE from
(
select GRADE,
  DEPTNO as PV_DEPTNO,
  GRADE as PV_GRADE
from DEMO_SRC.SRC_EMP SRC_EMP, DEMO_SRC.SRC_SALGRADE SRC_SALGRADE
where (1=1) And (SRC_EMP.SAL between SRC_SALGRADE.LOSAL and SRC_
SALGRADE.HISAL)
)
PIVOT(Count(PV_GRADE) for PV_DEPTNO in
(10 as ACCT_GRADE,
  20 as RESEARCH_GRADE,
  30 as SALES_GRADE))
```

There are many ways to achieve this result and many improvements can be done to the previous code. In particular, we are using two options to get the aggregation function and the name of the aggregation column; we prefixed these with the characters `PV_` to highlight them in the code that is generated in the end.

Also, to generate a subquery and to make sure that all the code fits in one single SQL query, we have taken advantage of the possibility to use a temporary interface to design the select statement that is part of the `From` clause. When generating a temporary interface, a key element is the selection of the staging area. Since we are not loading an existing table, we have to tell ODI where the code will be executed. The option staging area, different from the target, allows us to make that selection.

The exercise performed here was one of balance between the elements that were defined as options of the KM versus the ones that were part of the mappings of the KM. Based on individual use cases, you may prefer to use options where we were leveraging mappings, or vice versa.

A very good reference to see how to generate proper pivot codes is available in *Oracle® Database Oracle Database SQL Language Reference* at `http://docs.oracle.com/cd/B28359_01/server.111/b28286/statements_10002.htm#CHDCEJJE`.

There's more...

There are multiple techniques that can be leveraged to pivot data. Since we were using an Oracle database in our examples, we could leverage the `PIVOT` function of the database.

An alternative that would work for any database is to use a standard IKM and transform the data as needed using an aggregation function in the columns mapping. This approach would generate code similar to the following:

```
select grade
      ,count(CASE src_dept.deptno when 10 then grade end) ACCOUNTING_
GRADE
      ,count(CASE src_dept.deptno when 20 then grade end) ACCOUNTING_
GRADE
      ,count(CASE src_dept.deptno when 30 then grade end) SALES_GRADE
  from DEMO_SRC.SRC_EMP SRC_EMP, DEMO_SRC.SRC_SALGRADE SRC_SALGRADE
 where SRC_EMP.DEPTNO=SRC_DEPT.DEPTNO
   and (SRC_EMP.SAL between SRC_SALGRADE.LOSAL and
   SRC_SALGRADE.HISAL)
   group by grade;
```

However, this technique requires more work in the definition of the transformations, when our previous example hides most of the complexity in the `Knowledge` Module.

Additional examples and different pivoting techniques can be found on the site used by Oracle to share Knowledge Modules with the ODI community at `http://Java.net/projects/oracledi`.

Loading data using partition exchange

Table partitioning is a commonly used strategy in data warehouse systems, and although the many reasons for partitioning a table are beyond the scope of this book, suffice it to say that performance and high availability are among the primary reasons for doing so. From a data loading perspective, the gold standard ELT strategy for targeting a partitioned table is universally considered to be the **partition exchange loading** (**PEL**) method. This advanced technique involves five basic steps:

1. Create a standalone database table that is structurally identical to the partitioned table.
2. Load all source records into the standalone table that comply with the boundary definition of a specific partition within the partitioned table.
3. Create all secondary objects (local indexes, constraints) for the standalone table such that the final structure is identical to that of the partitioned table.
4. Exchange the contents of the standalone table with that of its corresponding partition segment in the partitioned table.
5. Drop the standalone table.

It is the intent of this recipe to demonstrate a simple example of this powerful data loading method using a specialized knowledge module. Please note that for the purpose of brevity, this example has deliberately been limited to process only one specific partition. A normal ODI application might include a package that would loop through the source data as a series of individual partition loads.

Getting ready

To follow along with the examples listed here, you will need an ODI project with the following knowledge modules: `LKM SQL to Oracle` and `IKM Oracle PEL`. (The IKM in this case is not an out of the box knowledge module, so it must be downloaded from the Packt website.) From a resource perspective, you will need to have imported the `DEMO_SRC` and `DEMO_TRG` data models as described in the *Preface*.

How to do it...

1. Create a variable called `PV_PARTITION_NAME` (this variable will be used by the IKM to pass in a specific partition name).
    - Set the **Datatype** option as `Alphanumeric`

- Set the **Keep History** option as `Latest Value`
- Set the **Default Value** option as `P201302`

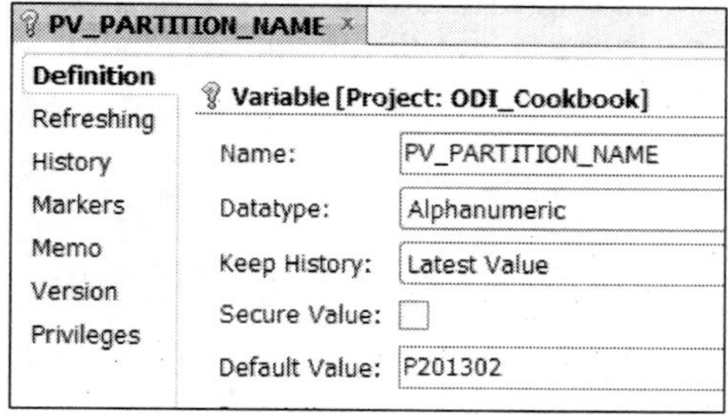

2. Expand the **Cookbook** project folder and right-click on the **Interfaces** container; select **New Interface**.
3. On the interface **Definition** panel, set the interface name as `Int_Load_Work_Hist`.
4. On the interface **Mapping** panel, do the following:
   1. Drag-and-drop the **SRC_WORK_HIST** data store from the **DEMO_SRC** data model onto the source area.
   2. Drag-and-drop the **TRG_WORK_HIST** data store from the **DEMO_TRG** data model onto the **Target Datastore** area.
   3. Drag-and-drop all the columns from source to target (or use auto-mapping of columns).

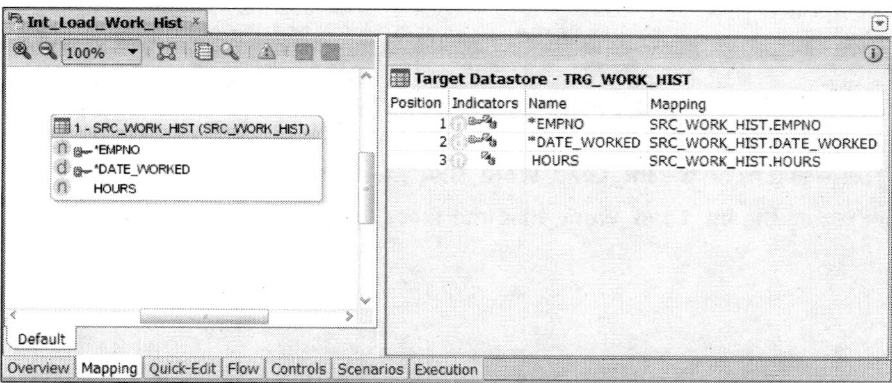

5. On the interface **Flow** panel, do the following:
    1. Set the LKM as **LKM SQL to Oracle**.
    2. Set the IKM as **IKM Oracle PEL**. Set the **APARTITION_VARIABLE** option with the `#PV_PARTITION_NAME` variable; all other IKM options can keep their default values.

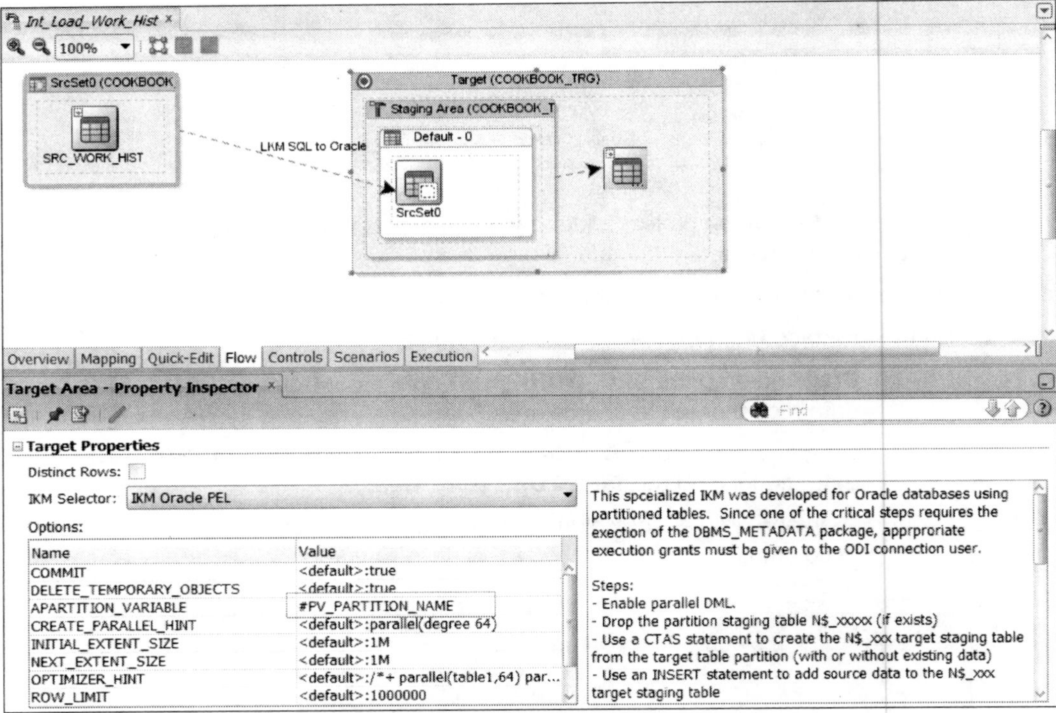

6. Save and close the **Int_Load_Work_Hist** interface.
7. Execute the **Int_Load_Work_Hist** interface.

How it works...

The magic of this particular recipe lies exclusively within the specialized knowledge module used by the interface. This KM used a series of steps uniquely designed to perform the five basic steps outlined in the introduction. A closer examination of the `IKM_Oracle_PEL` knowledge module will allow the reader to review the individual steps involved.

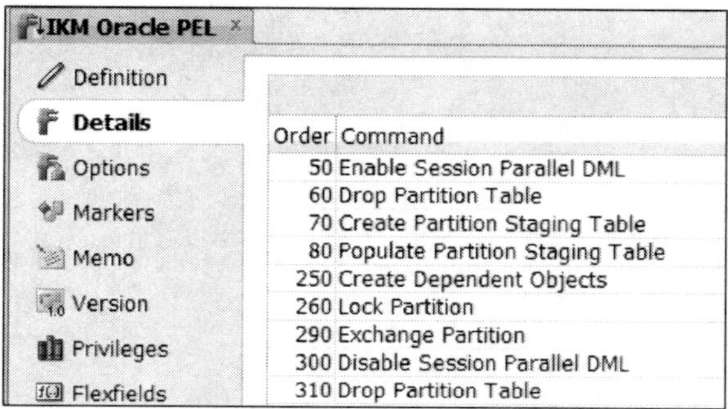

To summarize, the IKM makes a replica of the target table structure, populates that table with the `I$` staging data, creates all secondary dependent objects such that the new table is now identical to the partitioned target table, and lastly exchanges the new table with the variable-designated partition of the target table. The following illustration provides a high-level representation of the PEL methodology:

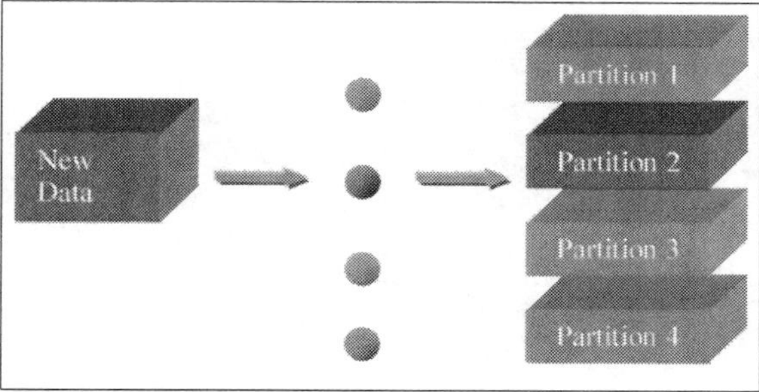

For this simple example to work properly, the partitioned target table had been limited to one local unique index and a primary key (this configuration was all that the knowledge module had been designed to include). For a more comprehensive solution, additional steps would need to be added to the KM in order to generate the DDL for multiple indexes and constraints.

8
Package Loops and File Processing

In this chapter, we will cover:

- Defining packages and loops for near real-time execution using a hybrid loop
- Using a file from a parameter variable
- Detecting files with a variable name
- Processing all files in a directory
- Processing a large number of files in parallel

Introduction

Experience has shown that many ODI developers limit their workflows by using only the most basic methods because they do not know how to implement more mature integration techniques. ODI offers a rich set of utilities and tools, looping controls, synchronous and asynchronous process invocations, and load plan management, which collectively can provide any developer the means to deliver elegant solutions to the most complex problems. This chapter is intended to explore several of the more advanced yet frequently occurring workflow situations that ODI can easily address. The recipes explained here will present some of the more mature techniques that can help a developer better take advantage of ODI orchestration.

Defining packages and loops for near real-time execution using a hybrid loop

There are many use cases where a specific job may require execution on a continual basis, perhaps the most common of which is when using a changed-data-capture process. A commonly occurring situation in **Changed Data Capture** (**CDC**) environments is the requirement that the ELT processes continuously monitor for data changes on the source system, rather than simply executing on a fixed schedule.

Unfortunately, a perpetual ELT process presents some logistical problems such as how to efficiently manage the job logs in the Operator navigator and how to afford an administrator the opportunity to terminate and restart the job. For example, if an ODI scenario is designed to recursively repeat an internal loop, all process activities will be collected into a single, enormous job log. On the other hand, if an ODI scenario is designed to reinvoke itself upon completion of its assigned tasks, the proliferation of individual job logs might overwhelm the operator manager.

This recipe is intended to demonstrate an implementation of a continuously running CDC process using a "hybrid" loop solution. To put it another way, this recipe will implement a CDC solution that uses a loop iterator for a set number of repetitions before respawning itself as a new session.

Getting ready

All references to tables in this recipe are taken from the data samples described in the *Preface* of this book. This recipe will also be reusing elements from the CDC section of this book. It will therefore be necessary to complete the *Chapter 6, Using CDC - consistent set* recipe prior to working with this example. This prerequisite includes establishing journalization on the `DEMO_SRC` data model as well as the reuse of the `Int_CDC_Consistent_Dept` and `Int_CDC_Consistent_Emp` interfaces.

How to do it...

1. Create a new package called `Pkg_Hybrid_Loop` and click on the **Diagram** panel.
2. Create and save a new variable called `PV_LOOP_CNTRL`.
    - Set the **DataType** option as `Numeric`
    - Set the **Keep History** option as `No History`

3. Drag-and-drop the `PV_LOOP_CNTRL` variable onto the canvas three times.

   For the first variable occurrence:

   1. Change the name to `Initialize CNTRL`.
   2. Select the **Type** option as **Set**.
   3. Click on the button **Assign**.
   4. Set the **Value** option to `0`.

   For the second variable occurrence:

   1. Change the name to `Increment CNTRL`.
   2. Select the **Type** option as **Set**.
   3. Click on the button **Increment**.
   4. Set the **Value** to `1`.

   For the third variable occurrence:

   1. Change the name to `Is CNTRL <= 5`.
   2. Select the **Type** option as **Evaluate Variable**.
   3. Set the **Operator** option as **<=**.
   4. Set the Value to `5`.

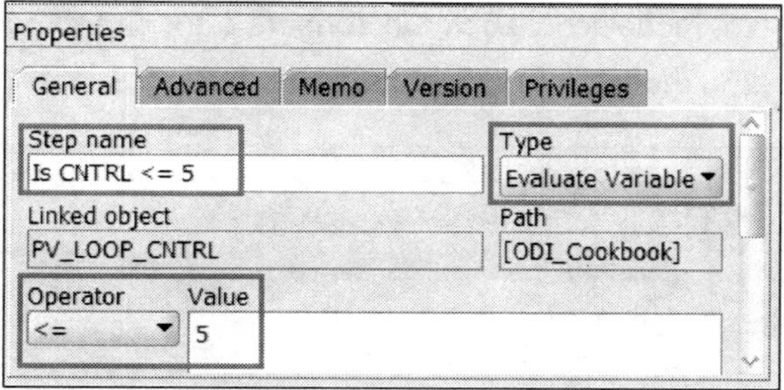

4. Expand the **Event Detection** Toolbox, click on the **odiWaitforLogData** utility, and then click it onto the canvas. Set the following properties:
   - The **Logical schema** parameter as `DEMO_SRC`
   - The **Subscriber** parameter as `SUB_A`

- The **CDC Set** parameter as <%=odiRef.getObjectName("L", "DEMO_SRC", "DEMO_SRC", "D")%>

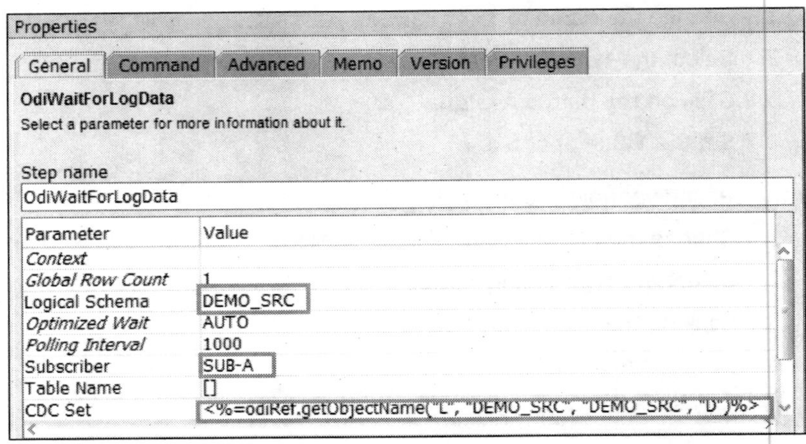

5. Drag-and-drop the **DEMO_SRC** data model onto the canvas two times.
    1. For both data model icons, select the **Journalizing Model** option from the drop-down list within the **Properties** panel.
    2. Click on the appropriate **Consumption** check-box for each model as follows:
        1. 1st model icon: **Lock Subscribers** & **Extend Window** options
        2. 2nd model icon: **Purge Journal** & **Unlock Subscribers** options

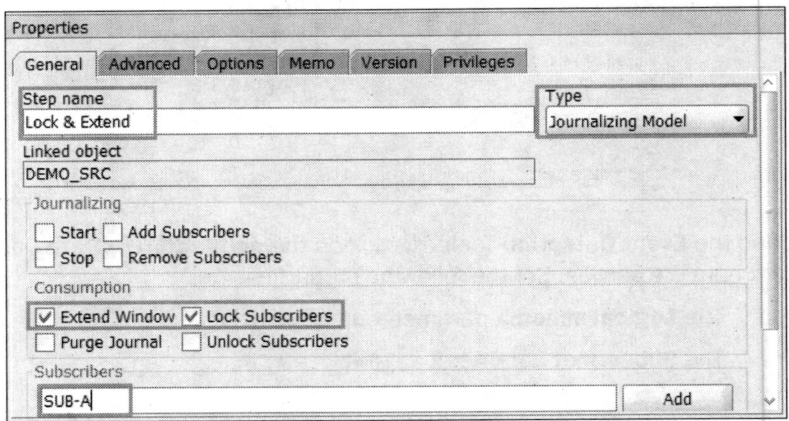

3. Change the step name to describe the action being taken for each model icon.

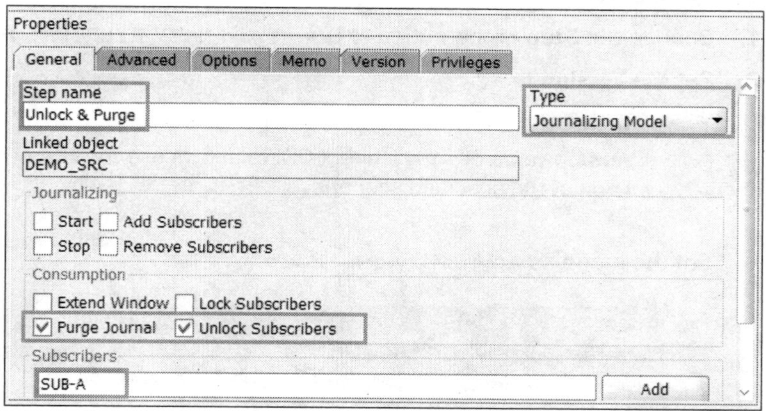

6. Drag-and-drop the following two interfaces from *Chapter 6, Inside Knowledge Modules: (SCD and CDC)*, onto the canvas:
   - `Int_CDC_Consistent_Dept`
   - `Int_CDC_Consistent_Emp`
7. Arrange and connect all of the package icons as shown in the following diagram:

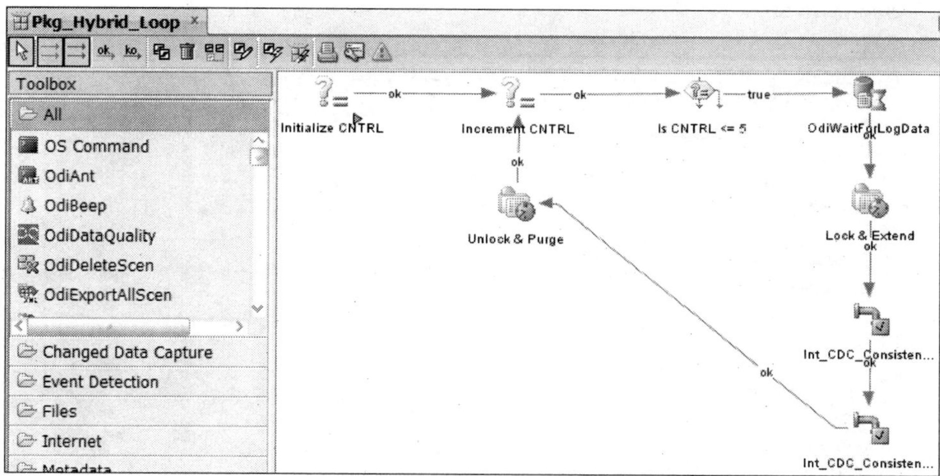

8. Save the package, but do not close it.
9. In the **Navigator** panel, right-click on the package name and select **Generate Scenario**.

10. Expand the scenario component folder underneath the **Pkg_Hybrid_Loop** package and then drag-and-drop the scenario onto the package diagram canvas (above the **evaluate variable** step).
    1. Change the **Step name** option to `Scenario PKG_HYBRID_LOOP`.
    2. Set the **Version** to `-1`.

A **Version** value of `-1` will direct ODI to always use the latest version of the specified scenario.

    3. Set the mode as `Asynchronous Mode`.

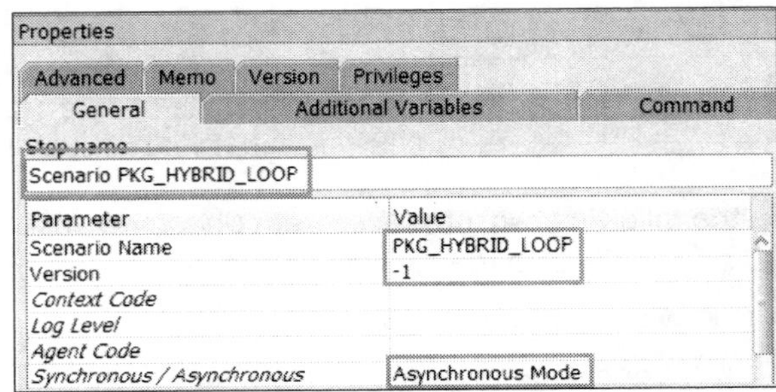

11. Connect the `KO` (false) condition of the **evaluate variable** step to the **launch scenario** step.

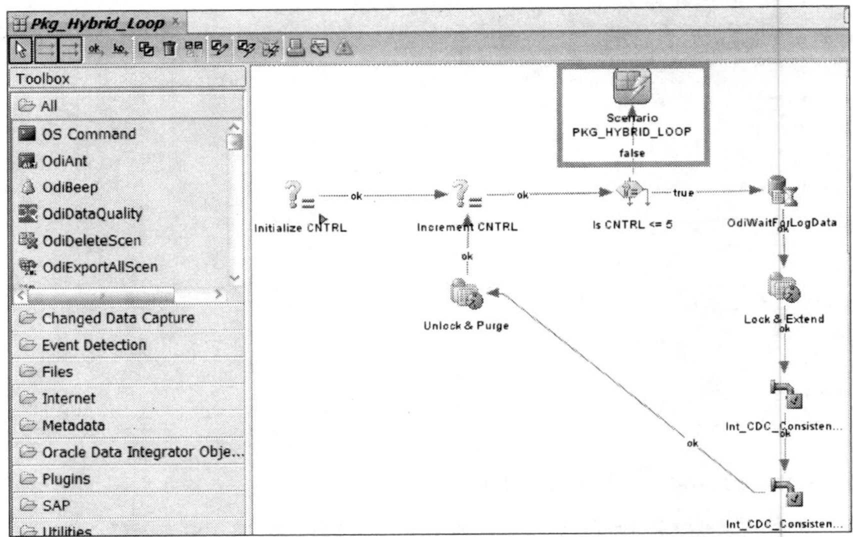

12. Resave and close the package.
13. In the **Navigator** panel, right-click on the **PKG_HYBRID_LOOP Version xxx** scenario and select **Regenerate**.

How it works...

Rather than looking for changed data on a fixed schedule, an efficient CDC workflow typically polls one or more of the journal tables for new transaction records to process. As was demonstrated by the consistent set CDC recipes in *Chapter 6, Inside Knowledge Modules: (SCD and CDC)*, a typical CDC workflow then locks and extends the change window, consumes all the available data for the specified subscriber (executing one or more interfaces), then releases the lock and purges all the relevant journal information. So far, so good.

The question now becomes how to best repeat the entire CDC process cycle without overloading any ODI resources (that is, operator logs). If we were to simply connect the basic package steps within an infinite loop, every step of every process cycle would be written into a single operator log, making it difficult to accurately monitor what ODI was doing at any given point in time. If however we immediately launched another session of the given scenario after each process cycle, we might flood the operator manager with too many individual logs.

This recipe presented a hybrid solution that used a combination of an internal process loop and an asynchronous scenario launch of itself. In this particular case, the CDC operations were repeated five times before terminating and spawning a new session of itself.

Using a file from a parameter variable

There are times when it may be necessary to load data from a file without knowing the exact name of the file prior to execution. To handle this unique situation, ODI provides a convenient method for developing an interface that references a data store with a variable resource name. All that is required at runtime is simply to pass a parameter containing the actual name of the file that needs to be processed.

This recipe will demonstrate how an interface can be developed initially using a known data store after which the resource name of that data store is replaced with an ODI variable. The interface can then be called from a package that accepts the true value or the resource (file) at runtime.

Getting ready

This recipe requires that the `DEMO_TRG` data model has been previously reverse engineered. Since this demonstration will load two text files, `WORK_HIST_011.txt` and `WORK_HIST_012.txt`, into the `TRG_WORK_HIST` table, be sure to place these files in the file directory/folder that has been defined in the Topology for the File Technology.

How to do it...

1. Create a new variable called PV_FILE_NAME. Set the **Data type** option as TEXT and the **Keep History** option as No History.
2. Within the DEMO_FILE data model, create a new data store called WORK_HIST; set the resource name as WORK_HIST_011.txt.
   1. On the **Files** tab:
      - Set the **File Format** option to **Delimited**
      - Set the **Heading (Number of Lines)** option to 0
      - Set the **Record Separator** option to **MS-DOS**
      - Set the **Field Separator** option to **Other** and then type (,) comma

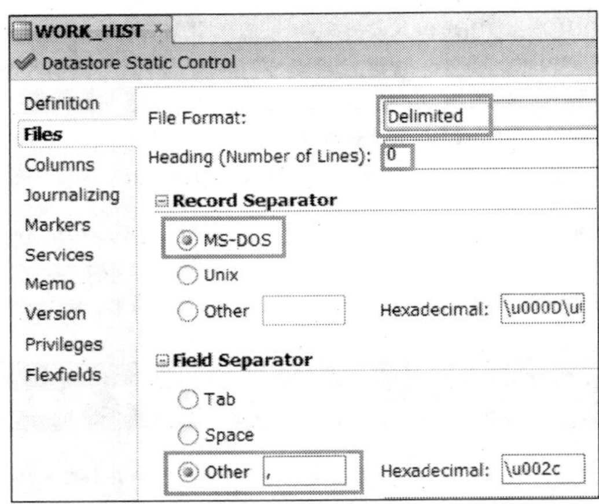

   2. On the **Columns** tab, click on **Reverse Engineer** (you may first be asked to save your work). ODI will scan the specified flat file and parse out three columns (C1, C2, C3) using data sampling methods for data typing.
      - Rename C1 to EMPNO
      - Rename C2 to DATE_WORKED; set the physical & logical length to 7
      - Rename C3 to HOURS; set the data type to Numeric; set the physical & logical length to 10

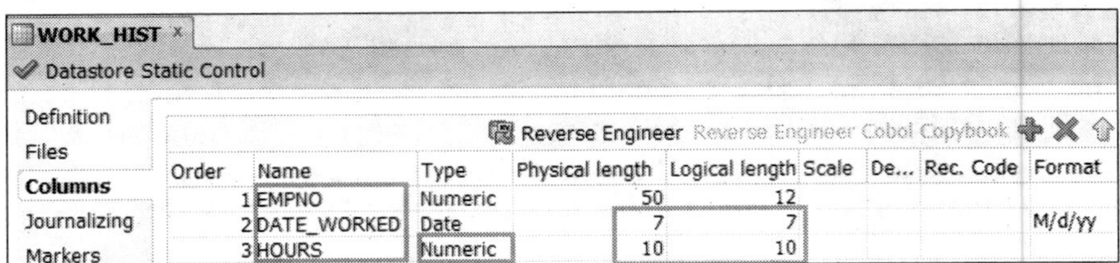

> Before proceeding to the next step, you may find it useful to save the data store in its current form and test the validity of its configuration by right-clicking on the data store name within the navigator and selecting the **View Data** option.

    3. Return to the **Definition** tab and change the **Resource Name** option to `#PV_FILE_NAME`. (Using a variable here will allow references to this data store to be more dynamic.)

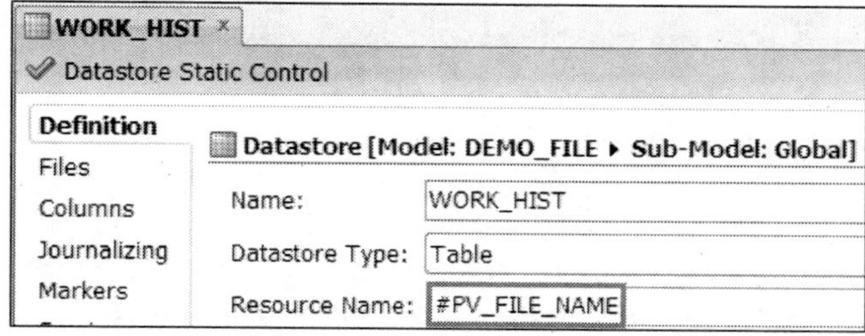

    4. Save and close the data store.
    5. Verify that the data store can read the file: right-click on **WORK_HIST** and select **DATA**. A display of file data should appear.

3. Create a new interface called `Int_Variable_File`.
    1. From the **DEMO_FILE** data model, drag-and-drop the **WORK_HIST** data store into the source area.
    2. From the **DEMO_TRG** data model, drag-and-drop the **TRG_WORK_HIST** data store into the target area.
    3. On the **Flow** tab, select the **LKM SQL to Oracle** and **IKM SQL Control Append** options (set **FLOW_CONTROL** as **false**).
    4. Save and close the interface.

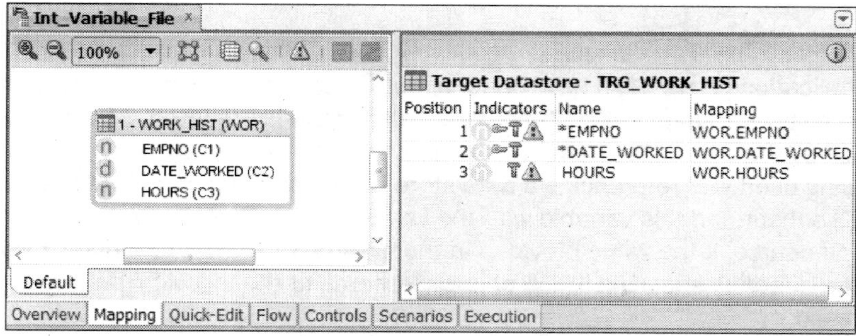

4. Create a new package called `Pkg_Variable_File`.
    1. Drag-and-drop the `PV_FILE_NAME` variable onto the diagram canvas. Set the **Type** option to **Declare Variable**.
    2. Drag-and-drop the **Int_Variable_File** interface onto the diagram canvas.
    3. Connect the two icons.
    4. Save and close the package.

5. Right-click on the **Pkg_Variable_File** package and select **Generate Scenario**. When the **Startup Parameter** display appears, choose **Use Selected**.
6. Expand the scenario component folder beneath the **Pkg_Variable_File** package and right-click on the **Pkg_Variable_File Version 001** scenario; select **Execute**. When the **Variable Usage** screen appears, deselect **Last used** and enter `WORK_HIST_011.txt` in the **Value** field.

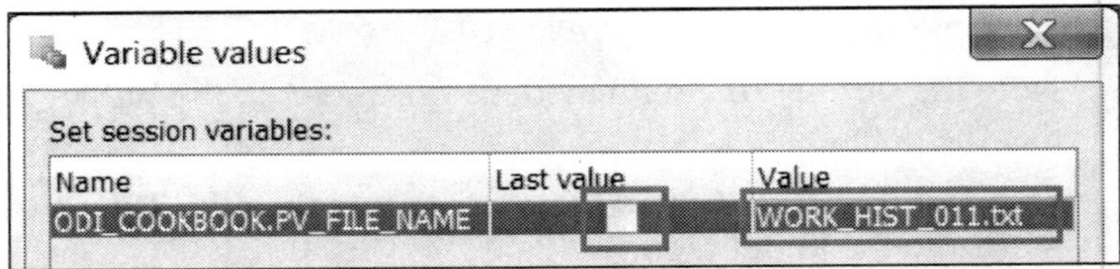

7. Verify a successful data load by reviewing the operator log or right-clicking on the **TRG_WORK_HIST** data store and selecting **DATA**.

How it works...

Once the applications have been developed, all future data store and topology references are resolved by the ODI agent at runtime. When a scenario is executed, ODI will identify every variable used by the embedded components and resolve their values. In this example, the interface being used was referencing a data store whose resource name was defined as a variable. ODI substituted this variable with the value passed into the scenario as a start-up parameter. Of course, if the value provided in the parameter did not reference a valid filename located in the directory specified in the physical schema of the topology, an error condition would be raised.

When an interface references an object using variables, those variables must either have a valid last value or be provided with a runtime value. In those situations, it is often necessary to execute the interface from within a package, and ultimately from within a scenario.

There's more...

Obviously the use of a variable within a data store is not limited to acquiring its value from a start-up parameter. Another popular method for setting the runtime value of a data store variable is to acquire its value from a table containing a list of filenames. You will see this technique in action in another recipe later in this chapter.

Detecting files with a variable name

Detecting files is actually a fairly trivial operation in ODI, but we have noticed that many people either do not know how to do it or even don't know that it is possible using ODI. Since detection is so simple, we will use this recipe to prepare the ground for the next two recipes.

Getting ready

For this recipe, we will detect when files are added to the `c:\temp` directory. Make sure that you have an instance of your file explorer ready. Create a directory `c:\temp\landing` and create three files in that directory: `EMP001.TXT`, `EMP002.TXT`, and `EMP003.TXT`. There is no need for any content in the files for this recipe. As part of this recipe, we will copy all three files into the `c:\temp` directory.

How to do it...

1. Create a new variable called `FILE_SIGNATURE`. Define that variable as `Alphanumeric`, and keep the latest value for the variable. There is no need for a default value or refresh statement.
2. Create a new package and call it `Detect Files`. Drag-and-drop the variable in the package. Set the type of action to **Set Variable** and enter the following as the value of the variable: `EMP*.TXT`.

3. From the Toolbox in the package, in the **Files** section, click on the `OdiFileWait` tool, then click in the package to add one instance of the tool. Once you have done so, connect the variable and the `OdiFileWait` tool as shown in the following screenshot:

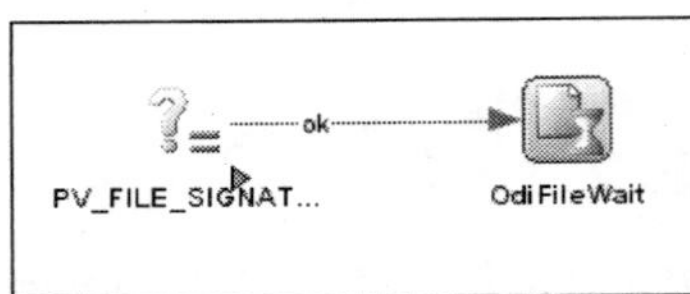

4. Click on the tool `OdiFileWait` to edit its parameters and set them as follows (keep the default value for all other options):
   - The `Step name` parameter as `Detect Files`
   - The `Action` parameter as `None`
   - The `Directory` parameter as `c:\temp\`
   - The `Filename Mask` option as `#FILE_SIGNATURE`
   - The `Timeout` parameter as `30000`
   - The `Error if file not found` parameter as `Yes`

5. We will now add two more steps for the outcome of the file detection. From the package toolbox, we will add one instance of the `OdiBeep` tool to connect to the successful output from the `OdiFileWait` tool, and an `OdiSendMail` tool to connect to the error output from `OdiFileWait`. For the `OdiSendMail` tool to work, you will have to set the parameters to connect to an SMTP server that works in your environment. Your package should now look like the following screenshot:

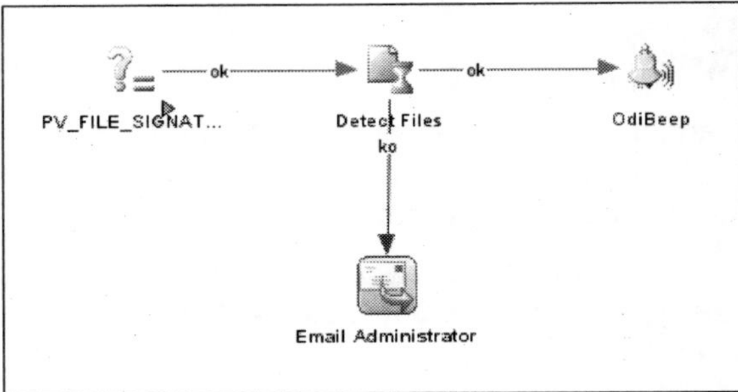

6. Execute the package without copying the files in the `c:\temp` directory. After 30 seconds, ODI should send an email as the files have not been detected as shown in the following screenshot:

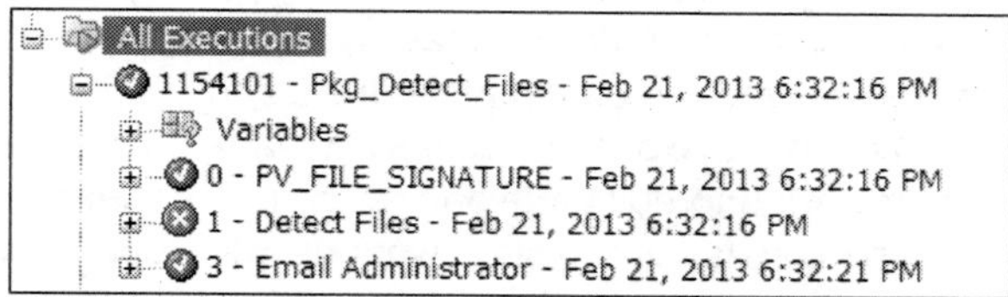

7. Now run the package again, and while the package is running, copy the three TXT files from `c:\temp\landing to c:\temp` (you have about 30 seconds to perform this operation before your package times out). As soon as the files are copied over, the package should detect the files and sound a beep.

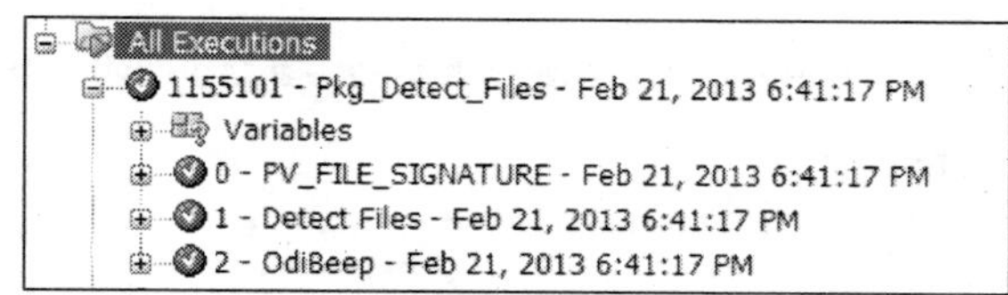

How it works...

As described in the introduction, the mechanisms here are relatively simple. ODI will poll the directory where the files are expected. The polling rate can be modified: it was one of the parameters of the `OdiFileWait` tool that we changed in our example. Based on your needs, you can also decide to never time out and wait indefinitely (set the timeout value to `0`). Our experience is that when files are expected and those files never appear, you probably have a problem somewhere, so setting a timeout value to raise an alert is usually a very good idea.

We have used a variable here to make the file pattern more dynamic, but we could also have hard-coded this value. Likewise, we do not have to wait for a pattern, for example, we could also explicitly wait for a specific file name (`EMP001.TXT` for instance).

There's more...

Usually when a process has to detect a file, you'll want to make sure that the file is not continuously detected. So it's a good practice at some point to move the file to another location before you go and try to wait for more files to become available for processing. The `Action` parameter of the `OdiFileWait` tool will allow you to move the files as they're being processed – or you can move the files using the `OdiFileMove` tool by another package step.

Processing all files in a directory

Now that we have a mechanism in place to detect files, it will be important to know which files are available in order to process them. Today we may be receiving EMP001.TXT, EMP001.TXT, and EMP003.TXT. Later we may receive other similar files. If the sequence of file names can easily be predicted, we can build the expected names in a variable and wait for the expected file. However if the file names are unpredictable and random, then we need to know what we have received before we can process them. This is what we will focus on within this recipe.

Getting ready

We can start from where we left off in the previous recipe and build the examples of this recipe into that package, or we can create an entirely new package. In either case, we will still need the files EMP001.TXT, EMP002.TXT, and EMP003.TXT in the c:\temp directory.

To make sure that our example is reusable, we will create a table with the following structure:

```
Create table FILESLIST (
  BATCH_ID number,
  FILE_TYPE varchar2(10),
  FILE_NAME varchar2(250)
);
```

We will have to reverse engineer this table because we will use it to load our list of files.

How to do it...

1. Create a new variable called BATCH_ID.
    1. Define that variable as Numeric, and keep the latest value for the variable. Set the **Refresh Statement** option to Select 0 from dual and select a logical schema that points to an Oracle database (such as DEMO_SRC or DEMO_TRG if you have followed the recipes in earlier chapters of this book).
    2. Right-click on the variable name and select **Generate Scenario** and uncheck **Startup Parameter** when you are prompted for the scenario parameters. Expand the tree below the variable name until you see the scenario name: right-click on that name and execute the scenario. If the scenario runs successfully, you should see one line in the **History** tab of the variable, with a seeding value of **0**.

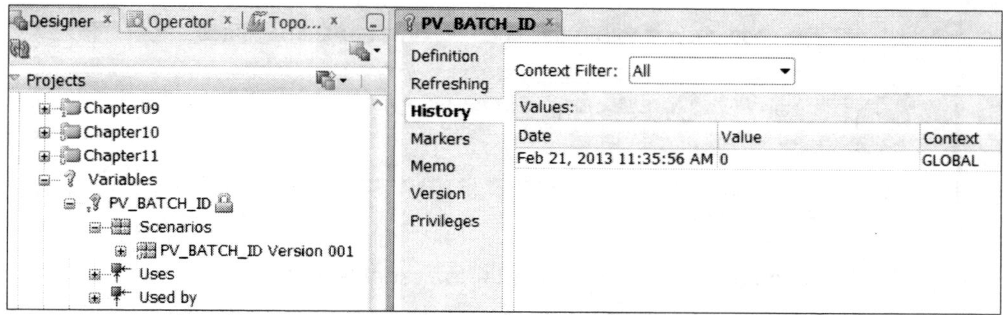

2. Either create a new package or modify the one that we created in the previous recipe. If you choose to modify the previous package, you can remove the **OdiBeep** step and replace it by dragging and dropping the `BATCH_ID` variable in the package. If you create a new package, drag-and-drop the variable in the package as your first step.
    1. Set the type to `Set Variable`
    2. Select the **Increment** option
    3. Set the increment value to `1`

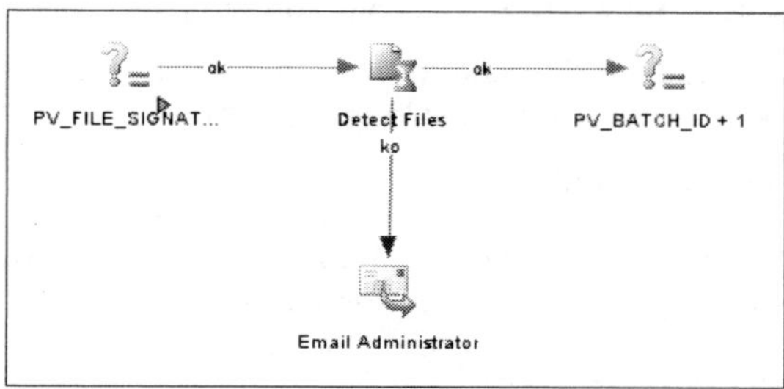

3. Now create an ODI procedure and call it `List Files`. Add a step, call it `List Files from OS`, set the technology to Jython, and enter the following code in the **Command** box:

```
import os
sCommand=''' dir /B c:\\temp\\#FILE_SIGNATURE > c:\\temp\\
FilesListEmp.txt'''
iError=os.system(sCommand)
if  iError <> 0 :
        raise '''OS command has signalled error %d for command %s'''
% (iError, sCommand)
```

> For people trying to run this code on Linux, you can replace
>
> ```
> ''' dir /B c:\\temp\\#FILE_SIGNATURE > c:\\
> temp\\FilesListEmp.txt'''
> ```
>
> with
>
> ```
> ''' "ls -1 /temp/#FILE_SIGNATURE > /temp/
> FilesListEmp.txt" '''.
> ```

4. Add this procedure to your package after the variable `BATCH_ID`.
5. In a **File** model that points to the `c:\temp` directory, declare the file `FilesListEmp.txt` as follows:
    1. **Name** as `FilesListEmp.txt`.
    2. **Resource** as `FilesListEmp.txt`.
    3. **Format** as `Delimited`.
    4. **Heading** as `0`.
    5. **Record Separator** as **MS-DOS** (set this as **Unix** if you are running on Unix or Linux).
    6. **Field separator** as `Tab` (basically something we will not have in the file).
    7. Manually add another column, name it `FILE_NAME`, set the type to `String` and the physical and logical length to `250`.
    8. Save the file definition.
6. Create an interface with the file `FilesListEmp.txt` as a source and the table `FILESLIST` as a target. Use the following mappings:

Column name	Mapping	Mappings Location
BATCH_ID	#BATCH_ID	Target
FILE_TYPE	'EMP'	Target
FILE_NAME	FIL.FILE_NAME	Staging area

> If you have generated your file on Linux, the filenames may come with the complete path for the files. If this is the case, you may want to use a substring transformation to only keep the filename. A transformation like the following will work:
>
> ```
> substr(FIL.FILE_NAME, instr(FIL.FILE_NAME, '/',
> -1)+1)
> ```

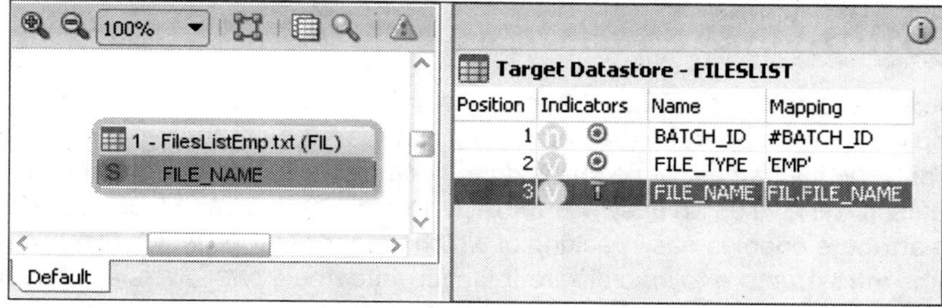

7. Select the **LKM File to SQL** and **IKM SQL Control Append** options (set **FLOW_CONTROL** as **false** in the **Flow** tab). Save the interface and add it to your package after the procedure. Connect the procedure to the interface.

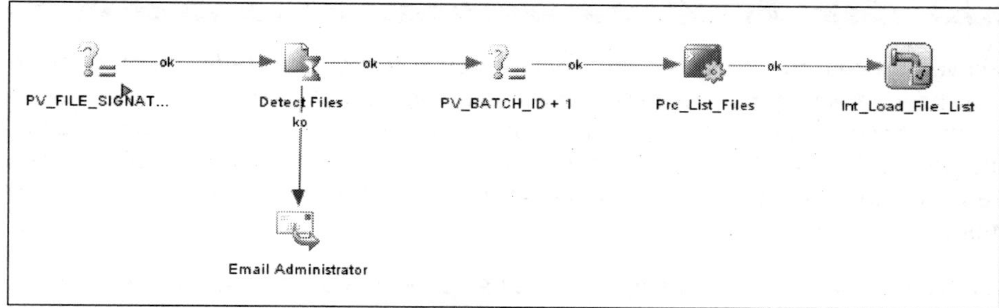

8. Run the package. After the package has run completely, you should find the list of files in the table: open the interface, right-click on the name of the target table and select **Data**. You will see all three files.

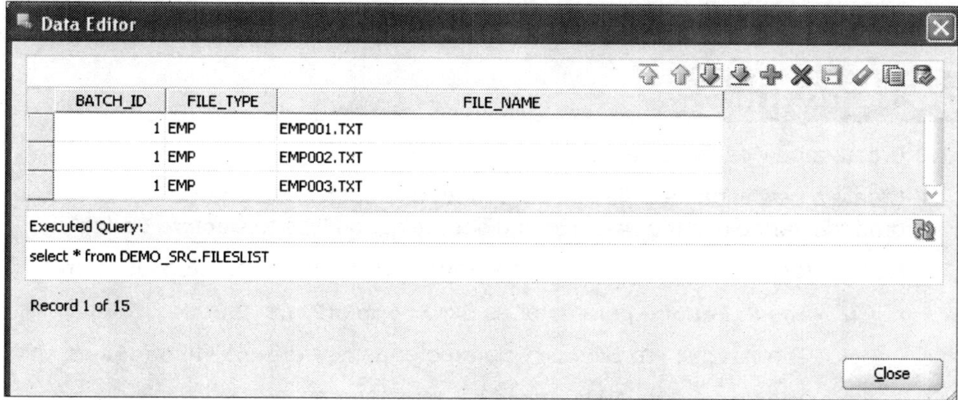

How it works...

The idea here is to have a list of files that can easily be processed. The most important point here is simply to use the operating system listing commands (with the proper parameters) to retrieve only the file names. Once this is done, loading the list of files into a table has many benefits; it will give us an easy way to track down what has been loaded and when (the `BATCH_ID` attribute enables easy tracking of which batches loaded which files). We can also use the same infrastructure to load different file formats (the `FILE_TYPE` attribute enables the differentiation of the table entries) and most important, we can now run any SQL we choose to retrieve the files associated with a given load or retrieve the filenames one by one for further processing.

Processing a large number of files in parallel

If you have worked through the two previous recipes, you should already have in place a framework for detecting the presence of a variable number of files in a designated location. You will also have developed a method for processing each of those files as they appear in a prepared list (that is, a table). But consider a situation where there are hundreds or even thousands of files to be processed. Managing all of those files serially would likely prove to be a bottleneck.

In this recipe, we will enhance the file-processing framework by introducing a way to execute the most critical components in parallel.

Getting ready

We will start from where we left off with the previous recipe and to do that, we will build on what we already have: a table that contains a list of files to be processed.

How to do it...

1. Create a new package called `ProcessFiles`.
2. Create a new variable called `FILE_PARAM` and set it as `Alphanumeric`. Drag-and-drop the variable in the package and set the action type to **Declare Variable**.
3. Add the tool `OdiMoveFile` to the package and set the parameters as follows:
    - The `FileName` parameter as `c:\\temp\#FILE_PARAM`.
    - The `Target Directory` parameter as `c:\\temp\\Processed`.
    - The `Move Sub Directories` parameter as `No`.

- Leave all the other options to their default value. Connect the variable and the tool in the package so that the tool is executed after the variable has been declared.

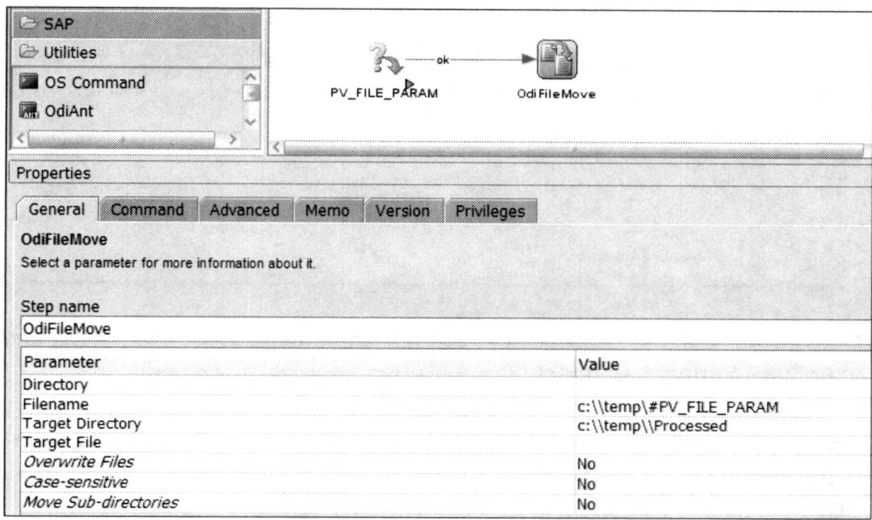

4. Save and close the package. Right-click on the package name in the object tree and select **Generate Scenario**.
5. Create a variable called `LoopFileNum`. This variable is `Numeric` and has neither default value nor refresh statement.
6. Create a second variable called `LoopFileName`. This variable is `Alphanumeric` and has no default value. In the **Refresh** tab, select the logical schema that points to the location where the `FILESLIST` table was created, and type the following code for the select query:

```
select FILENAME
from (select FILE_NAME FILENAME, rownum ROW_NUM
      from DEMO_SRC.FILESLIST
      where BATCH_ID = #BATCH_ID and FILE_TYPE = 'EMP')
where ROW_NUM = #LoopFileNum
```

7. Open the package created in the previous recipe (`Detect File`).

8. Drag-and-drop the variable `LoopFileNum` at the end of the package (just after the last step) and set the action type to **Set Variable**. Assign a value of `1` to the variable. Connect the last step to the variable.

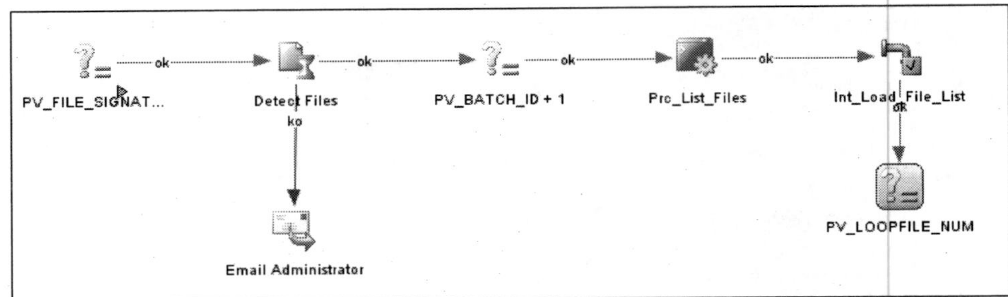

9. Drag-and-drop the variable `LoopFileName` into the package and set the action type to **Refresh Variable**. Connect `LoopFileNum` to `LoopFileName`.

10. Drag-and-drop the scenario that was created in step 4 of this recipe (you have to drill under the package name in the tree to find the scenario). Change the execution mode to `Asynchronous`, and set the `SessionName` parameter to `#LoopFileName`. In the **Additional Variables** tab, add an entry to select the current project and, the variable `FILE_PARAM`, and then set the value to `#LoopFileName`.

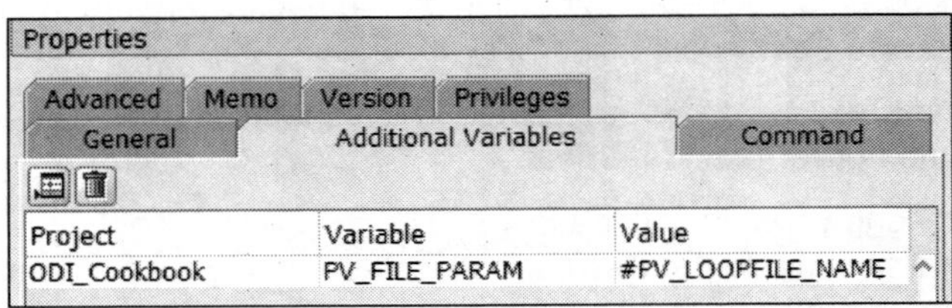

Connect `LoopFileName` to the scenario. If `LoopFileName` fails, connect it to an `OdiBeep` tool (this would mean that you have exhausted the list of files to be processed).

11. Drag-and-drop the variable `LoopFileNum` again in the package and set the action type to **Set Variable.** Increment the value by `1`. Connect the scenario to this instance of `LoopFileNum`. Connect this instance of `LoopFileNum` to `LoopFileName`.

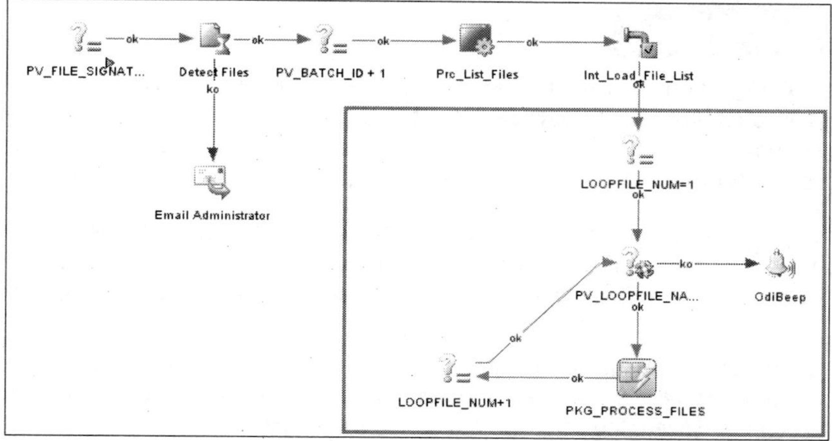

12. Save and execute the `Detect File` package. The package will spawn a separate process of the `ProcessFile` scenario for each file, and each one of these processes will be named after the file that it loads. In addition, all file processing jobs will be executed in parallel.

13. After all the jobs have been completed, you can confirm that everything worked according to expectations by verifying that the files have been moved to the `c:\temp\Processed` folder.

How it works...

The most challenging part of running the same process multiple times in parallel is to understand which instance may have failed out of the entire set. Imagine if we were running the above scenario for hundreds of files instead of just three. And then imagine if one of those loads had failed; how quickly could you know which file was causing a problem?

With the design proposed in this recipe, not only can we use the exact same job definition for all files, but we can immediately see which file is being processed from the operator view. In case of a problem, we would know which one has to be reprocessed or investigated for errors.

Whenever you design an application that can invoke asynchronous processing, it is extremely important to understand the processing capacity of the designated server. In order to prevent a system overload, use the Topology navigator to modify the `Agent` parameter (the **Maximum Number of Sessions** option) as a means of limiting the number of concurrent sessions.

There's more...

In this recipe, we only focused on the detection of the files and on how to easily identify the sessions in charge of each file. Obviously these sessions might be doing a lot more than just moving the files around, but hopefully this will give you a framework for processing large numbers of files.

Keep in mind though that if you are running the same process multiple times in parallel, you may encounter table collisions during the generation of staging (`C$`, `I$`) tables. If this is the case, you can apply the techniques described in *Chapter 5, How to use Substitution methods in Java*.

9

XML and Web Services

In this chapter, we will cover the following tasks:

- Defining a connection to XML within ODI
- Processing complex files with ODI
- Processing XML data within an RDBMS not in memory
- Invoking web services from ODI
- Invoking asynchronous ODI web services with callbacks
- Configuring container-based authentication with ODI web services

Introduction

XML and web services are becoming common place in enterprise data integration, and ODI provides many features that allow organizations to take full advantage of their **service oriented architectures** (**SOA**). These features allow ETL developers to incorporate XML and their SOA infrastructure into their ETL processing. ODI and SOA directly complement one another; both can read, write, and transform flat files, XML, relational data, and so on, and both directly integrate with web services, however both technologies have their strengths. SOA is great at message-based integration, while ODI is great at performing bulk integrations and heavy transformations of data.

ODI is SOA native, and this allows ODI to take full advantage of existing SOA services. The SOA services do not need to be recreated in ODI since ODI can directly invoke web services; the opposite is also true. If there is a bulk transformation that already exists in ODI, this can easily be invoked from the SOA environment. As we will see in this chapter, with the proper ingredients, you can dramatically expand the scope of a standard integration implementation by combining your data integration and SOA environments with ODI.

The following sources will be extremely helpful as you investigate these techniques *Oracle Data Integration Documentation*, provided in *Oracle® Fusion Middleware Developer's Guide for Oracle Data Integrator* (available here: `http://docs.oracle.com/cd/E23943_01/integrate.1111/e12643/toc.htm`) explains all the generic concepts.

For more detailed explanations about specific options and fields, Oracle Data Integrator provides the ODI Studio online help, which will answer many questions. You can access this additional help from any screen inside the ODI Studio, where it will provide contextual help on the different concepts you are looking at. To view this, press the *F1* key on your keyboard when you have the focus on the window you need help with.

In this chapter, we will begin with the basics of defining a connection to an XML file, continuing with transforming and processing complex files, then put all the concepts together by using web services within ODI.

Defining a connection to XML within ODI

In this section, we will look into how to create a new connection to an existing XML file technology. The connection will be created as a new data server with the XML technology. Technologies are defined in the Topology navigator, so all you need to do to get started is to make sure that this navigator has been selected.

In this recipe, we will create a new data server based on the XML file that is delivered with the ODI demonstration environment. This XML file is named `GEO_DIM.xml` and is located on the ODI Companion CD and zipped in the `oracledi-demo.zip` file within the `[demo home] \oracledi\demo\xml` directory. ODI has an XML JDBC driver, which will be used to connect to the XML file. The XML driver can also utilize a DTD or XSD file, which is used to generate the logical data stores used by ODI to represent the XML file and hierarchical relationships within the XML file. If the DTD or XSD does not exist, this information will be inferred during the reverse engineering process based on the XML metadata. An XSD file will be automatically generated based on the XML metadata. We will review this in detail after the following step-by-step instructions.

How to do it...

1. First make sure that all the technologies are visible: there is a drop-down menu on the top right of the Topology navigator; the option **Hide Unused Technologies** must not be selected.

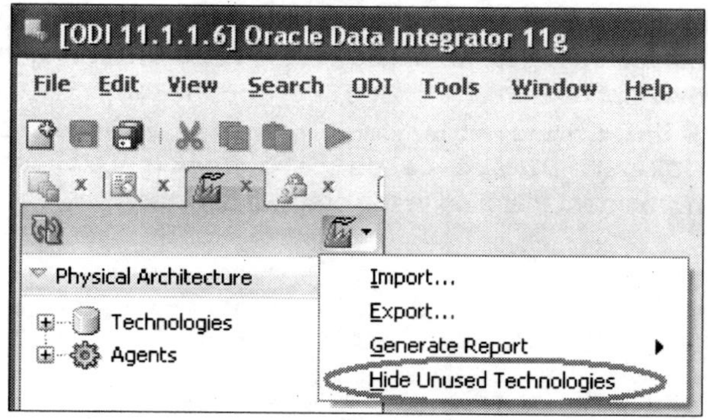

Then expand **Technologies**, right-click on the **XML technology**, and select **New Data Server**. ODI will create a new data server, which will open in the **Data Server Editor**.

2. Within the **Data Server Editor**, set the XML **Data Server** properties as follows:

   In the **Definition** tab, set the **Name** to `XML_GEO_DIM`, **Array Fetch Size** and **Batch Update Size** are left to default of **30**, the other properties are not set and left blank. For more information on the additional parameters click *F1* for the ODI online help.

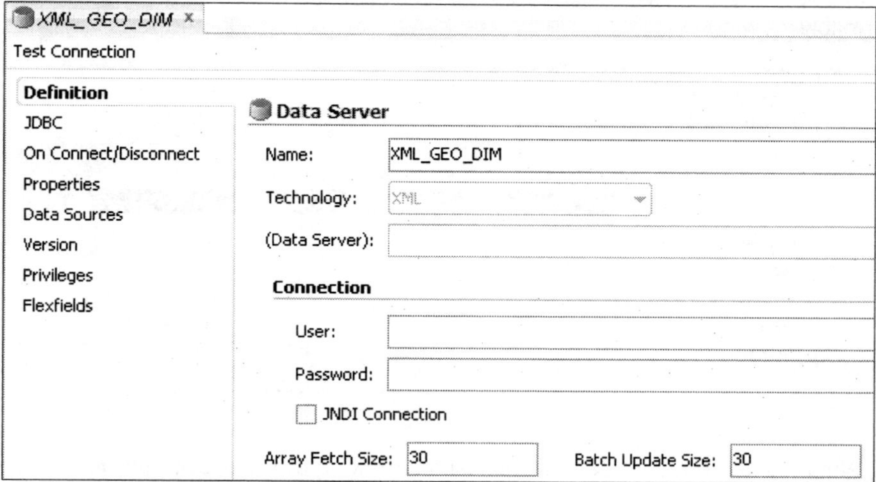

Click on **JDBC**. Here we will setup the JDBC connectivity to the `GEO_DIM` XML file. Similar to other technologies, we will define the **JDBC Driver** and the **JDBC URL** options. The **JDBC Driver** option is `com.sunopsis.jdbc.driver.xml.SnpsXmlDriver`, and the **JDBC URL** is `jdbc:snps:xml?f=../../../demo/xml/GEO_DIM.xml&re=GEOGRAPHY_DIM&ro=false&case_sens=true&s=GEO&d=GEO_DIM.dtd` [the demo environment installed in the oracledi directory].

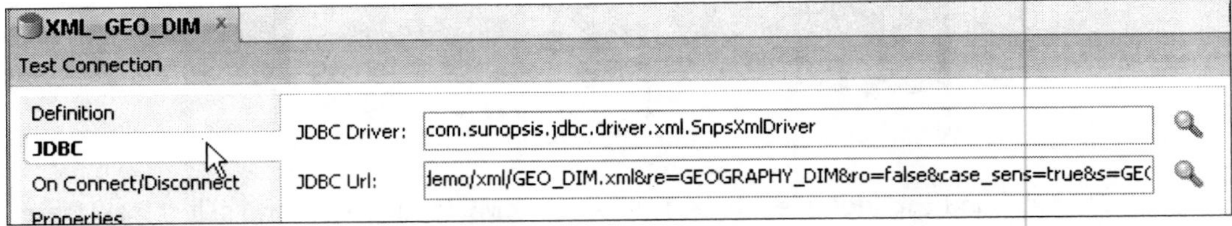

Click on the **Test Connection** button to make sure that the connection information is correct and ODI can connect to the XML file.

Click **OK** when prompted to save before testing.

Ignore the information window saying you have to register a schema when you are prompted to save. Then click on the **Test** button when you are prompted by the following window:

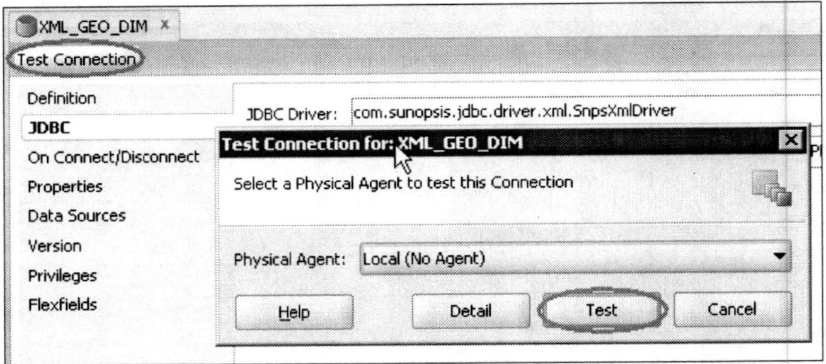

When your connection test is successful, click on the **Test Connection** button again. When prompted, select **Detail** to confirm the version number of the JDBC driver and that of the database.

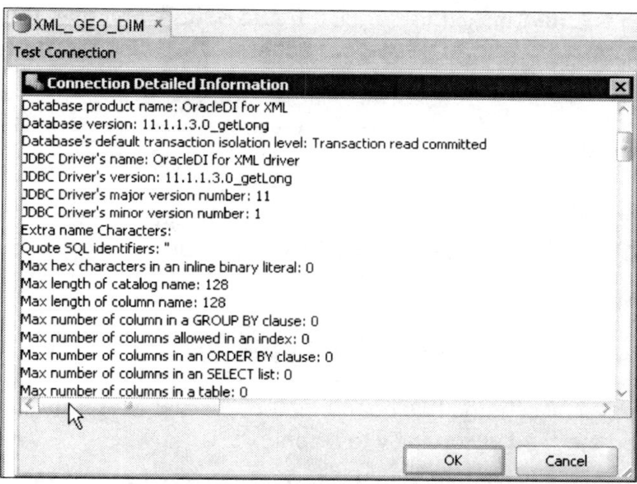

3. Close the `XML_GEO_DIM` data server. A connection to the `GEO_DIM` XML file has now been created, however we need to create the physical schema:
    - Right click on the `XML_GEO_DIM` data server and click on **New Physical Schema**.
    - On the **Definition** tab, set the **Schema (Schema)** value and **Schema (Work Schema)** value to **GEO**, which should be the only option in the drop-down list. Uncheck **Default** and leave all the other parameters as defaults.

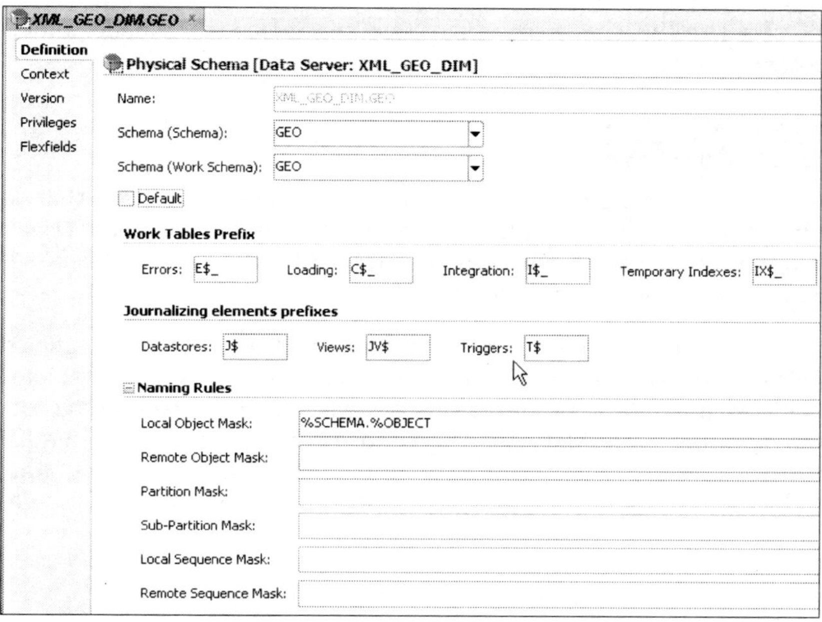

- Select the **Context** tab, click the **Add** button, and map the `Global` **Context** to the `XML_GEO_DIM` **Logical Schema**. By typing the logical schema, this will create the new **Logical Schema** `XML_GEO_DIM`.

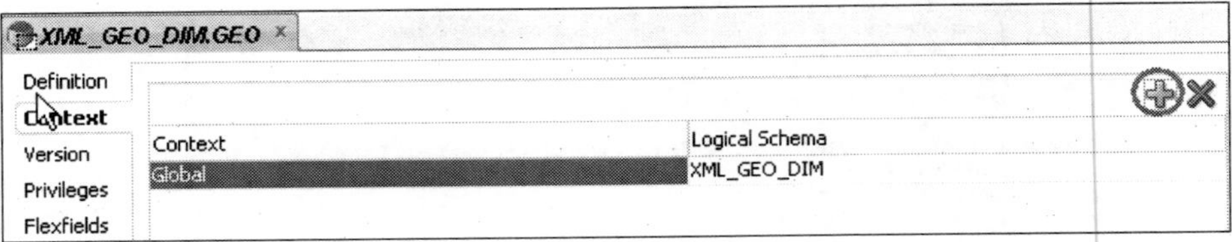

- Save and close the **Physical Schema**.

4. Once the physical schema has been created, verify the logical schema was also created and mapped accordingly to a context.
    - Expand the **Logical Architecture** accordion, expand **XML technology**, and click on **Logical Schema** `XML_GEO_DIM`.

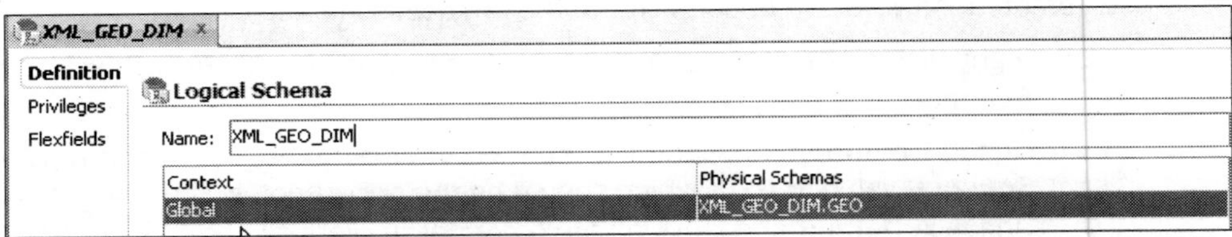

5. The `GEO_DIM` XML file can now be reverse engineered into a model within the ODI designer navigator.

How it works...

XML files are natively supported within the standard ODI architecture. Each XML file is represented by a data server in the ODI Topology. The Oracle Data Integrator Driver for XML allows ODI to connect to the XML file as well as to the DTD or XSD; no additional setup or configuration is required for this connectivity.

The XML data server creation process follows the standard procedure for creating data servers within ODI. The JDBC Driver and the JDBC URL are the key setup parameters needed for the XML connectivity. The JDBC URL is where additional parameters can be added for additional configuration of the XML connectivity. For instance, in this recipe, the JDBC URL is `jdbc:snps:xml?f=../../../demo/xml/GEO_DIM.xml&re=GEOGRAPHY_DIM&ro=false&case_sens=true&s=GEO&d=GEO_DIM.dtd`.

The parameters used are as follows:

- `f`: XML file Location, this can be HTTP, FTP, or URL file
- `re`: root Element, used when several root elements exist or to reverse engineer a specific message definition
- `ro`: read Only, specify if the XML file is opened in read only
- `case_sens`: case Sensitive Mode
- `s`: schema Name, relational schema where XML data will be loaded
- `d`: DTD/XSD File Location, file location can be HTTP, FTP, or URL file

Additional XML JDBC URL parameters are documented in the ODI documentation:

`http://docs.oracle.com/cd/E17904_01/integrate.1111/e12644/appendix_xml_driver.htm`

Once the data server is created, a physical and logical schema can be created for the data server. As with any physical server, a data schema and work schema are needed; the schema was defined within the JDBC URL `s=GEO`, and this schema is used for both the data and work schema. The logical schema creation also follows the standard process for ODI.

Once the XML data server, physical schema, and logical schema are created and the JDBC test is successful, the XML file can be reversed engineered within a model and the data stores can be used as a source or target within an ODI interface. Using XML files within ODI integrations is just as easy as using a relational table or a flat file. XML files can be joined and filtered as part of the source data set. The XML can also be transformed by applying SQL functions to the mapping expression, as with other technologies in ODI.

There's more...

Real applications for this recipe are used more often than you may think. Every integration project will have a requirement for XML file integration at some point. XML has quickly become the de facto standard for sharing data over the Internet. This section covers a full spectrum of use cases such as integration within a single web application, integration across applications including cloud to on-premise /on-premise to cloud, integration across enterprises, and business-to-business integration.

Processing complex files with ODI

A new and highly underutilized feature introduced in ODI 11.1.1.5.0 was the ability to leverage complex files such as a source and target for integrations. Previously, ODI could handle many different types of files out of the box, such as delimited, fixed length, XML, and many other variations. But how would you handle a flat file sent from a vendor that has multiple record formats within the same file? The file could have many different types of delimiters as well as record formats. For example, the following line of a file has many different delimiters as well as objects within the line:

```
123456,^Joeseph Kraichely^15th Street,1923,Soulard,63104,US, MO, 314-
555-1212
```

This row contains a person record, `person` is a complex object made up of an `ID`, `Name`, and an `Address`. Each of these can be defined in the schema descriptor for the file, this is stored in an native XSD (nXSD). The `nXSD` file defines how the records are delimited and how each delimited item is stored in the overall object. In this recipe, `ID`, `Name`, and `Address` are part of the `person` object, `Address` can be broken out into its own complex element. Once we have decided on a logical structure to store the complex file data, we use either a text editor or the Native Format Builder Wizard to create the `nXSD` file.

More information on the Native Format Builder Wizard can be found at `http://docs.oracle.com/html/B25307_02/nfb.htm`

For creating the nXSD schemas, an XML editor can be used or the Native Format Builder, which is installed with Oracle SOA Suite. I find the Native Format Builder to be useful as a starting point. However, for detailed control over the `nXSD` file, I prefer editing the XSD file directly.

Getting ready

For this recipe, the nXSD schema would be as follows:

```
<schema attributeFormDefault="qualified"
elementFormDefault="qualified"
    targetNamespace="http://xmlns.oracle.com/ias/pcbpel/fatransschema/
demo"
    xmlns:tns="http://xmlns.oracle.com/ias/pcbpel/fatransschema/demo"
    xmlns="http://www.w3.org/2001/XMLSchema"
    xmlns:nxsd="http://xmlns.oracle.com/pcbpel/nxsd"
    nxsd:version="NXSD" nxsd:stream="chars">

    <element name="person" type="tns:person"/>
    <complexType name="personType">
```

```
        <sequence>
        <element name="Customer" type="tns:partnerType"/>
        </sequence>
        </complexType>
    <complexType name="Customer">
        <sequence>
        <element name="uid" type="string" nxsd:style="terminated"
        nxsd:termindatedBy=","/>
        <element name="name" type="string" nxsd:style="surrounded"
        nxsd:surroundedBy="^"/>
        <element name="address" type="tns:addressType"/>
        </sequence>
    </complexType>
    <complexType name="addressType">
        <sequence>
        <element name="street1" type="string"
        nxsd:style="terminated"
        nxsd:termindatedBy=","/>
        <element name="street2" type="string"
        nxsd:style="terminated"
        nxsd:termindatedBy=","/>
        <element name="city" type="string" nxsd:style="terminated"
        nxsd:termindatedBy=","/>
        <element name="postal-code" type="string"
        nxsd:style="terminated"
        nxsd:termindatedBy=","/>
        <element name="country" type="string"
        nxsd:style="terminated"
        nxsd:termindatedBy=","/>
        <element name="state" type="string"
        nxsd:style="terminated"
        nxsd:termindatedBy=","/>
        <element name="phone" type="string"
        nxsd:style="terminated"
        nxsd:terminatedBy="${eol}"/>
        </sequence>
    </complexType>
</schema>
```

When reverse engineered, ODI would generate three logical data stores for this complex file: `Person`, `Customer`, and `Address`. The `Person` data store contains the metadata about the complex file, and `Customer` and `Address` contain the data for the complex file. A primary foreign key relationship is also created between `Customer` and `Address` to allow for querying and storing the data correctly.

A good starting point is the *Oracle Data Integrator Driver for Complex Files Reference*. At the time of writing, this chapter can be found here:

`http://docs.oracle.com/cd/E21764_01/integrate.1111/e12644/appendix_complex_driver.htm`

How to do it...

1. For this recipe, the following data will be used:

```
123456,^Joeseph Kraichely^15th St.,1924,Soulard,63111,US,
MO,314-555-1212
123345,^Big Red^Marvin Gardens,800,Red
City,94000,US,CA,650-555-1212
001|Widget XYZ|20000,2,+40000+
002|Widget 123|10000,5,+50000+
003|Widget @#$|20000,2,+40000+
004|Widget ...|10000,5,+50000+
005|Widget %|1000,20,+20000+#110000
```

2. Save this file as `Purchase.txt` and note the location. In this example, the file will be saved as `c:\Purchase.txt`, and all references to this file will use this location.

   In this recipe, there are many different delimiters as well as multiple record types. The data in the file represents an invoice with the purchaser, seller, and the line items. Within the `PURCHASER` and `SELLER` object there is another related object: `ADDRESS`. The following ODI diagram shows the overall logical architecture and relationships:

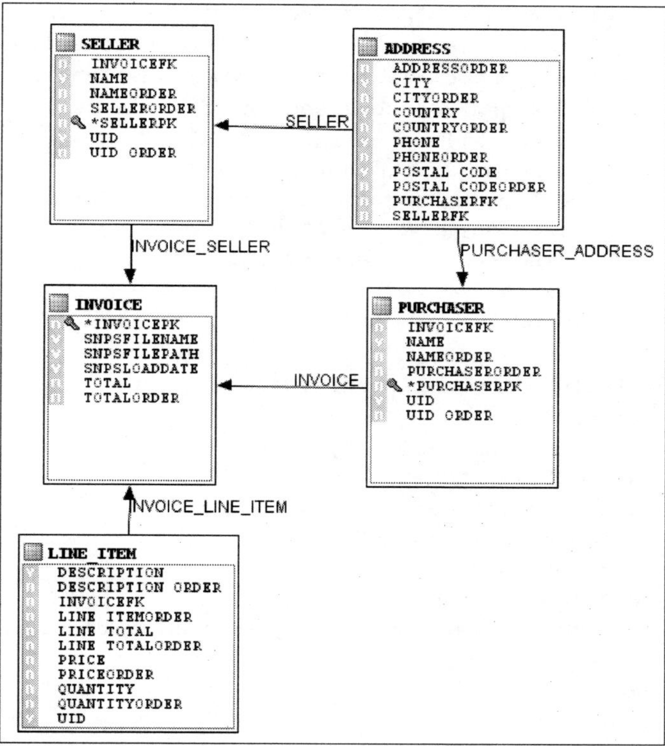

3. Once the data and relationships of the complex file are understood, an `nXSD` file needs to be created. The `nXSD` file outlines the schema and it's relationships as well as how to parse the file. The following `nXSD` file is used to define the schema as well as the parsing for this recipe file:

```
<schema attributeFormDefault="qualified"
elementFormDefault="qualified"
                targetNamespace="http://xmlns.oracle.com/ias/
pcbpel/fatransschema/demo"
                xmlns:tns="http://xmlns.oracle.com/ias/pcbpel/
fatransschema/demo"
        xmlns="http://www.w3.org/2001/XMLSchema"
        xmlns:nxsd="http://xmlns.oracle.com/pcbpel/nxsd"
        nxsd:version="NXSD" nxsd:stream="chars">

    <element name="invoice" type="tns:invoiceType"/>

    <complexType name="invoiceType">
        <sequence>
```

```
        <element name="purchaser" type="tns:partnerType"/>
        <element name="seller" type="tns:partnerType"/>
        <element name="line-item" type="tns:line-itemType"
            maxOccurs="unbounded" nxsd:style="array"
            nxsd:cellSeparatedBy="${eol}"
            nxsd:arrayTerminatedBy="#"/>
            <element name="total" type="double"
            nxsd:style="terminated"
            nxsd:terminatedBy="${eol}"/>
    </sequence>
</complexType>

<complexType name="partnerType">
    <sequence>
    <element name="uid" type="string"
    nxsd:style="terminated"
    nxsd:termindatedBy=","/>
    <element name="name" type="string"
    nxsd:style="surrounded"
    nxsd:surroundedBy="^"/>
    <element name="address" type="tns:addressType"/>
    </sequence>
</complexType>


<complexType name="addressType">
    <sequence>
    <element name="street1" type="string"
    nxsd:style="terminated"
    nxsd:termindatedBy=","/>
    <element name="street2" type="string"
    nxsd:style="terminated"
    nxsd:termindatedBy=","/>
    <element name="city" type="string"
    nxsd:style="terminated"
    nxsd:termindatedBy=","/>
    <element name="postal-code" type="string"
    nxsd:style="terminated"
    nxsd:termindatedBy=","/>
    <element name="country" type="string"
    nxsd:style="terminated"
    nxsd:termindatedBy=","/>
    <element name="state" type="string"
    nxsd:style="terminated"
```

```
        nxsd:termindatedBy=","/>
        <element name="phone" type="string"
        nxsd:style="terminated"
        nxsd:terminatedBy="${eol}"/>
        </sequence>
    </complexType>

    <complexType name="line-itemType">
        <sequence>
        <element name="uid" type="string"
        nxsd:style="terminated"
        nxsd:termindatedBy="|"/>
        <element name="description" type="string"
        nxsd:style="surrounded"
        nxsd:surroundedBy="|"/>
        <element name="price" type="double"
        nxsd:style="terminated"
        nxsd:terminatedBy=","/>
        <element name="quantity" type="integer"
        nxsd:style="terminated"
        nxsd:terminatedBy=","/>
        <element name="line-total" type="double"
        nxsd:style="surrounded"
        nxsd:surroundedBy="+"/>
        </sequence>
    </complexType>

</schema>
```

For this recipe, save this file as `Purchase.xsd` and note the location. In this example, the file will be saved as `c:\Purchase.xsd` and all references to this file will use this location

4. Now that the schema has been defined and validated, the complex file data server will need to be created within the ODI Topology. First make sure that all the technologies are visible: there is a drop down menu on the top right of the **Topology** navigator; the **Hide Unused Technologies** option must not be selected.

   Then, expand **Technologies**, right-click on the **Complex File** technology, and select **New Data Server**. ODI will create a new data server that will open in the **Data Server** editor.

5. Within the **Data Server** editor, set our complex data server properties as follows:

   In the **Definition** tab, set the **Name** to `COMPLEX_FILE_Purchase`; **Array Fetch Size** and **Batch Update Size** are left to default of `30`; the other properties are not set and are left blank.

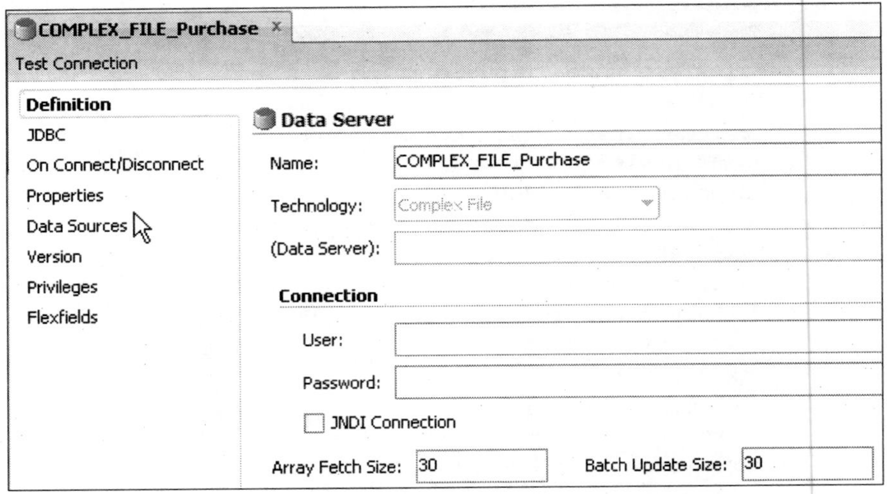

   Click on **JDBC**. Here we will setup the JDBC connectivity to the `Purchase.txt` file. Similar to other technologies, we will define the **JDBC Driver** and the **JDBC Url** value. The **JDBC Driver** value is `oracle.odi.jdbc.driver.file.complex.ComplexFileDriver`, and the **JDBC URL** value is `jdbc:snps:complexfile?f=c:/Purchase.txt&d=c:/Purchase.xsd&re=invoice&ro=true`

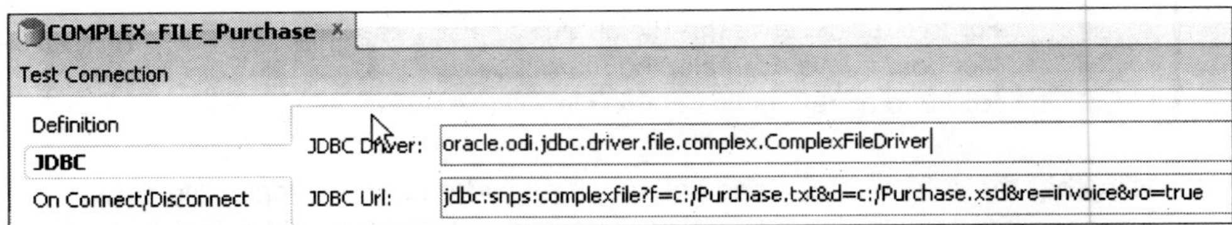

   Click on the **Test Connection** button to make sure that the connection to the information is correct is correct and ODI can connect to the complex file

   Click on **OK** when prompted to save before testing.

Ignore the information window saying you have to register a schema when you are prompted to save. Then, click on the **Test** button when you are prompted by the following window:

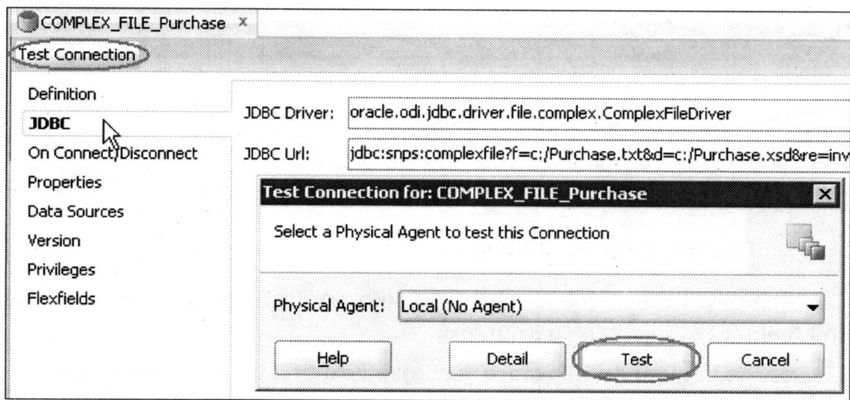

If your connection failed, review the parameters you have just entered.

6. Close the `COMPLEX_FILE_PURCHASE` data server. A connection to the `Purchase.txt` file has now been created, however we need to create the physical schema.

   Right-click on the `COMPLEX_FILE_PURCHASE` data server and click on New Physical Schema.

   On the **Definition** tab, set the **Schema (Schema)** and **Schema (Work Schema)** values to **PURCH**, which should be the only option in the drop-down list. Uncheck **Default**, and leave all the other parameters as defaults.

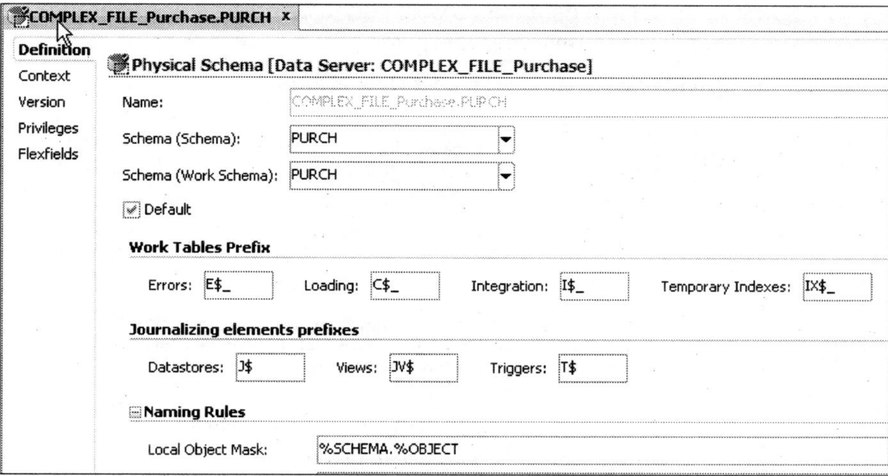

Select the **Context** tab, click the **Add** button, and map the `Global` **Context** to the **Logical Schema** `COMPLEX_FILE_PURCHASE`; the **Logical Schema** value will be created automatically when the **Physical Schema** is saved.

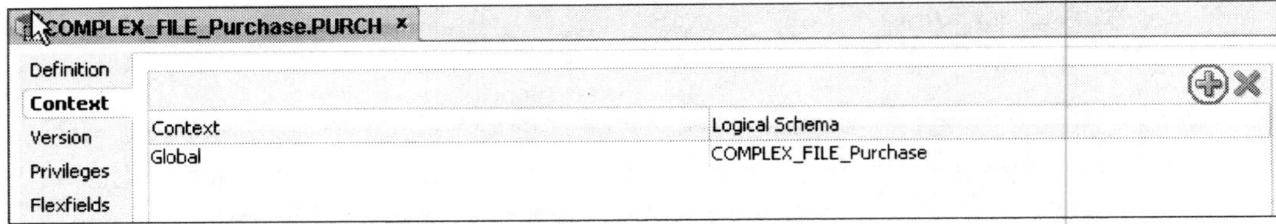

Save and close the **Physical Schema**.

7. Once the physical schema has been created, verify the **Logical schema** was created and mapped accordingly to a context.

   Expand the **Logical Architecture** accordion, expand the **XML technology**, and double click on `COMPLEX_FILE_PURCHASE`.

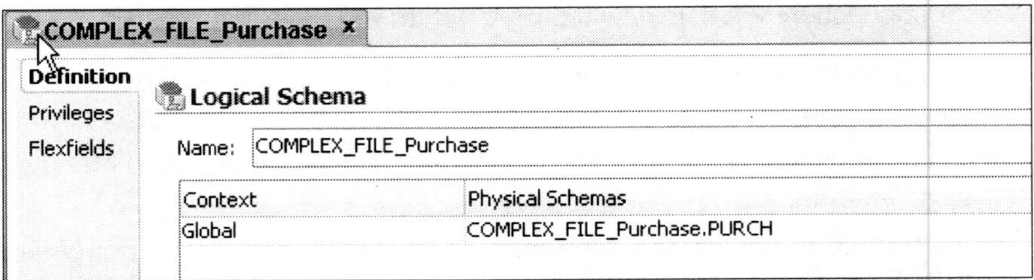

8. The connectivity is now setup to the `Purchase.txt` complex file. To use the file in an integration, the logical data stores will need to be reverse engineered. To do this, make sure you are in the **Designer** navigator.
9. Expand the **Models** accordion and select **New Model**.

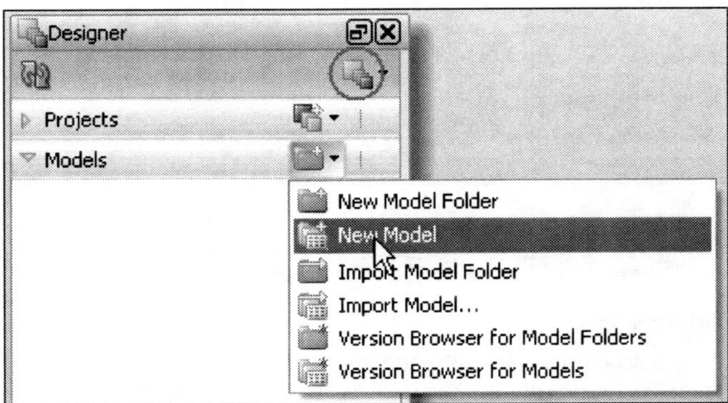

10. On the **Definition** tab, specify the name as `CP_PURCHASE`, the code will be automatically filled, set the **Technology** as **Complex File**, and set the **Logical Schema** to **COMPLEX_FILE_PURCHASE**.

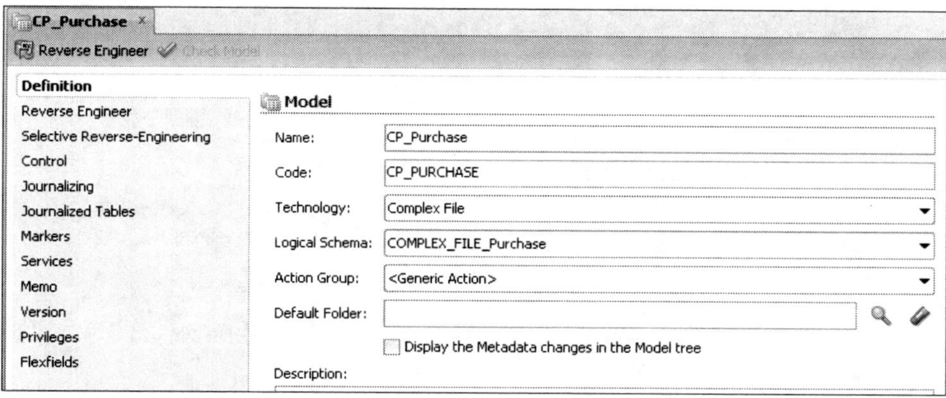

11. Click on the **Reverse Engineer** button to create the `Purchase.txt` logical data stores.

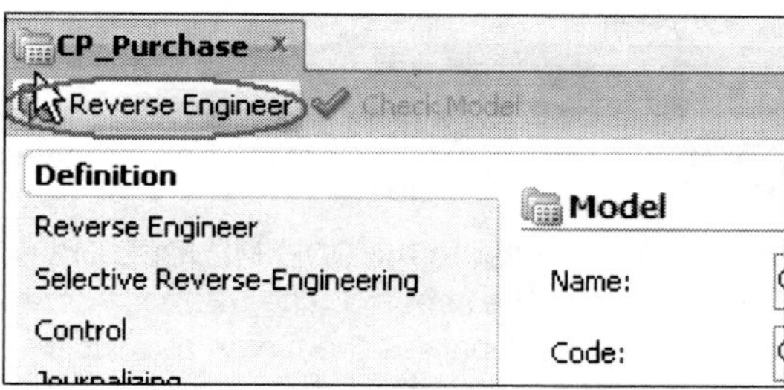

12. The following data stores are generated from the reverse engineering process.

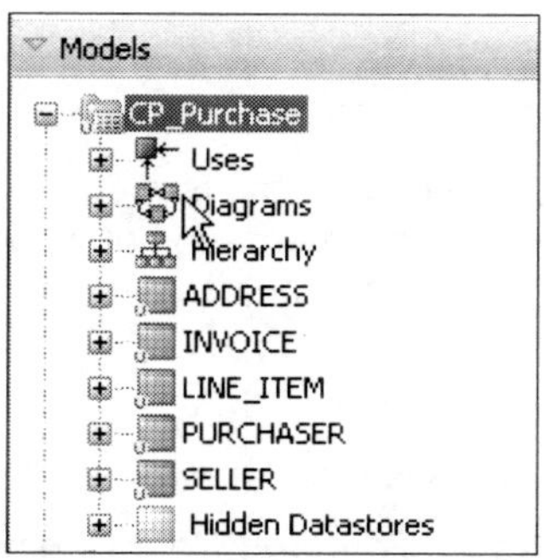

13. The data stores can now be used in an interface. The primary and foreign keys are generated during the reverse engineering process and the relationships will be drawn when adding to the sources panel within an interface as shown:

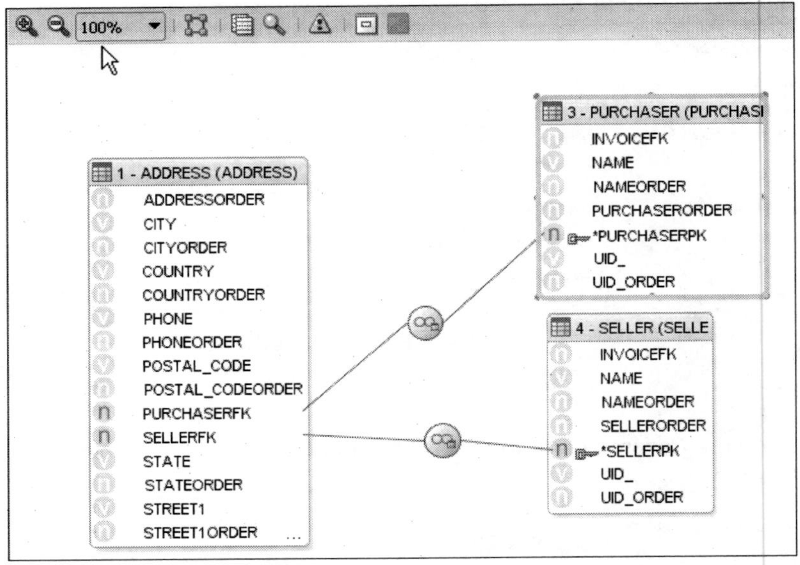

How it works...

The ODI Complex File Driver is very similar to the ODI XML JDBC Driver. Both utilize a schema that is defined in an XSD file to derive the schema. The `nXSD` file contains the parsing information as to how the driver actually parses the file. In this recipe, we just scratched the surface of what is possible within the complex file driver. With more than 30 constructs defined for the native format schema, the complex file technology can be adapted to virtually any structure for storing data in a file.

There's more...

There are many additional examples and use cases within the *Oracle® Fusion Middleware User's Guide for Technology Adapters* documentation at `http://docs.oracle.com/cd/E21764_01/integration.1111/e10231/nfb.htm#autoId38`.

For example:

- Removing or adding namespaces to XML with no namespace
  - By utilizing the Native Format Builder with native XML files, namespaces can be added to inbound XML files with no namespaces, and you can also remove namespaces from outbound XML files.

- Defining the `Choice Condition` schema for a complex file structure
    - By utilizing the Native Format Builder with a complex file with multiple record types, the choice condition can be used to build three types out of outbound structures.
- Defining choice condition with LookAhead for a complex file structure
    - Building on the previous example, the choice condition can also be utilized with LookAhead to verify a record type with information that occurs after the record starts.

Processing XML data within an RDBMS not in memory

By default, ODI will perform XML processing within the default in-memory database, HSQL. For out of the box JVM settings, small XML files, less than 2-3 megabytes, the in-memory database will perform as expected. However, for larger XML files, or when there is a large amount of files, it is easy to exceed the reserved amount of memory for processing within the JVM. When the JVM memory size is exceeded, the JVM will crash, and it is necessary to tune the JVM settings to allow for the large amount of memory the in-memory database will require. The XML JDBC Driver can also be set up to use a relational database for this processing. Similar to the in-memory database, a relational schema will be created in the RDBMS to match the logical schema. The physical schema in the relational database will be managed by ODI; the artifacts will be created, updated, and deleted as needed by the ODI XML JDBC Driver. The set up to use an RDBMS for XML processing is relatively straightforward, however many developers overlook this option, since it is not set up by default. In this recipe, we will setup an XML file as a source within ODI, which we will use a relational database schema for processing. We will create a relational schema to store the physical schema for the XML file and set up the connectivity to this file.

A good starting point is the *Oracle® Fusion Middleware Connectivity and Knowledge Modules Guide for Oracle Data Integrator*. At the time of writing, this chapter can be found here:

`http://docs.oracle.com/cd/E17904_01/integrate.1111/e12644/appendix_xml_driver.htm`

How to do it...

1. First we will create a new relational schema for the ODI XML JDBC Driver to manage the XML schema within. ODI supports many RDBMS's as an option to store the XML schema. For this recipe, we will use the Oracle database. The following SQL can be used to create the user:

The DBA role is added for simplification and should not be used for a production environment.

```
-- USER SQL
CREATE USER ODI_XML IDENTIFIED BY oracle1
DEFAULT TABLESPACE "USERS"
TEMPORARY TABLESPACE "TEMP";
-- ROLES
GRANT "DBA" TO ODI_XML ;
```

If you followed the first recipe in this chapter, the instructions here are very similar, however, since there are some differences, it is easier to create a new data server for this exercise.

2. Connectivity to the relational database can be setup in multiple ways. For this recipe, we will use a properties file, which has all the necessary parameters to connect to the database. This file needs to be created in the `odi/oracledi/userlib` directory within the application data directory. An easy way to find this directory is to navigate to the `%appdata%` directory. For ODI Agent installation, the file would need to be copied to the `lib` directory of the agent. The following properties will be used for this recipe:

```
driver=oracle.jdbc.driver.OracleDriver
url=jdbc:oracle:thin:@localhost:1521:xe
user=ODI_XML
password=fDyamifqOyM4kuvbr9Q1
schema=ODI_XML
drop_on_connect=Y
create_tables=AUTO
create_indexes=Y
truncate_before_load=Y
ids_in_db=Y
drop_tables_on_drop_schema=Y
use_prepared_statements=Y
use_batch_update=Y
batch_update_size=30
commit_periodically=Y
num_inserts_before_commit=1000
reserve_chars_for_column=3
reserve_chars_for_table=3
```

Be sure to update the password and to use the `encode.bat(sh)` executable to create the encrypted password.

The parameters can also be set at the data server level within the JDBC URL for more information, refer to the ODI documentation located at `http://docs.oracle.com/cd/E17904_01/integrate.1111/e12644/appendix_xml_driver.htm`

Save the properties in the file `%appdata%\odi\oracledi\userlib\geo_dim.properties`.

3. Now that the relational schema and the external database properties file have been setup, the XML data server will need to be created within the ODI Topology. First make sure that all the technologies are visible: there is a drop-down menu on the top right of the Topology navigator; the **Hide Unused Technologies** option must not be selected.

   Then expand **Technologies**, right-click on the **XML technology**, and select **New Data Server**. ODI will create a new data server, which will open in the **Data Server** editor.

4. Within the **Data Server** editor, set our XML **data server** properties as follows:

   In the **Definition** tab, set the **Name** to `XML_GEO_DIM_DB`, **Array Fetch Size** and **Batch Update Size** are left to default of `30`, the other properties are not set and are left blank:

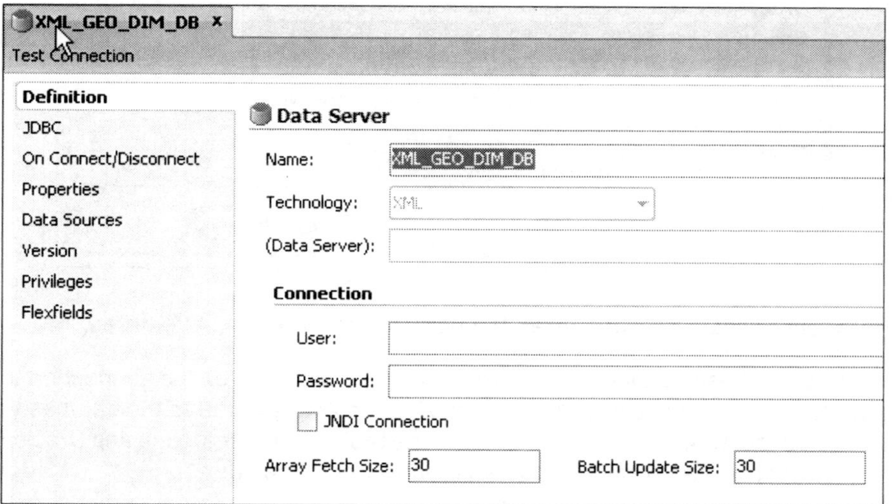

Click on **JDBC**. Here we will setup the JDBC connectivity to the `GEO_DIM` XML file. Similar to other technologies, we will define the **JDBC Driver** and **JDBC URL** value. The **JDBC Driver** value is `com.sunopsis.jdbc.driver.xml.SnpsXmlDriver`, and the **JDBC URL** value is `jdbc:snps:xml?f=c:/GEO_DIM.xml&re=GEOGRAPHY_DIM&ro=false&case_sens=true&s=GEO&d=c:/GEO_DIM.dtd&dp=geo_dim.properties&lf=c:/GEO_DIM.log&ll=31`:

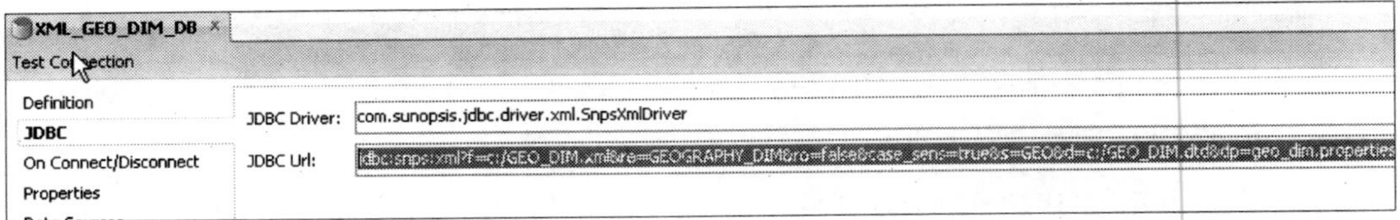

Click on the **Test Connection** button to make sure the connection information is correct and ODI can connect to the XML file.

Click **OK** when prompted to save before testing.

Ignore the information window saying you have to register a schema when you are prompted to save. Then, click on the **Test** button when you are prompted by the following window:

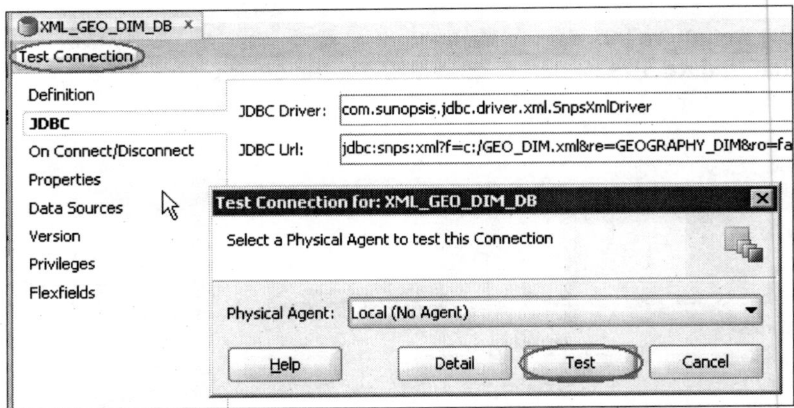

If your connection failed, review the parameters you have just entered.

5. As ODI verifies the connection to the XML file, it also verifies the connection to the external database as well as synchronizing the XML schema to the database along with the data. Use an SQL tool to verify the tables were created; using Oracle SQL Developer we can verify the following tables were created:

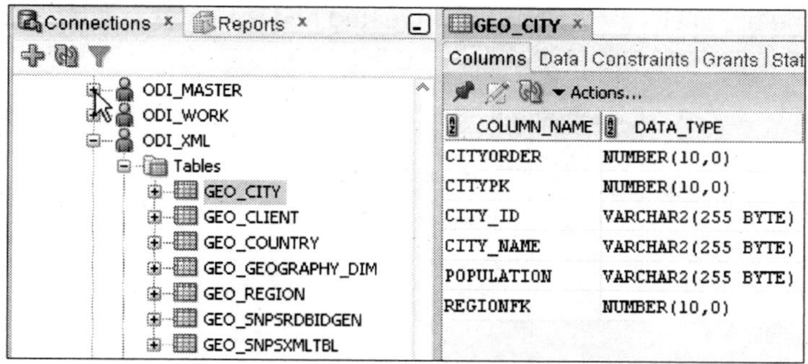

6. Close the `XML_GEO_DIM_DB` data server. A connection to the `GEO_DIM` XML file has now been created, however we need to create the physical schema.

   Right-click on the `XML_GEO_DIM_DB` data server and click on New Physical Schema.

   On the **Definition** tab, set the **Schema (Schema)** and **Schema (Work Schema)** values to **GEO**, which should be the only option in the drop-down list. Uncheck **Default**, leave all the other parameters as defaults.

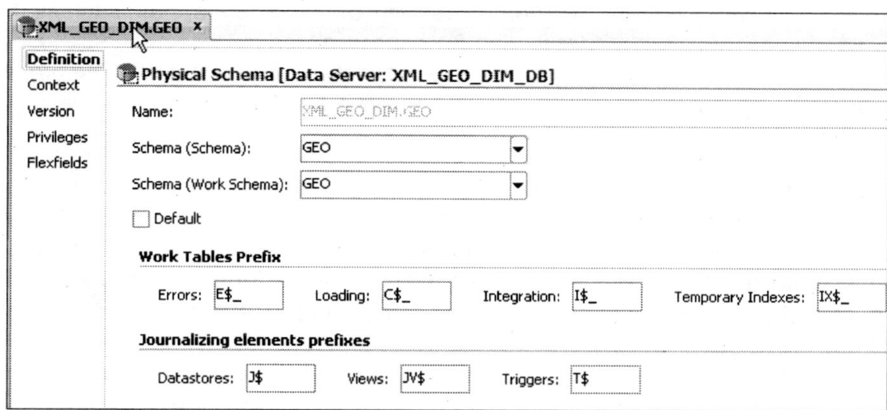

   Select the **Context** tab, click the **Add** button, and map the `Global` **Context** to the **Logical Schema** `XML_GEO_DIM_DB`.

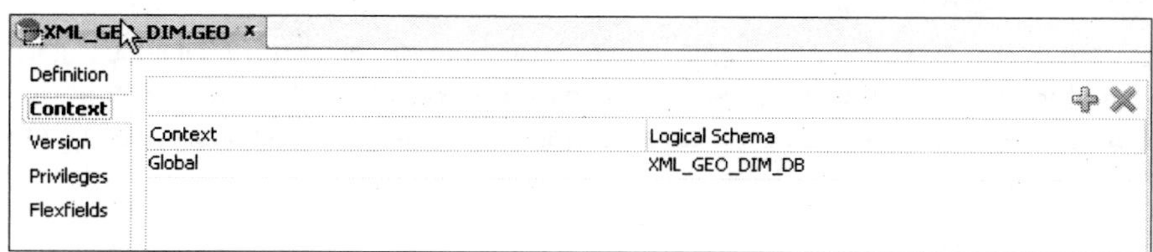

   Save and close the **Physical Schema**.

7. Once the physical schema has been created and the context is mapped, the logical schema is created automatically and mapped accordingly to a context.

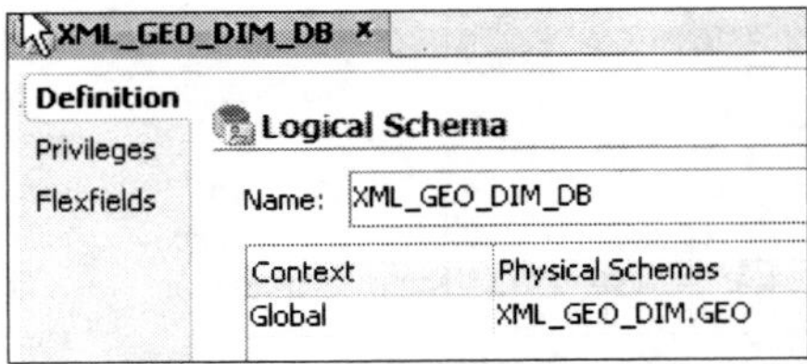

8. The `GEO_DIM` XML file can now be reverse engineered into a model within the ODI Designer navigator.

How it works...

ODI's default method for processing XML data is to perform the processing within the in-memory database. This database is actually a relational in-memory database that the ODI XML JDBC driver is set to connect to out of the box. The ODI XML JDBC Driver can easily be configured to work with a physical relational database management system such as the Oracle Database as well as other databases. This is completed by passing the ODI XML JDBC Driver the correct property/value pair for the external database connectivity. The properties can be passed as part of the JDBC URL or within a properties file that exists within the ODI classpath.

Utilizing an external database for XML processing is highly recommended for larger files or large amounts of files, which could possibly exceed the JVM memory settings. This will allow for faster processing of the XML as well as allow for better memory and resource management, since the database is managing these resources and not the JVM. Another benefit of using the physical relational database is that the tables can be queried directly if needed from within ODI or other tools. This allows for direct updating of the XML data in the physical table. Also, if the final target is the same physical database, the insert from the XML staging area to the target table will not have to travel over the network, therefore increasing performance.

There's more...

As mentioned in the *Complex File* recipe, the complex file driver and the ODI XML JDBC driver are very similar. The complex file driver can also be setup to store its physical schema in an external database. The steps to setup an external database for a complex file are the same as what was used in this recipe.

Invoking web services from ODI

SOA and data integration are very complimentary to one another. It is now common place to have an integration and data integration overlap, with web services being called from data integration and data integration routines being called from web services. In this recipe, we will use ODI to execute a web service. The cool part about the recipe is that the web service that we will call is actually an ODI integration compiled to an ODI scenario.

A good starting point is *Oracle® Fusion Middleware Developer's Guide for Oracle Data Integrator - Running Integration Processes*. At the time of writing, this chapter can be found here:

`http://docs.oracle.com/cd/E21764_01/integrate.1111/e12643/running_executions.htm#BABDHJJF`

Before you start this recipe, a standalone or JEE Agent needs to be created. If you do not have a standalone or JEE Agent, follow the appropriate recipe in *Chapter 10, Advanced Coding Techniques using the ODI SDK* to create one.

How to do it...

1. Start the ODI Agent. Then start the ODI Studio and create a new package as follows:

   Package: `SLEEP_20`

   Add ODI tool: `ODI_Sleep`

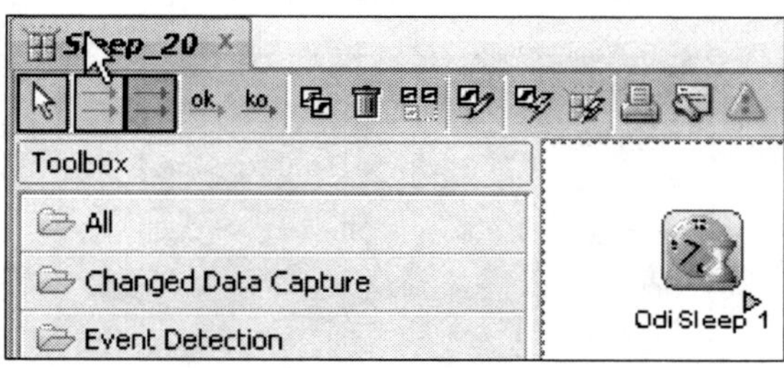

Set **Parameter** as `Wait Delay` and it's **Value** as `20000` (20 Seconds):

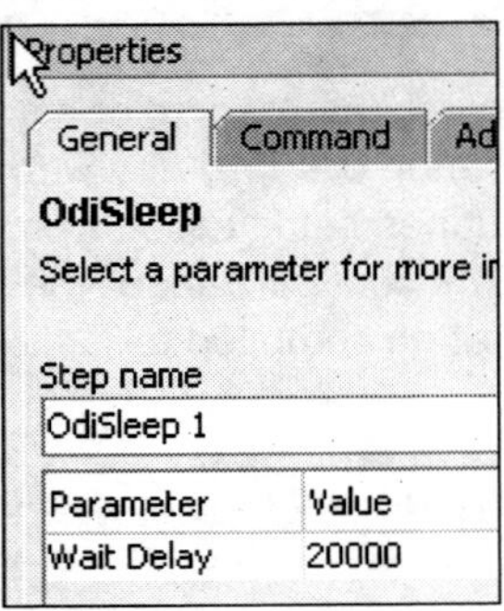

Save the `SLEEP_20` package, generate an ODI scenario for the `SLEEP_20` package with default name `SLEEP_20 Version 001`:

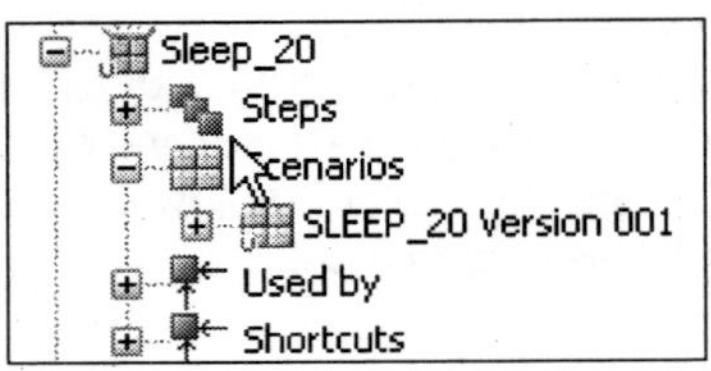

2. By default, both the standalone and the JEE ODI Agent are configured with public web services. The ODIInvoke public web service allows any ODI scenario to be executed as long as the correct security and SOAP request is passed to the web service. In this recipe, we will execute the ODI scenario `SLEEP_20` synchronously as a web service by calling the `ODIInvokeWebService` tool from within an ODI package. Create a new package with the name `ODIInvoke_WS_Sleep`:

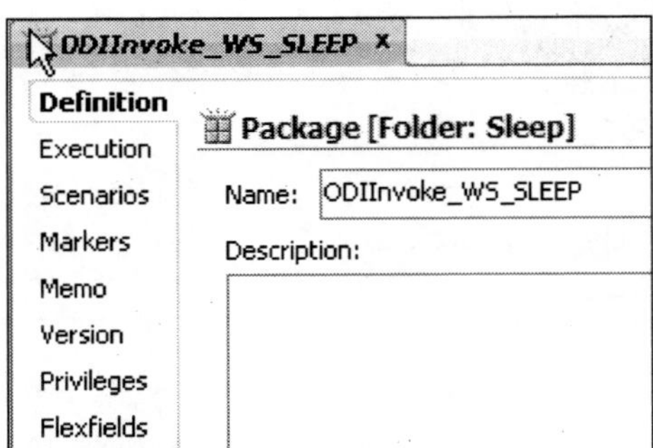

3. Click on the **Diagram** tab and expand the Internet folder; drag the `ODIInvokeWebService` tool onto the diagram:

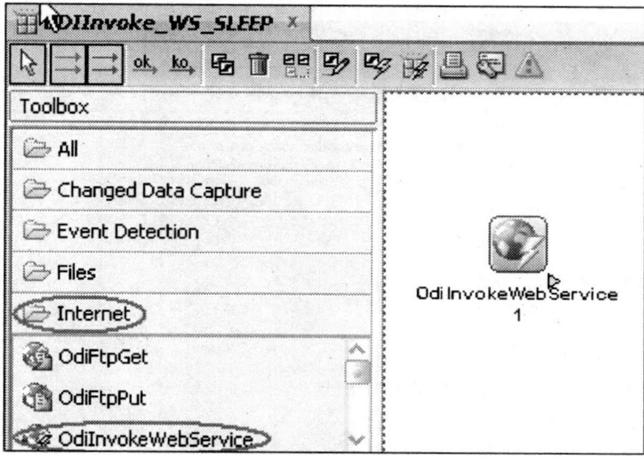

4. Click on **Properties**, set the **Step name** to `INVOKE_WS_SLEEP_20`, and click on the **Advanced...** button.

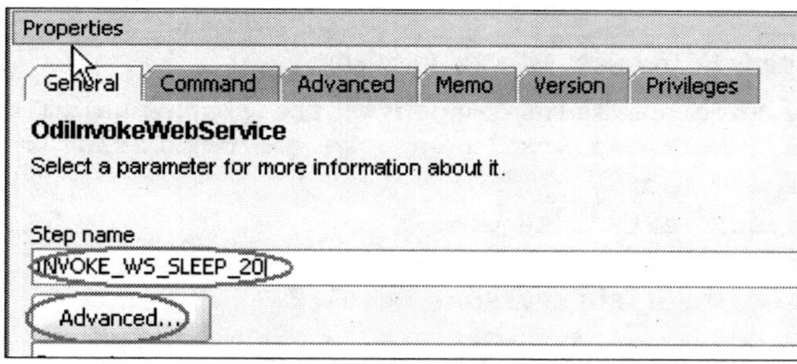

5. Clicking the **Advanced...** button will open the ODI WSDL browser and SOAP editor. Our agent is currently running and listening on port 8001.

   Paste the following into the URL on the **WSDL URL** option: `http://localhost:8001/oraclediagent/OdiInvoke?wsdl`

Click on the Connect to WSDL button. For this recipe, we will use the `invokeStartScen` port; select this port and view the sample SOAP request.

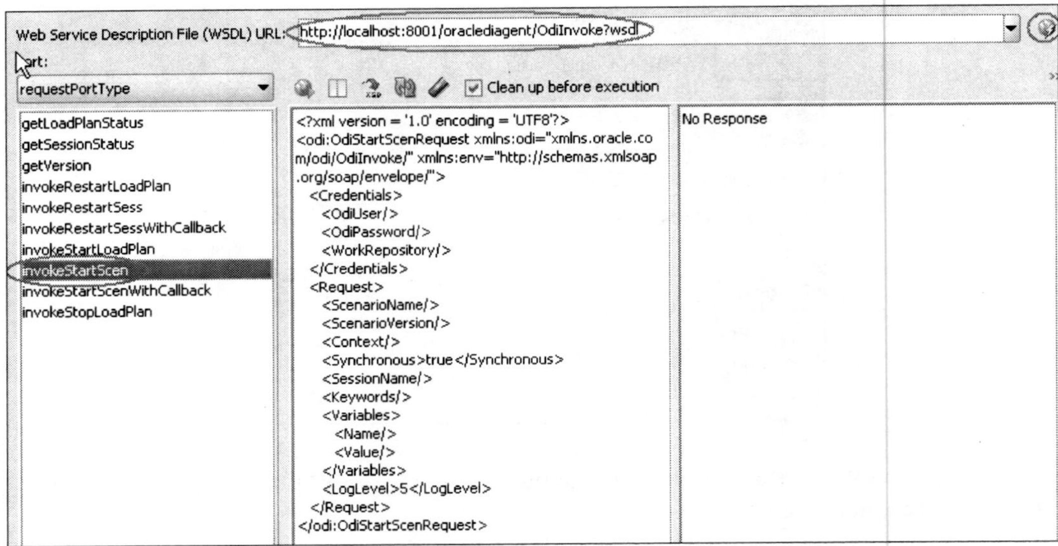

Replace the SOAP request with the following:

```
<soapenv:Envelope xmlns:soapenv="http://schemas.xmlsoap.org/soap/
envelope/" xmlns:odi="xmlns.oracle.com/odi/OdiInvoke/">
    <soapenv:Body>
    <odi:OdiStartScenRequest>
    <Credentials>
        <OdiUser>SUPERVISOR</OdiUser>
        <OdiPassword>SUNOPSIS1</OdiPassword>
        <WorkRepository>WORKREP1</WorkRepository>
    </Credentials>
    <Request>
    <ScenarioName>SLEEP_20</ScenarioName>
        <ScenarioVersion>001</ScenarioVersion>
        <Context>GLOBAL</Context>
        <Synchronous>1</Synchronous>
        <LogLevel>5</LogLevel>
    </Request>
</odi:OdiStartScenRequest>
    </soapenv:Body>
</soapenv:Envelope>
```

Click the Execute Web Service button. Notice the synchronous setting of request was set to `1` for true. When the execution is finished (after 20 seconds), the response will be returned. The response contains the session ID of the executed scenario.

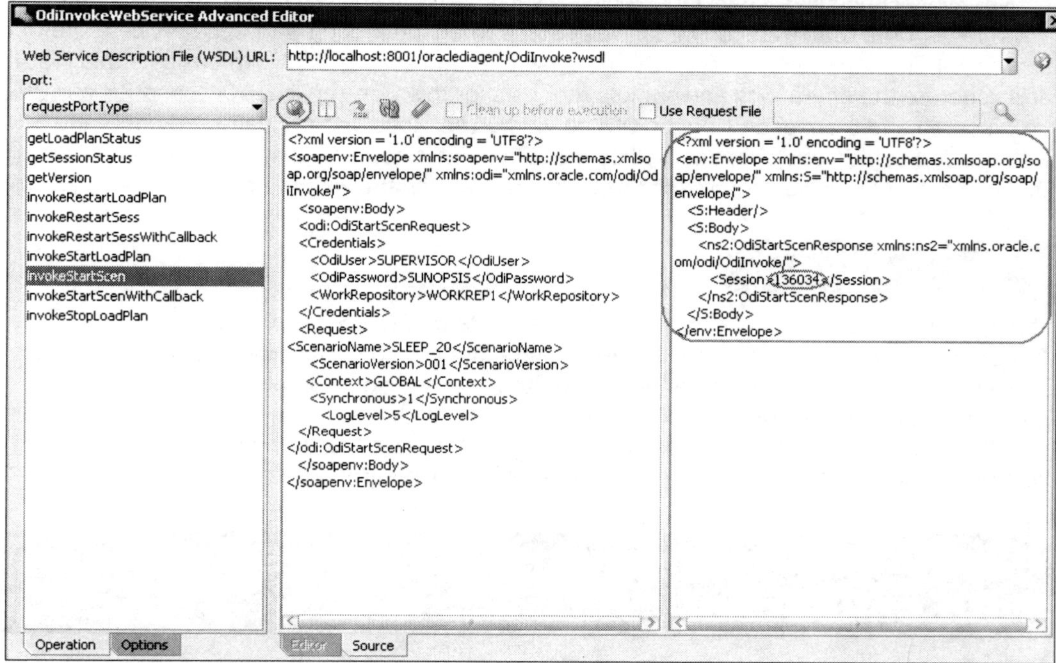

In this recipe, the scenario was executed on session 5001; this can be verified in the ODI Operator.

Changing the synchronous value to `0` will execute the web service asynchronously, allowing control to be passed back to the calling operation once the web service is started.

Click **OK** and save the package. You have now successfully called a web service from an ODI integration. Execute the package and review the results in the ODI operator.

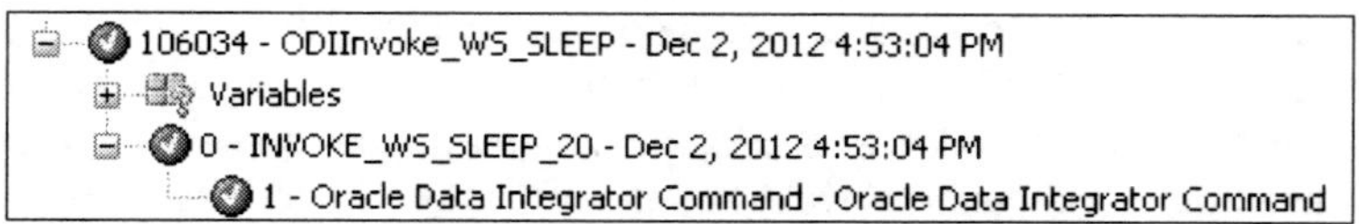

How it works...

Since ODI is 100 percent Java, the development environment can easily integrate with other native Java technologies. Oracle Weblogic Server is also built on Java and ODI clearly takes advantage of the Oracle Fusion Middleware stack when interacting with web services. The ODI tool `InvokeWebService` allows ODI to browse to a web service WSDL, interrogate this WSDL, and generate the operations and sample requests for this web service. ODI scenarios can also be executed and managed using the ODI public web services that are delivered out of the box with the ODI standalone agent as well as the JEE Agent. Once an agent is set up, any client that can call out to a web service can execute an ODI scenario with the proper SOAP request.

There's more...

This recipe calls an ODI public web service to execute an ODI scenario. The `ODIInvokeWebService` tool can be used to execute any compliant web service. There are many public web services available for use on the Internet. For example, there are many mapping sites, which provide geocoding web services. With these web services, an address is provided in the request and the geographic coordinates will be returned in the response. This type of web service could easily be added to an existing integration.

Invoking asynchronous ODI web services with callbacks

As we saw in the previous recipe, SOA and data integration are very complimentary to one another. Web service integration is great, but for advanced web service processing and orchestration, executing a web service with a callback method is a must. Executing web services with callbacks does require additional configuration and may seem like an advanced web service topic, however web services with callbacks are a standard in every SOA deployment.

The configuration and execution of a web service with a call back in ODI is relatively straightforward. The web service is executed as normal, however within the calling request, a callback address is set. This address is a port where the application server is listening for a response from the web service. When the application server gets a response posted, it interrogates the response for a match that it might be waiting for and then acts appropriately. In this recipe, we will use ODI to execute a web service and use WS-Addressing to define the callback and the message ID of the callback. For this recipe, a simple Java callback listener was created, which can be compiled and deployed in an application server. When using most SOA tools, the execution and callback would all be defined in the tool itself. However, this is out of the scope of this recipe.

A good starting point is *Oracle® Fusion Middleware Developer's Guide for Oracle Data Integrator - Running Integration Processes*. At the time of writing, this chapter can be found here:

`http://docs.oracle.com/cd/E21764_01/integrate.1111/e12643/running_executions.htm#BABDHJJF`

Before you start this recipe, a standalone or JEE agent needs to be created. If you do not have a standalone or JEE Agent, follow the appropriate recipe in *Chapter 10, Advanced Coding Techniques using the ODI SDK* to create one.

How to do it...

This recipe executes the web service from within the ODI tool. A simple callback listener is provided, which is called back on in the replyto->address of `http://127.0.0.1:8080/requestprinter/printme`. Step 1 outlines creating this simple Java callback listener that will print the callback request to a file. If using Oracle BPEL or a similar SOA environment, the callback would be provided by the tool.

1. The following is a very simple Java program that can be compiled and deployed on an application server (Tomcat in our recipe environment). Compile and deploy the sample callback listener to your application server:

```
package mypkg;

import java.io.*;
import java.util.*;
import javax.servlet.*;
import javax.servlet.http.*;

public class RequestPrinter extends HttpServlet {
    @Override
    public void doGet(HttpServletRequest request,
HttpServletResponse response)
    throws IOException, ServletException {
    }
 // Do the same thing for GET and POST requests
    @Override
    public void doPost(HttpServletRequest request,
HttpServletResponse response)
```

```
        throws IOException, ServletException {
        InputStream in=request.getInputStream();
        StringBuffer xmlStr=new StringBuffer();
        int d;
        while((d=in.read()) != -1){
            xmlStr.append((char)d);
        }
             File file = new File("c:/callBackResponse.txt");
        if (file.exists()!=true) {
        file.createNewFile();
        }
        OutputStreamWriter writer = new OutputStreamWriter(
        new FileOutputStream("c:/callBackResponse.txt", true),
        "UTF-8");
        BufferedWriter fbw = new BufferedWriter(writer);
            fbw.write(xmlStr.toString());
            fbw.newLine();
            fbw.close();
        }
    }
```

2. Start your ODI Agent. Start the ODI Studio and create a new package and a scenario as follows:

   Set **Parameter** as `Wait Delay` and it's **Value** as `20000`. Generate an ODI scenario for the `SLEEP_20` package with the default name `SLEEP_20 Version 001`. By default, both the standalone and the JEE ODI agent are configured with public web services. The ODIInvoke public web service allows any ODI scenario to be executed as long as the correct security is past in a request to the web service. In this recipe, we will execute a scenario as web services using the `ODIInvokeWebService` tool. First create a new package with the name `ODIInvoke_WS_Sleep`:

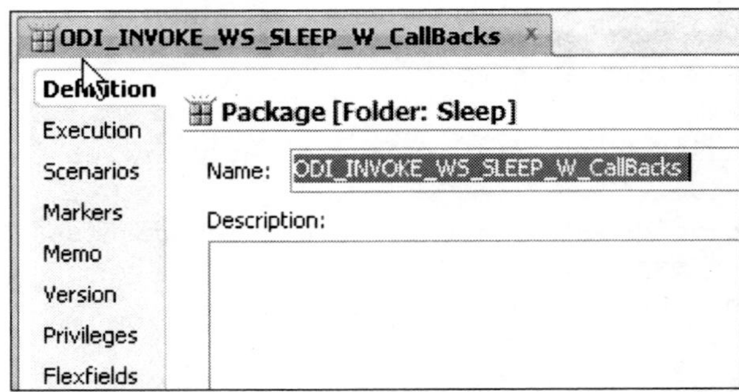

3. Within the package `ODI_INVOKE_WS_SLEEP_W_CallBacks`, create steps, which use the `ODIInokeWebService` tool.

   The first step will be named `INVOKE_WS_SLEEP_20` and use the following SOAP request; notice we are now using the port `InvokeStartScenWithCallback`:

```
<soapenv:Envelope xmlns:soapenv="http://schemas.xmlsoap.org/soap/
envelope/" xmlns:odi="xmlns.oracle.com/odi/OdiInvoke/">
<soapenv:Header xmlns:wsa="http://www.w3.org/2005/08/addressing">
<wsa:Action soapenv:mustUnderstand="1">xmlns.oracle.com/odi/
OdiInvoke/invokeStartScenWithCallback</wsa:Action>
<wsa:ReplyTo soapenv:mustUnderstand="1">
<wsa:Address>http://127.0.0.1:8080/requestprinter/printme</
wsa:Address>
</wsa:ReplyTo>
<wsa:MessageID soapenv:mustUnderstand="1">WSCALL_1</wsa:MessageID>
</soapenv:Header>
        <soapenv:Body>
   <odi:OdiStartScenWithCallbackRequest>
   <Credentials>
      <OdiUser>SUPERVISOR</OdiUser>
      <OdiPassword>SUNOPSIS1</OdiPassword>
      <WorkRepository>WORKREP1</WorkRepository>
   </Credentials>
   <Request>
<ScenarioName>SLEEP_20</ScenarioName>
      <ScenarioVersion>001</ScenarioVersion>
     <Context>GLOBAL</Context>
      <Synchronous>1</Synchronous>
         <LogLevel>5</LogLevel>
   </Request>
</odi:OdiStartScenWithCallbackRequest>
   </soapenv:Body>
</soapenv:Envelope>
```

Review the additional WS Addressing tags added to the XML header. The actions `ReplyTo` and `MessageID` must be set appropriately. For this recipe, we used a simple `MessageID` that is readable for example purposes.

4. Verify the `Callback` address is running and accepting requests:

Tomcat Web Application Manager

Message:	OK

Manager			
List Applications	HTML Manager Help	Manager Help	Server Status

Path	Version	Display Name	Running	Sessions	Commands
/	None specified	Welcome to Tomcat	true	0	Start Stop Reload Undeploy Expire sessions with idle ≥ 30 minutes
/docs	None specified	Tomcat Documentation	true	0	Start Stop Reload Undeploy Expire sessions with idle ≥ 30 minutes
/examples	None specified	Servlet and JSP Examples	true	0	Start Stop Reload Undeploy Expire sessions with idle ≥ 30 minutes
/manager	None specified	Tomcat Manager Application	true	1	Start Stop Reload Undeploy Expire sessions with idle ≥ 30 minutes
/requestprinter	None specified		true	0	Start Stop Reload Undeploy Expire sessions with idle ≥ 30 minutes

5. Click **OK**, save the package, then execute the `ODI_INVOKE_WS_SLEEP_W_CallBacks` package. When the package executes, the session will be started, which can be verified in the operator. However, since we have set the synchronous parameter of the SOAP request to `1`, the `callback` response will not be called until the execution is finished (20 seconds). Once the execution is finished, the `callback` response will be saved in the `callbackresponse` file. You can verify the response by matching the messageID of `WSCALL_1`.

The synchronous parameter is confusing and not intuitive. `InvokeStartScenWithCallback` is always an asynchronous web service call. The synchronous parameter defines how the ODI scenario will be called. Setting the synchronous value to `0` calls the scenario asynchronously, which will return the callback immediately after the session is successfully started in ODI. Setting the synchronous value to `1` will return the callback response only after the ODI scenario has completed.

6. You have now successfully called a web service with callbacks using WS-Addressing from ODI.

How it works...

The ODI public web services can all be configured to execute using callbacks. Using WS-Addressing the actions such as `replyto`, `faulto`, and `messageID` can all be set within the SOAP header. Any calling client that supports callbacks can utilize this methodology to execute the ODI public web services. A key note is that the web services must be executed synchronously or the callback will occur as soon as the method is executed. In the case of `invokeStartScen` being invoked asynchronously, the response is returned to the callback once the session is successfully started, not when the session is complete. In both cases, the web service call is invoked asynchronously and ODI will perform the next step in the integration flow.

Configuring container-based authentication with ODI web services

ODI public web services that are deployed in an Oracle WebLogic Server can take advantage of container-based authentication on execution. This means ODI public web services can be executed without providing the username and password in the SOAP request, as long as the username and password is passed to the application server by a supported method. This includes HTTP basic authentication, WS-Security Headers, SAML tokens, and other Oracle WebLogic **Oracle Platform Security Services** (**OPSS**) supported methods.

In this recipe, we will execute an ODI public web service using the ODIInvokeWebService tool in an ODI package. The container-based authentication method will use basic HTTP authentication. We will invoke the `InvokeStartScen` from the ODIInvoke WSDL running within a JEE Agent deployed within Oracle WebLogic Server. For this recipe, ODI is set up to authenticate externally to the embedded LDAP server within Oracle WebLogic Server. The setup and confirmation for this is outlined in *Chapter 2, Defining a connection to XML within ODI*, and once the WebLogic LDAP server and OPSS are configured appropriately, executing a public web service using container-based authentication is very simple.

A good starting point is *Oracle® Fusion Middleware Developer's Guide for Oracle Data Integrator - Running Integration Processes*. At the time of writing, this chapter can be found here:

`http://docs.oracle.com/cd/E21764_01/integrate.1111/e12643/running_executions.htm#BABDHJJF`

> Before you start, ensure the LDAP Server is configured for use with OPSS, ODI is using external authentication, and there is a JEE Agent deployed within Oracle Weblogic Server.

How to do it...

1. For this recipe, we will use the scenario and package, which executes a web service that was created earlier in this chapter in the *Invoking web services from ODI* recipe. If the `ODI_Invoke_WS_SLEEP` package and the `SLEEP_20` scenario do not exist, please create them using this recipe.

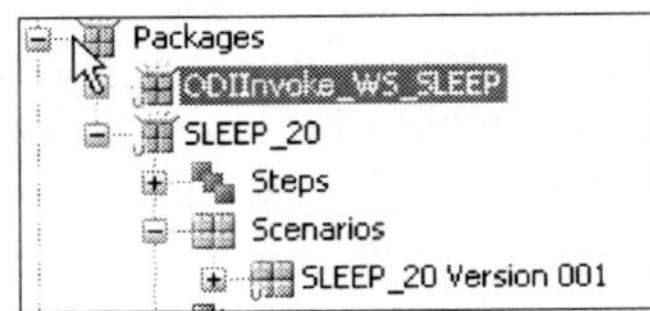

2. Open/Edit `ODI_INVOKE_WS_SLEEP`:
   - Click on the `INVOKE_WS_SLEEP_20` step
   - Click on the **Advanced** button to open the WSDL browser
   - Click on the **Options** tab on the left pane
   - Click on the **HTTP Authentication** checkbox
   - Enter the ODI username and password
   - Remove the following elements from the request:

```
<OdiUser>SUPERVISOR</OdiUser>
<OdiPassword>SUNOPSIS1</OdiPassword>
```

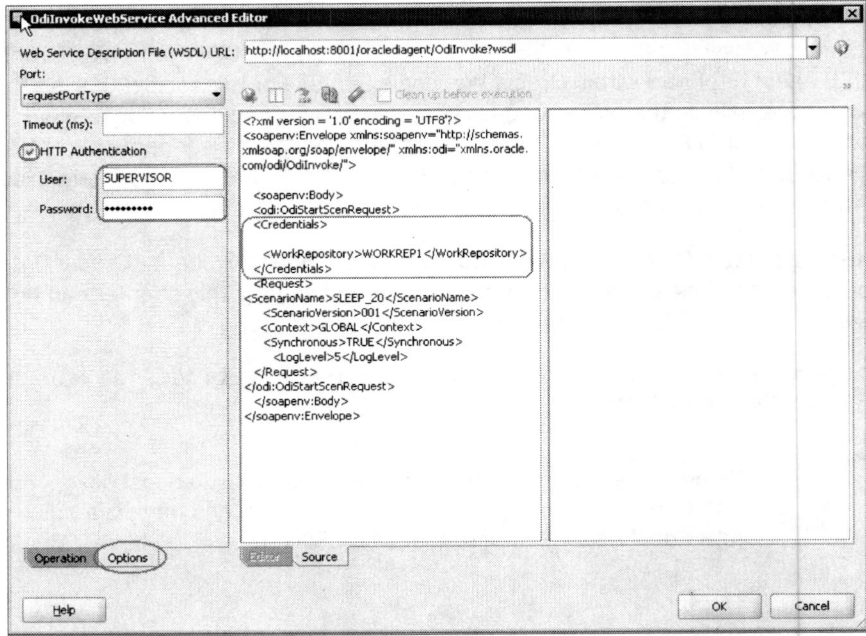

3. With external authentication set up and OPSS configured for the JEE Agent, this is all that needs to be configured to execute the web service with container-based authentication. Click on the Invoke Web Service button to execute the web service. The web service should successfully execute, returning the response on the right panel:

4. We have now successfully executed an ODI public web service using container-based authentication!

How it works...

Container-based authentication can utilize various authentication methods; for this recipe, basic HTTP authentication was used. The ODI public web services can utilize container-based authentication to pass credentials directly within the headers and not within the SOAP request itself. In this recipe, the `InvokeStartScen` web service is invoked within a JEE Agent deployed within Oracle WebLogic Server. Since this JEE Agent is configured for external authentication, the username and password can be passed through HTPP authentication and therefore do not need to be passed within the SOAP Request.

10
Advanced Coding Techniques Using the ODI SDK

In this chapter, we will cover the following:

- Creating the Master and Work repositories using the SDK
- Creating a project using the SDK
- Automating the import of artifacts using the SDK
- Creating models and datastores using the SDK
- Automating the creation of an interface using the SDK
- Invoking and monitoring a scenario using the SDK

Introduction

The ODI **Software Development Kit** (**SDK**) provides a set of Java classes allowing developers to automate most ODI operations such as creating the repositories, importing or exporting objects, modifying interfaces or packages, as well as analyzing the repository content for reporting purposes. The SDK is also used behind the scenes for most tasks happening within the Oracle Data Integrator Studio.

You can leverage the ODI SDK Java classes in your Java or Groovy programs for many use cases, such as integrating ODI within another application, jump starting ODI projects by automating several development or administration tasks, generating interfaces dynamically based on configuration files, migrating existing code to ODI, and so on. The recipes in this chapter will help advanced developers to dive into the ODI SDK concepts.

The recipes in this chapter use Groovy as a scripting language to leverage the ODI Java **Application Programming Interface** (**API**). Groovy provides a syntax similar to Java and allows for rapid prototyping of Java programs. In addition to those benefits and beginning with ODI 11.1.1.6, ODI Studio comes with an embedded Groovy editor and console that makes it even easier to use. Of course, you can also utilize the ODI SDK in your favorite Java **Integrated Development Environment** (**IDE**) such as JDeveloper or Eclipse. If you plan on using the Groovy editor in ODI Studio, make sure your ODI installation is using a **Java Development Kit** (**JDK**) and not a **Java Runtime Environment** (**JRE**).

If you are planning on using your own IDE such as JDeveloper with the ODI SDK, make sure to include all the libraries located in the `<ODI_HOME>/oracledi.sdk/lib` folder to your program classpath.

You can find more information about Groovy at `http://groovy.codehaus.org/`. It is also recommended to review the ODI documentation chapter on *Using Groovy Scripting in Oracle Data Integrator* (appendix *C* in *Oracle Fusion Middleware Developer's Guide for Oracle Data Integrator*), which at the date of this publication was available at: `http://docs.oracle.com/cd/E23943_01/integrate.1111/e12643/appendix_c.htm#sthref258`.

We will neither be listing nor describing each and every ODI SDK class used in this chapter. Furthermore, the goal of these recipes is not to write the best possible Java or Groovy code, but rather to give you an overview of what can be done through the SDK. It is recommended that while studying these recipes, the reader refer to the ODI SDK documentation, which at the date of this publication could be found at `http://docs.oracle.com/cd/E23943_01/apirefs.1111/e17060/toc.htm`.

Creating the Master and Work repositories using the SDK

The ODI SDK Java classes provide complete administration capabilities including the ability to create and upgrade Master and Work repositories. In this recipe, we will be developing a Groovy script that creates a Master and a Work repository, allowing developers embedding ODI into their own applications to automate this task.

Getting ready

With the ODI SDK, you can fully implement the repositories creation in only a few lines of code. You can follow the instructions using the Groovy editor in ODI Studio 11.1.1.6 and higher. You need to have two Oracle schemas created, `SDK_MREP` and `SDK_WREP`, and grant the `CONNECT` and `RESOURCE` database roles to those schemas. To keep it simple we have used the schema names as their passwords. No other prerequisites are required.

How to do it...

1. In ODI Studio, go to **Tools**, then click on **Groovy** and select **New Script**, as you can see in the following screenshot:

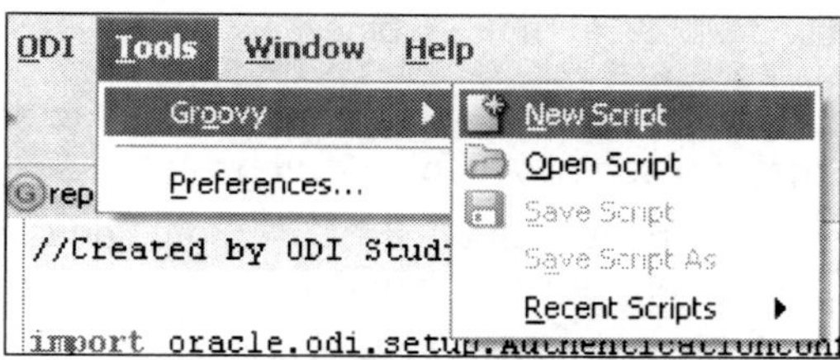

2. In order to use the ODI SDK to create the repositories, we first need to import several Java classes such as `IMasterRepositorySetup`, `IWorkRepositorySetup`, `MasterRepositorySetupImpl`, and `WorkRepositorySetupImpl`. These classes define and implement the API methods needed to create the Master and Work repositories.

   We also need to import the `OdiInstance` class, which plays a central role in the ODI SDK since it represents an instance of a Master repository or a Master and Work repository pair.

   We insert the following lines in the Groovy editor:

```
import oracle.odi.setup.AuthenticationConfiguration;
import oracle.odi.setup.IMasterRepositorySetup;
import oracle.odi.setup.IWorkRepositorySetup;
import oracle.odi.setup.TechnologyName;
import oracle.odi.core.config.MasterRepositoryDbInfo;
import oracle.odi.core.config.PoolingAttributes;
import oracle.odi.setup.JdbcProperties;
import oracle.odi.core.repository.WorkRepository;
import oracle.odi.setup.support.MasterRepositorySetupImpl;
import oracle.odi.setup.support.WorkRepositorySetupImpl;
import oracle.odi.core.OdiInstance;
import oracle.odi.core.config.OdiInstanceConfig;
import oracle.odi.core.security.Authentication;
```

3. Now that the right Java classes have been imported, we will start writing the code to implement the creation of the repositories.

   We begin by adding a `try` block to catch exceptions. This will help handle any potential execution errors. Add the following lines to your script:

```
try {
}
catch (Exception e)
{
auth.close();
  odiInstance.close();
  println(e);
}
```

   Next we will add some code in the `try` block.

4. We start by defining some Java variables in our program to enable the ODI SDK API methods to use the right settings for our environment.

   1. First we specify the ODI Supervisor username and password. This information is set when ODI is installed:

```
String odiSupervisorUser = "SUPERVISOR";
String odiSupervisorPassword = "SUPERVISOR";
```

   2. Then we add the database username and password information; as you can see, the repository creation process requires the use of a database user with DBA or SYSDBA privileges:

```
String dbaUser = "system";
char[] dbaPwd = "oracle";
```

Your passwords may be different, so make sure to use credentials that match your environment.

   3. We continue by adding the information required to connect to the database schema that will host the Master repository. In this recipe, we will use an Oracle database and set the repository ID to `0`:

```
TechnologyName masterRepositoryTechnology = TechnologyName.
ORACLE;
String masterRepositoryJdbcUrl = "jdbc:oracle:thin:@
localhost:1521:orcl";
String masterRepositoryJdbcDriver = "oracle.jdbc.
OracleDriver";
String masterRepositoryJdbcUser = "SDK_MREP";
String masterRepositoryJdbcPassword = "SDK_MREP";
int masterRepositoryId = 0;
```

4. We finish the variables definition with the Work repository settings. We will create a design-time repository and we set the repository ID to `1`:

```
TechnologyName workRepositoryTechnology = TechnologyName.
ORACLE;
String workRepositoryJdbcUrl = "jdbc:oracle:thin:@
localhost:1521:orcl";
String workRepositoryJdbcDriver = "oracle.jdbc.
OracleDriver";
String workRepositoryJdbcUser = "SDK_WREP";
String workRepositoryJdbcPassword = "SDK_WREP";
String workRepositoryName = "SDK_WORKREP";
WorkRepository.WorkType wRepType = WorkRepository.WorkType.
valueOf("DESIGN");
int workRepositoryId = 1;
```

Remember to save your work frequently within the Groovy editor. To do so, within ODI Studio, use the **Save All** button, or go to **Tools** then click on **Groovy** and select **Save Script As** or **Save Script** if you have already saved an earlier version of your script.

5. Once we are done with specifying all the variables, we enter the following code to create the Master repository:

```
IMasterRepositorySetup masterRepositorySetup = new
MasterRepositorySetupImpl();
AuthenticationConfiguration authConf =
AuthenticationConfiguration.createStandaloneAuthenticationConfigur
ation(odiSupervisorPassword.toCharArray());
JdbcProperties mRepJdbcInfo = new JdbcProperties(masterRepositor
yJdbcUrl, masterRepositoryJdbcDriver, masterRepositoryJdbcUser,
masterRepositoryJdbcPassword.toCharArray());
masterRepositorySetup.createMasterRepository(mRepJdbcInfo,
dbaUser, dbaPwd, masterRepositoryId, masterRepositoryTechnology,
true, authConf, null);
```

We use the ODI Supervisor password along with the database and Master repository information that we specified previously.

6. We can now proceed with the creation of the Work repository, but first we need to define an `OdiInstance` object to connect to our newly created Master repository. Add the following lines of code to specify an `OdiInstance` object representing your Master repository:

```
MasterRepositoryDbInfo mRepDbInfo= new MasterRepositoryDb
Info(masterRepositoryJdbcUrl, masterRepositoryJdbcDriver,
masterRepositoryJdbcUser, masterRepositoryJdbcPassword.
toCharArray(), new PoolingAttributes());
```

```
OdiInstance odiInstance = OdiInstance.createInstance(new
OdiInstanceConfig(mRepDbInfo, null));
Authentication auth = odiInstance.getSecurityManager().createAuthe
ntication(odiSupervisorUser, odiSupervisorPassword.toCharArray());
odiInstance.getSecurityManager().setCurrentThreadAuthentication(au
th);
```

7. We type a few lines of code to initialize the Work repository:

```
IWorkRepositorySetup workRepositorySetup = new WorkRepositorySetup
Impl(odiInstance);
JdbcProperties wRepJdbcInfo = new JdbcProperties(workReposito
ryJdbcUrl, workRepositoryJdbcDriver, workRepositoryJdbcUser,
workRepositoryJdbcPassword);
workRepositorySetup.createWorkRepository(wRepType, wRepJdbcInfo,
workRepositoryId, workRepositoryName, workRepositoryTechnology,
true, null);
```

8. Finally, we add the following code to close the `Authentication` and `OdiInstance` objects:

```
auth.close();
odiInstance.close();
```

9. Then we execute this Groovy script to set up our Master and Work repositories. To do so, select the **Groovy script** tab in ODI Studio and click on the green **Execute** button.

How it works...

The Groovy script in this recipe is using several ODI SDK Java classes, which play a key role in the creation of repositories:

- `MasterRepositorySetupImpl` implements the `IMasterRepositorySetup` interface and provides methods to create or upgrade Master repositories.
- `AuthenticationConfiguration` defines the Master repository authentication approach. It can represent a standalone configuration as highlighted in this recipe or an external authentication configuration using the **Oracle Platform Security Services** (**OPSS**) framework. More information about OPSS can be found, at the time of writing, on the Oracle Technology Network at `http://www.oracle.com/technetwork/middleware/id-mgmt/index-100381.html`.
- `OdiInstance` corresponds to an instance of a Master repository in our case, but it can also represent an instance of a Work and Master repository pair.
- `Authentication` is used along with the ODI Supervisor credentials to log into the Master repository and authenticate ourselves.
- `WorkRepositorySetupImpl` implements the `IWorkRepositorySetup` interface and provides methods to create or upgrade Work repositories.

In order to create a Master and a Work repository, we first used the `MasterRepositorySetupImpl` class to create an `IMasterRepositorySetup` object that gives us access to API methods to create the Master repository. Then we defined the standalone authentication configuration using the `AuthenticationConfiguration` class and stored the Master repository connection details (JDBC Url, JDBC User, and so on) into a `JdbcProperties` object. Those objects are required to invoke the `createMasterRepository()` method that initiates the creation of the Master repository.

Once the Master repository is created, we had to define an `OdiInstance` object associated with it before we could create our Work repository. We started by creating a new `MasterRepositoryDbInfo` object, which stores the Master repository configuration, then we passed it as a parameter to the `OdiInstance.createInstance()` method. This call returned the `odiInstance` object, which we then used to authenticate ourselves through the `Authentication` class.

With the `OdiInstance` object created and the authentication done, we can proceed with the creation of the Work repository. We started by using the `WorkRepositorySetupImpl` constructor, which takes the `odiInstance` object as a parameter. Then we stored the Work repository connection details into a `JdbcProperties` object. Finally, we invoked the `createWorkRepository()` method to finalize the Work repository creation and we released the `Authentication` and `OdiInstance` resources.

There's more...

You can do more with the ODI SDK in terms of repository management than just creating the Master and Work repositories. The SDK also provides methods to upgrade the repositories from one release to another (for example, 11.1.1.5.*x* to 11.1.1.6.*x*) and create other runtime Work repositories in addition to design-time Work repositories.

Creating a project using the SDK

The ODI SDK allows you to easily create an instance of a project, which can be useful in order to rapidly create a project infrastructure when doing a prototype. In this recipe, we will be creating a project and adding a folder to it.

Getting ready

You can follow the instructions using the Groovy editor in ODI Studio 11.1.1.6 and higher. In this recipe, we will reuse the repositories created in the previous recipe, *Creating the Master and Work repositories using the SDK*. Follow the necessary steps of this recipe to create them; you can also use the **Repository Creation Utility** (**RCU**), which is typically the recommended approach, or ODI Studio. No other prerequisites are required.

How to do it...

1. In ODI Studio, go to **Tools**, then click on **Groovy** and select **New Script**.
2. In this recipe, we will again have to import several Java classes such as `MasterRepositoryDbInfo`, `WorkRepositoryDbInfo`, or `Authentication` in order to first connect to an existing Master and Work repository pair. We also need to import the `OdiInstance` class, which plays a central role in the ODI SDK as it represents an instance of our Master and Work repository pair. Type the following lines in the Groovy editor:

```
import oracle.odi.core.config.MasterRepositoryDbInfo;
import oracle.odi.core.config.WorkRepositoryDbInfo;
import oracle.odi.core.config.PoolingAttributes;
import oracle.odi.core.OdiInstance;
import oracle.odi.core.config.OdiInstanceConfig;
import oracle.odi.core.security.Authentication;
import oracle.odi.core.persistence.transaction.
ITransactionDefinition;
import oracle.odi.core.persistence.transaction.support.
DefaultTransactionDefinition;
import oracle.odi.core.persistence.transaction.
ITransactionManager;
import oracle.odi.core.persistence.transaction.ITransactionStatus;
```

3. We will also import classes that are specific to a project, like `OdiProject` and `OdiFolder`, which define and implement the API methods to create and manage the ODI project artifacts. Add the following to your Groovy script:

```
import oracle.odi.domain.project.OdiProject;
import oracle.odi.domain.project.OdiFolder;
```

4. Next we add a `try` block to catch exceptions. This is always useful to catch errors and show the exception text. The rest of the code will be entered in the `try { }` part. Add the following lines to your script:

```
try {
}
catch (Exception e)
{
  auth.close();
  odiInstance.close();
  println(e);
}
```

5. We can now add some variables to our try block. The `odiSupervisorUser` and `odiSupervisorPassword` variables store the ODI Supervisor credentials:

```
String odiSupervisorUser = "SUPERVISOR";
String odiSupervisorPassword = "SUPERVISOR";
```

> In ODI 11.1.1.6 and higher, you can also reuse your repository connection in the Groovy editor using the predefined `odiInstance` variable. You will need to log into your repositories in ODI Studio; it will not work when not connected.

Then we specify the information to connect to the database schema that hosts our Master repository:

```
String masterRepositoryJdbcUrl = "jdbc:oracle:thin:@
localhost:1521:orcl";
String masterRepositoryJdbcDriver = "oracle.jdbc.OracleDriver";
String masterRepositoryJdbcUser = "SDK_MREP";
String masterRepositoryJdbcPassword = "SDK_MREP";
String workRepositoryName = "SDK_WORKREP";
```

6. Next we add the following lines of code to create an `OdiInstance` object that will be representing our Master and Work repositories:

```
MasterRepositoryDbInfo mRepDbInfo= new MasterRepositoryDb
Info(masterRepositoryJdbcUrl, masterRepositoryJdbcDriver,
masterRepositoryJdbcUser, masterRepositoryJdbcPassword.
toCharArray(), new PoolingAttributes());
WorkRepositoryDbInfo wRepDbInfo= new WorkRepositoryDbInfo(workRepo
sitoryName, new PoolingAttributes());
OdiInstance odiInstance = OdiInstance.createInstance(new
OdiInstanceConfig(mRepDbInfo, wRepDbInfo));
Authentication auth = odiInstance.getSecurityManager().createAuthe
ntication(odiSupervisorUser, odiSupervisorPassword.toCharArray());
odiInstance.getSecurityManager().setCurrentThreadAuthentication(au
th);
```

7. Before we can create new objects, we have to initialize a transaction that allows us to access and modify the information stored in the repositories. Enter the following lines of code to define a new transaction:

```
ITransactionDefinition txnDef = new
DefaultTransactionDefinition();
ITransactionManager tm = odiInstance.getTransactionManager();
ITransactionStatus txnStatus = tm.getTransaction(txnDef);
```

8. Then we will create a project called `ODI SDK Project` and a folder called `SDK Folder`. These objects will both be persisted in the Work repository:

```
OdiProject sdkProject = new OdiProject("ODI SDK Project","ODI_SDK_
PROJECT");
OdiFolder sdkFolder = new OdiFolder(sdkProject,"SDK Folder");
odiInstance.getTransactionalEntityManager().persist(sdkProject);
```

You can use the `println()` or `print()` methods in Groovy to add some text in your scripts that will be displayed in the **Groovy Console** window in ODI Studio. It is also possible to write some logging information into a log file.

9. Lastly, we commit the changes to the repositories using the `ITransactionManager` object created earlier and we close the `Authentication` and `OdiInstance` objects:

```
tm.commit(txnStatus);
auth.close();
odiInstance.close();
```

10. We can now execute this Groovy. To do so, select your **Groovy script** tab in ODI Studio and click on the green **Execute** button. When the script finishes successfully, you will see a new project in ODI Studio with a structure similar to the following screenshot:

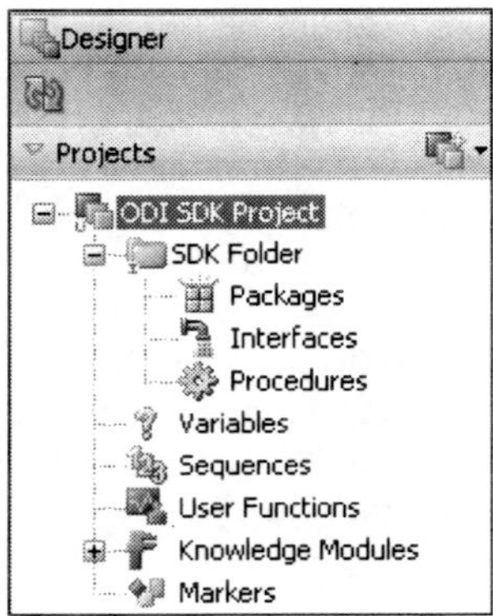

How it works...

In order to create a new project and a folder, we used several ODI SDK Java classes. Listed below are some of the key Java classes utilized in this recipe:

- `OdiInstance` plays a central role when manipulating objects in the repositories; it represents an instance of a Work and Master repository pair in this recipe. The `OdiInstance` class also gives us access to the `IOdiEntityManager` object linked to the current transaction, allowing us to persist objects at the Java level.

- ITransactionManager defines the transaction management process, allowing us to commit Java artifacts into the repositories database.
- Authentication is used along with the ODI Supervisor credentials to log into the Master and Work repositories and persist objects at the Java level before they get committed into the repositories.
- OdiProject provides methods to create and manipulate projects.
- OdiFolder represents projects folders and offers methods to manage them.

The project creation process started with the definition of an OdiInstance object named odiInstance, which is created using the Master and Work repositories information. This odiInstance object allows us to authenticate ourselves and get a transaction to add or edit objects in the repositories. The transaction is obtained through the creation of a ITransactionManager object called tm and the use of its getTransaction() method.

Finally, we used the OdiProject and OdiFolder constructors to create two new objects, respectively named ODI SDK Project and SDK Folder. We then invoked the getTransactionalEntityManager() method of our OdiInstance object to access the IOdiEntityManager object attached to the current transaction. This allowed us to cache the newly created objects into a persistence layer at the Java level using the persist() method. This functionality is available throughout the ODI SDK API to minimize database access: objects are cached while they're being developed without requiring the SDK program to again access the repository database. Objects will be committed into the repository database using the commit() method of the ITransactionManager class. We only have to persist parent objects since this will also persist its children. In our example, only the project is persisted, and since the project folder is a child of the project, it is cached at the same time.

The commit() method of the ITransactionManager object is then used to save the changes in the Work repository, and in the end we released the Authentication and OdiInstance resources.

There's more...

As we will see in the following recipes, creating a project is only the beginning. All design-time objects such as interfaces, models, packages, datastores, and so on, can also be managed using the SDK.

Automating the import of artifacts using the SDK

It is possible to automate the import and export of most ODI objects through the ODI SDK. This feature can be used to promote objects from development to quality assurance or to design packaging and deployment processes around your ODI projects. In this recipe, we will import Knowledge Modules into a project.

Getting ready

You can follow the instructions using the Groovy editor in ODI Studio 11.1.1.6 and higher. In this recipe, we will reuse the project created in the previous recipe, *Creating a project using the SDK*. Follow the necessary steps of this recipe to create it or recreate it using ODI Studio. No other prerequisites are required.

How to do it...

1. Follow steps 1 and 2 from the recipe *Creating a project using the SDK*.
2. In this recipe, we use the import of Knowledge Modules into a project as an example, so we start by importing classes related to projects: `OdiProject` and `IOdiProjectFinder`. We then import the `ImportServiceImpl` class that implements the `IImportService` interface and provides access to the import API methods. Add the following lines of code in your Groovy editor:

   ```
   import oracle.odi.domain.project.OdiProject;
   import oracle.odi.domain.project.finder.IOdiProjectFinder;
   import oracle.odi.impexp.support.ImportServiceImpl;
   import oracle.odi.impexp.IImportService;
   ```

3. Follow steps 4 and 5 from the recipe *Creating a project using the SDK*.
4. Then we add as a variable the location of the Knowledge Modules, XML files in the Oracle Data Integrator home directory. Add the following line of code and make sure it points to the right folder in your environment:

   ```
   String kmInstallFolder = "C:/fmw/Oracle_ODI_1/oracledi/xml-
   reference/";
   ```

   This variable will be used during the import to locate the KMs' content.

5. Follow steps 6 and 7 from the recipe *Creating a project using the SDK*.
6. Next we use the project finder class `IOdiProjectFinder` to retrieve `ODI SDK Project` that we created in the previous recipe:

   ```
   OdiProject sdkProject = ((IOdiProjectFinder)odiInstance.
   getTransactionalEntityManager().getFinder(OdiProject.class)).
   findByCode("ODI_SDK_PROJECT");
   ```

7. Finally, we create an `IImportService` object using our `OdiInstance` object to get access to the import methods. Then we use the `importObjectFromXml()` method to import three KMs into our project: `IKM SQL Control Append`, `CKM Oracle`, and `LKM SQL to Oracle`:

   ```
   IImportService impService = new ImportServiceImpl(odiInstance);
   impService.importObjectFromXml(IImportService.IMPORT_MODE_
   DUPLICATION, kmInstallFolder + "KM_IKM Oracle Incremental Update.
   xml", sdkProject, false);impService.importObjectFromXml(IImportSe
   ```

```
rvice.IMPORT_MODE_DUPLICATION, kmInstallFolder + "KM_CKM Oracle.
xml", sdkProject, false);
impService.importObjectFromXml(IImportService.IMPORT_MODE_
DUPLICATION, kmInstallFolder + "KM_LKM SQL to Oracle.xml",
sdkProject, false);
```

8. Follow steps 9 and 10 from the recipe *Creating a project using the SDK*. When the script finishes successfully, you should see KMs under your project structure similar to the following screenshot:

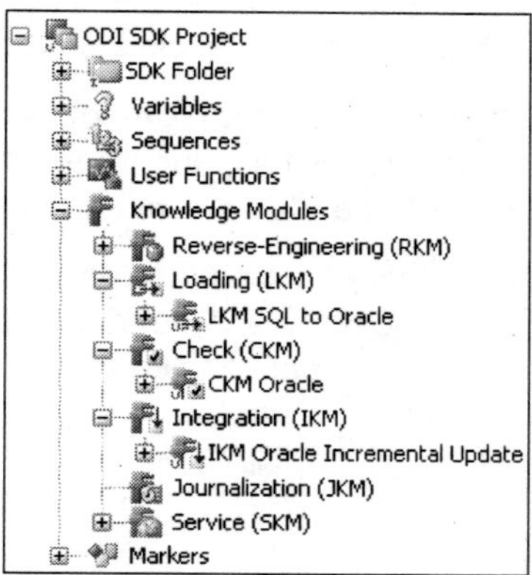

How it works...

In order to import some KMs into a project, we used several ODI SDK Java classes. We will now highlight some of the key Java classes utilized in this recipe:

- `OdiInstance` plays a central role when manipulating objects in the repositories. It represents an instance of a Work and Master repository pair in this recipe, and allows us to obtain an `IImportService` object attached to our repositories.
- `ITransactionManager` defines the transaction management process, allowing us to commit artifacts into the repositories database.
- `IOdiProjectFinder` provides a method, `findByCode()`, that allows developers to locate a project using its code.
- `OdiProject` provides methods to create and manipulate projects.
- `IImportService` offers import methods for various ODI artifacts; design objects such as interfaces, packages, and so on, as well as security or topology objects. `IImportService` allows the import of individual objects, sets of objects, and solutions.

Once we had created an `OdiInstance` object and retrieved a transaction to import objects into the repositories, we used the `IOdiProjectFinder` class to find the project `ODI SDK Project` using its internal code, `ODI_SDK_PROJECT`. Finder classes such as `IOdiProjectFinder`, `IOdiLogicalSchemaFinder`, or `IOdiDataStoreFinder` are available for most entities manageable through the SDK. Finder classes usually provide several methods to easily find and retrieve a given ODI object using its internal code, its name, or other parameters.

Then we created a new `IImportService` using the `ImportServiceImpl` constructor and by passing the `OdiInstance` object as a parameter. Finally, we used the `importObjectFromXml()` method to import Knowledge Modules into our project.

The `commit()` method of the `ITransactionManager` object is used at the end of the script to save the changes to the Work repository, and we released resources by calling the `close()` methods of the `OdiInstance` and `Authentication` objects.

You may have noticed that in this recipe, we do not use any method to persist the imported objects before committing them into the repository. Import and export methods available in the SDK in ODI 11g use a different mechanism to cache the objects and do not require developers to invoke a persist method.

There's more...

It is possible to import any ODI object using the ODI SDK Java classes; export capabilities are also provided that complement the import features. In addition, smart import and smart export services are available through the ODI SDK using the `SmartImportServiceImpl` and `SmartExportServiceImpl` classes.

Creating models and datastores using the SDK

The SDK offers full control over the metadata defined in the ODI repositories. Developers can write scripts to create or modify datastores, models, as well as other artifacts linked to those objects such as constraints. In this recipe, we will be adding two new models and datastores to our environment.

Getting ready

You can follow the instructions using the Groovy editor in ODI Studio 11.1.1.6 and higher. In this recipe, we will reuse the repositories created in the recipe *Creating the Master and Work repositories using the SDK*. Follow the necessary steps of this recipe to create them. You can also use the **Repository Creation Utility** (**RCU**) or ODI Studio. You will also need to create the `DEMO_SRC` and `DEMO_TRG` schemas in your database and the `DEMO_SRC` and `DEMO_TRG` logical schemas for the Oracle technology described in the *Preface* of this book. No other prerequisites are required.

How to do it...

1. Follow steps 1 and 2 from the recipe *Creating a Project using the SDK*.
2. Since the model creation process requires information about logical schemas and contexts, we add their appropriate finders, `IOdiLogicalSchemaFinder` and `IOdiContextFinder`, as well as their respective classes, `OdiLogicalSchema` and `OdiContext`. Finally, we import several classes related to models and datastores: `OdiModel`, `OdiDataStore`, `OdiColumn`, and `OdiKey`. Add the following lines of code in your Groovy editor:

```
import oracle.odi.domain.topology.finder.IOdiLogicalSchemaFinder;
import oracle.odi.domain.topology.finder.IOdiContextFinder;
import oracle.odi.domain.topology.OdiLogicalSchema;
import oracle.odi.domain.topology.OdiContext;
import oracle.odi.domain.model.OdiModel;
import oracle.odi.domain.model.OdiDataStore;
import oracle.odi.domain.model.OdiColumn;
import oracle.odi.domain.model.OdiKey;
```

3. Follow steps 4 through 7 from the recipe *Creating a Project using the SDK*.
4. We start the creation of our two models with the one representing our source system. A model requires a logical schema and a context, so we first use `IOdiLogicalSchemaFinder` and `IOdiContextFinder` to search for a logical schema called `DEMO_SRC` and the default context in our environment. With that information, we leverage the `OdiModel` constructor to create a new model, which is then persisted at the Java level:

```
OdiLogicalSchema srcLogicalSchema = ((IOdiLogicalSchemaFinder)
odiInstance.getTransactionalEntityManager().
getFinder(OdiLogicalSchema.class)).findByName("DEMO_SRC");
OdiContext sdkContext = ((IOdiContextFinder)odiInstance.
getTransactionalEntityManager().getFinder(OdiContext.class)).
findDefaultContext();
OdiModel srcModel = new OdiModel(srcLogicalSchema, "DEMO_SRC",
"DEMO_SRC");
srcModel.setReverseContext(sdkContext);
odiInstance.getTransactionalEntityManager().persist(srcModel);
```

5. We create a target model representing our Data Warehouse in a similar manner:

```
OdiLogicalSchema trgLogicalSchema = ((IOdiLogicalSchemaFinder)
odiInstance.getTransactionalEntityManager().
getFinder(OdiLogicalSchema.class)).findByName("DEMO_TRG");
OdiModel trgModel = new OdiModel(srcLogicalSchema, "DEMO_TRG",
"DEMO_TRG");
trgModel.setReverseContext(sdkContext);
odiInstance.getTransactionalEntityManager().persist(trgModel);
```

6. Now that the models are created, we can add two datastores, one representing a source table and the other one corresponding to a target table. We start with the definition of a source datastore named `SRC_EMP` and its columns. Add the following lines of code to your script:

```
OdiDataStore srcDatastore = new OdiDataStore(srcModel, "SRC_EMP");
OdiColumn srcCol = new OdiColumn(srcDatastore, "EMPNO");
srcCol.setDataTypeCode("NUMBER");
srcCol.setMandatory(true);
srcCol.setLength(4);
srcCol.setScale(0);

srcCol = new OdiColumn(srcDatastore, "ENAME");
srcCol.setDataTypeCode("VARCHAR2");
srcCol.setLength(10);
srcCol.setScale(0);

srcCol = new OdiColumn(srcDatastore, "JOB");
srcCol.setDataTypeCode("VARCHAR2");
srcCol.setLength(9);
srcCol.setScale(0);

srcCol = new OdiColumn(srcDatastore, "MGR");
srcCol.setDataTypeCode("NUMBER");
srcCol.setLength(4);
srcCol.setScale(0);

srcCol = new OdiColumn(srcDatastore, "HIREDATE");
srcCol.setDataTypeCode("DATE");

srcCol = new OdiColumn(srcDatastore, "SAL");
srcCol.setDataTypeCode("NUMBER");
srcCol.setLength(7);
srcCol.setScale(2);

srcCol = new OdiColumn(srcDatastore, "COMM");
srcCol.setDataTypeCode("NUMBER");
srcCol.setLength(7);
srcCol.setScale(2);

srcCol = new OdiColumn(srcDatastore, "DEPTNO");
srcCol.setDataTypeCode("NUMBER");
srcCol.setLength(2);
srcCol.setScale(0);
```

7. Similarly, we create a target datastore named `TRG_EMP` with a primary key defined on the `EMPNO` column:

```
OdiDataStore trgDatastore = new OdiDataStore(trgModel, "TRG_EMP");
OdiColumn trgCol = new OdiColumn(trgDatastore, "EMPNO");
trgCol.setDataTypeCode("NUMBER");
trgCol.setMandatory(true);
trgCol.setLength(4);
trgCol.setScale(0);
OdiKey sdkPrimaryKey = new OdiKey(trgDatastore, "PK_" +
trgDatastore.getName());
OdiKey.KeyType keyType = OdiKey.KeyType.valueOf("PRIMARY_KEY");
sdkPrimaryKey.setKeyType(keyType);
sdkPrimaryKey.addColumn(trgCol);

trgCol = new OdiColumn(trgDatastore, "ENAME");
trgCol.setDataTypeCode("VARCHAR2");
trgCol.setLength(10);
trgCol.setScale(0);

trgCol = new OdiColumn(trgDatastore, "JOB");
trgCol.setDataTypeCode("VARCHAR2");
trgCol.setLength(9);
trgCol.setScale(0);

trgCol = new OdiColumn(trgDatastore, "MGR");
trgCol.setDataTypeCode("NUMBER");
trgCol.setLength(4);
trgCol.setScale(0);

trgCol = new OdiColumn(trgDatastore, "HIREDATE");
trgCol.setDataTypeCode("DATE");

trgCol = new OdiColumn(trgDatastore, "SAL");
trgCol.setDataTypeCode("NUMBER");
trgCol.setLength(7);
trgCol.setScale(2);

trgCol = new OdiColumn(trgDatastore, "COMM");
trgCol.setDataTypeCode("NUMBER");
trgCol.setLength(7);
trgCol.setScale(2);

trgCol = new OdiColumn(trgDatastore, "DEPTNO");
trgCol.setDataTypeCode("NUMBER");
trgCol.setLength(2);
trgCol.setScale(0);
```

8. Follow steps 9 and 10 from the recipe *Creating a Project using the SDK*. When the script finishes successfully you will see a model structure similar to the following screenshot:

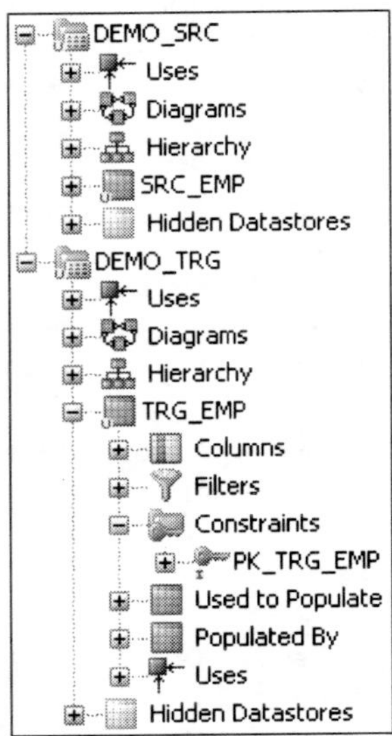

How it works...

In order to create some models and datastores, we used several ODI SDK Java classes. Here is a highlight of some of the key Java classes utilized in this recipe:

- `OdiInstance` plays a central role when manipulating objects in the repositories. It represents an instance of a Work and Master repository pair in this recipe, and allows us to persist objects at the Java level using the `IOdiEntityManager` methods.
- `IOdiLogicalSchemaFinder` is a finder class providing a method, `findByName()`, that can locate a specific logical schema using its name.
- `OdiLogicalSchema` offers methods to create and manipulate logical schemas.
- `IOdiContextFinder` provides several methods to find a specific context or the context marked as default.
- `OdiContext` allows developers to define contexts in the topology.
- `OdiModel` provides mechanisms to manage models.
- `OdiDataStore` gives methods to create datastores as well as access or edit their settings.
- `OdiColumn` offers functionality to handle the datastores' columns.
- `OdiKey` represents constraints such as primary keys, alternate keys, or references.

Once we had created an `OdiInstance` object and retrieved a transaction to import objects into the repositories, we used the `IOdiLogicalSchemaFinder` and `IOdiContextFinder` classes to find the source and target logical schemas as well as the default context. The logical schemas information is passed as a parameter to the `OdiModel` class constructor, while the context is set as the reverse engineering context through the `OdiModel.setReverseContext()` method. The two models `DEMO_SRC` and `DEMO_TRG` are then persisted at the Java level using the `OdiInstance` API methods. Newly created objects have to be persisted before further modifications can be made, such as adding datastores in our recipe. Note that the datastores will not have to be explicitly persisted since their parents, the models, have already been persisted.

After the models are created, we used the `OdiDataStore` class constructor to create two datastores under the new models: `SRC_EMP` under `DEMO_SRC` and `TRG_EMP` under `DEMO_TRG`. Columns are added to the datastores using the `OdiColumn` constructor and edited through various column management methods such as `setDataTypeCode()` or `setLength()` that set the datatype and the length of a column. We also used the `OdiKey` class to add a constraint to the target datastore `TRG_EMP`; the constant `PRIMARY_KEY` from the `OdiKey.KeyType` enumeration is leveraged to mark this constraint as a primary key.

Finally, the `commit()` method of the `ITransactionManager` object is used to save the changes to the Work repository and resources are released through the use of the `close()` method of the `OdiInstance` and `Authentication` classes.

There is more...

In this recipe, we have created the metadata definitions of `SRC_EMP` and `TRG_EMP` manually, but the ODI SDK also provides the ability to automatically reverse engineer a datastore using a Reverse Engineering Knowledge Module in a package. In addition, it is possible to leverage the SDK to read metadata from an external source such as a CSV or an XML file and programmatically create some objects.

Creating an interface using the SDK

It is possible to create design-time objects such as interfaces using the ODI SDK Java classes. This can be very useful to build dynamic interfaces on the fly using metadata contained in excel spreadsheets or flat files, or to simply design data flows without using the GUI.

Getting ready

You can follow the instructions using the Groovy editor in ODI Studio 11.1.1.6 and higher. In this recipe, we will reuse the project created in the recipe *Creating a project using the SDK* and the models and datastores created in the recipe *Creating models and datastores using the SDK*. Follow the necessary steps to create the required objects; you can also create them manually from ODI Studio.

This recipe uses two Oracle tables called `SRC_EMP` and `TRG_EMP` described in the *Preface* of this book. No other prerequisites are required.

How to do it...

1. Follow steps 1 and 2 from the recipe *Creating a project using the SDK*.
2. Import classes that are specific to interfaces, such as `InteractiveInterfaceHelperWithActions`, `InterfaceActionAddSourceDataStore`, or `InterfaceActionOnTargetDataStoreComputeAutoMapping`; those helper classes provide mechanisms to easily manipulate interfaces using the ODI SDK. Add the following lines in the Groovy editor:

```
import oracle.odi.domain.project.finder.IOdiFolderFinder;
import oracle.odi.domain.topology.finder.IOdiContextFinder;
import oracle.odi.domain.model.finder.IOdiDataStoreFinder;
import oracle.odi.domain.topology.OdiContext;
import oracle.odi.domain.model.OdiDataStore;
import oracle.odi.domain.project.OdiFolder;
import oracle.odi.domain.project.OdiInterface;
import oracle.odi.domain.project.interfaces.DataSet;
import oracle.odi.interfaces.interactive.support.
InteractiveInterfaceHelperWithActions;
import oracle.odi.interfaces.interactive.support.actions.
InterfaceActionAddSourceDataStore;
import oracle.odi.interfaces.interactive.support.actions.
InterfaceActionSetTargetDataStore;
import oracle.odi.interfaces.interactive.support.actions.
InterfaceActionOnTargetDataStoreComputeAutoMapping;
import oracle.odi.interfaces.interactive.support.aliascomputers.
AliasComputerDoubleChecker;
import oracle.odi.interfaces.interactive.support.clauseimporters.
ClauseImporterDefault;
import oracle.odi.interfaces.interactive.support.mapping.automap.
AutoMappingComputerColumnName;
import oracle.odi.interfaces.interactive.support.mapping.
matchpolicy.MappingMatchPolicyColumnName;
import oracle.odi.interfaces.interactive.support.
targetkeychoosers.TargetKeyChooserPrimaryKey;
```

3. Follow steps 4 through 7 from the recipe *Creating a project using the SDK*.

4. The interface can now be created. We start by locating the project folder under which the interface will be created using the `IOdiFolderFinder` class. We then pass the project folder, the interface name, and the default context to the `OdiInterface` constructor to initialize our interface. Add the following to your script:

```
OdiFolder sdkFolder = ((IOdiFolderFinder)odiInstance.
getTransactionalEntityManager().getFinder(OdiFolder.class)).
findByName("SDK Folder").get(0);
OdiContext sdkContext = ((IOdiContextFinder)odiInstance.
getTransactionalEntityManager().getFinder(OdiContext.class)).
findDefaultContext();
OdiInterface sdkInterface = new OdiInterface(sdkFolder, "Load TRG_
EMP", sdkContext);
```

5. We create an `InteractiveInterfaceHelperWithActions` object to help with the addition of the interface through the SDK. `InteractiveInterfaceHelperWithActions` is a helper class, which implements several methods to easily modify interfaces:

```
InteractiveInterfaceHelperWithActions sdkIntHelper = new Inte
ractiveInterfaceHelperWithActions(sdkInterface, odiInstance,
odiInstance.getTransactionalEntityManager());
```

6. We then add the source datastore `SRC_EMP` to the interface. First we locate it using I`OdiDataStoreFinder` and then we add it using the `InterfaceActionAddSourceDataStore` helper action class:

```
OdiDataStore sdkSrcDatastore = ((IOdiDataStoreFinder)odiInstance.
getTransactionalEntityManager().getFinder(OdiDataStore.class)).
findByName("SRC_EMP", "DEMO_SRC");
DataSet dataSet = sdkInterface.getDataSets().get(0);
sdkIntHelper.performAction(new InterfaceActionAddSourceDataStore
(sdkSrcDatastore, dataSet, new AliasComputerDoubleChecker(), new
ClauseImporterDefault(), new AutoMappingComputerColumnName()));
```

7. Similarly, we add the target datastore `TRG_EMP` using `InterfaceActionSetTargetDataStore` and we use the auto-mapping capabilities to create one-to-one mappings between our source and target datastores.

It is also possible to add a mappings expression into target columns manually using the `InterfaceActionOnTargetMappingSetSql` class in combination with the `InteractiveInterfaceHelperWithActions.prepareAction()` method.

Finally, we ensure the source sets are in a correct state using the `computeSourceSets()` method and we prepare the interface to be persisted:

```
OdiDataStore sdkTrgDatastore = ((IOdiDataStoreFinder)odiInstance.
getTransactionalEntityManager().getFinder(OdiDataStore.class)).
findByName("TRG_EMP", "DEMO_TRG");
sdkIntHelper.performAction(new InterfaceActionSetTargetDat
aStore(sdkTrgDatastore, new MappingMatchPolicyColumnName(),
new AutoMappingComputerColumnName(), new
AutoMappingComputerColumnName(), new
TargetKeyChooserPrimaryKey()));
sdkIntHelper.performAction(new
InterfaceActionOnTargetDataStoreComputeAutoMapping());
sdkIntHelper.computeSourceSets();
sdkIntHelper.preparePersist();
```

8. Follow steps 9 and 10 from the recipe *Creating a project using the SDK*. When the script finishes successfully, you should see an interface like the one seen in the following screenshot:

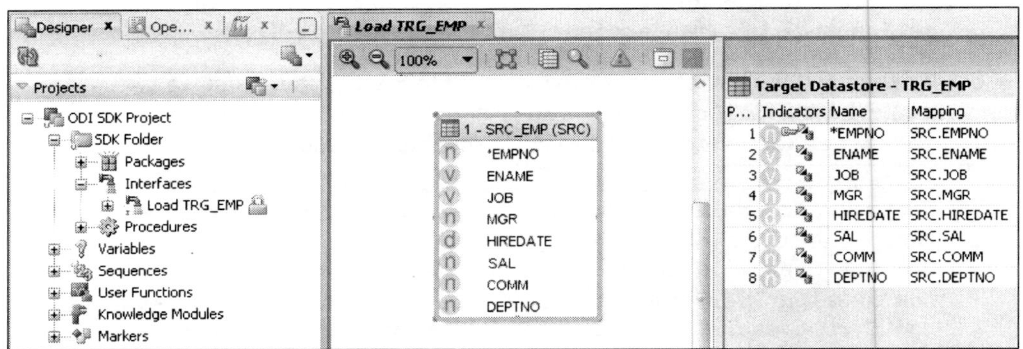

How it works...

In order to create an interface, we used several ODI SDK Java classes. The following list highlights some of the key Java classes utilized in this recipe:

- `InteractiveInterfaceHelperWithActions` is an helper class, which must be utilitized to work with interfaces in the SDK, it provides key methods to modify interfaces. It is used along with interface action classes such as `InterfaceActionAddSourceDataStore` or `InterfaceActionOnTargetDataStoreComputeAutoMapping`.
- `InterfaceActionAddSourceDataStore` is an interface action class used when adding a source datastore into an interface.

- `InterfaceActionSetTargetDataStore` is another interface action class used when adding the target datastore into an interface.
- `InterfaceActionOnTargetDataStoreComputeAutoMapping` is also an interface action class utilized to map automatically all the columns of a target datastore in an interface.
- `OdiInterface` represents an instance of an interface; it can be used to get some information about an interface, such as its description, internal ID, and so on.

Once we had created an `OdiInstance` object and retrieved a transaction to import objects into the repositories, we used the `IOdiFolderFinder` and `IOdiContextFinder` classes to find the project folder under which the interface will be added as well as the default context. This information is passed as a parameter to the `OdiInterface` class constructor along with the interface name, `Load TRG_EMP`.

After the interface is initialized, we created a new `InteractiveInterfaceHelperWithActions`, which plays a key role in the interface creation process along with interface action classes. Helper classes are commonly used in **object-oriented programming** (**OOP**), and in this case provide a wrapper around the interface object to make it easier to manipulate, such as adding source datastores, defining mappings, and so on using the helper action classes. Action classes such as `InterfaceActionAddJoin` or `InterfaceActionOnTargetMappingSetSql` must be used in combination with an `InteractiveInterfaceHelperWithActions` object and its `prepareAction()` method. With the `InteractiveInterfaceHelperWithActions` object defined, we started by adding a source datastore to the interface. We used the `IOdiDataStoreFinder` class to locate a datastore named `SRC_EMP` and we used the `OdiInterface.getDataSets()` method to get the first and only source dataset included in our interface. The `OdiDataStore` and `DataSet` objects are used to add `SRC_EMP` to the interface through the `InterfaceActionAddSourceDataStore` action class. Helper action classes, such as `InterfaceActionAddJoin`, `InterfaceActionAddLookup`, or `InterfaceActionOnTargetColumn`, are leveraged in combination with a helper class to customize interfaces.

In a similar manner, we located the target datastore, `TRG_EMP`, and added it to the interface using the `InterfaceActionSetTargetDataStore` action class. With both the source and target datastores in place, we used the `InterfaceActionOnTargetDataStoreComputeAutoMapping` helper action class to map automatically all the target datastore columns. The ODI SDK auto-mapping capabilities are the same as the ones found in ODI Studio. ODI analyzes the names of the source and target columns and, if they are identical, it will map them together. Finally, we invoked the `computeSourceSets()` method to ensure the consistency and integrity of the interface source sets, then a call to the `preparePersist()` method prepares the interface to be stored in the Work repository. The `InteractiveInterfaceHelperWithActions.preparePersist()` method encapsulates a call to the `IOdiEntityManager.persist()` method that we have used previously along with other ones.

Lastly, the `commit()` method of the `ITransactionManager` object is used to save the changes to the Work repository and resources are released through the use of the `close()` method of the `OdiInstance` and `Authentication` classes.

There's more...

We created a simple interface with one-to-one mappings in this recipe, but understand that the ODI SDK provides more advanced capabilities to edit interfaces, such as assigning specific mapping expressions using the `InterfaceActionOnTargetMappingSetSql` class, or modifying the mapping execution location using `InterfaceActionOnTargetMappingSetLocation` and much more.

See Also

Since interfaces rely on metadata defined in models and datastores, you might be interested in the recipe *Creating models and datastores using the SDK*, which walks you through creating metadata using the ODI SDK Java classes.

Invoking and monitoring a scenario using the SDK

The ODI SDK offers API methods to generate and run scenarios. These capabilities can be used to integrate the execution of ODI processes into an application. In this recipe, we will generate a scenario from an interface, execute it using a local Agent, and monitor its execution.

Getting ready

You can follow the instructions using the Groovy editor in ODI Studio 11.1.1.6 and higher. For this recipe, we will reuse the interface created in the recipe *Creating an interface using the SDK*. Follow the necessary steps of that recipe to create the interface (you can also create it manually from ODI Studio or use any of your interfaces). No other prerequisites are required.

How to do it...

1. Follow steps 1 and 2 from the recipe *Creating a project using the SDK*.
2. Import the `IOdiInterfaceFinder` and `OdiInterface` classes, because executing an interface requires that it be first found and initialized. Add `OdiScenarioGeneratorImpl` and `IOdiScenarioGenerator`, which are used to generate a scenario out of various objects. Finally, we import `RuntimeAgent` and several classes related to sessions in order to invoke the scenario and monitor its related session.

Add the following lines of code in your Groovy editor:

```
import oracle.odi.runtime.agent.RuntimeAgent;
import oracle.odi.domain.project.finder.IOdiInterfaceFinder;
import oracle.odi.domain.project.OdiInterface;
import oracle.odi.generation.support.OdiScenarioGeneratorImpl;
import oracle.odi.generation.IOdiScenarioGenerator;
import oracle.odi.runtime.agent.invocation.ExecutionInfo;
import oracle.odi.domain.runtime.session.finder.IOdiSessionFinder;
import oracle.odi.domain.runtime.session.OdiSession;
```

3. Follow steps 4 through 6 from the recipe *Creating a project using the SDK*.
4. We start by searching for an interface named `Load TRG_EMP` located in the `SDK Folder` of the `ODI SDK Project` project using `IOdiInterfaceFinder`. Since we know there is only one interface in that folder with that name, we extract the first entity from the interface collection using the `get(0)` method. Then we search for a scenario named `LOAD_TRG_EMP` that should already exist using `IOdiScenarioFinder`. If it doesn't already exist, we create a new `IOdiScenarioGenerator` object to generate a scenario using the `generateScenario()` method. Before we can create the new scenario, we need to initialize a transaction, and finally we commit the changes to the repositories using the `ITransactionManager` object we created earlier:

```
  OdiInterface sdkInterface = ((IOdiInterfaceFinder)odiInstance.
getTransactionalEntityManager().getFinder(OdiInterface.class)).
findByName("Load TRG_EMP", "ODI_SDK_PROJECT", "SDK Folder").
get(0);
  if (!((IOdiScenarioFinder)odiInstance.
getTransactionalEntityManager().getFinder(OdiScenario.class)).
findLatestByName("LOAD_TRG_EMP")) {
     println("Generating Scenario from Interface...");
     ITransactionDefinition txnDef = new
     DefaultTransactionDefinition();
     ITransactionManager tm =
     odiInstance.getTransactionManager();
     ITransactionStatus txnStatus =
     tm.getTransaction(txnDef);
     IOdiScenarioGenerator sdkIntScenario = new
     OdiScenarioGeneratorImpl(odiInstance);
     sdkIntScenario.generateScenario(sdkInterface,
     "LOAD_TRG_EMP", "001");
     tm.commit(txnStatus);
  }
```

5. Next we create an instance of a local agent using the `RuntimeAgent` class constructor. Then we leverage its `startScenario()` method to invoke a scenario named `LOAD_TRG_EMP`:

```
  RuntimeAgent runtimeAgent = new RuntimeAgent(odiInstance,
odiSupervisorUser, odiSupervisorPassword.toCharArray());
  ExecutionInfo sdkExecInfo = runtimeAgent.startScenario("LOAD_
TRG_EMP", "001", null, null, "GLOBAL", 5, null, true);
```

6. Finally, we define an `OdiSession` object that represents the session from the scenario we just executed. Thanks to the `OdiSession` object, we can display useful information about the session such as its status using `getStatus()`, or its error message using `getErrorMessage()`. Enter the following lines of code in your script:

```
OdiSession sdkSession = ((IOdiSessionFinder)odiInstance.
getTransactionalEntityManager().getFinder(OdiSession.class)).
findBySessionId(sdkExecInfo.getSessionId());
println("Completed Interface Execution. Session " + sdkSession.
getName() + " (" + sdkSession.getSessionId() + ").") ;
println("Status: " + sdkSession.getStatus());
println("Return Code: " + sdkSession.getReturnCode());
  String sdkError = sdkSession.getErrorMessage();
  if (sdkError != null) {
    println("Error Message: " +
    sdkSession.getErrorMessage());
  }
```

The session information will be displayed in the Groovy console in a similar manner to what you can see in the following screenshot:

```
Starting Interface Execution...
Generating Scenario from Interface...
Executing Scenario...
Completed Interface Execution. Session LOAD_TRG_EMP (20001).
Status: DONE
Return Code: 0
Script exited.
```

7. Subsequently, we release resources using the `OdiInstance` and `Authentication` classes and the `close()` methods:

```
auth.close();
odiInstance.close();
```

8. We can now execute this Groovy script to generate and execute the scenario. To do so, simply select your **Groovy script** tab in ODI Studio and click on the green **Execute** button. When the script finishes successfully, you should see a scenario and a session executed as shown in the following screenshot:

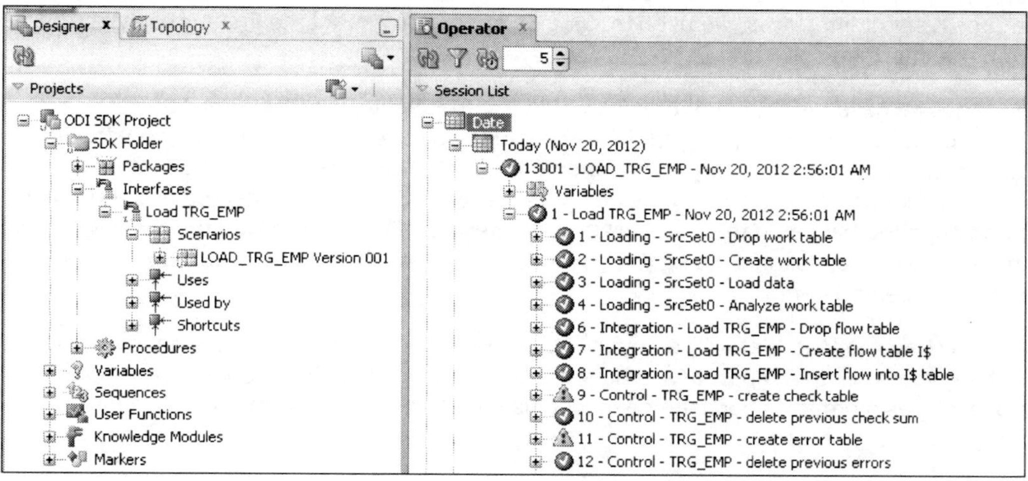

How it works...

In order to create, invoke, and monitor a scenario, we used several ODI SDK Java classes. The following list highlights some of the key Java classes utilized in this recipe:

- `OdiScenarioGeneratorImpl` offers methods to generate or regenerate scenarios from various entities such as interfaces or packages
- `RuntimeAgent` corresponds to a local agent and provides methods to start scenarios, stop or restart sessions, and so on
- `ExecutionInfo` stores information about a session execution such as its internal ID or return code
- `IOdiSessionFinder` is a finder class providing several methods to locate sessions based on their internal ID, the name of the agent who executed it, a scenario name, and so on
- `OdiSession` represents a session and has several mechanisms to access execution information

Once we had created an `OdiInstance` object and retrieved a transaction to import objects into the repositories, we used the `IOdiInterfaceFinder` class to locate an interface. Three parameters are passed to the `IOdiInterfaceFinder.findByName()` method: the interface name, `Load TRG_EMP`, the project code, `ODI_SDK_PROJECT`, and the project folder name, `SDK Folder`. Since the `IOdiInterfaceFinder.findByName()` method returns a set of interfaces, we used the `get()` method to extract the first and only interface from the interface collection.

Now that we have the interface that we would like to execute, we created a new `IOdiScenarioGenerator` using the `OdiScenarioGeneratorImpl` class constructor. `OdiScenarioGeneratorImpl` implements the `IOdiScenarioGenerator` interface, which cannot be invoked directly. Using the `generateScenario()` method, we generated a new scenario based on the `Load TRG_EMP` interface. Finally, we saved the newly generated scenario to the repositories using the `commit()` method of the `ITransactionManager` object we created earlier.

You may have noticed that we do not invoke any `persist()` method in this recipe, similarly to the *Automating the import of artifacts using the SDK* recipe. The scenario generation process uses a different persistence mechanism that does not require an explicit call to a `persist()` method.

Next we created an instance of a local agent through the `RuntimeAgent` class constructor and we used it to start the scenario execution with the `startScenario()` method. The last parameter, `pSynchronous`, of the `startScenario()` method is important as it determines if the execution will be done in synchronous mode or asynchronous mode. In this recipe, we used a synchronous execution, which means that the overall session is blocked until the scenario execution completes. In asynchronous mode, the overall session execution doesn't wait for the scenario execution to complete and continues to run until all of its steps have been started. The `startScenario()` method returns an `ExecutionInfo` object, which represents the execution details of a scenario in this recipe and is used to retrieve the session internal ID. This identifier is then passed to the `IOdiSessionFinder` class in order to initialize an `OdiSession` object representing the actual scenario execution.

Finally, we used the `OdiSession` object named `sdkSession` to display various information about the session such as its name with `getName()`, its internal ID with `getSessionId()`, or its return code with `getReturnCode()`. An `if` block is added to show the error message along with the Java stack trace in case of errors.

There's more...

The ODI SDK provides many execution management features, for example, it is possible to stop or restart a session using the `RuntimeAgent` class, which represents a local agent, or the `RemoteRuntimeAgentInvoker` class, which allows the invocation of operations on a remote agent. A developer can also create load plans using the SDK, fully modify them, and orchestrate their executions. In addition, Java classes to schedule scenarios (`OdiScenarioSchedule`) and load plans (`OdiLoadPlanSchedule`) are provided.

11
More on ODI

For this last chapter, we will conclude with the following topics:

- Invoking an external program that requires a password
- Tuning a standalone ODI agent
- Loading a file containing a LOB
- Using ODI versioning
- Performing a Smart Export/Smart Import
- Accessing an Excel spreadsheet
- Impacting the data flow by changing the staging area location
- Automating smart import/export with the ODI SDK

Introduction

We have covered a lot of concepts and techniques in this book so far, and there is a lot more that needs to be covered. The subjects that we have put together in this chapter were selected on the basis of the frequency of questions we've been asked on different forums or by customers that we were helping out rather than following a core theme, as was the case for the previous chapters.

For the most part, the recipes in this chapter are a different take on topics that have already been discussed in earlier chapters. Here, we are either using metadata differently than would be expected or we are digging a little deeper into concepts that we have already touched on. Truth be told, this is a little bit of a catch all chapter, but we thought these recipes too important to be left aside, so here you go!

To integrate ODI with external tools, we will look into how to invoke an external program that requires a password or other connectivity parameters, and how to connect to an Excel spreadsheet using ODBC. To help with performance, we will look into how to tune a standalone ODI agent and how to impact the data flow by changing the staging area location. To load large data, we will work on an example of a KM that can load files containing LOBs. And finally, to help with lifecycle management, we will look into the use of ODI versioning as well as how to use smart export/import.

Invoking an external program that requires a password

There are many instances of external programs that will require a password to be used. For instance, you may be required to establish a VPN connection before you can even connect to your databases.

The example we will use here, because it is easier to demonstrate, will be to decrypt an encrypted file using an external program.

Getting ready

The external program that we will use to build in this recipe is AES Encrypt, an open source encryption application that can be downloaded at `http://www.aescrypt.com/download.html`. After downloading the console version of the program for your operating system, unzip the executable and put it in a folder next to the file that you will want to encrypt and decrypt. The steps of this recipe assume that we have copied the executable in the `c:\temp` directory. If you are using another operating system or if you decide to put the program in a different folder, you will have to adapt the instructions of this recipe accordingly.

How to do it...

1. Open a command line console and go to the `c:\temp` directory. Add a text file of your choice in this directory. Here we are using a file called `foo.txt`:

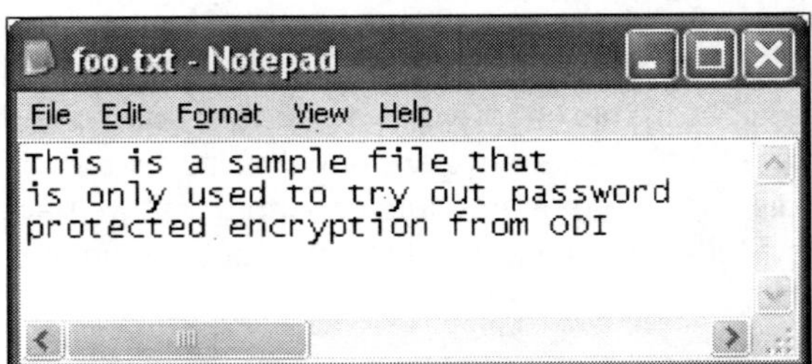

2. Run the following from the command line:

```
c:\temp> aescrypt -e -p oracledi foo.txt
```

This will generate an encrypted file named `foo.txt.aes` that is protected with the password `oracledi`. If you try to edit the content of this new file, you will see that it has indeed been encrypted:

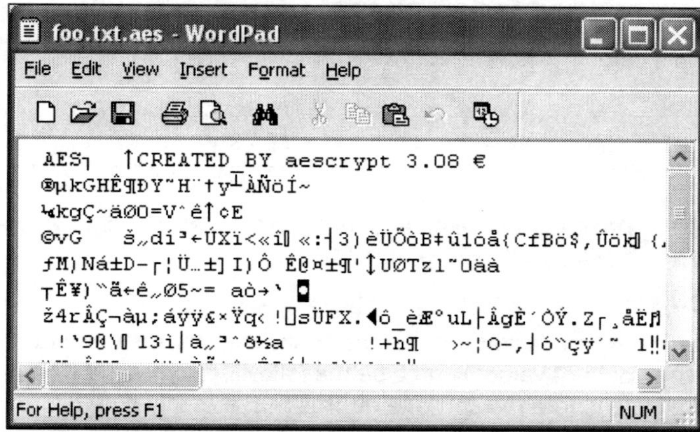

Rename the original `foo.txt` file to `foo.txt.ori`. We will now use ODI to decrypt the file and restore the original content.

3. In ODI **Topology**, create a new **Data Server** in the **File** technology called `AESCRYPT`. We will use this data server as a placeholder for the password that we need for this operation. We can also use this to locate the file that we will work on. You can leave the **User** name empty (we do not need it here), but do set the **Password** value to `oracledi`.

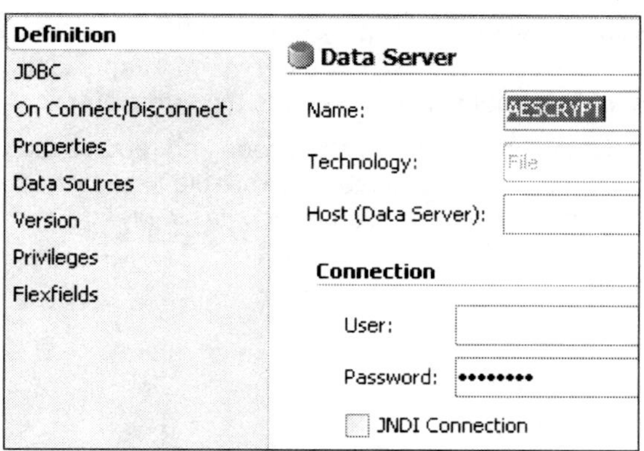

In the **JDBC** tab, select the **ODI File JDBC Driver** and use the default **JDBC URL**: `jdbc:snps:dbfile`.

4. Create a physical schema under that server. Set both the **Schema** name and **Work Schema** name to `c:\temp`.

   Create a logical schema to point to this physical schema for the default context: `FILE_AESCRYPT`

   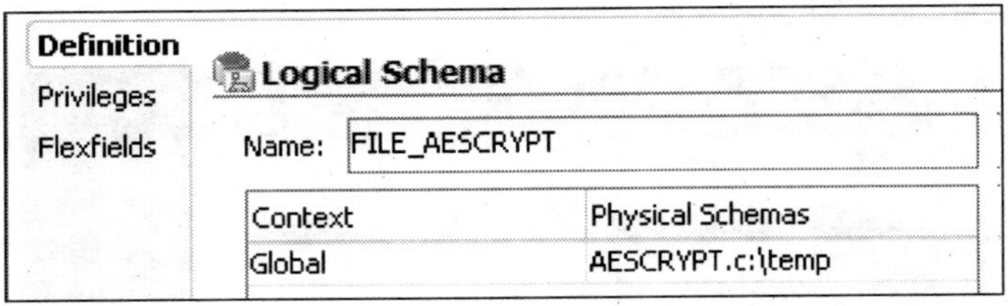

5. Switch to the **Designer** operator, and in the project of your choice, create a procedure called `Ch11_Password_Decrypt_File`.

   Add a new step to this procedure, and call this `Decrypt`.

   In the **Command on Target** tab, set the **Technology** to **OS Command** (leave all other fields to their default values) and type the following command (this is all one line of code, so please ignore the carriage returns that are only due to formatting):

```
<%=odiRef.getInfo("SRC_SCHEMA")%>\aescrypt -d -p <@=odiRef.
getInfo("SRC_PASS")@> <%=odiRef.getInfo("SRC_SCHEMA")%>\foo.txt.
aes
```

The technology OS Command can be used to execute any type of command at the OS level. One note of caution though: if the script or program that you execute returns anything else than `0`, ODI will consider that the program failed. Typically there are two techniques that can be combined to solve this problem:

Redirect any output or errors to other files. For instance, `dir 1>dir.out 2>dir.err`, where 1 represents the standard output and 2 represents the errors output.

Use Jython code to execute the code and retrieve the return code in a variable. Then evaluate this variable to see whether the returned value indicates an error or is simply informational.

In the **Command on Source** tab, set the **Technology** to **File**, set the logical **Schema** name to **FILE_AESCRYPT**, and leave all other fields to their default values. There will be no code on the source side.

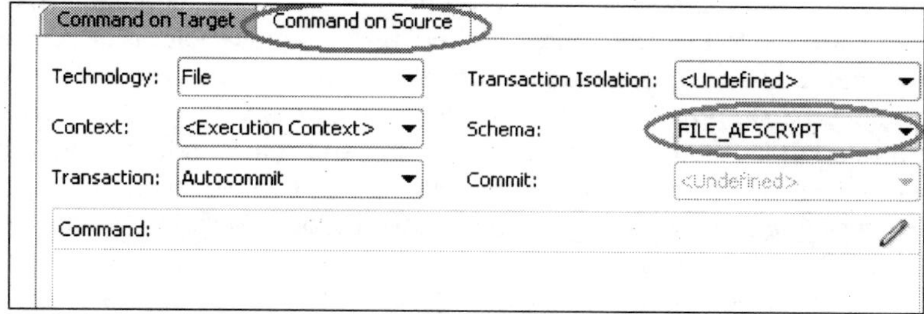

6. Save the procedure and run it.
7. Now, if you go to the **Operato**r window to look into the details of the code that was generated, you can see that the password is not revealed in the operator logs. We are looking in the following screenshot at the code generated for the task:

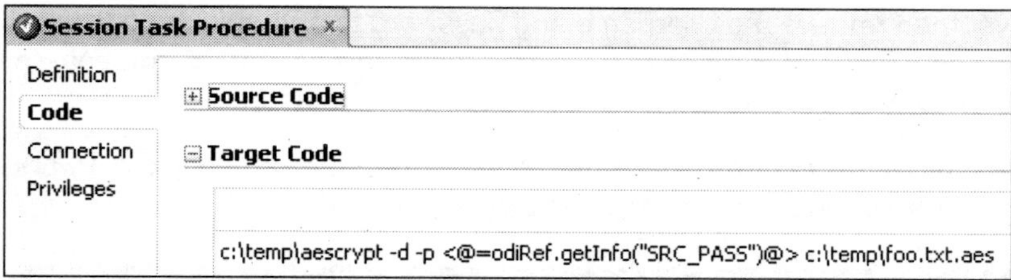

8. Now back to the console, we can see that the original un-encrypted file, `foo.txt`, was restored along with its original content. You can choose to keep or delete the encrypted file `foo.txt.aes`.

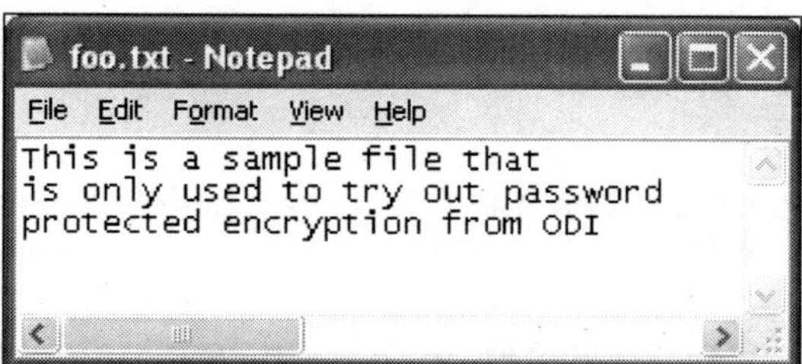

How it works...

It is very common to have code written on both the source and target commands of a KM (LKMs and multi-technology IKMs) or in a procedure step. One technique that is not necessarily well known is to use the source technology as a placeholder for connectivity information that can be used in the code on the target side. In our example, the technology on the target side is OS Command, which does not give us much flexibility in terms of configuration and connectivity parameters. So, we use an artificial source connection to point to the data server that contains the information we need. Then we leverage that information as needed by leveraging the `odiRef.getInfo` substitution method to extract the required parameters. In addition, ODI makes sure that the password that we retrieve and pass into the external tool is never revealed in the operator logs, as it is encapsulated with the `<@@>` syntax.

There's more...

The selection of logical schemas in the source and target connections allows us to leverage any of the parameters defined in either connection. If we were to establish a VPN connection for instance, we could leverage the Host (Data Server) entry to retrieve the name of the remote server then retrieve the username and password to authenticate against this server. When dealing with external components, which require this type of information, think of leveraging **Topology** to securely store the connectivity information.

The additional benefit is that if you leverage ODI contexts, the same logic will work across all environments, from development to production.

Tuning a standalone ODI agent

An ODI agent orchestrates all ODI executions. As such, it is a central piece of the infrastructure. Properly tuning the agent and understanding what requires tuning will help you better manage your infrastructure.

Getting ready

All we need for this recipe is to have a standalone agent already installed on one of your systems. If you do not have an agent available, you can run the ODI installer and select the ODI Standalone Agent option. For the recipe that follows, we assume that the agent was installed on a Windows machine, in the folder `c:\oracledi\products\11.1.1.6`. If your agent is installed in a different directory or on a different operating system, keep this in mind as you follow these steps.

How to do it...

1. Go to the `bin` directory of the agent:

   `c:\oracledi\products\11.1.1.6\oracledi\agent\bin`

2. Edit the file `odiparams.bat` (you will have to edit the `odiparams.sh` file on Linux or Unix systems).
3. In the file, identify the parameters `ODI_INIT_HEAP` and `ODI_MAX_HEAP`. You will notice that the default values are `32` and `256` respectively. Double these values to `64` and `512`, then save the file:

```
REM #
REM # Java virtual machine
REM #
set ODI_JAVA_HOME=D:\oracledi\product\11.1.1.6_GA\jrockit

REM #
REM # Other Parameters
REM #
set ODI_INIT_HEAP=64m
set ODI_MAX_HEAP=512m
set ODI_JMX_PROTOCOL=rmi

REM #
REM # Additional Java Options
REM #
set ODI_ADDITIONAL_JAVA_OPTIONS=
```

4. If your agent is already running, you will have to stop and restart the agent to take these new values into consideration.

How it works...

The parameters we have modified control how much memory is initially allocated to the ODI agent (`ODI_INIT_HEAP`) and what is the maximum amount of memory that the agent can request (`ODI_MAX_HEAP`). These parameters are very important because they control the amount of memory available to the agent. Most actions performed by the agents are running in memory:

- When data is fetched with a JDBC connection, this data will be transferred through the agent memory space
- If you use the ODI memory engine, this in-memory database will actually use the memory space of the agent
- The default behavior of the ODI JDBC driver for XML is to load data into the in-memory database, and as such, it uses more of the agent's allocated memory

These operations are in addition to the orchestrations that the agent always performs:

- Reading the scenarios from the repository
- Completing the scenario code according to the context selected for the execution of that scenario
- Updating the logs with execution results and statistics

The more operations you ask for the agent to run in memory, the more memory you will need to allocate to the agent.

Keep in mind that if you are running several agents on the same server, each agent will have its own memory space. This can be useful to segregate memory intensive operations, but this will also use more of the available memory on that server.

The same will be true with JEE agents, but in this case, the memory parameters will be part of the configuration of the server itself. Refer to your WebLogic Server documentation for more details.

When we are using JDBC to connect to the source and target servers, we can influence how much memory will be used to transfer data from source to target. If you edit any of the data servers in the **Topology** navigator, you will see two parameters at the bottom of the window: **Array Fetch Size** and **Batch Update Size**:

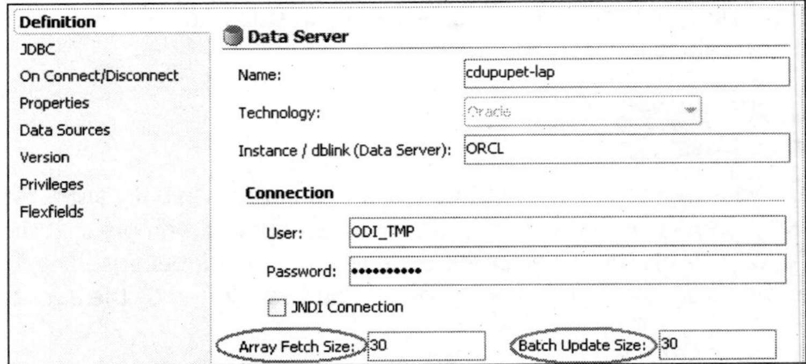

The JDBC protocol is defined so that records are processed in limited batches to make sure that memory is not exhausted immediately with very large queries. By default, these two parameters have a value of `30` when ODI ships, which means that JDBC will process the records 30 at a time. By increasing the value of these parameters, you can improve performance by retrieving more records each time. Just keep in time that by doing so, you are using more of the agent's memory.

> When changing the values of the **Array Fetch Size** and **Batch Update Size** parameters, it is recommended to have the same value for the **Array Fetch Size** on the source data server and the **Batch Update Size** on the target data server. Different values can result in buffering at the agent level, which can be counter-productive in terms of performance.

There's more...

Increasing the agent's memory parameters will only work as long as there is enough memory available on the server hosting the agent. Before looking into increasing the value of these parameters, we should always try to use less memory. Techniques that do not leverage the memory space of the agent usually have better performance, if only because the agent does not have to handle the data anymore and simply behaves as an orchestrator:

- Instead of using JDBC, try and use database loading utilities: external tables, sqlldr, and data pump are some examples available on Oracle databases. Similar utilities are available on other databases: ODI ships out of the box with KMs that support most of these utilities.
- The in-memory engine has one large drawback: it runs in-memory, and as such is more limited than actual databases. Let's be clear: it will perform well only as long as there is enough physical memory available. After that, we are talking about degrading performance, as memory blocks are swapped to disk to leverage virtual memory. You are usually better off using an actual database, and databases today do cache data in memory when it makes sense to do so.
- If you are handling very large XML files that cannot fit easily in memory, use the driver's property `db_props` and point to a `.properties` file that contains all the necessary parameters to connect to an external database. The benefit of this approach is that it allows you to process a lot more files in parallel (files processed in parallel all share the same agent memory space), and also much bigger files. You can look back to *Chapter 9, XML and Web Services*, where this topic is discussed in details.

Loading a file containing a LOB

Loading large objects always requires special considerations. Here, we will create a multi-technology IKM (that is, an IKM that connects to a remote source data server) that loads `CLOB`s and `BLOB`s using an external table definition.

Getting ready

For this recipe, we will need to create three files on disk:

- `CLOB.TXT`: use notepad and write `This is a CLOB` in this file. Save it on disk in your `c:\temp` directory.
- `BLOB.DOC`: use a word processor program and create this file. Write `this is a BLOB` in the file and save it in your `c:\temp` directory.
- Use notepad and create the file `DATA.TXT` with the following record:

```
"Sample record with CLOB and BLOB", "CLOB.TXT", "BLOB.DOC"
```

- Save this file in your `c:\temp` directory.
- Create a table to load the LOBs in your database:

```
Create table LOB_SAMPLE(
Description VARCHAR2(100),
CLOB_Data CLOB,
BLOB_Data BLOB
);
```

- You will have to reverse engineer the file `DATA.TXT` in a file model. Define the file with no header, use the comma as the field separator, and use the following names for the three columns: `Description`, `Clob_File`, and `Blob_File`. Use the double quote character (`"`) for the text delimiter.
- You will have to reverse engineer the `LOB_SAMPLE` table.
- You will need a project where the KM `IKM SQL Control Append` has been imported.

How to do it...

1. Make a copy of `IKM SQL Control Append` and rename the new KM `IKM File SQL Append (LOB)`.
2. Expand the KM in the tree and remove all the options except for `INSERT`, `COMMIT`, and `DELETE_TEMORARY_OBJECTS`.

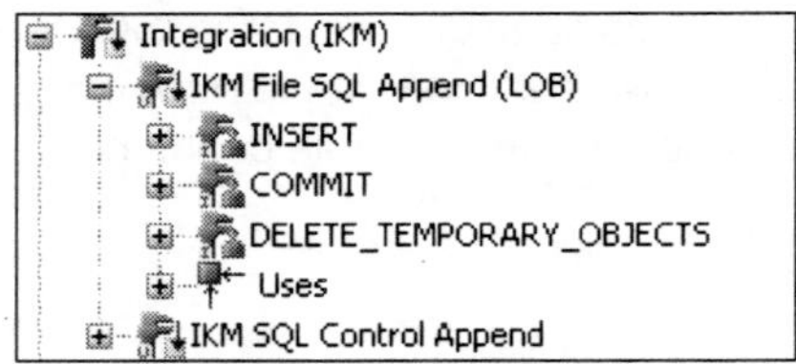

3. Edit the IKM. In the **Definition** tab, select the option **Multi-Connections**. Then, set the source **Technology** to **File** and the target **Technology** to **Oracle**.

4. We will simplify the IKM, so delete all the steps except for the following ones:
    - `Drop flow table`
    - `Create flow table I$`
    - `Insert new rows`
    - `Commit Transaction`
    - `Drop flow table`
5. Add a new step, name this step `Create Oracle Directory`, and copy this code:

```
create or replace directory dat_dir AS '<%=snpRef.
getSrcTablesList("", "[SCHEMA]", "", "")%>'
```

   Move this step up to make it the second step in the list after the first `Drop flow` table.

6. Edit the two steps named `Drop flow` table. At the very bottom of the steps details, expand the **Option** entry and select **Always Execute**: in the original IKM, these steps were conditioned by the **FLOW_CONTROL** option, which we have removed.
7. Edit the step `Create Flow table I$`. At the very bottom of the step details, expand the **Option** entry and select **Always Execute**. Then replace the original code with this:

```
create table <%=odiRef.getTable("L", "INT_NAME", "A")%>
(
    <%=snpRef.getColList("", "[COL_NAME]\t[DEST_WRI_DT]",
    ",\n\t", "","")%>
    )
    ORGANIZATION EXTERNAL
    (
    TYPE ORACLE_LOADER
    DEFAULT DIRECTORY dat_dir
    ACCESS PARAMETERS
    (
        RECORDS DELIMITED BY NEWLINE
        CHARACTERSET "WE8ISO8859P1 "

        BADFILE    '<%=snpRef.getSrcTablesList("",
        "[RES_NAME]", "", "")%>.bad'
        LOGFILE        '<%=snpRef.getSrcTablesList("",
        "[RES_NAME]", "", "")%>.log'
        DISCARDFILE '<%=snpRef.getSrcTablesList("",
        "[RES_NAME]", "", "")%>.dsc'
SKIP        <%=snpRef.getSrcTablesList("",
    "[FILE_FIRST_ROW]", "", "")%>
    FIELDS  TERMINATED BY  '<%=snpRef.getSrcTablesList("",
    "[SFILE_SEP_FIELD]", "", "")%>'
```

```
    <% if(snpRef.getSrcTablesList("", "[FILE_ENC_FIELD]",
    "", "").equals("")){%>
    <%} else {%>OPTIONALLY ENCLOSED BY
    '<%=snpRef.getSrcTablesList("", "[FILE_ENC_FIELD]", "",
    "")%>' AND '<%=snpRef.getSrcTablesList("",
    "[FILE_ENC_FIELD]", "", "")%>' <%}%>
    MISSING FIELD VALUES ARE NULL
    (
    <%=snpRef.getColList("", " " +"<? if
    (\u0022[DEST_WRI_DT]\u0022.equals(\u0022CLOB\u0022))
    {?> [EXPRESSION] <?}else if
    (\u0022[DEST_WRI_DT]\u0022.equals(\u0022BLOB\u0022))
    {?> [EXPRESSION] <?}else{?>[COL_NAME] <?}?>"
    +»CHAR([LONGC])», «,\n\t\t\t», «»,»»)%>
    )
    COLUMN TRANSFORMS (<%=odiRef.getColList(«», «[COL_NAME]
    from LOBFILE ([EXPRESSION]) from (dat_dir)
    CLOB»,»,/n»,»»,»UD1»)%>
    <%=odiRef.getColList(«,», «[COL_NAME] from LOBFILE
    ([EXPRESSION]) from (dat_dir) BLOB»,»,/n»,»»,»UD2»)%>)

    )
    LOCATION (<%=snpRef.getSrcTablesList(«»,
    «'[RES_NAME]'», «», «»)%>)
    )
PARALLEL 2
REJECT LIMIT UNLIMITED
```

8. Simplify the code of the step `Insert new rows` to only keep the following:

```
insert into <%=odiRef.getTable("L","TARG_NAME","A")%>
(
    <%=odiRef.getColList("", "[COL_NAME]", ",\n\t", "", "((INS and
!TRG) and REW)")%>
    <%=odiRef.getColList(",", "[COL_NAME]", ",\n\t", "", "((INS
and TRG) and REW)")%>
)
select <%=odiRef.getColList("", "[COL_NAME]", ",\n\t", "", "((INS
and !TRG) and REW)")%>
    <%=odiRef.getColList(",", "[EXPRESSION]", ",\n\t", "", "((INS
and TRG) and REW)")%>
From <%=odiRef.getTable("L","INT_NAME","A")%>
```

9. Now save the IKM and create a new interface called `Load LOBs` where you are using the file `DATA.TXT` as a source and the table `LOB_SAMPLE` as a target. In the **Overview** tab, select **Staging Area Different From Target** and select the **File** logical schema that points to the `DATA.TXT` file in the schema drop down (no worries, we will not actually create anything in the staging area). Then, map the columns as follows:

Source columns	Target Columns	Mappings
Description	Description	DAT.Description
`Clob_File`	`CLOB_Data`	`Clob_File`
`Blob_File`	`BLOB_Data`	`Blob_File`

> We have removed the alias name from the mapping of both LOBs using `Clob_File` and `Blob_File` instead of `DAT.Clob_File` and `DAT.Blob_File`, otherwise this would generate invalid code for the external table definition used in the KM.

10. In the **QuickEdit** tab, select the option **UD1** for the `CLOB` column, and the option **UD2** for the `BLOB` column.
11. In the **Flow** tab, click on the target data server to select the `IKM File SQL Append (LOB)`.
12. Save and run the interface. You can check for successful execution in the operator navigator. If you run a `select` statement against the table `LOB_SAMPLE`, you can confirm that you have just loaded a `CLOB` and a `BLOB`.

How it works...

In this recipe, we are taking advantage of multiple elements that are at our disposal in the redaction of KMs.

Multi-technology IKMs can only be used when the staging area is not on the target server, hence their name, since they can connect to a different technology to access the staging area.

By forcing the staging area on the source data server, we eliminate the need for an LKM; source and staging are now on the same server.

As a result, by using this multi-technology IKM, we bypass the creation of both `C$` and `I$` staging tables. First, since we do not have an LKM, there is no `C$` table. Second, since we use an external table to map the file into the database, the data will go straight from the file into the target table, removing the need for an `I$` table. One thing to remember with such IKMs though: you must use the source technology as your staging area as we did in step 9 of this recipe. This can be quite counter-intuitive when you are using a flat file as your source, but since we are not creating any staging table, we are safe doing so.

Next, because of the specific nature of CLOBs and BLOBs, we need to use the name of the columns of both the target table and source table to generate the proper code that will create the external table (this is the reason why we are removing the alias name from the mappings in step 9). This allows us to leverage the tags [COL_NAME] and [EXPRESSION] to retrieve the target and source column names respectively, as we did in step 8:

```
COLUMN TRANSFORMS (<%=odiRef.getColList(", "[COL_NAME] from LOBFILE
([EXPRESSION]) from (dat_dir) CLOB",",/n","","UD1")%>
```

Finally, we take advantage of the flags available in the **QuickEdit** view to explicitly mark the CLOBs and BLOBs columns as UD1 and UD2, so that the proper code from the KM can be applied to these columns specifically.

There's more...

We have over-simplified the KM to focus on the load of the LOBs, but the techniques used here can be expanded upon. By relying on other techniques as described in this book, you can avoid the manipulation of the aliases in the mappings, for instance. This could have been done by using the .replace() function available in Java.

Likewise, listing the CLOBs and BLOBs in the COLUMN TRANSFORMS section of the external table definition could have been handled with a for loop.

Several KMs have been written by the ODI community. A Google search on ODI and LOB returns too many results for us to list them all here, but they are worth a look if you are interested in this subject. A good starting point is http://java.net/projects/oracledi, where KMs are shared by the ODI developers community.

Using ODI versioning

Versioning source code is a key element for a successful development lifecycle. All ODI objects can be exported as XML files if you want to store them in an external source control system, but one limitation of this approach is that the comparison of different versions of the same objects are not trivial in the XML form.

To make version comparisons easier, you can leverage versioning of objects directly within ODI. This recipe will show you how to take advantage of this feature.

Getting ready

To play with versioning, we will need some objects. You can use any objects of your choice, but for our step-by-step instructions, we will first create an interface based on the SRC_EMP and TRG_EMP tables as described in the *Preface* of this book.

To follow the steps described here, do the following:

- If you have not done so earlier, create a model where you reverse engineer the `SRC_EMP` table from our source sample.
- If you have not done so earlier, create a model where you reverse engineer the `TRG_EMP` table from our target sample.
- Make sure that you have a project where the `IKM SQL Control Append` KM has been imported. If both source and target schemas are defined under the same data server in **Topology**, you will not need an `LKM`. If they are defined on separate data servers, you can use `LKM SQL to Oracle`, as we are dealing with very low volumes of data here.

How to do it...

1. Create a new interface called `Load Employees` with `SRC_EMP` as a source and `TRG_EMP` as a target. All the mappings are straight mappings (no transforms). Use the `IKM SQL Control Append` in the **Flow** tab and set the **FLOW_CONTROL** option to `False`. Set the option **TRUNCATE** to `True` because there is most likely data left over from earlier recipes in your target table. Save the interface. Run the interface to make sure that it runs successfully.
2. In the **Overview** tab of the interface, select the **Versions** panel on the left. Click on the green **+** sign to add a new version; keep the default version number (**1.0.0.0**) and add this **Description**: `Straight mapping from SRC_EMP to TRG_EMP`. Then click on **OK** to create the version. You should now have a version listed as follows:

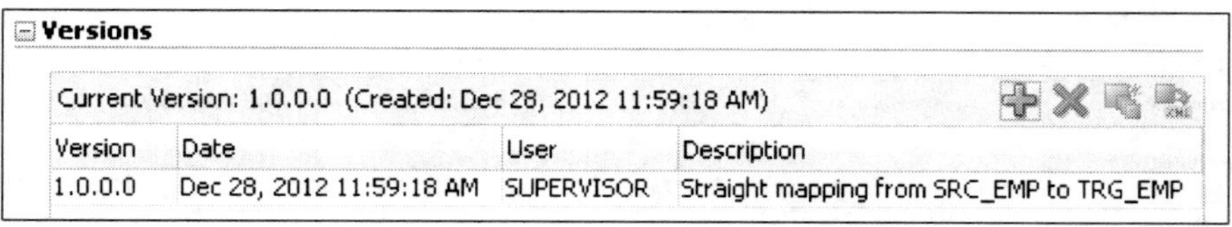

3. Now go back into the interface **Mapping** tab and replace the current mapping for `HIREDATE` with `sysdate`. In the **Flow** tab, set the option **FLOW_CONTROL** to `True`. Save, close, and re-open the interface. If you go to the **Versions** panel in the **Overview** tab, you can see that the object has been modified since a version was created:

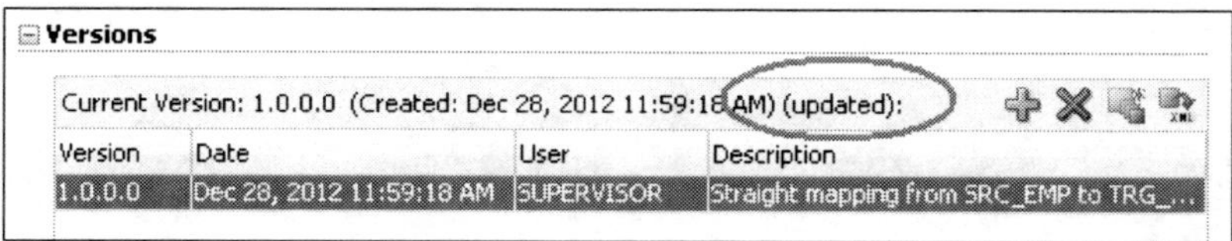

4. Now click on the green **+** sign to create a new version. Change the `Version` number to `2.0.0.0`. In the **Description** field, enter this: `Changed HIREDATE to sysdate`. Click on **OK** to create the version.

5. With several versions available, it is now possible to compare the multiple iterations of the object. You can perform a comparison by using the **Versions** browser available from the main menu, **ODI/Version Browser...**, or you can compare the different versions directly from this screen. If you press the *Ctrl* key, you can select both versions with your mouse cursor. Once both are highlighted, you can right-click on the selection and select **Compare...**.

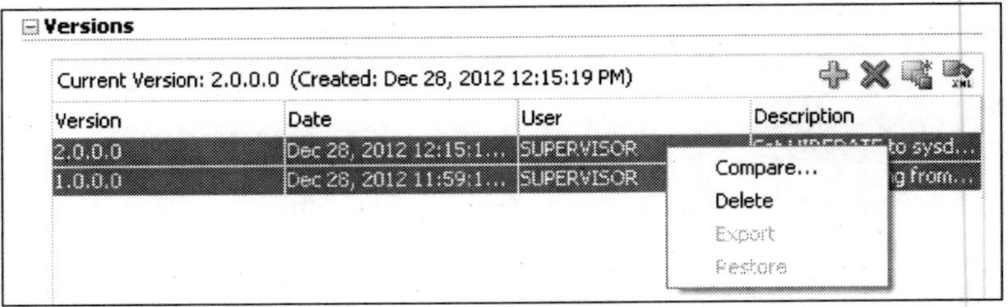

6. Both versions of the object will be presented side by side, with a highlight on the differences between the objects:

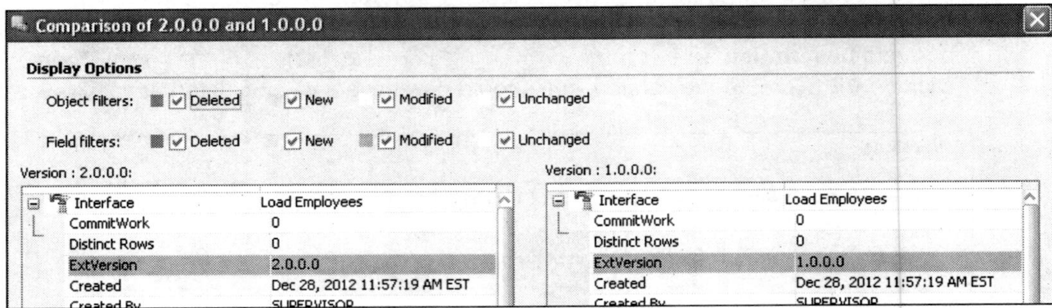

7. If you scroll down the description of the objects, you see more of the highlighted differences:

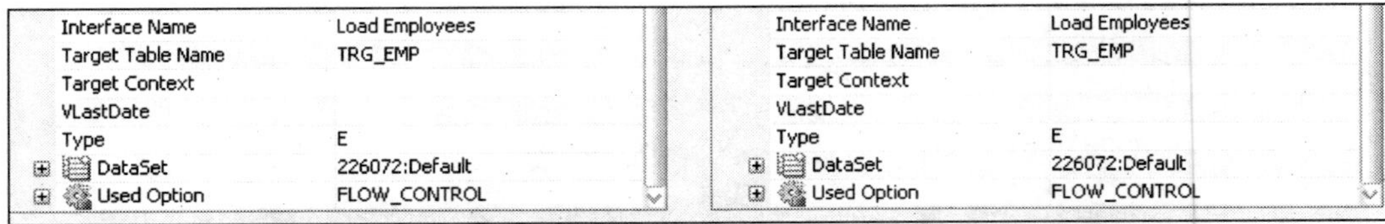

To get more details on the changes from version to version, click on the **+** sign in front of the highlighted elements (we have removed some entries in the following image to highlight our focus):

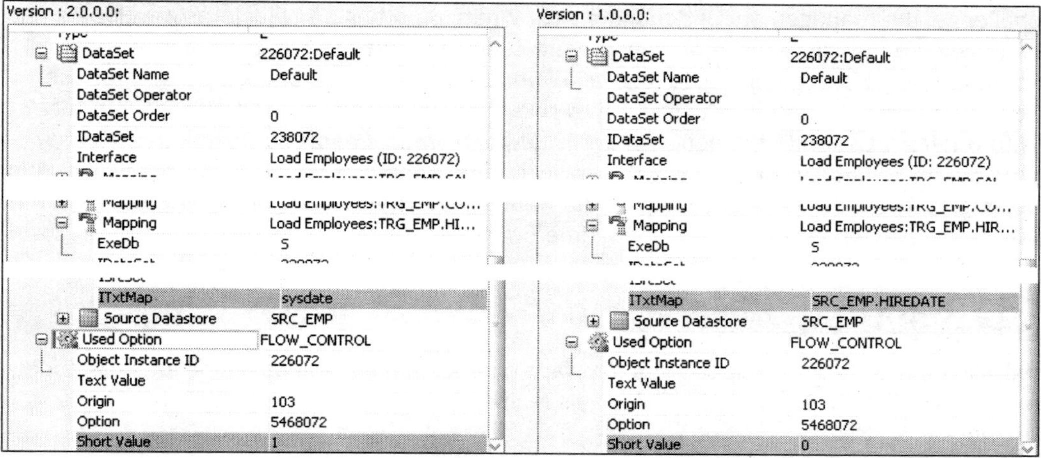

We can see here both the old and current version of the mapping that we have changed, along with the change in the option of our KM.

How it works...

When a user creates a version in ODI, a copy of that object is saved in the Master repository, along with the version number and the description associated to that version. When different versions of the same object are being compared, it is the objects from the Master repository that are compared. Versioning is not limited to interfaces, it is also possible to version individual objects, such as `Packages` and `Load Plans`, but also objects that are collections of objects such as `Folders`, `Models`, `Model Folders`, and `Projects`.

The version browser allows you to filter the list of objects by object types (`Interfaces`, `folders`, `models`, and so on) and to further limit your list by selecting the name of the objects that match that type.

There's more...

At any point in time, there is only one current version of any object in the Work repository. All previous versions are saved in the Master repository. Any version can be restored in the Work repository in order to replace the current one. The `restore` function is available from the **Versions** tab of the objects (`Interfaces`, `folders`, `packages`, and so on) as well as from the **Versions** browser.

Performing a Smart Export/Smart Import

Up until version 11.1.1.6.0 of ODI, exporting and importing objects presented a particular challenge: the management of dependencies. When importing an object, the developers had to make sure that all dependent objects were in place before the object itself was imported. For instance, before importing an interface, models and KMs referenced by that interface had to already be in place. But what if they had not been exported along with the interface? With version 11.1.1.6.0, the notion of **Smart Export/Smart Import** solves the dependency problem. In addition, it will give you the ability to merge the new imported objects with existing objects; you can always select whether you want to keep the existing objects or overwrite them with the imported ones, one object at a time.

Getting ready

We will reuse the `Load Employees` interface created in the previous recipe for illustration purposes. However, you can also follow this recipe by using another object of your choosing.

How to do it...

1. In the **Designer** navigator, click on the Designer drop-down icon to display the options menu and select **Export...**, as depicted on the following screenshot:

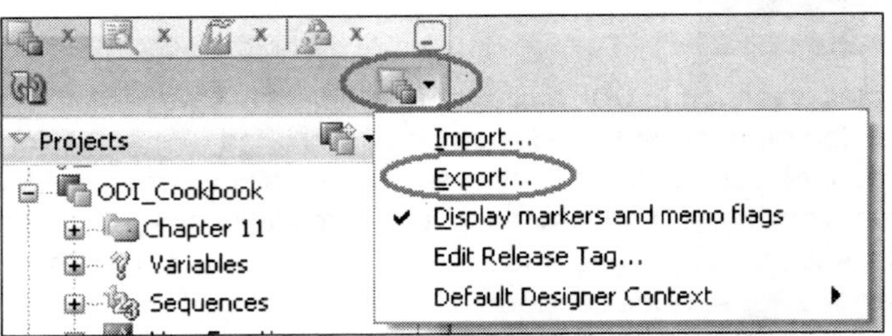

From the window that pops up, select **Smart Export** and click on **OK**.

2. Drag-and-drop the interface `Load Employees` into the **Selected objects** panel:

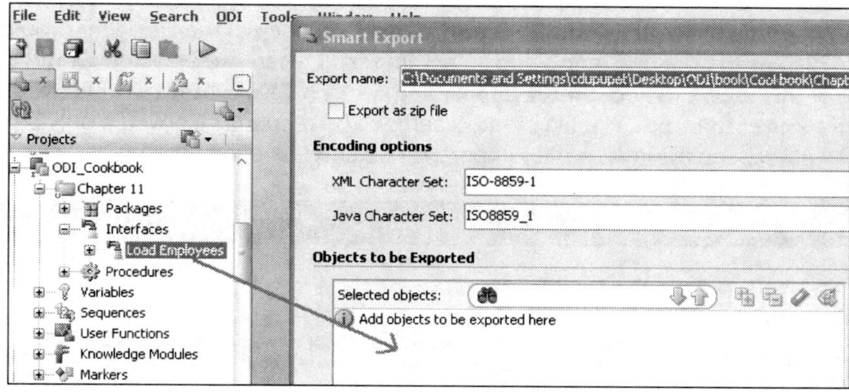

3. ODI will compute the dependencies and list all the objects that are needed if you want to re-import this interface later:

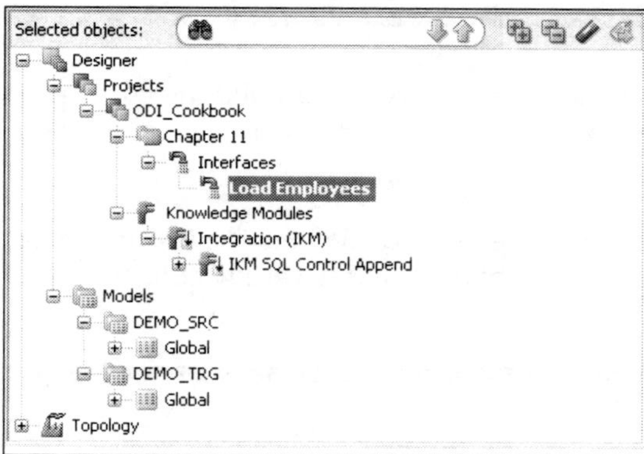

We can see here that the KM and the models that we have used to build the interface are properly listed. **Topology** references are also present, assuming the user has enough privileges to access that information.

> You may have more than one project listed here if your models reference KMs (RKMs, CKMs, and JKMs) that are in these other projects. Best practice would be to use Global Knowledge Modules rather than having cross-project dependencies.

4. Now that we have all the elements we need, select the option **Export as a ZIP file** at the top of the window and click on **Export**. After reading the Export Report, press **Close**.

5. To import a file generated with **Smart Export**, go back to the Designer drop-down icon to display the options menu and select **Import...** where we selected **Export...** in Step 1 of this recipe. Select **Smart Import** and click on **OK**. A wizard will help you select the `SmartExport.zip` file created earlier. The response file would only be needed if we were replaying an earlier import, so we can leave this blank.

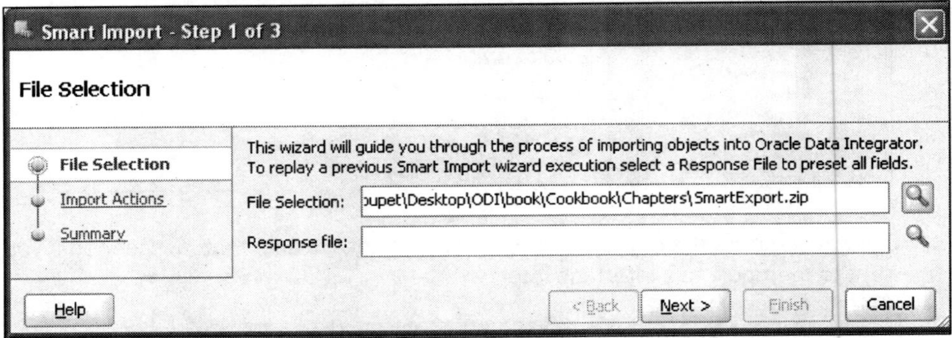

6. The wizard will compare incoming objects with the content of the repository and will offer actions (merge, overwrite, create a copy, ignore, reuse).

> The lowest elements of the tree (like interface here) cannot be merged, you have to choose which interface version to use.

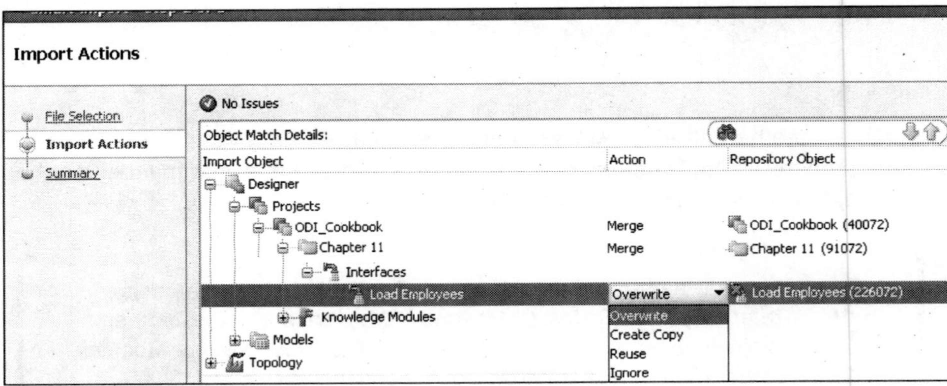

7. Once you have reviewed the options for the import (we will keep the default here to **Overwrite** the existing objects with the ones that we are importing) you can click **Next** to see if there are any potential issues identified by the wizard, and if none are listed, you can click **Finish** to proceed with the import.

How it works...

The **Smart Export** and **Smart Import** are based on new SDK APIs available as of ODI 11.1.1.6.0. They validate dependencies before the export takes place and before the import takes place. If missing dependencies are detected, the import can still be done, but imported objects will be highlighted and missing objects will be listed so that developers can later import the missing objects to fix this inconsistency. This whole concept is extremely important, as it alleviates developers from the burden of keeping track of these dependencies.

At import time, when the object that is being imported already exists in the repository, the user has the ability to choose among the following options:

- **Overwrite**: Overwrite an existing object when importing a new version of that object
- **Create Copy**: Create a copy of the object that is being imported so that both the existing copy and the imported copy coexist after import
- **Reuse**: Reuse the existing object and discard the imported object, but objects linked to the discarded object can still be imported
- **Ignore**: Ignore the imported object and its dependencies

There's more...

The **Smart Export** and **Smart Import** features are not limited to the **Designer** navigator; they can be found in the **Topology** navigator as well.

The same features can also be leveraged from the ODI SDK for a programmatic approach to object exports and imports. Some customers have chosen this approach to automated source code management and code promotion.

Accessing an Excel spreadsheet

As much as we might want all data to reside in databases, a large amount of data still resides in other formats. In this recipe, we will look into how to read data from an Excel spreadsheet, as this can present some unique challenges.

Getting ready...

To connect to an Excel spreadsheet, ODI requires two components: the ODBC driver provided by Microsoft and the ODI ODBC/JDBC bridge that ships with ODI.

> If you are using Excel on a Windows 64-bit platform, you will have to make sure that you have a 64-bit version of the ODBC driver. You can download the proper drivers from the Microsoft support website. The 64 bit ODBC driver for Office 2010 is available at the Microsoft download center at this URL: `http://www.microsoft.com/en-us/download/details.aspx?displaylang=en&id=13255`

Before getting started, we will need an Excel spreadsheet. To make things simple, you can create a spreadsheet with the following data:

EMPNO	ENAME	JOB	HIREDATE	DEPTNO
10	J Tanake	Intern	1/1/2013	10
11	I Shawnee	Intern	1/1/2013	10
12	W Welkert	Intern	1/1/2013	20
13	K Thulsberg	Intern	1/1/2013	20

Save the spreadsheet in the `c:\temp` directory and call it `interns.xlsx`.

How to do it...

1. The first thing we have to do is to expose the data to through the ODBC driver. With the spreadsheet open in Excel, select all the data (including the header row) and name the area `Interns` (you can type that name in the top left corner).

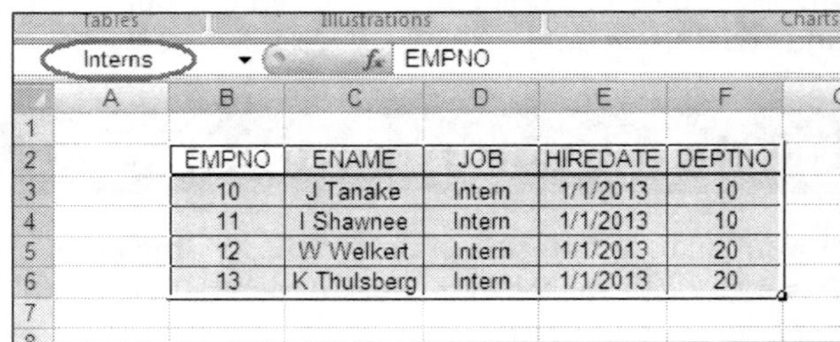

Save and close the spreadsheet.

2. Open the Microsoft **Data Sources (ODBC)** tool:

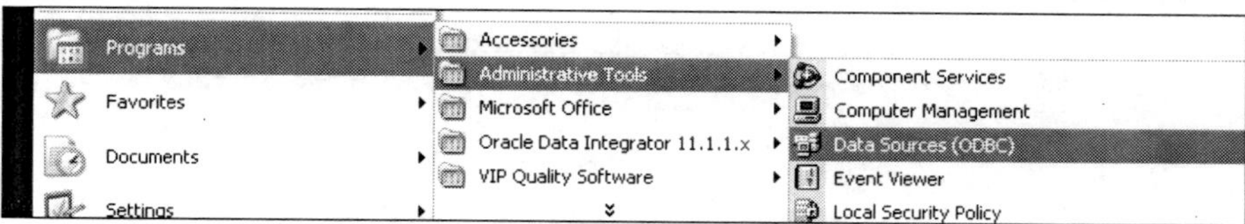

In the ODBC Data Source Administrator, you can add either a **User DSN** or a **System DSN**; the process is the same, but the **User DSN** will only be visible for the user currently logged-in; a system DSN will be available to all users. Click on **Add...** to create a new DSN and select the **Microsoft Excel Driver** option:

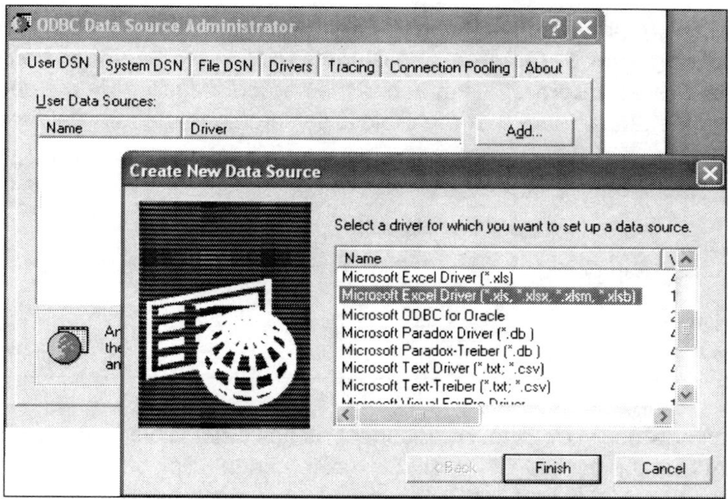

Click on **Finish** and you will be prompted to name the connection and select the file; we type here `Interns` for the **Data Source Name**, and you have to click on **Select Workbook** to select the file `c:\temp\interns.xlsx`. When you click on **OK**, the new data source will be listed in the original window.

3. In ODI, select the **Topology** navigator to add a new data server under the technology Microsoft Excel. Use the name `XL_Interns`. Neither username nor password are required. In the **JDBC** tab, select the **Sun JDBC-ODBC driver** `sun.jdbc.odbc.JdbcOdbcDriver` and update the **JDBC URL** with the name of the data source: `jdbc:odbc:Interns`. Under this data server, create a physical schema (you can keep the default name of `XL_Interns_Default`). Then, create a logical schema called `XL_Interns` to point to this physical schema.

4. In the **Designer** navigator, create a model called `EXCEL_Interns`. Set the **Technology** to **Microsoft Excel**, and select the `XL_Interns` logical schema:

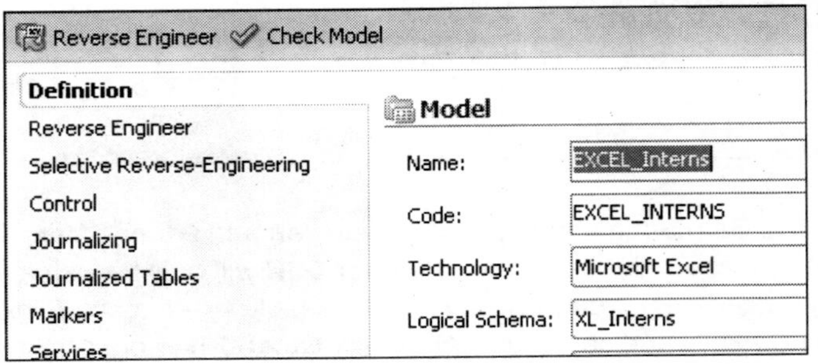

Then click on the **Selective Reverse-Engineering** tab and select **Selective Reverse-Engineering**, **New Datastores**, and **Objects to Reverse Engineer**. You should see one table listed: **Interns**. This matches the named area that we created in the spreadsheet. Make sure that the table is selected and click on **Reverse Engineer**:

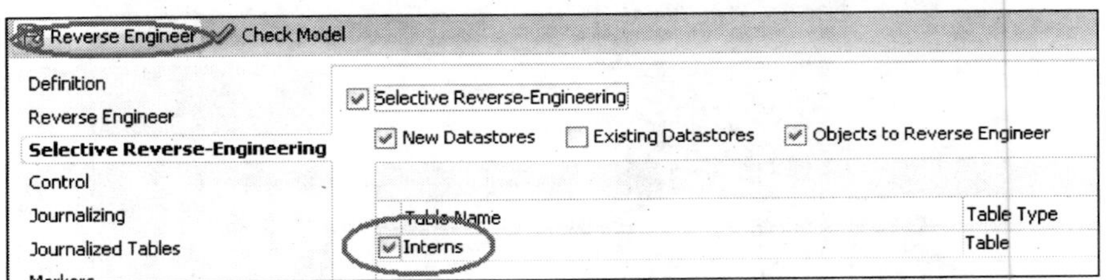

5. You can now use your Excel spreadsheet as any other table in your interfaces. To confirm that the data is fully available, you can right-click on the table name under the newly created model in the object tree and select the data entry in the menu: you will see the data from the spreadsheet:

Data: Interns

	EMPNO	ENAME	JOB	HIREDATE	DEPTNO
1	10.0	J Tanake	Intern	2013-01-01 00:00:00.0	10.0
2	11.0	I Shawnee	Intern	2013-01-01 00:00:00.0	10.0
3	12.0	W Welkert	Intern	2013-01-01 00:00:00.0	20.0
4	13.0	K Thulsberg	Intern	2013-01-01 00:00:00.0	20.0

How it works...

The behavior is actually quite simple: the ODBC driver exposes all the named areas as tables. ODI uses a JDBC driver that in turn invokes the ODBC driver. The tables become visible to ODI, which can reverse engineer the metadata. Once again, the metadata is served up by the ODBC driver, which chooses the data types for the different columns.

There is an alternative syntax for the ODBC driver that combines the previous steps 2 and 3 in the sense that you can skip step 2, and enter all the necessary information when specifying the JDBC URL. Note that this syntax will vary depending on the version of Microsoft Excel that you are using.

For versions of Microsoft Excel older than 2007, you have to use the following syntax for the JDBC URL:

```
jdbc:odbc:Excel Files;DBQ=<file_path>
```

For versions of Microsoft Excel including 2007 and later, you have to use the following syntax for the JDBC URL:

```
jdbc:odbc:Driver={Microsoft Excel Driver (*.xls, *.xlsx, *.xlsm,
.xlsb)};DBQ=<file_path>;DriverID=22;READONLY=true;
```

These syntaxes still leverage the Microsoft ODBC driver, and as such require the same naming of the tables within the spreadsheet.

> You will also want to double check the data types returned by ODBC, as the driver can be picky; a number with an empty cell could be interpreted as a string for instance. Microsoft recommends to not mix text and numbers in the same column, or to set the format of the cells in the spreadsheet to force the format returned by the driver. More details are available on the Microsoft support website: `http://support.microsoft.com/kb/141284`.

There's more...

There are a number of situations that can be problematic with Excel spreadsheets. The first one is that you may not be running your ODI agent on a Windows machine. There are two possible solutions here:

- Install a separate ODI agent on the Windows machine such that the ODBC driver, data source definition, and the file become local resources to that agent.

- Instead of using an ODBC approach, you can try to connect directly with 3rd party JDBC drivers. JDBC drivers for Excel are available from `http://xlsql.SourceForge.net` ,`http://odiexperts.com`, and `http://www.hxtt.com`, among others. You will want to check ownership and possible restrictions around the use of these drivers with their respective owners.

The next challenge is the fact that we have to create a named area in the spreadsheet. This is a limitation of the ODBC driver, which can be annoying if your receive spreadsheets that do not have named areas. One thing to keep in mind is that the naming is only needed for the reverse engineering process. Once ODI knows of the structure of the spreadsheet, you can modify the definition of the ODI datastore (aka table) to point to the sheet itself. So if you kept the default name of `Sheet1` in your spreadsheet, you can replace the name in the resource name of the data store with `[SHEET1$]` (brackets and uppercase are all required). Try it out and view the data: the result will be the same!

Impacting the data flow by changing the staging area location

When an interface is created, ODI will by default create the staging area on the target server. There are many reasons for this design choice:

- Data is usually loaded into servers that are larger than the ones data is extracted from: data warehouses for instance will host a lot more data than individual systems, and as a result these systems will tend to offer a lot more processing power.
- Centralizing data coming from disparate sources is more convenient in a central location. As long as everything has to be loaded on the target system eventually, staging on the target will save us additional data movement.
- Often times, source systems cannot be used for staging because of restricted permissions (read only).

However, there are cases where staging data away from the target is necessary. For example, if a process writes to a flat file, there is no way to transform data by leveraging the engine on the target side: there is none to use in that case. There are other cases (such as packaged applications for instance) where staging on the target system is not necessarily recommended. In yet other cases, staging some of the data will be more efficient on the source system: moving a small lookup table from the target system to the source can save a lot in terms of extraction costs.

For all these cases, developers will want to stage data away from the target system on a case-by-case basis. The purpose of this recipe is to show you how to perform this action.

Getting ready

If you have used the setup proposed in the *Preface* of this book, you will have two separate Oracle data servers, one for the `DEMO_SRC` schema and one for the `DEMO_TRG` schema. We will take advantage of this setup to illustrate the changes in data flows when the staging area is moved away from the target schema.

For this recipe, we will need the `SRC_EMP` table from `DEMO_SRC`, as well as the `TRG_EMP` and `TRG_DEPT` tables from the `DEMO_TRG` schema.

You will also need a project where the following KMs have been imported:

- `LKM SQL to Oracle`
- `LKM SQL to SQL`
- `IKM SQL Control Append`
- `IKM SQL to SQL Control Append`

We will also use the predefined in-memory engine technology. Make sure that you have a server defined under that technology, and that the default schema under that server is associated to a logical schema (we will use a logical schema named `MEMORY_ENGINE`).

We are using the memory engine in this recipe because it does not require us to take any other technology into account. For real life scenarios, I recommend a commercial database for staging purposes because the memory engine will consume some of the memory space of the ODI agent, and as such will eventually become limited.

How to do it...

1. Create an interface called `Load Remote Employees` with the tables `SRC_EMP` and `TRG_DEPT` on the source side. Join the tables on `DEPT_NO`. Use `TRG_EMP` as the target, and make straight mappings from `SRC_EMP` to `TRG_EMP`.

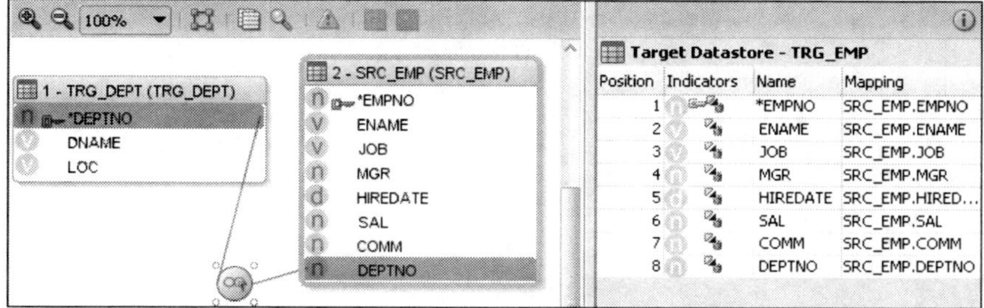

2. Click on the **Flow** tab of the interface to look at the staging of tables: the `SRC_EMP` table is staged in the `Work` schema of the target server, but the `TRG_DEPT` table is not staged because it already resides on the target server.

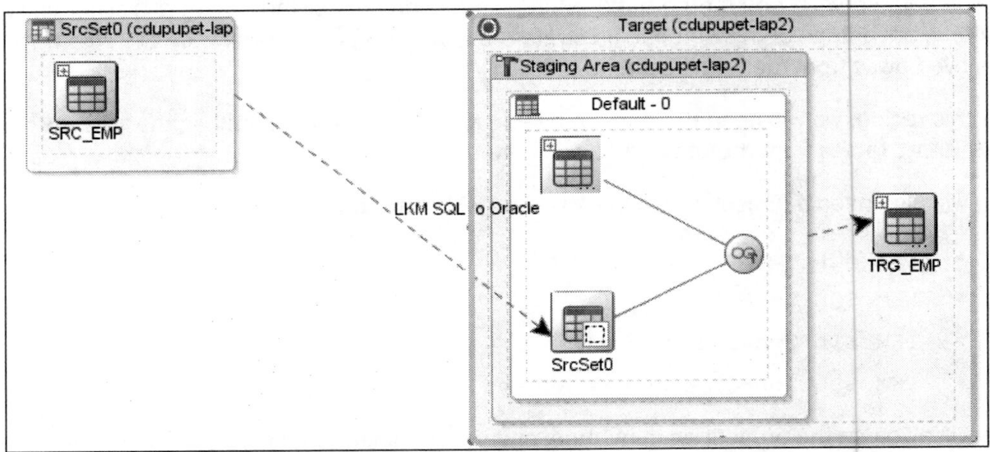

You can look at the default KMs selection. Make sure that the **LKM SQL to Oracle** was selected to load data into the target server, and `IKM SQL Control Append` was selected to combine staged data and local data into the target table.

3. Going back to the **Overview** tab of the interface, click on **Staging Area Different From Target** and select the logical schema that points to your source schema (`DEMO_SRC` in this screenshot):

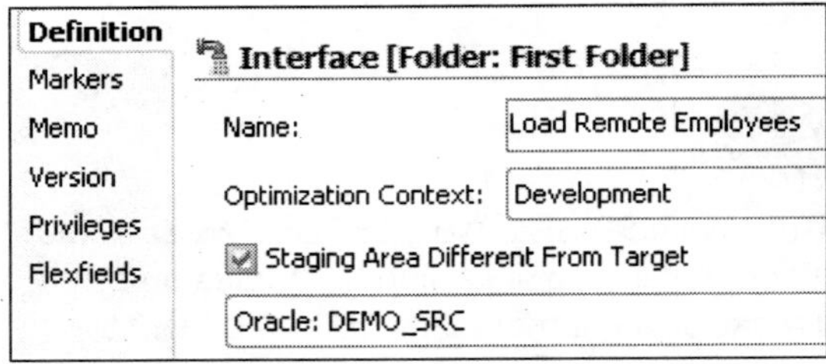

4. Click on the **Flow** tab again, and you will see that this time, the `TRG_DEPT` table is staged on the source schema, but the `SRC_EMP` table is not staged anymore.

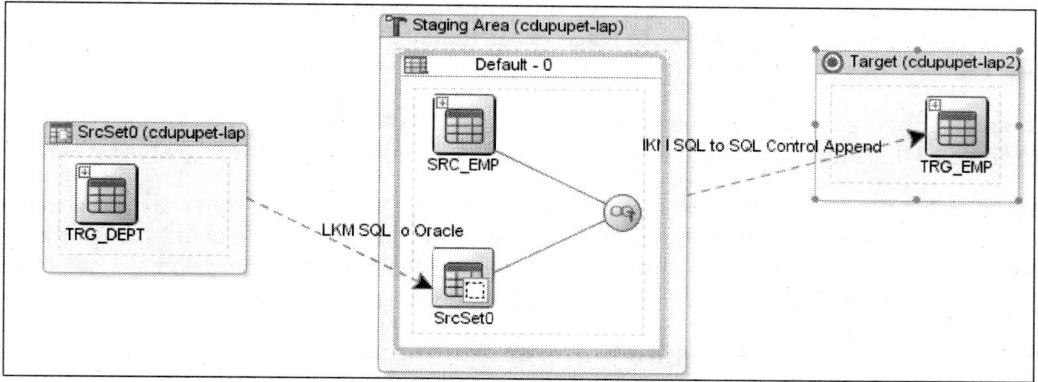

The LKM has not changed, but you will most likely have to click on the target to select the proper IKM in this case: `IKM SQL to SQL Control Append`.

5. Now, back to the **Overview** tab, change the staging area to the in-memory engine MEMORY ENGINE.
6. Finally, back to the **Flow** tab. Both the `SRC_EMP` and the `TRG_DEPT` table are staged. This is now similar to a traditional ETL architecture where all resources are brought into a single engine.

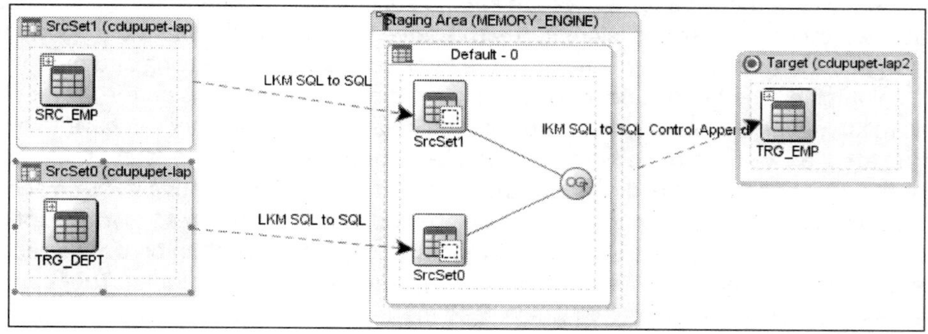

Here you may have to select the proper KMs for each source table: **LKM SQL to SQL**. Keep using **IKM SQL to SQL Control Append** to go from the staging area to the target. If you need to select this KM, you can do so by clicking on the target schema represented in the **Flow** tab.

How it works...

The logic for the creation of staging tables is a combination of KM selection and the location of the staging area. ODI knows not to stage tables that are on the same data server. This is why the `TRG_DEPT` table is not staged when we are staging on the target server.

If, however, you are staging in a server where none of the sources are available, ODI will have to stage all the sources, as illustrated when we used the memory engine as a staging area.

What we have to keep in mind when we choose where to stage data is what the impact will be in terms of data movement. All other things being equal, do I move more data by staging on the target side or on the source side? Once this concept is properly understood, the selection of the most efficient KM should guarantee the best possible performance for your interface.

Now, of course, all the other things are never equal. There are issues with user privileges (perhaps it's not allowable to stage on the source or target system) as well as technologies limitations (you cannot stage on a flat file or on a JMS connection). After taking these factors into consideration and knowing what your options are, you should be able to define the best strategy for staging your data.

Finally, keep in mind that the selection of the location of the staging area can be different from interface to interface, enabling you to optimize each individual case.

There's more...

One concept where the developers need to set the staging area is when creating a temporary interface. A temporary interface is created with source tables coming from the data models and a target table that is created directly in the interface, either by dragging and dropping source columns on the target side, or by directly creating target columns on the target side. For ODI to know where this temporary table will be created, the developer will have to choose a staging area, as we have done here in this recipe. The properties of the target table will contain the name of that table along with the schema to use when creating it (`Data` schema or `Work` schema). Obviously, for the table to be created, the `CREATE_TARG_TABLE` option in the IKM will have to be set to `True`. These temporary interfaces can then be used directly as sources in other interfaces (no need to reverse engineer the temporary table). They can even be used as sub-select statements, in which case there is not even a need to physically create the temporary table.

Automating Smart Export/Smart Import with the ODI SDK

The basis of life cycle management is ensuring that there are separate and distinct environments for development, test, production, and any additional environment needed by the enterprise. As objects are created and modified within ODI, the object as well as any dependent object can be moved from the development environment to the test environment and finally deployed to the production environment. Along with this movement of objects, the baseline of each object as well as any modification to this object need to be stored and versioned in a source control system. ODI objects can easily be imported and exported with ODI's smart import/export. The exported XML files can then be easily integrated with a source control system or a lifecycle management system; however this is an interactive process. Often an enterprise has an existing set of best practices for source control management as well as life cycle management. ODI's smart/import export functionality can easily be integrated into this set of best practices by utilizing the ODI SDK and appropriately calling the ODI smart import or export from within the source code control program or from within the enterprise's lifecycle management system.

In this recipe, we will reuse the `LoadEmployees` interface from the *Performing a smart import/export* recipe in *Chapter 11, More on ODI*, to perform an automated smart export and import. Using the following recipe, you could integrate and automate the import and export objects within ODI.

This recipe uses a simple Java program to automate export and import of the ODI interface and its dependant knowledge modules.

How to do it...

1. Ensure you have JDK 1.6 installed along with the ODI SDK as outlined in *Chapter 7, Advanced Coding Techniques*.
2. Update and compile the included `smartExport.java` program to perform the smart export using the ODI SDK.
3. The Java program `smartExport.java` must be updated as follows:
    1. Line 36: JDBC URL updated appropriately, will match ODI Studio value.
    2. Line 37: JDBC driver updated appropriately, will match ODI Studio value.
    3. Line 38: JDBC Master repository username updated appropriately, will match ODI Studio value.
    4. Line 39: JDBC Master repository password updated appropriately, will match ODI Studio value
    5. Save the `smartExport.java` file.

4. Compile the `exportJava` program by executing the following from the command line:

```
<your Java home>/javac -classpath ./;<your ODI home>/oracledi.sdk/
lib/.;<your ODI home>/oracledi.sdk/lib/* smartExport.java
```

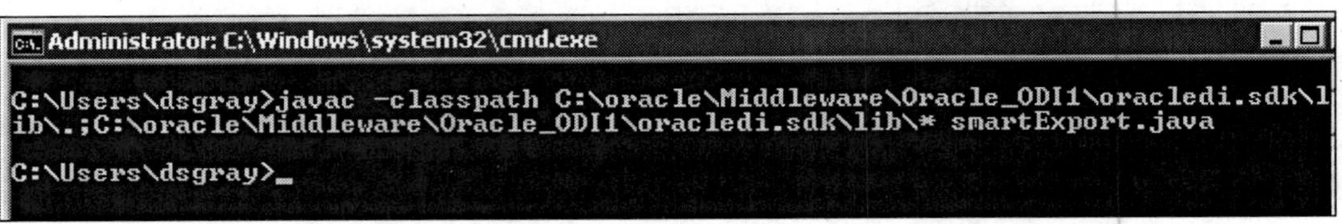

5. The `smartExport.java` program uses command line arguments as follows:
   1. Command Line Argument 1: Work Repository Name.
   2. Command Line Argument 2: Work Repository User.
   3. Command Line Argument 3: Work Repository Password.
   4. Command Line Argument 4: Smart Export XML File Path.
   5. Command Line Argument 5: Project Code.
   6. Command Line Argument 6: Interface Name.

6. To execute the smart export of the `LoadEmployees` interface from the `smartExport.java`, program enter the following from the command line

```
<your Java home>/java -classpath ./;<your ODI home>/\oracledi.sdk
\lib\.;<your ODI home>/\oracledi.sdk\lib\*;;./ojdbc6.jar smartEx
port WORKREP1 SUPERVISOR SUNOPSIS c:\chap11Export.xml TEST test1
```

Command line arguments must be entered in order.

The following messages will scroll through that consists of a listing of the correct command line arguments, as well as a message that the interface was found.

```
Administrator: C:\Windows\system32\cmd.exe

C:\Users\dsgray>java -classpath ./;C:\oracle\Middleware\Oracle_ODI1\oracledi.sdk
\lib\.;C:\oracle\Middleware\Oracle_ODI1\oracledi.sdk\lib\*;;./ojdbc6.jar smartEx
port WORKREP1 SUPERVISOR SUNOPSIS c:\chap11Export.xml TEST test1
The following command line arguments were passed:
arg[0]: WORKREP1
arg[1]: SUPERVISOR
arg[2]: SUNOPSIS
arg[3]: c:\chap11Export.xml
arg[4]: TEST
arg[5]: test1
Feb 24, 2013 11:28:08 PM org.eclipse.persistence.default
INFO: EclipseLink, version: Eclipse Persistence Services - 2.3.1.v20110920-r1012
4
Feb 24, 2013 11:28:08 PM org.eclipse.persistence.default
INFO: work-session login successful
Feb 24, 2013 11:28:08 PM org.eclipse.persistence.default
INFO: master-session login successful
Feb 24, 2013 11:28:08 PM org.eclipse.persistence.default
INFO:  login successful
---***--- setMustDeleteReferenceObjectsOneByOne called for: oracle.odi.domain.ru
ntime.loadplan.OdiLoadPlanStep mapping stepVariables setting to: true
---***--- setMustDeleteReferenceObjectsOneByOne called for: oracle.odi.domain.ru
ntime.lpi.OdiLoadPlanInstanceExceptionLog mapping variableLogs setting to: true
---***--- setMustDeleteReferenceObjectsOneByOne called for: oracle.odi.domain.te
xts.WorkText mapping txtXRefs setting to: true
FOUND : test1

C:\Users\dsgray>_
```

7. The exported smart export file can be manually verified from the ODI Studio UI using the steps outlined in the previous recipe.
8. The imported XML file can easily be imported into a source code control system or lifecycle management, so the file can be checked in and versioned.

   For both the source code control system and the lifecycle management system, the system itself can call the `smartExport.java` program or the system can natively use the ODI SDK inline to perform the export.

   The import or deployment of the ODI object to a new environment such as development to test or from a code branch to the mainline can also be performed through the ODI SDK.

Using the ODI Studio for the smart import gives detailed control over the import. Using the SDK without a response file for the import ODI will automatically decide which action - merge, overwrite, create copy, and so on to use during the smart import process.

The included `smartImport.java` program can be used to import the `smartExport.xml` file which was exported in the previous steps.

9. Update and compile the included `smartImport.java` program to perform the smart import using the ODI SDK.
10. The java program `smartImport.java` must be updated as follows:
    1. Line 49: JDBC URL updated appropriately, will match ODI Studio value.
    2. Line 50: JDBC driver updated appropriately, will match ODI Studio value.
    3. Line 51: JDBC Master repository username updated appropriately, will match ODI Studio value.
    4. Line 52: JDBC Master repository password updated appropriately, will match ODI Studio value.
    5. Save the `smartImport.java` file.
11. Compile the `smartImport.java` program by executing the following from the command line:

    ```
    <your Java home>/javac -classpath ./;<your ODI home>/oracledi.sdk/
    lib/.;<your ODI home>/oracledi.sdk/lib/* smartImport.java
    ```

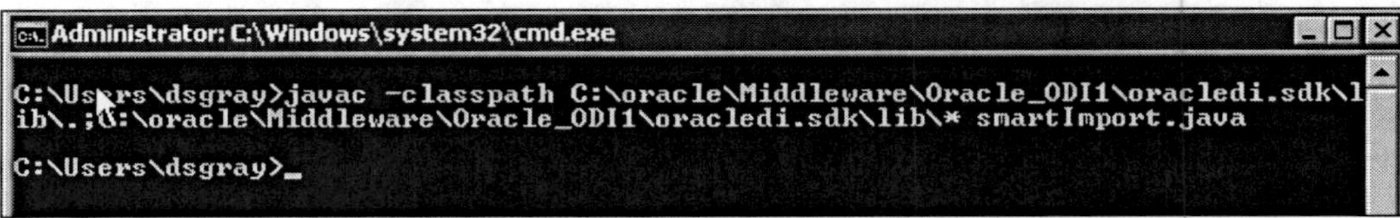

12. The `smartImport.java` program uses command line arguments as follows:
    1. Command Line Argument 1: Work Repository Name.
    2. Command Line Argument 2: Work Repository User.
    3. Command Line Argument 3: Work Repository Password.
    4. Command Line Argument 4: Smart Export XML File Path.
13. To execute the smart import of the `LoadEmployees` interface from the `smartImport.java` program enter the following from the command line:

    ```
    <your Java home>java -Djavax.xml.parsers.SAXParserFactory=oracle.
    xml.jaxp.JXSAXP
    arserFactory -classpath ./;<your ODI home>\oracledi/client/modu
    les/oracle.xdk_11.1.0/xmlparserv2.jar;<your ODI home>\oracledi.
    sdk\lib\.;<your ODI home>\oracledi.sdk\lib\*;;./ojdbc6.jar smar
    tImport WORKREP1 SUPERVISOR SUNOPSIS c:\chap11Export.xml
    ```

> The Oracle SAX Parser must be used as outlined in the command line or the execution will return with a an error:
>
> ODI - 10104- file smartExport.xml is not a smart export file and cannot be imported by Smart Import.
>
> Command line arguments must be entered in order.

The following messages will scroll through:

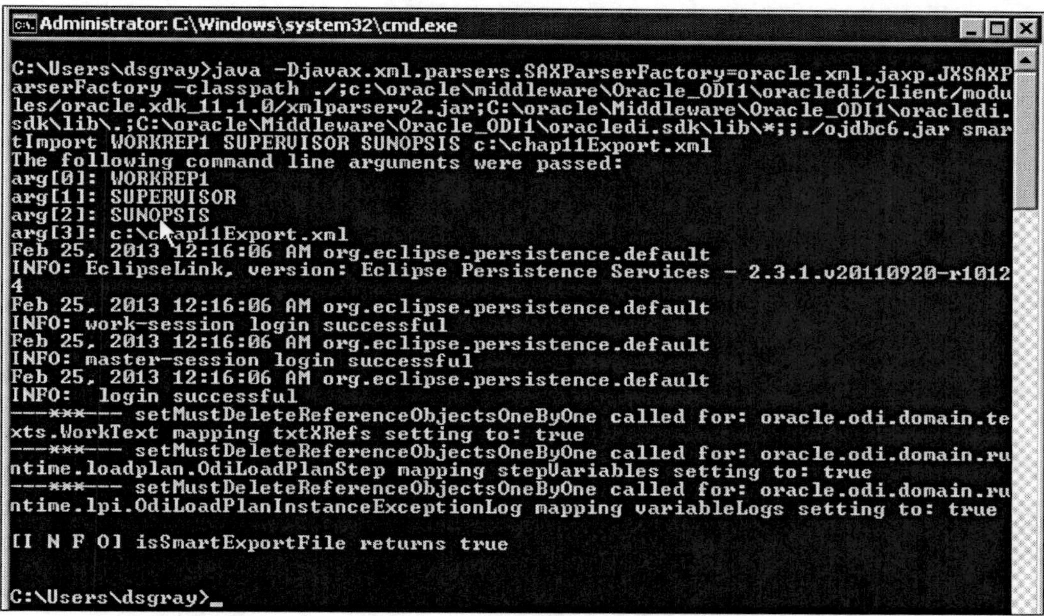

14. Verify the `LoadEmployees` interface was imported correctly.

How it works...

Lifecycle management and source code control management are central to any enterprise ODI implementation. ODI does provide out of the box functionality for integrating exported objects' xml definitions with these types of systems; however this is an interactive process. Utilizing the ODI SDK, it is possible to integrate ODI into the enterprises' best practices around life cycle management as well as source control management. The ODI SDK allows for automation of exporting and import ODI objects, allowing this process to be managed outside of ODI.

There's more...

A lot can be accomplished with the code samples delivered within this recipe. Additionally ODI has a full JAVA SDK that allows for automating virtually every available function within ODI. For more information on this refer to *Chapter 7, Advanced Coding Techniques*.

Index

T

U

V

W

X

Thank you for buying
Oracle Data Integrator 11*g* Cookbook

About Packt Publishing

Packt, pronounced 'packed', published its first book "*Mastering phpMyAdmin for Effective MySQL Management*" in April 2004 and subsequently continued to specialize in publishing highly focused books on specific technologies and solutions.

Our books and publications share the experiences of your fellow IT professionals in adapting and customizing today's systems, applications, and frameworks. Our solution-based books give you the knowledge and power to customize the software and technologies you're using to get the job done. Packt books are more specific and less general than the IT books you have seen in the past. Our unique business model allows us to bring you more focused information, giving you more of what you need to know, and less of what you don't.

Packt is a modern, yet unique publishing company, which focuses on producing quality, cutting-edge books for communities of developers, administrators, and newbies alike. For more information, please visit our website: `www.PacktPub.com`.

About Packt Enterprise

In 2010, Packt launched two new brands, Packt Enterprise and Packt Open Source, in order to continue its focus on specialization. This book is part of the Packt Enterprise brand, home to books published on enterprise software - software created by major vendors, including (but not limited to) IBM, Microsoft and Oracle, often for use in other corporations. Its titles will offer information relevant to a range of users of this software, including administrators, developers, architects, and end users.

Writing for Packt

We welcome all inquiries from people who are interested in authoring. Book proposals should be sent to `author@packtpub.com`. If your book idea is still at an early stage and you would like to discuss it first before writing a formal book proposal, contact us; one of our commissioning editors will get in touch with you.

We're not just looking for published authors; if you have strong technical skills but no writing experience, our experienced editors can help you develop a writing career, or simply get some additional reward for your expertise.

Oracle Enterprise Manager 12*c* Administration Cookbook

Over 50 practical recipes to install, configure, and monitor your Oracle setup using Oracle Enterprise Manager

Foreword by Shashank Patwardhan, Head of Application Management Services, Europe, TechMahindra Limited

Dhananjay Papde Tushar Nath Vipul Patel [PACKT] enterprise

Oracle Enterprise Manager 12*c* Administration Cookbook

ISBN: 978-1-849687-40-9 Paperback: 324 pages

Over 50 practical recipes to install, configure, and monitor your Oracle setup using Oracle Enterprise Manager

1. Recipes for installing, configuring, and getting up and running with Oracle Enterprise Manager
2. Set up automatic discovery, create and clone databases, and perform provisioning
3. Monitor Oracle Fusion Middleware, and remotely use incident and problem management using iPad/iPhone

---

OCA Oracle Database 11*g*: Database Administration I: A Real-World Certification Guide

Learn how to become an Oracle-certified database administrator

Steve Ries [PACKT] enterprise

OCA Oracle Database 11*g*: Database Administration I: A Real-World Certification Guide

ISBN: 978-1-849687-30-0 Paperback: 582 pages

Learn how to become an Oracle-cerfitied database administrator

1. Prepare for Oracle Database Administration I certification
2. Learn real world skills in database administration
3. Written in an example driven format with step-by-step real world examples

Please check **www.PacktPub.com** for information on our titles

Managing Multimedia and Unstructured Data in the Oracle Database

A revolutionary approach to understanding, managing, and delivering digital objects, assets, and all types of data

Marcelle Kratochvil

Managing Multimedia and Unstructured Data in the Oracle Database

ISBN: 978-1-849686-92-1 Paperback: 504 pages

A revolutionary approach to understanding, managing, and delivering digital objects, assets, and all types of data

1. Full of illustrations, diagrams, and tips with clear step-by-step instructions and real time examples
2. Get up to speed on all the aspects of this new technology
3. Learn how to work with rich multimedia and control it

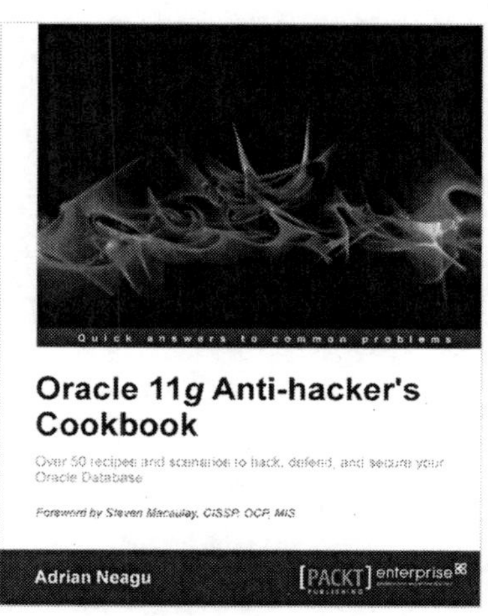

Oracle 11*g* Anti-hacker's Cookbook

ISBN: 978-1-849685-26-9 Paperback: 302 pages

Over 50 recipes and scenarios to hack, defend, and secure your Oracle Database

1. Learn to protect your sensitive data by using industry certified techniques
2. Implement and use ultimate techniques in Oracle Security and new security features introduced in Oracle 11g R2
3. Implement strong network communication security using different encryption solutions provided by Oracle Advanced Security

Please check **www.PacktPub.com** for information on our titles

Lightning Source UK Ltd.
Milton Keynes UK
UKOW03f1507290515

252563UK00003B/78/P